HISTORY OF PHYSICAL EDUCATION AND SPORT

REVISED EDITION

Earle F. Zeigler
The University of Western Ontario
London, Ontario, Canada

with chapters by

Maxwell L. Howell, Univ. of Queensland, Australia
and Reet Howell, Brisbane, Queensland, Australia;
Robert G. Glassford and Gerald Redmond,
University of Alberta, Canada;
Robert Knight Barney, The University of
Western Ontario, Ontario, Canada;
Garth A. Paton, University of New Brunswick,
New Brunswick, Canada

ISBN 0-87563-309-9

Published by
STIPES PUBLISHING COMPANY
10 - 12 Chester Street
Champaign, Illinois, U.S.A.
61820

Preface

History has always been a popular topic within the field of physical education, and increasing worldwide interest in sport has been a significant force in this heightening of concern for historical analysis and interpretation. The addition of the words "and Sport" in the Stipes Series is most important, reflecting a broadening of emphasis within the profession. Also, it was not just a chance occurrence that the National Association for Sport and Physical Education emerged within the formation of the American Alliance for Health, Physical Education, Recreation, and Dance. Further, the growth and development of the North American Society for Sport History (including its *Journal of Sport History*) and the earlier inauguration of the scholarly Canadian Journal of Sport History have been highly important steps forward. Moreover, we have witnessed the beginning of the *British Journal of Sports History* in 1984.[1]

This volume was published originally in 1979 as one of three volumes in The Prentice-Hall Foundations of Physical Education and Sport Series under the editorship of John E. Nixon. For several reasons (not of Dr. Nixon's doing), this series did not develop further and was eventually discontinued. Nevertheless there has been a continuing demand for this basic history text for use in a variety of core courses that have sprung up within the sub-disciplinary emphasis that began to develop in the mid1960s. Many leaders have come to believe that the idea of a required or "service" physical education experience for all undergraduates needs to be supplemented by a second "introduction to the discipline" of sport and physical education approach. Just as we find required and elective courses available to university first-year students in all disciplines on campus, a need has arisen for a similar course in sport and physical education, an introduction to the theory and practice of developmental physical activity in sport, dance, play, and exercise. Such a course should then be followed (and supplemented) by short introductory core courses. This volume on physical education and sport history is suited admirably for such a core experience.

---

[1] Now called the *International Journal of the History of Sport.*

Second, some decisions had to be made originally about how a brief history could be best written. It was decided that, in these days of increasing specialization, more than one of two people should be involved in the project. Also, with a book this size, some choices had to be made as to what could (and what should) be included. Obviously, a section on ancient physical activities and sport was still needed. So we asked Professor Maxwell L. Howell, now of the University of Queensland, Australia, and Dr. Reet Howell, a recognized sport and physical education author also in Brisbane, if they wished to be involved in this venture again. We were pleased that they accepted because they are recognized worldwide for their overall knowledge and experience with developmental physical activity in the ancient world. The Howells felt that only minor revisions were necessary for Section One.

When this text was planned originally, very few people had specialized in writing in English about physical activity and sport in the Middle Ages. Thus, the editor finally decided to accept the assignment of writing about this period in Section Two himself, admittedly with some misgiving, when one knowledgeable author had to withdraw from the project and another felt that he did not have the time at that point. There has been some evidence that the final result did not detract from the remainder of the volume. It must be admitted, of course, that a bias existed here in the delimitation of coverage, because Western Europe was really an outpost of civilization (at least during the so-called "Dark Ages" of the Western world). (Since the late 1970s, there has been evidence of a rising interest in the period. The editor now has a listing of some 20 people with an interest in this area and hopes to begin an exchange of information among the members of this group.)

The next subdivision, Section Three of this compact volume, had to be about the development of physical education and sport in the modern period in parts of the world other than North America. To accomplish this impossible task reasonably adequately in the allotted eighty pages of manuscript, the editor turned to Professors R. G. (Gerry) Glassford and Gerald Redmond, both of the University of Alberta, very well-known physical education and sport historians who have travelled to many parts of the world in the course of their work and professional experiences. These men exceeded the expectations of the editor in accomplishing this assignment initially, and stated that it would be possible to update the material with relatively few changes for the revised edition.

Next the editor had turned to his long-time colleague, Professor Robert Knight Barney of The University of Western Ontario, to undertake Section Four treating the history of sport and physical activity in the United States and Canada. Students of physical education and sport history will already be well aware of Bob Barney's sound scholarship in writing about the history of the Turner Movement in North America.

For this revised edition, however, with the concurrence of Dr. Barney, it was decided to subdivide North America (excluding Mexico at this time) into two sections on the United States of America and Canada, respectively. Professor Barney agreed to do the revision for the United States.

Section Five on physical education and sport in Canada will be researched and written by Professor Garth A. Paton, former Dean and current Chairman of the Graduate Program at the University of New Brunswick, Fredericton, Canada. Dr. Paton teaches physical education and sport history and management. His chapter entitled "The Historical Background and Present Status of Canadian Physical Education" appeared in a 1975 history reader (Zeigler, Stipes). Paton will incorporate the earlier material about Canada by Barney in the first edition into this second edition of the text.

To bring the volume to a close, the editor has retained the final section (now #6) from the first edition. This chapter places physical education and sport in a historical perspective by converting the unilateral narrative of the earlier chapters to an approach that delineates the persistent, recurring problems that have been recorded in sufficient quantity for reasonably intelligent qualitative analysis (e.g., the influence, or *social force*, of economics, the impact, or *professional concern*, of amateurism and professionalism). With this approach, a conscious effort has been made to keep the reader from thinking that history is of antiquarian interest only.

The editor appreciated over 40 years ago, as a result of an experience with Professor John S. Brubacher of Yale University and The University of Michigan, that students need to comprehend not only the sweep of history, but also the nature of such persistent historical social forces and professional concerns as the influence of societal values and norms or the concept of 'progress'. Following this, his course of action has been to help students determine how these persistent, recurring problems or issues might be resolved according to what seem to be the leading philosophic stances or positions in the Western world. More recently, the editor has also come to appreciate the necessity for the student to place sport and physical education in a reasonable sociological perspective based on tenable theory. Moreover, we in this field have much to learn from the developing social-science aspects of anthropology. Those who seek to administer programs in this profession should have this type of theoretical undergirding *before* they study management theory and practice as applied to sport and physical education. The profession desperately needs intelligent, inquiring scholars, inspired teachers of teachers, and dedicated professional practitioners. You, the reader, may not yet be fully aware of it, but our future depends on you!

Once again, it is a distinct pleasure to recognize a continuing very happy relationship with the Stipes Publishing Company dating back to 1964. The late R. L. (Rooney) Stipes, Jr. and Mr. Robert Watts have been wonderful people with whom to work over the years in the production of some 11 books and monographs. Professors Glassford and Redmond wish to acknowledge the research assistance on the modern period of Richard Baka, Jean Leiper, and Barbara Schrodt (now all professors in their own right).

E.F. Z.

DEDICATION

To the late Dr. Ion Ioannides of Athens, Greece — friend, physical educator, sport history scholar, administrator, former consultant for Physical Education in Greece's Ministry of Education; a cultured gentleman who worked tirelessly for an ideal in the planned establishment of a Delphic Cultural Center at Psatha in the hope that the best traits and aspects of classical antiquity could be made to live again more fully in his native land and across the world.

CONTENTS

                                                                Page

PREFACE iii

Section

One   PHYSICAL ACTIVITIES AND SPORT
           IN EARLY SOCIETIES 1
           Maxwell L. Howell and Reet Howell

Two   PHYSICAL EDUCATION AND SPORT
           IN THE MIDDLE AGES 57
           Earle F. Zeigler

Three   PHYSICAL EDUCATION AND SPORT
           IN MODERN TIMES 103
           Robert G. Glassford and Gerald Redmond

Four   PHYSICAL EDUCATION AND
           SPORT IN THE UNITED STATES OF
           AMERICA 173
           Robert Knight Barney

Five   PHYSICAL EDUCATION AND SPORT
           IN CANADA 220
           Garth A. Paton and R. K. Barney

Six   PHYSICAL EDUCATION AND SPORT
           IN A HISTORICAL PERSPECTIVE 246
           Earle F. Zeigler

INDEX 305

Section One
Physical Activities and Sport in Early Societies

Maxwell L. Howell
Reet Howell

In recent years there has been a surge of interest in the socio-cultural area in physical education, particularly in the role and relevance of sport, games, and play in society. The socio-cultural area has been defined by Howell as follows:

> The socio-cultural area, defined tentatively, is the study of man in social and cultural settings in his relation to sport and physical education—his thoughts and feelings in relation to self and others in the context of sport and physical education, and the history of those developments; and the role of sport and physical education in various cultures, civilizations and societies. Strictly speaking the word socio is a combining form, meaning social, society, sociological. Cultural is, of course, that which is relating to culture, and is the training and refinement of mind, interests, tastes and manners; it is the condition of being thus trained or refined. It is the intellectual side of civilization, the improvement or refinement by education and training. (1975, p. 11)

Scholars have been turning their attention to the ancient Western world and so-called "primitive" societies, utilizing one or more of the subdisciplines of the socio-cultural areas; each subdiscipline is equally important for putting together the jigsaw puzzle of the place of sport in a particular society. The subdisciplines are: history of sport and physical education, philosophy of sport and physical education, sociology of sport, archaeology of sport and physical education, anthropology of physical activities, history of art in sport and physical education, comparative physical education and sport, and the social psychology of sport and physical education. Figure 1–1 shows these fields of study in the socio-cultural area (Howell, 1975, p. 11).

In endeavoring to reconstruct the play habits of ancient civilizations, the scholar has to contend with the meagerness of evidence, but

Maxwell L. Howell holds a chair as Professor, Human Movement Studies, University of Queensland, Brisbane, Australia. Reet (Mrs. M.L.) Howell is engaged full-time in research and writing.

1

Figure 1–1. The Eight Subdisciplines in the Socio-Cultural Area

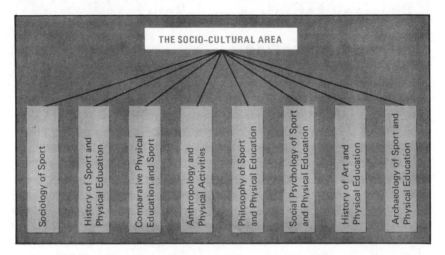

THE SOCIO-CULTURAL AREA

Sociology of Sport

History of Sport and Physical Education

Comparative Physical Education and Sport

Anthropology and Physical Activities

Philosophy of Sport and Physical Education

Social Psychology of Sport and Physical Education

History of Art and Physical Education

Archaeology of Sport and Physical Education

when evidence is replicated and substantiated, an astute researcher can produce an imaginative, artistic reconstruction of the past. As Cantor stated:

> Once the historian has gleaned the factual data, his role is like that of a sculptor as he transforms the hard stone of his factual material into a meaningful pattern. The historian is not merely a reporter; he is an interpreter of what happened in the past.[1]

Taking history as an example, historians have, in the main, been concerned with economic and political history. Social history has been neglected. Do the flow of money, industrial developments, the lives of presidents, kings, and queens, adequately portray a civilization? Mr. Doolley put it this way:

> I know histhry isn't thrue, Hinnessy, because it ain't like what I see ivry day in Halsted Sthreet. If any wan comes along with a histhry iv Greece or Rome that'll show me th' people fightin', gettin' dhrunk, makin' love, gettin' married, owin' th' grocery man and bein' without hard-coal, I'll believe they was a Greece or Rome, but not before. . . . Histhry is a postmortem examination. It tells ye what a country died iv. But I'd like to know what it lived iv. (Ware, 1940, p. 3)

Sport and games are an essential part of that social history, and their study has likewise been neglected. Indeed, sports may mirror a society; hence the sport historian might provide invaluable data toward the understanding of a particular civilization.

It must be emphasized that play did not start with the advent of the great civilizations. Indeed, play preceded civilization, though our evi-

---

[1]Norman F. Cantor, *Western Civilization: Its Genesis and Destiny*, Vol. 1, p. 2. Copyright © 1969 by Scott, Foresman and Company. Reprinted by permission of the publisher.

dence of such play is sparse. People ran and jumped and played games before the city-states existed. They hunted and fished, though basically for economic reasons. But as man sat in caves and crude shelters at night around warm fires, his mind was set to invention, and games such as knucklebones and simple board games inevitably developed. On festive and other occasions there would be tapping on objects for rhythm and performing of dances.

Human history began at least half a million years ago. Writing began approximately 3000 B.C. with the invention of cuneiform writing and then hieroglyphics. With the invention of writing we have the beginning of recorded history; the period prior to that, almost half a million years, is termed prehistory.

Play appeared during this vast amount of time, but we have little evidence of it. We are dependent on the findings of archaeologists and anthropologists, and the more mobile the culture, the more difficult it is to find information about it. As Cantor said:

> ... scientists have worked diligently to bring order and meaning to the study of prehistory through systematizing the artifacts they have uncovered, and they have developed a schema for categorizing human societies according to the tools and implements each made and used. The broad categories are well known and present a progression through many thousands of years. The Lower Paleolithic Era (Old Stone Age) of primitive, chipped stone tools began more than a million years ago. The Upper Paleolithic Era, which began about 35,000 B.C., witnessed vast improvements in the working of stone, including highly specialized and multiple-part tools. It gave way gradually to the Neolithic Era (New Stone Age) after about 7000 B.C., when stone tools were delicately ground, shaped, and polished. Stone was superseded by metal in the Bronze Age, which began in the fourth millenium B.C. and was followed by the Iron Age after 1500 B.C. Prehistoric times, then, were marked by successive changes and improvements in tools and weapons. (1968, p. 16)

"Modern" man gradually evolved, and by about 40,000 years ago he was similar in appearance to man of today. And of course we still have the remnants of the Stone Age in such races as the Australian aboriginal. Cave paintings and archaeological finds from the Neolithic period, in particular, have shown men hunting and dancing, have revealed children's dolls and games like knucklebones. Nevertheless, the evidence of play in the prehistoric period has not as yet been adequately researched.

Be that as it may, we have been able to witness the adoption of sports and games in civilizations as they emerged, and we have noted their diffusion. As Woody has so aptly put it:

> Where propitious external conditions and human competence combined to fashion great permanent settlements, as in Mesopotamia, China, Egypt, India, labor and leisure became more sharply defined, and both had increasing importance. Labor produced wealth; accumulated wealth became concentrated in a few hands; and leisure became the grand prize of those few who possessed great wealth. Labor was the lot of the great majority.

Historically, extended leisure depended on some kind of surplus wealth, public or private, whence one of many might draw sufficiently for maintenance. The individuals who composed the classes which controlled wealth put this valuable leisure potential to various uses; in extensive sportive activity, outdoors and indoors; in the development and pursuit of intellectual and aesthetic arts. (1957, p. 4)

THE RIVER VALLEY CIVILIZATIONS

The Tigris and Euphrates rivers were the key to the development of the River Valley civilizations, which were known as Mesopotamia. The function of the great rivers was similar to that of the Nile. From their origins in the north of Mesopotamia, these great rivers and their tributaries flowed to the Persian Gulf. The rivers were erratic and had to be assisted by irrigation, by the use of an extensive canal system, but the fertile land left by the river water encouraged the development of an agricultural community. The regularity and success of the production led to the growth of the city-states by roughly 3000 B.C.

The very flatness of the land between the rivers, while encouraging agriculture, occasioned other problems. Military control was difficult to maintain in the region—no one area was able to assert control. The original power came from Sumer in the south, was transferred to Babylonia in the center, and eventually to Assyria in the north.

The basis of ancient Sumer was the city-state, and the economy was basically an agricultural one. The majority of the population were peasants, though the society had artisans, scribes, merchants, and slaves. The center of the society was the temple, and the temple community controlled everything. These ziggurats, or large temples, have been unearthed by various archaeologists. Cuneiform writing was invented by these people to keep records of various transactions.

By 2350 B.C. Sumerian dominance ended through the military efforts of Sargon of Akkad, but the Babylonians adopted most of the Sumerian ways. Approximately 1100 B.C. the Assyrian civilization dominated the area, and control was centered in Assur in the north. These fierce fighters eventually fell in 612 B.C. to the Chaldeans and the Medes.

Some of the great archaeologists who have made considerable contributions to the understanding of Mesopotamia are: Paul Emile Botta, an amateur who found Nineveh and whose finds are now in the Louvre; Georg Fredrich Grotefend, a German schoolteacher who solved the mystery of cuneiform writing on a bet, after famous Oriental scholars had been unsuccessful; Major Henry Creswicke Rawlinson, the father of Assyriology, who translated Nebuchadnezzar's dictionary; Austin Henry Layard, another amateur, who discovered Nimrud (these extensive finds are now in the British Museum); George Smith, a banknote engraver in

London and an amateur Assyriologist, who unraveled the *Gilgamesh Epic;* the German Robert Koldewey, who excavated Babylon; and Sir Leonard Woolley, who discovered Ur. These men, and countless others, made significant contributions to our understanding of the Sumerian, Babylonian, Hittite, and Assyrian civilizations.

The first real evidence of sports and games is found in the Early Dynastic period of the Sumerian civilization (3000–1500 B.C.). In addition to archaeological artifacts, there is literary evidence as well (Palmer, 1967, p. 3).

Combat sports are seen in artifacts which show boxing and wrestling. Boxing is seen, in all probability, in a clay tablet from a tomb at Sinkara, dating from the second millennium B.C. (Contenau, 1954, p. 131); this scene could, however, depict dancing.

Earlier representations, from the fourth to the third millennia B.C., depict wrestling (Strommenger, Plate 46), and possibly boxing. The most famous representation of wrestling is a copper statuette of two figures, heads interlocked and hands gripping the belt on their opponent's hips (Woolley, 1961, Figure 21). This is perhaps an earlier form of the belt wrestling of bible times and Sumo wrestling of Japan. The objects on the heads of the wrestlers, like large pots, have been the subject of much discussion. It has been argued that the object of the event was to upset the pottery from the heads of the wrestlers, but a more logical opinion is that the objects had no relationship to wrestling, but that the artifact was a household ornament and objects such as flowers were placed in the pottery. And perhaps we have literary support in one of the tablets of the *Epic of Gilgamesh:*

> They met in the Market-of-the-Land
> Enkidu barred the gate
> With his foot.
> Not allowing Gilgamesh to enter.
> They grappled each other,
> Holding fast like bulls.
> They shattered the doorpost,
> As the wall shook. . . .
>
> As Gilgamesh bent the knee—
> His foot on the ground—
> His fury abated
> And he turned away.[2]

Archaeological evidence relating to warfare has implications of play activities. If an individual is to master the use of a chariot, it is easy for the sport historian to envision challenge races; and if bows and arrows

[2] From "The Epic of Gilgamesh," transl. E. A. Speiser in James B. Pritchard (ed.), *The Ancient Near East: An Anthology of Texts and Pictures,* p. 50. Copyright © 1959 by PUP. Reprinted by permission of Princeton University Press.

are utilized, it is logical to infer that events would be staged to demonstrate skill and accuracy. The Sumerians introduced the phalanx, and in the Stele of the Vultures (Parrot, 1961, p. 135) soldiers are depicted carrying axes and spears or lances. They are led by Eannarum riding in his chariot. The use of the chariot in war was another Sumerian innovation. The king, incidentally, holds a lance in his left hand and a curved mace or throwing stick in his right. It takes little imagination to understand the training necessary to perfect the phalanx and the chariot, and yet there were doubtless play aspects to the development of such military efficiency.

Also, although we are without evidence as to training in equestrianism, it had to be reasonably advanced. As Oppenheim stated:

> The occurrence of the horse on the painted pottery and on the Tell Halaf statues seems to me a further proof that the much debated question whether the beasts before the chariots in Ur are asses or mules (or horses) must be answered in favour of the latter suggestion. I should be astonished at the courage of the warrior who should dare let his chariot be drawn into the fight by asses. The amusing mishaps of the sporting English officers driving asses in gymkhanas in Cairo show that asses cannot be properly driven. (1933, p. 157)

And there is some evidence that some chariots were utilized for racing. Mallowan wrote:

> The bronze quadriga discovered in the Shara Temple of Tell Asman gives us a curious illustration of the beginnings of traction. A tiny chariot just big enough to accommodate a precariously balanced driver, was of strictly limited practical value: it was designed for speed and was symbolic of speed. (1948, p. 53)

And Pritchard has found, in a version of the *Epic of Gilgamesh,* literary evidence of chariot racing:

> Thy he-ass in lading shall surpass thy mule,
> Thy chariot horses shall be famed for racing,
> [Thine ox] under yoke shall not have a rival. (Pritchard, 1959, p. 52)

There is no profusion of hunting scenes among the evidence we have. Numerous cylinder seals depict Gilgamesh and Enkidu fighting wild animals, and the use of the mace is evident. The Gilgamesh-Enkidu representations, however, have to be taken with a grain of salt. As Parrot stated:

> The earlier theme of the two friends Enkidu and Gilgamesh fighting wild animals, is one of their favorites and they treat it with exuberance and even gaiety, for the triumph of the two heroes is always a foregone conclusion. They are more than slayers of wild beasts; they make sport with them through paces of the most diverse kinds. Lions and buffaloes are no match for these Herculean athletes, who have no trouble in swinging them aloft or cracking their joints like matchsticks. (1961, p. 187)

The translations of cuneiform tablets show the records of the delivery of gazelles, deer, wild boars, and roasted birds, so we know that extensive hunting was practiced. We know of the use of the mace, the lance, the sling, and bows and arrows. A stele at the Iraq Museum (Parrot, 1961, p. 72) shows a lion hurt, and the lance being used in a dramatic fashion, as well as a bow and arrows.

Various musical instruments have been excavated. The harp discovered at Ur is the most famous representation, but there are also a flute, a lute, the double pipes, a type of oboe, percussion clubs, clappers, sistra, rattles, and drums. In addition, of course, the hands were utilized in clapping. When there is music there is dancing. The love poems cited in Kramer establish this with certainty:

> Last night as I the queen was shining bright,
> As I was shining bright, was dancing about
> As I was singing away while the bright light overcame the night. . . .
>
> My girl friend, she took me with her to the public square,
> There a player (?) entertained (?) us with dancing. (1963, p. 251)

Boating and fishing were extensively practiced by the Sumerians. Some fifty types of fish are noted by Kramer (1963, p. 110), and there is evidence of fishing nets and bronze fish hooks (Lloyd, 1936, p. 110).

The meticulous archaeologist Woolley found four gaming boards in the royal graves at Ur. Each had some twenty cells and a drawer to hold the gaming pieces; a complete set was found in one drawer (Woolley, 1934, p. 274–79). The boards are inlaid with red limestone and lapis lazuli, occasionally engraved with animals. The rosette is commonly shown.

The white marble gaming board from Tell Halaf (*Iraq,* 1946, Photo VIII) resembled those found at Ur. One end is hollow, presumably to hold pieces.

The Hittite civilization provides additional evidence of physical activities in ancient Mesopotamia. Much of the evidence comes from activities related to war. The chariot, again, was utilized, as well as weapons similar to those used by the Sumerians, and one must infer that these objects were used to develop skill, occasionally in a competitive manner. A light, horse-drawn chariot was introduced.

A most important document was unearthed at Hattusas; some thousand lines of the clay tablet refer to the training and breeding of horses. Indeed, it is our first handbook on equestrianism. Much of the text is concerned with the preparation of horses for chariot races (Diem, 1960, p. 106). A seven-month training period was recommended. A training track was utilized, and as the program developed, the length of the training sessions and the work load were increased. Gradually the horse was familiarized with the chariot, again the work load being gradually increased. The diet and care of the horses were also stressed.

A considerable number of artifacts show hunting. The bow is often shown on the representations; it is short, with long arrows, being adapted for a crowded chariot. Hunting from the chariot was, understandably, a pastime of the rich. A spear was also used, particularly for lion hunting, and slings have been found. One lion hunt relief shows hunting dogs (Akurgal, 1962, Plate 96). Other artifacts show the hunting of the bull, the bear, the stag, and the boar. Falconry was also practiced; two artifacts show a falcon being utilized (Garstang, 1929, p. 231).

Guterbock (1950, p. 95) describes the various festivals of the Hittites, particularly those that accompanied war. There was entertainment at these festivals, and this was apparently music and dancing, but it is possible that other forms of entertainment were practiced. There are a number of artifacts that depict forms of acrobatics. Boxing and wrestling are also in evidence, and even gladiatorial combat is a possibility. The instruments that the Sumerians used were duplicated: concussion clubs, drums, clappers and cymbals, wind instruments such as pipes, horns, and trumpets, and the stringed instruments such as the harp, lyre, and lute. Dancing accompanied the music on many occasions.

One of the most interesting aspects of the Hittite civilization is the use of swimming in warfare, although we have no evidence of its practice as a recreational activity. In various artifacts we see swimming and the use of floats, which were inflated skins. A tube went into the swimmer's mouth so he could fill the skin and thus keep afloat (Diem, 1960, p. 106). Various strokes were seen in scenes from the Battle of Kadesh, and it is tempting to generalize that the Hittites knew the front crawl, the sidestroke, and the breast stroke (Pritchard, 1954, p. 113; Breasted, 1903, Figure 160). Perhaps the most astonishing illustration is the one showing two Hittite soldiers performing a method of artificial respiration, and various reaching assists being utilized to rescue drowning soldiers (Breasted, 1903, Figure 160).

Very little evidence of other games appeared from the Hittite civilization. There is the possibility of dice being used, or knucklebones, as well as toys.

There is still a need to examine the other civilizations in Mesopotamia. All we have discovered is that many of the activities are related to both warfare and the aristocracy, and there is little evidence of play activities among the peasants.

Little is known of the sports and games of the Phoenicians (Roebuck, 1966) and the early Hebrews, though Zeigler (1968, p. 24) notes that among the latter, physical culture was necessary for military purposes, and healthy activities were promoted, particularly on the Sabbath.

Woody (1949, p. 106) says of the Sabbath: "a time for recreation of mind and body, but idleness was condemned." Vilnay (1968) mentions the following sports in ancient Israel: running in biblical times (Benjamin ran 42 kilometers, 600 meters uphill, to inform Eli, the Great Priest, of Israel's defeat by the Philistines); a gymnasium in Greek and Roman times in Jerusalem; games in Herod's time to honor Emperor Augustus; games in the second and third centuries A.D. at various sites; swimming, dancing, stadia and hippodromes in Roman times. On the other hand, Orthodox Jews tended to remain away from the games that were held, and the city of Tur-Shimon was supposed to have been destroyed because its sons played ball on the Sabbath.

There is more evidence of physical activities in Assyrian life. Chariot driving (Hall, 1932, Plate XXV–1) was a necessary part of the army, as was the use of the bow and arrow (Hall, 1932, Plate XXV–2). Hunting was widely practiced. Lion hunting was practiced by the king and higher officials (Maspero, 1908, p. 265). It is thought that parks were attached to the royal palace (Layard, 1853, p. 552), and, indeed, that the Assyrians may have been the innovators of such parks, and that these were afterwards maintained by the Persians (Layard, 1853, p. 328). Beaters were used to hunt the lion, and dogs were used as well (Maspero, 1908, p. 264). Rawlinson interprets one artifact as follows:

> At other times, when it was felt that the natural chase of the animal might afford little or no sport, the Assyrians called out to their assistants, and having obtained a supply of lions from a distance, brought them in traps or cages to the hunting ground, and then turned them out before the monarch. (1875, p. 297)

Occasionally a king was shown in hand-to-hand combat against a lion, using a sword (Maspero, 1908, p. 266). The hunt against wild bulls was also practiced (Moscati, 1957, Plate X), as well as other animals such as the onager or wild ass, the stag, the ibex or wild goat, the gazelle, the ostrich, and the hare.

Fishing was practiced (Rawlinson, 1875, Plate V), the fisherman being portrayed holding a line with no float attached. One artifact shows a fisherman peacefully fishing seated on an inflated skin (Rawlinson, 1875, Figure 3).

Musical instruments such as the lyre, the harp, the double flute, the tambourine, the cymbals, the santour, and the trumpet were used, and artifacts show groups of musicians (Rawlinson, 1875, Plate XIX). Dances were naturally performed. Regarding festivals, Maspero states:

> The remainder of the day is passed in banquets and amusement—dancers, singers, players upon the harp and upon the flute, jugglers, who perform feats of strength, storytellers who relate fables or merry tales. (1908, p. 231)

Bird training was probably performed as well. As Bonomi says, commenting on the battle scene:

> We are disposed, therefore, to regard these eagles, hovering over the chiefs, as birds trained to accompany them in battle. In other parts of these sculptures from Nimroud, we find the birds contending with the wounded, and chiefly attempting to pick out their eyes, thus exhibiting their natural instinct, as eagles and falcons, when contending with large and powerful prey, at once attack the eyes of their victims. (1852, p. 239)

Many artifacts show men crossing rivers and streams using inflated skin sacks for support (Bonomi, 1852, p. 239), and one engraving shows a person swimming unaided, doing what appears to be the crawl stroke (Bonomi, 1852, p. 239).

Charioteers were also of prime importance among the Persians (Frye, 1963, pp. 103–4). The bow was used extensively (Ghirshman, 1964, p. 381). As Herodotus (1871, p. 53) wrote, " . . . to ride, to use the bow, and to speak the truth" were the essentials of Persian life. On the tomb of Darius, moreover, was the following inscription, again indicative of the place of certain physical activities in the civilization: "I was a friend to my friends; as a horseman and bowman I proved myself superior to all others . . ." (Ghirshman, 1954, p. 152). Hunting was, therefore, a necessary part of the way of life of the Persians. In one seal Darius is shown slaying a lion with bow and arrow, from a chariot (Porada, 1965, p. 176). Other scenes depict lions, deer, the ibex, and asses being hunted by bow and arrow, sword, javelin, or spear.

The Persians were ardent horsemen and the way they bred and trained horses was known throughout western Asia (Ghirshman, 1954, p. 94). The Persian riders did not use a saddle and they used snaffled bits to control their horses. Hitti notes (1951, p. 480): "Several caliphs and courtiers engaged in more innocent pastimes such as hunting, dicing and horse racing."

It is not possible to claim without question that a form of polo (chuvigan) originated among the Persians, but this is generally believed (Diem, 1960, pp. 336–39). Hitti stated that polo " . . . was introduced from Persia (into Syria) probably toward the end of the Umayyad period and soon became a favourite and fashionable sport with the Abbasids" (1951, p. 480).

All Persians in the military were expected to be "experts in all manly exercises" (Benjamin, 1888, p. 68), and visiting dignitaries had festivals arranged for them to test their prowess. For example, "Gueriwez was entertained in a manner worthy of his rank, and athletic games were arranged in his honor" (Benjamin, 1888, p. 74). Also, "But in the exercises with the bow, the javelin, and the mace, and in exhibitions of horsemanship, Zal outstripped every competitor, and by the remarkable feats of his skill and strength and courage, aroused the amazement of the king and his entire court" (Benjamin, 1888, p. 32).

The Sassanians, the Parthians, and possibly the Persians jousted on horseback. One Sassanian rock sculpture shows three pairs fighting, as Ghirshman says (1962, p. 125): " . . . like knights in a medieval tournament." One relief shows a lance being used to unseat an opponent (Ghirshman, 1962, pp. 129–30).

Wrestling was also performed in Persia. One stamp seal shows two nude wrestlers (Schmidt, 1957, Plate 12). Another seal is thought to depict running, the figure appearing to be beardless, bareheaded, and nude (Schmidt, 1957, Plate 12).

Musicians, dancers, and acrobats were also in evidence. As Ghirshman stated in describing some artifacts:

> In the wine cup are images; you can glimpse smoothly swaying forms of lovely women. . . .
>
> Then again on a handsome silver jug we see musicians and tumblers performing while four dancing girls display their charms. . . . (1962, p. 214)

Various authors (Frye, 1963, p. 231; Ghirshman, 1954, p. 347) have made reference to the fact that chess was played in Persia, and Hitti (1951, p. 480) stated that dice was played. At the Persepolis excavation, what were thought to be gaming pieces were discovered (Schmidt, 1957, p. 103).

There is no other country that has survived 6,000 years of existence in the way that Egypt has. No other land mass that has had so little to work with has been able to thrive and prosper to such an extent. There are a number of reasons why the inhabitants of the valley prospered six thousand years ago as well as today. For one thing, the valley was pretty much isolated from the neighboring areas and was thus relatively secure from invasion and plunder. It is surrounded by craggy, rocky hills, some reaching heights of up to 800 feet.

The valley is an arid mass of sandy desert, entirely without water. There is no vegetation except in those places low enough to accommodate an occasional oasis, where the moisture allows for fertile soil. But there are too few such oases to make any real difference. Rather the difference lies with the Nile River. Indeed, Egypt is the gift of the Nile. The Nile provides fertile, rich land from the rising and lowering of its water level, caused by the source from which the river runs. As Cottrell says:

> For the marvelous fertility of Egypt is due to a unique geographical circumstance. The great lakes, Victoria and Albert, like cisterns fed by the equatorial rains, provide the

impetus which drives the mighty river through a thousand miles of parched desert which otherwise would swallow it. But the annual flooding is due to another cause. Once a year the high mountains of Abyssinia intercept the rain clouds of the Indian Ocean as they move north. The falling rain fills the dried-up beds of the Atbara and the Blue Nile, tributaries of the White Nile. (1963, p. 16)

When the river lowers, it leaves behind mud and silt which provide a rich, fertile soil. As the Nile's assets became known, the nomads that wandered from place to place seeking ideal soil and living conditions began to settle on its banks.

The earliest farmers in the Nile Valley settled sometime between 5,000 and 4,000 B.C. Their crops consisted of wheat and barley and, in addition to harvesting their grains, they also hunted, fished, and even raised cattle.

The Egyptians were by no means primitive in their farming techniques in comparison to other civilizations that were developing at or near the same time. At the most they set a precedent in farming methods, but that perhaps is only the start of their amazing achievements. These people who first settled in the Nile Valley are called predynastic by archaeologists because they came before the first dynasties of the Egyptian Pharaohs, founded about 3200 B.C. There were no drastic infiltrations at this time by outsiders, although later there was a gradual influx of more advanced people from the South and East.

Artifacts from as far back as 4000 B.C., revealing pottery, vases, and slate pallettes for grinding eye-paint, demonstrate the craftsmanship and artistic talent of the more advanced Egyptians of the dynastic period.

The line of evolution can be seen in the evidence of the burial preparations for the deceased. It begins with, perhaps, the first grave— a pit in the ground, appropriately called a pit grave. The next to evolve was a mastaba tomb, a rectangular structure made from mud-brick; and finally the magnificent stone pyramids. One might assume that the Egyptians were obsessed with death. The artifacts show intricate details, beautiful reliefs of everyday life, and people preparing for their death. If one did assume such an obsession, one would be incorrect, for the fact remains that the Egyptians were instead obsessed with life and believed they were destined to live eternally. Their motive in creating such remarkable tombs was to provide all the enjoyment of their present life when they passed on into eternal life. Most of the evidence illustrating everyday life is depicted on the walls of the tombs, with painted frescoes, bas-reliefs; there has also been clothing and furniture found within the tombs. In some cases these artifacts were completely intact after 5,000 years.

Some authorities think that perhaps the reason the Egyptians spent so much time, wealth, and labor on death was their belief that the preservation of the body aided in the survival of the soul. Another reason, perhaps, was that the dry, hot climate contributed, along with the sand, as a medium for preservation. Though embalmed, bodies found in predynastic pit-graves of 4000 B.C. are often found with skin and hair still intact.

When the nomadic tribes first came to the Nile Valley, they all settled along the banks at different places. They all had their own religious beliefs and practices. When a need arose to unite these people, perhaps when an irrigation system needed to be developed for the annual flooding of the river, they were all united under one ruler. This concept brought strife and rebellion. Then the country was divided into Upper Egypt and Lower Egypt. In 3200 B.C. Narmar, a powerful chieftain from the south, swept up toward Upper Egypt and captured it. This was the first time Egypt had been brought under a single crown, and it was the beginning of the dynasties.

By this time a high state of civilization had already developed, though the pyramids would not be created until four centuries later. These beginning rulers were buried in the mastaba tombs. The tombs were robbed of the valuables that were placed there, yet there is still ample evidence in these tombs to give one a picture of how life was lived, particularly the games.

The Third Dynasty (2800–2720 B.C.) reveals an already developing economic and manpower resource. Djoser, the first King of that Dynasty, founded a capital at Memphis, ten miles south of Cairo. There the first so-called step pyramid was built to be the tomb of the royal master. This was man's first attempt to build a great building of stone. This tomb and the seventy that were to follow represent the Egyptian's never-ending preoccupation with death.

When one looks at the educational developments of the Egyptians, it is noticeable that they were practical in their learning. To convey their thoughts they constructed a system of symbols, called hieroglyphics. These little pictures represented tools, elements such as water and earth, and animals. The symbols are recognizable even today. The scribes, who were considered a part of the elite, were the ones who mastered the art of writing. Instructed by older scribes, they copied, using papyrus to record their instruction. The instructor would give them any number of works to record—fairy tales, passages from a religious text or a magic book, and preferably, ancient poems, as great thoughts of life were incorporated in these books and the student would therefore gain wisdom.

The literature traced the lives of gods, rulers, and conflicts, and these were developed into stories and folk myths. As the civilization advanced so did their educational techniques. Their language became more complex, their stories contained greater detail. These people were indeed advanced. Subsequent civilizations gained much knowledge from the habits and practices of the Egyptian people, and from their devices and their approaches to agriculture.

The overall fact, however, is that the Nile dominated the Egyptian civilization in much the same manner as the Tigris and the Euphrates dominated the Mesopotamian civilizations.

Many individuals contributed to the modern unraveling of the Egyptian civilization: Napoleon, mainly because he brought 175 of the French intelligentsia with him when he invaded Egypt, and in addition to a number of significant finds and records (the originals of which were ceded to England and are in the British Museum), a soldier found the Rosetta stone, the key to the deciphering of the hieroglyphics; Jean-François Champollion, the French language genius who eventually deciphered the stone; the former Italian strongman Giovanni Battiata Belzoni, an avid collector who discovered Seti's tomb and opened up the second pyramid at Gizeh; Richard Lepsius, the great cataloguer, whose finds are in the Berlin Museum; the Frenchman Auguste Mariette, who found the Avenue of the Sphinxes at Sakkara and founded the Egyptian Museum; the Englishmen William Mathew Flinders Petrie and Howard Carter, who are responsible for significant finds, Carter's discovery of Tutankhamen, in particular, capturing the imagination of the world.

The following physical activities are seen in the Egyptian civilization (Palmer, 1967, pp. 31–87); acrobatics and gymnastic games, tug-of-war, hoop and kicking games, ball and stick games, juggling, knife throwing, club throwing, wrestling, swimming, guessing games, games of chance, and board games.

There are many Egyptian artifacts of acrobats. Most participants appear to be women, and it is quite possible they were a professional class. Hieroglyphic symbols depict acrobatics (Chapouthier, 1938a, Figures 21 and 22), and two limestone figures (Breasted, 1948, Plates 84 and 85a) and another source (Maspero, 1912, Figure 287) show female figures in the "back bend" position.

The tomb of Beni-Hasan (dating from 2000–1800 B.C.) has provided us with many athletic scenes, and chief among them are those that exhibit what appear to be exercises and gymnastics (Newberry, 1893, Part I, Plate XXIX; Part II, Plates VIII, XIII, XVI; Diem, 1960, Plates 75, 78; Montet, 1958, p. 101; Evans, 1935, Figure 450).

Other gymnastic-type games are in evidence. One large relief from the Tomb of Mereruka at Sakkara (Pritchard, 1954, Figure 217) shows three and possibly four activities. We see the game of "pick-a-back." A youth appears to be maintaining himself on the shoulders and arms of his three nude companions. Two groups of three are indulging in what appears to be "tug-of-war." Three runners appear ready to start in the relief, and would appear to be connected to another two figures, who are represented by the artist as above each other. It is felt that this is merely artistic license and indeed primitive art, and that they are meant to be near each other. The game represented here is believed to be "kid on the ground," which is represented elsewhere in Egyptian artifacts.

> The game of "kid on the ground" was a kind of obstacle race. Two boys sat on the ground facing each other, arms and legs stretched out and fingers extended, and with the left heel resting on top of the right foot. These two boys were the obstacle which the other players had to jump without getting caught. The obstacle could of course try to catch the legs of the jumpers and so "bring the kid to the ground." The jumper was not allowed to pretend to jump and then not do so, but as he began his run he called out "Look out, boys! Here I come!" (Montet, 1958, p. 101)

The swinging game of the Egyptians (Smith, 1958, Figure 221; Newberry, 1893, Part II, Plate IV) was most interesting, and there are two tomb paintings depicting the activity. A form of the game is described by Montet:

> . . . two big girls stood back to back and stretched their arms out sideways. Four other little girls stood with their feet close to them and took their outstretched hands, holding themselves rigid as if they were hanging from them. When the word was given the whole group whirled around at least three times—unless they all fell down and brought the game to an end. (1958, p. 102)

The artist had depicted the center figures as facing the same direction, but it is felt that they should have been represented back to back, as described by Montet.

A representation from the Tomb of Ptah-hotep shows a crawling and balancing activity (Smith, 1958, Figure 211). A man is crawling on his hands and knees while two small boys, holding each other's legs, balance precariously on each side of the man's body.

A painting from the same tomb (Smith, 1958, Figure 215) depicts an odd game. One boy is shown kneeling on the ground, his body turned around to face or possibly seize an opponent, who has touched him with a leg, or perhaps even kicked him. Other legs are shown on the first youth. One conception of the game is that the players surround the youth and kick at him randomly, and if the kneeling boy can seize one of his adversaries, that boy then would occupy the center position.

An interesting painting from the Tomb of Beni-Hasan (Newberry, 1893, Part II, Plate XVI) shows two youths with hooked sticks playing with a hoop. The shape of the sticks and the fact that there is but one hoop does suggest that it was a competitive game.

Ball games were also played in ancient Egypt (Cottrell, 1960, Figure 32; Wilkinson, 1878, p. 65; Naville, 1901, Plate C). One painting (Naville,

1901, Plate C) from the Temple of Deir-el-Bahari depicts Thothmes III holding a wavy stick in his right hand and a large ball in his left hand. Two dwarf-size prophets are shown nearby proferring two balls to Thothmes III. Simri (1965) believes this representation to be the first artifact demonstrating a ball game fulfilling a religious or magical function. Naville says that the purpose of the ceremony was "to strike the ball to (in honor of) Hathon the protectress of Thebes" (1901, p. 4).

Four representations from the Tomb of Beni-Hasan show girls with long braided hair playing ball games in either a dance or exercise. A painting from Tomb fifteen shows what undoubtedly is juggling (Newberry, 1893, Part II, Plates IV, XIII) and we see what appear to be two, three, and four balls in use and four different attitudes of the jugglers. The other two paintings show what are possibly team games. In the first (Newberry, 1893, Part II, Plates IV, XIII) we see two girls seated "side-saddle" on the backs of other girls, and one is apparently throwing balls to the other (Figure 1–2). This has some similarities to a Greek game. The final painting (Newberry, 1893, Part II, Plates IV, XIII) shows what appears to be a team game, three girls against three girls. One girl is apparently throwing to the other side, where another girl is in the act of catching the ball. The other four players are represented with arms outstretched as if to catch a ball. This has occasionally been likened to an earlier form of the Greek game "Episkyros."

Figure 1–2. Ball Game. Mural painting in a tomb near Beni-Hasan. Egyptian, Dynasty XII, about 1900 B.C.

From *The Art of Ancient Egypt* (Vienna: The Phaidon Press, 1936), Figure 246.

Knife throwing (Newberry, 1893, Part II, Plate VII) is represented in a painting from the Tomb of Beni-Hasan. In the left-hand segment two youths are shown withdrawing long, thin knives from a block of wood while one prepares to throw. On the right-hand side two figures are shown; two knives are in the wood, one being withdrawn, while a thrower with a knife in each hand prepares to throw.

Two stick-fighting sequences are in evidence (Wilkinson, 1878, p. 72; Diem, 1960, Plates 91, 92). The left forearm and hand of the figure are protected by leather and/or wood, that arm being held high to ward off blows. A stick is held in the right hand. A form of this game has been preserved to the present day in Japan.

An activity that resembles our modern club swinging has been found in Tomb fifteen at Beni-Hasan (Newberry, 1893, Part II, Plate VII). Three males are shown at various stages of swinging a weighted bag of some kind.

The representations of wrestling are possibly the most complete artifacts of any physical activity in ancient times. A limestone relief from the Tomb of Ptah-hotep (Phaidon Press, 1936), dating from 2480 B.C., shows three pairs of wrestlers. The first pair is engaged and one of the wrestlers has been put in a disadvantageous position, preparatory to a toss. The other two scenes show figures being thrown in a most dramatic fashion. An ostracon in the Cairo Museum (Maspero, 1908, Figure 285) shows two wrestlers in the "referee's hold," one hand seizing the other's neck, the other hands being grasped.

The remaining artifacts are all from the Tomb of Beni-Hasan. A detail of the wrestlers shown in the tomb (Phaidon Press, 1936, Figure 251) demonstrates that they are wearing a form of loin belt, perhaps comparable to that worn by the Sumerians (Figure 1–3). The belts are clearly seen in one representation (Wilkinson, 1878, p. 71), where a wrestler holds out a belt while another attaches it. One part of the belt appears to act as a protection for the hip, its position being vertical to the upright body. These drawings show the athletes putting on the belts, facing each other, going into the referee's hold, one being grasped by the leg and then turned and eventually floored.

The representation from the north wall of Tomb fifteen (Newberry, 1893, Part II, Plate VII) can only be described as remarkable. Two hundred and twenty separate groups of wrestlers are shown, and there is rarely duplication of position. These scenes are worthy of closer study. The wrestlers are distinguished by the use of two colors, red and red-brown. It is obvious that a great number of moves and counters were known to the Egyptian wrestlers and they practiced assiduously. The east wall of Tomb seventeen (Newberry, 1893, Part II, Plate V) is a similar scene of considerable magnitude, embracing 122 separate groups of wrestlers.

Figure 1–3. Wrestlers. Mural painting in a tomb near Beni-Hasan. Dynasty XII, Egyptian, about 1900 B.C.

From *The Art of Ancient Egypt* (Vienna: The Phaidon Press, 1936), Figure 251.

Swimming is also in evidence (Figure 1–4). Hieroglyphic symbols from the Chapel of Iv-Mery (Smith, 1958, Figure 10), dated from 3000–2700 B.C., have been taken to be swimming—apparently a form of crawl and/or sidestroke. Mehl (1927, Figure 11) also notes a hieroglyphic symbol for swimming. A wall painting from Sakkara (Smith, 1958, Figure 166) also shows people in the water, and, in all probability, swimming. There are also four elegant cosmetic boxes (Phaidon Press, 1936, Figure 292; Woldering, 1963, Plate 48; Mehl, 1927, Figure 5) on which the handles are carved in the shape of what are presumably swimmers.

Guessing games appear to have been very popular, which is understandable when their simplicity is considered. These were basically finger games, similar to Japanese finger games of today. There are three such artifacts (Wilkinson, 1878, pp. 55, 61, 70), all essentially similar. The game was called "atep" and it had various forms, but it usually involved

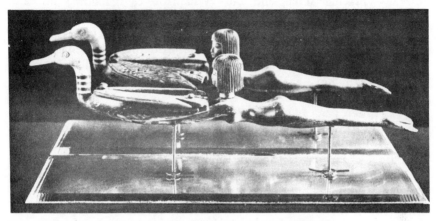

From *The Art of Ancient Egypt* (Vienna: The Phaidon Press, 1936). Figure 296.

two players, one guessing the number of fingers in the other's concealed hand or guessing odd or even. There was a game using four large thimbles (Newberry, 1893, Part II, Plate VII), probably with an object concealed underneath, that can also be classified as a guessing game.

Board games were played extensively, particularly by the upper class, as evidenced by the tomb finds. Falkener (1961) had endeavored to reconstruct these games, but the main ones were "tau," "senat," and "bowl."

Draughtsmen (Wilkinson, 1878, pp. 59–60)—from the Tombs of Ramses II and other Pharaohs, and in the private collections of Sir John Gardiner Wilkinson—are of various shapes, though those found in the Tomb of Queen Hatchepsut (Falkener, 1961, p. 31), along with knucklebones, are of a more regular design.

The game of "bowl" is shown in a tomb painting (Falkener, 1961, p. 83) with two players and two spectators, though all the figures could possibly be players. Thirteen concentric circles are drawn, and small marble-like objects are shown.

A game board of ivory and ebony veneer (Pritchard, 1954, Figure 46) was found in the Tomb of Ren Seneb. Ivory pieces are stuck in the board to show progression, and animal heads are carved at their ends. Three game boards (Carter, 1963, Volume III, Plate XLII) were also found in the annex of the Tomb of Tutankhamen. Playing pieces were also found.

There are also numerous artifacts of people playing board games. In the Tomb of Ramses III (Wilkinson, 1878, pp. 59–60) we have a tomb painting of Ramses III playing a game that resembles draughts, and at

Beni-Hasan and Thebes are tomb paintings of people kneeling at very low tables playing "senat" and "tau" (Wilkinson, 1878, Figures 206.1 and 208).

Other representations are of men playing a game resembling draughts (Smith, 1958, Figure 200), Nefertiti playing "senat" in the Tomb of Nefertiti (Mekhitarian, 1954, p. 140), and finally, a papyrus showing a lion and a gazelle playing "tau" (Phaidon Press, 1936, Figure 272).

Egyptian games and sports are considerably in evidence, then, in the period from 3000 to 1500 B.C. No attempt has been made here to consider the magnitude of their role in the society of the time, due to the limitations of the material and the inferences that would have to be made. The aim has simply been to outline the range of the activities, considering that we are discussing a civilization over 4,000 years old. Most of the evidence presented is indisputable, except in particular points related to the activity. The following physical activities, in summary, were in evidence: acrobatics, tumbling, dancing, exercises for various parts of the body, possibly resistance exercises, yoga or a race on the knees, "pick-a-back," a jumping game ("kid-on-the-ground"), tug-of-war, a crawling and balancing game, a kicking game, ball games, juggling, a hoop game, a stick game, knife throwing, dueling with sticks, the swinging of weights, wrestling, swimming, finger and guessing games, and board games.

THE MINOAN-MYCENAEAN CIVILIZATION

The Minoan civilization, in the Bronze Age, was the first European civilization. It was found on the island of Crete, which is approximately 160 miles long and 35 miles wide. The Minoan period was approximately from 3000 to 1100 B.C. It has been classified into the Early (3000–1950), Middle (1950–1550) and Late (1550–1100) periods. This Bronze Age civilization was discovered by Sir Arthur Evans at the beginning of this century, and he classified and named it after the legendary King Minos of the Labyrinth.

There is little known of the Early Minoan period and it passed rather abruptly into the middle Minoan about 1950 B.C. Large cities with great palaces (Knossos, Mallia, and Phaestos) and rich villas sprang up in central Crete with great administrative centralization. The use of the half-hieroglyphic, half-syllabic script, Linear A, became widespread. The arts flourished, particularly the luxury arts of goldworking and fresco painting. The most beautiful Minoan works belong to this period.

About 1650 B.C. a series of earthquakes struck. Most of the great Cretan structures were demolished or severely damaged, and the power passed to mainland Greece, in particular to Mycenae. However, the Cretan cities and palaces were quickly rebuilt. About 1450 B.C. a gigantic cataclysm occurred on Thera, a volcanic island some hundred miles to the north of Crete. Crete was later occupied by another culture (possibly Mycenaean). Knossos was finally sacked in the twelfth century by the Dorians, thus going to ruin at the same time as the Homeric or Mycenaean cities of Pylos, Tiryns, and Mycenae.

Crete is a most beautiful, idyllic island with many beaches, fertile plains, and cypress forests. The people in that era were centered in settlements near the coast, and excavations have revealed impressive buildings of stone and wood, some with elaborate frescoes, reliefs and pottery, systems of indoor plumbing and well-lighted and well-ventilated homes. They had a love of flowing line and brilliant color, of music, of beautiful clothing and slender bodies. They had a remarkably peaceable character; almost nowhere do Cretan artifacts contain the celebrations of warlike or militaristic exploits or personalities so typical of contemporary Egyptian or Mycenaean cultures. This attitude is also reflected in their sports and games.

Mycenae is generally taken as the first Bronze Age site identified in Greece; it was discovered by the amateur Heinrich Schliemann. Mycenaean refers to the people of Greece in the Late Bronze Age. There are no records which establish a chronology of dynasties; therefore we know nothing of their philosophy and literature. Some of their art remains: a few pieces of sculpture and the foundations of several buildings. Their towns were major architectural works and involved large-scale engineering.

The later Greeks (Hellenes) were so staggered by the traces of Mycenaean masonry that they assumed that the walls must have been built by semi-divine giants such as Cyclops, and the term Cyclopean survives today to denote the Mycenaean method of building walls with monumental blocks of stone. Their palaces were decorated with magnificent frescoes. They knew and used the art of writing, Linear B, which was an early dialect of Greek. Their dating, from 3000 to 1100 B.C., overlapped the Minoan civilization.

From the Minoan[3] there are many representations of various physical activities. Among these are four representations of tumbling and aspects of acrobatics. The discovery—by the French school at the Palace of Mallia (Chapouthier, 1938a, pp. 1–62)—of the gold covering of the pommel of a bronze sword revealed a remarkable figure of an acrobat in an extreme back arch position, the toes pointed and the soles of the feet

[3]The term Minoan is not given an ethnic connotation in this section, but is simply used to mean the people who lived in Crete during the Bronze Age from roughly 3000 to 1200 B.C.

touching the head of the acrobat, with the arms under the face in a forearm balance or "tiger" stand position. A bluish seal (Evans, 1935, Vol. IV, Part II, pp. 500–502) shows two tumblers in a flowery field. They are shown in the handstand position, arms semibent. The seal stone is very symmetrically represented, the legs of the tumblers crossing both bodies, which appear lean and strong. Another seal stone, now at Athens, also shows two acrobats in a hand or forearm stand position; the body arch is not as pronounced as in the other examples, the legs do not cross over, but the resemblance is intensified by the presence of three flowers or stalks between the acrobats. This is possibly Mycenaean rather than Minoan (Sakellariou, No. 131).

Perhaps the best-known physical activities of the Minoan period were those related to bull grappling and the so-called "taureador" sports. A primary feature of these, particularly the latter, was their acrobatic nature. The representations of the bull games far outnumber those of any other games in the Minoan period. The bull is a common subject of Minoan artists and is shown to us on seal stones, frescoes, plaster reliefs, bronzes, rings, pendants, and vases.

There is evidence of both bull vaulting and bull grappling. It is also apparent that such activities were performed ceremonially, at the Palace of Minos at Knossos, as well as in the country, the country activities being, perhaps, an imitation of the more elaborate palace games. Their purpose, significance, and the ceremonial surrounding them is largely unknown.

The "Taureador Fresco," restored by Evans and co-workers, is by far the most famous artifact of bull vaulting (Evans, 1935, Vol. III, Figure 144) and is thought to represent the most probable manner in which the feat was performed. This performance was also reconstructed diagrammatically for Evans by Mr. Theodore Fyfe (Evans, 1935, Vol. III, Figure 156): the acrobat is shown seizing the horns of the bull near the tips, the body of the performer being between the horns; the head of the bull lifts to throw the performer, who holds on to the horns and uses his or her own momentum plus the tossing of the bull's head to effect a front somersault (incorrectly designated as a back somersault by Evans [1935, Vol. III, p. 222]), landing on the back of the bull.

The main fresco itself shows a galloping bull, with three acrobats, two female and one male. The female "Taureadors" are shown with light skin color, the male is of "ruddy hue" (Evans, 1935, Vol. III, p. 211). The dress is very similar, all wearing loincloth and girdle, but the colors of the females' apparel are different. They all have long hair, but the female figures show short curls over the forehead and temple. "Their foot-gear consists of short gaiters or stockings and pointed moccasin-like shoes" (Evans, 1935, Vol. III, p. 212). Bands are worn around the wrists of the performers similar to the thongs worn by Greek boxers, and double necklaces are worn as well.

The fresco shows one female acrobat holding the horn or horns, the male over the back of the bull in the later stages of a front somersault, while the third figure (female) appears to be standing, with arms outstretched as if to assist the landing of the acrobat. From the reconstruction it would be difficult to see how the performer could land on the back of the bull; he would more likely finish the somersault off the bull, with the aid of the third acrobat.

The evidence is by no means clear-cut as to the actual method of the performance, if indeed it had a consistent pattern. The size of the enclosure, the ability of the performers, the speed of the bull, and the bull's reaction were possibly all variables which added to the excitement of the performance and its lack of consistency.

Bull grappling, which was continued up to the present time in rodeos, was evidenced by Mycenaean artifacts, particularly the Vapheio Cup; nevertheless, there are enough remains available to demonstrate that the activity was performed in Minoan times.

The remains of a crystal plaque from Knossos (Evans, 1935, Vol. III, Plate XIX and Figures 60, 61, pp. 108–111) show what appears to be a rope stretched between two trees to prevent the flight of the bull. A man seems to be jumping forward to seize the horns and throw the bull. A lenticular seal (Kenna, 1960, p. 125), in the Ashmolean Museum, Oxford, might also be considered as evidence. A galloping bull is leapt at from behind and seized by the horns. Another man lies prone on the ground, attesting to the danger. A similar lenticular seal (Kenna, 1960, Plate 10, p. 125) of spartan basalt may also be evidence as a bull is grasped from behind by the horns as if he is to be grappled. Perhaps the most conclusive evidence is a sealing (Kenna, 1960, Plate 10, p. 125) from the Fifth Magazine at Knossos, also in the Ashmolean Museum. This depicts a bull-grappling scene where the man's right arm passes over the neck of the bull and the base of the horn is grasped with the left hand. It is not dissimilar to the rodeo "tossing" position used today.

As mentioned, many of the performances of the bull games were apparently in the country, but some were obviously conducted in or near the palaces. Some archaeological evidence bears on where such activities might have been held.

> Peculiar likewise is the remarkable degree of similarity . . . among the central courts of the three major palaces (Minos at Knossos, Phaestos, Mallia). All were paved with flagstones; all had one or more porticoes, probably with upper galleries, on the long sides; all had their long axis running north and south; and all measure about 80 feet broad by 170 feet long. This standardization, as it were, of the court might even

suggest that it was built to definite specifications, like a football field or a tennis court (Graham, 1962, pp. 74–75).

Graham (1962, pp. 75–76) says that there can be no doubt that these central courts were used for bull games. "Representations of the bull games sometimes hint at an architectural background, and Evans was of the opinion that the "Grandstand Fresco" [Evans, 1935, Vol. III, pp. 36–65], as he called it, depicted a large crowd of Cretan men and women watching these sports in a setting of columns and tri-columnar shrine. . . ."

Dance was a seemingly important aspect of the Cretan way of life (Oesterley, 1923). Frescoes, seal stones, and a terra-cotta model depict this activity.

Probably the best known artifact is the terra-cotta model found at Palaikastro (Evans, 1935, Vol. III, pp. 73–80). Three female votaries are shown dancing with outstretched arms, in a near semicircle around a central female figure who is playing the lyre. It has been variously interpreted as a chain (Marinatos, [n.d.], p. 153), a ring (Evans, 1935, Vol. III, p. 73), or a simple round (Glotz, 1925, p. 290) dance. The dancers are facing inward, looking toward the lyre player, who, it has been suggested (Evans, 1935, Vol. III, p. 73), is the Minoan goddess herself with her sacred dove in front of her.

The evidence of dance in the Minoan period points to both group and individual dances. Group dances are perhaps represented in the harvester's dance, and in the beautiful fresco from Knossos, the so-called "Miniature Fresco of the Sacred Grove and Dance" (Evans, 1935, Vol. III, pp. 66–80), in which we see perhaps five hundred spectators among a grove of olive trees, women occupying the best seats; they are observing a dance, perhaps being performed by a Goddess:

> In the open space in front . . . groups of women on a blue ground are seen performing what seems to be a ceremonial dance. Their hair streams out behind them in separate tresses, in a manner that in some cases is clearly indicative of a quick rhythmic movement, and the attitude and arrangement of the figures as far as it can be reconstructed is certainly suggestive of a sensuous meandering course—such as is associated with the traditional Knossian dance in the Ariadne's honour. Their dress reproduces the fashionable cut of the ladies of the Temple scene. They wear short-sleeved jackets open at the bosom, diaphanous chemises, and flounced gowns, the prevailing saffron hue of which had perhaps religious associations. In nearly all cases they have one arm raised or held out before them, as in the act of adoration, towards some sacred personage or object on the left. (Evans, 1935, p. 67)

The individual type of dances are mainly those which Evans calls dances of "ecstatic possession" (1935, Vol. III, p. 69), or "orgiastic" dances. The "Fresco of a Dancing Lady" (Evans, 1935, Vol. III, pp. 369–71; pp. 70–71) is typical, showing the hair of the dancer flying out, exemplifying the spinning of the dancer. It is occasionally a male in ecstatic possession (Evans, 1935, Vol. II, p. 614). We see single female figures in the Vapheio finds (Furtwangler, [n.d.], p. 45; Evans, 1901, pp. 99*ff.* and Figure 52) and at Phaestos (Savignoni, 1904, p. 578).

It is also fairly evident that among the objects described we also see the sacred dance, which may be subclassified into the sacred processional dance, the encircling of a sacred object, the ecstatic dance, sacred dance at harvest festivals, and the sacred dance as a burial or mourning rite (Oesterley, 1923).

The most famous representation of boxing in Minoan times is that of the funnel-shaped rhyton of black steatite from the Palace of Hagia Triada, dated about 1550–1500 B.C. (Evans, 1935, Vol. I, Figure 511). The rhyton is composed of four "zones," and at least two of them, perhaps three, represent boxing.

The lower band shows what apparently are boys boxing. They do not wear helmets or any hand protection and they have masses of curly hair. Three men are shown standing in what seems to be the normal Minoan boxing stance—legs well spread, the leading (usually the left) arm well out but slightly bent as if in a "hook" or a "jab," the other arm held well back of the body and apparently waist high as if to throw an "uppercut" or "straight" right, but certainly not in a position to guard the head or the body. Two boxers are down on the ground. One has his right leg bent, with the right foot on the ground. His right arm is held up close to his head as if to prevent blows, and he is holding himself off the ground by his extended left arm. The head is not toward his antagonist but looking down toward his left hand. The other knockdown on this band shows a boxer who has been knocked down so hard that he is on the upper part of his back, with his feet above his head.

The second band from the bottom also depicts boxing, and the zone is divided horizontally and vertically. There has been comment, particularly on what the vertical division is (Marinatos, [n.d.], p. 147), ranging from evidence of stands and hence arenas for spectators (Gardiner, 1931, p. 10), to standards or banners raised for festive occasions (Marinatos, [n.d.], p. 147). In any case, we see three panels in this zone: (a) a victor and a defeated boxer (the opponent is on the ground on his knees, head toward the ground); (b) a victor only; and (c) a defeated boxer only. The characteristic stance is evident but there are two important differences between these figures and those in the lower panel. These boxers "wear close-fitting helmets, possibly of leather similar to the later wrestling caps; their hands seem to be padded, the forearm also protected by some sort of guard" (Gardiner, 1931, pp. 9–10). The helmet appears too big to resemble the later wrestling cap, but there appears to be little doubt that we are seeing an earlier form of the Roman *caestus* rather than the straps of oxhide which the bull vaulters appear to be using and which were used in Greece for boxing, particularly in the sixth and fifth centuries B.C.

Two artifacts from the Palace of Minos, both now at the Heraklion Museum, emphasize some of the points already made. The first, a fragment of a steatite rhyton (Evans, 1935, Vol. I, Figure 510), clearly shows a covering for the hands, wrist, and forearm, as if a glove and/or *caestus* were used. The stance is characteristic: a fallen opponent is between the legs of the victor, the head appears to be uncovered, though the forehead is overly square as if there were some kind of guard. Another Knossos find (Evans, 1935, Vol. I, Figure 509) shows a boxer in characteristic stance, a fallen opponent barely shown. Again, a column is shown in the sealing, and Evans says (1935, Vol. I, pp. 689–90): "This . . . corresponds with the structural arrangement of the 'Grand Stands' on either side of the Shrine on the 'Temple Fresco' of Knossos, where pillars of the same peculiar character are depicted. The 'Grand Stands' there enabled crowds of spectators to look on at agnostic contests held, no doubt, in honour of the great Minoan Goddess."

Evidence of wrestling is certainly not conclusive. The main support for the activity is in the upper zone of the rhyton from the Palace of Hagia Triada (Bossert, 1937, Plate 272), the so-called "boxer rhyton." The handle of the rhyton was obviously made separately and obscures a part of what is generally taken to be two wrestlers. Their bodies are close together and they appear to be grappling rather than hitting one another.

Hunting is commonly represented in Minoan art. We have been left examples of the hunting of the lion, stag, wild goat, calf, ewe, wild boar, oxen, and bull. The animals are hunted with bow and arrow, spear, dagger, sword, nets, and often with the assistance of hounds. The prevalence of fish motifs suggests that fishing was commonly practiced as well.

That archery was practiced was noticeable in the hunt (Evans, 1935, Vol. IV, Figure 556, pp. 574–76). In addition to these representations, we have vase fragments depicting archery (Zervos, [n.d.], Plate 480). Other than these instances, it is not seen in a game or a sport scene, though it is perhaps reasonable to infer that in practicing accuracy it would have found such forms.

That running was practiced, even though in this case as a military exercise, is evidenced by the "Captain of the Blacks" fresco (Evans, 1935, Vol. II, Plate XIII, pp. 755–57). A Minoan captain is depicted leading a black troop, all at a run. The captain is clearly seen with two spears. The arm and leg positions of the captain and what are undoubtedly black mercenaries are those of distance running.

A three-sided prism seal (Kenna, 1966, p. 151) of cream-brown steatite, from the private collection of R. W. Hutchinson, clearly shows a running man. The style is that of a sprinter, with arms up high and legs stretched. An interesting find was that of Hogarth at Kato Zakro in 1901. A clay sealing (Hogarth, 1902, p. 78) shows three figures moving to the right. The figures appear to be female and the arms are held as if they are running. The style would lead one to judge that distance running was being depicted.

Mention should be made at this point of the possibility of a strigil being used in Minoan times. The find was by Hazzidakis (1921, Figure 32). Ridington ([n.d.], p. 68) also refers to the discovery of the strigil as an example of the interest of Minoans in athletics, and reinforces the view by noting that the word for strigil is of pre-Greek origin. If this were the strigil it would leave room for considerable speculation, and though the opinion of Hazzidakis must be respected, the lack of supporting evidence must place the find in the highly doubtful, even unlikely, category.[4]

The "Swimmers" dagger from the Tholos tomb at Vapheio (Marinatos, 1927, pp. 63–71) is the only artifact that represents swimming, and it is Mycenaean. Male swimmers, entirely naked, are seen performing what appears to be sidestroke. Inlaid gold wires depict the sea (Marinatos, 1927, p. 70).

A red lentoid jasper or pebble (Kenna, 1966, p. 203) is the only certain artifact depicting juggling or ball throwing. A man is shown playing with two balls, throwing them in the air, and he is standing between two steers.

A remarkable terra-cotta model (Evans, 1935, Vol. IV, pp. 24–27) from the Phaestos shrine, found by Italian archaeologists, shows a female figure on a swing. The figure, because of the doves on the two side pillars, has been taken to be the Goddess herself.

Various finds at Palaikastro, in both houses and cemeteries, have been taken to be toys (Bosanquet and Dawkins, 1923, pp. 110–11). In the main they were miniature vases which undoubtedly were used as toys, perhaps in a game resembling today's "house." The miniature vases correspond with those of larger vases in common use.

Excavations of a large double cavern southwest of Psychro revealed several terra-cotta objects (Hogarth, 1900, pp. 94–116) like cotton reels; Hogarth believed these to be pawns in a game. A three-sided prism bead of white steatite from Kastelli Pediada (Kenna, 1966, p. 92) shows a man playing some kind of a game at a table. His hand is raised as if he were making a move with one of the pieces. Evans says:

> The table-like object . . . with its square divisions leads us to a remarkable series of comparisons. It is in fact a Minoan draughtboard and in the triangular object beneath

[4]This is the opinion of Dr. Catlin of the Ashmolean Museum.

the hand of the seated personage we must recognize a conical draughtsman. (1935, Vol. I, pp. 124–25)

A six-faced Minoan III ivory signet (Evans, 1935, Vol. I, p. 125) has been taken by Evans to be a Minoan adaptation of an Egyptian "draughtboard" sign *man*. The draughtsmen show a characteristic knobbed head.

The most outstanding find, however, was the Royal "Draught Board" at Knossos (Evans, 1935, pp. 472–85). The board is inlaid with gold, ivory, and crystal. This magnificent work has possibly three divisions: the four discs which would appear to represent the "goal" of the game, a middle area of ivory inlays that were possibly used for marking scores, and a separate area below of ten disks of smaller diameter than those in the "goal." Evans is of the following opinion:

It looks as if the game proper had been played on this [i.e. the ten discs], one player starting on each wing, and the successive occupation of the squares of the "citadel" being dependent on results obtained below. The victory in each case may have been marked by placing a piece on one of the upper disks, two wins on either side making of course a drawn game. (1935, Vol. I, p. 475)

From this and other evidence, it seems certain that some forms of board games were played in the Minoan period.

J. D. Evans (Plate 59), in more recent excavations, noted that cattle astragali were probably used as gaming pieces. The dating is Neolithic, but Mosso (1908, pp. 148–49) also commented on the frequency of such Neolithic objects at Phaestos. These were probably used for a type of knucklebones, a game which has persisted to the present day. They predate the Minoan period, but they are mentioned here on the assumption that the game persisted throughout the period.

A broken slab of hard limestone discovered at Knossos (Evans, 1935, Vol. III, p. 396) and similar stones found in Kavusi (though of the Hellenic or Greek period) (Boyd, [n.d.], pp. 141–43) have been taken to be evidence of pavement games. The slab shows seven holes or cups and it has been deduced that the complete object would have consisted of twelve such cups. Two are double cups of larger size. But, as Evans said (1935, Vol. III, pp. 391–92):

The comparative material at hand shows that the arrangement constantly varied. The number of small holes in the circle ranges in the known examples from 10 to 39. Sometimes there is a central cup, in other cases it is absent. In the Knossian specimen we see two double holes, and at times there is a hole contained in a side projection.

A limestone disc found at Mallia by French archaeologists (Chapouthier, 1938a, Plate VI) shows 34 surrounding cups with a larger bowl in the center. Chapouthier and Joly have attributed a religious significance to the Mallia table and have called it a "Table of Offerings." The possibility does exist, however, that it is a similar type of pavement game. This type of game was played with dice or pebbles (Evans, 1935, Vol. III, p. 395).

It can be seen that the possibility of pavement games such as knucklebones and cup games is very strong. The exact manner in which these games were played is lost to us.

In conclusion, the archaeological evidence that we have supports the view that a considerable number of games were played in the Minoan-Mycenaean period. From the archaeological remains it is difficult to support the conclusion of Ridington that "... the Minoan-Mycenaean civilization was of notable influence in the development of the Greek athletic festival" ([n.d.], p. 86). It is true, however, that we have evidence of spectators, of boxing, wrestling, running (though no evidence of an actual contest), all of which were part of the Greek festival.

It should again be noted that the picture is incomplete and undoubtedly will always be so. That some of the activities may not have been sports and games is very possible. The *manner* in which the games were played in the Minoan-Mycenaean civilization is, of course, fraught with speculation.

GREEK CIVILIZATION

The increasing range of sports and games is particularly apparent in the Egyptian and the Minoan-Mycenaean civilizations and then reaches its pinnacle, up to that point in society's development, with the Greek civilization. It should again be emphasized that many more sports and games might have been played in the civilizations cited, and doubtless were, but the historian is limited to the evidence, literary and archaeological. As societies developed, their art became more sophisticated, and as writing increased, so did the opportunity for such evidence of games to be recorded. It should be noted, however, that it is doubtful if the games of the lower class were being recorded, and so the evidence that comes down to us may merely represent those activities of the upper classes.

So much has been written on the Greek civilization that it is difficult to summarize briefly the evidence of sports and games. From the sixth to the fourth centuries B.C., in particular, there appeared to be a balance among all of one's daily activities, and sport appeared to play a greater role in normal life than in any other society to this point.

In approximately 1700 B.C. the Achaeans dominated in Greece—we call them Mycenaean in culture—and they lasted from about 1500 to

1200 B.C. About 1184 B.C. they invaded Troy. By the twelfth century the Dorians took over in southern Greece and Crete, and even got to Asia Minor. By the ninth century B.C., the classical Greeks began to emerge, living in city-states such as Corinth, Athens, and Sparta. Despite their differences, they all called themselves "Hellenes."

The land they lived in was rugged, essentially goat and donkey country, with a closeness to the sea. Though rugged, Greece, and for that matter Crete and the other islands of the Aegean, have a compelling beauty. Overpopulation and other factors caused the expansion of Greece throughout the Mediterranean, from about 750 B.C. One colony, Byzantine, became Constantinople, which we now call Istanbul. Their colonies were in the Black Sea, in Spain, in Italy. Their pottery, for example, became famous throughout the Mediterranean.

The Greek army became famous, Athens and particularly Sparta becoming legendary for their militarism. The Greek *hoplite* took his place among the great warriors of the world.

By the fifth century B.C., Athens was the dominant power in Greece, and the city swarmed with ideas—from historians, philosophers, dramatists, and so on. There was a heretofore unheard-of development intellectually, politically, and artistically. We see in Greece the development of the world's first democracy, and the foundation for Western traditions. But by 168 B.C. (Battle of Pydra), 63 B.C. (the annexation of Syria), and 30 B.C. (the annexation of Egypt) Rome had swallowed up the Greek world.

The development of the crown games of Greece—the Isthmian, Pythian, Nemean, and Olympic—was unrivaled in the ancient world. Local festivals appeared in the city-states, and sports and games were a primary part of these festivals. The gymnasia emerged also, affording the citizens a place to meet and talk, to exercise, and to perform various physical activities. Greek pottery—which was eagerly sought throughout the Mediterranean world and, though fragile, has been preserved to the present—bears clear representations of many of the sports and games of ancient Greece (Figures 1–5, 1–6, 1–7, 1–8, 1–9, and 1–10). Greek literature also abounds in references to physical activities (Hardy, 1970).

The following activities are in evidence: acrobatics, running (sprinting and distance running, the hoplite race, and torch races) (Figure 1–9), swimming, the pentathlon, the jump (Figure 1–5), the discus, the javelin (Figure 1–6), ball games of various kinds, boxing, wrestling (Figure 1–8), the pankration (a combination of boxing and wrestling) (Figures 1–7 and 1–10), the swing, the seesaw, *mora* (a hand guessing game), the spinning disc, *ephidrismos* (a form of blind man's buff), *ostrakinda* (a dice game in which the losers had to carry their partners pick-a-back), playing with

Figure 1–5. Jumper in midair with weights. Greek, Museum of Fine Arts, Boston.

From H. A. Harris, *Greek Athletes and Athletics* (Bloomington and London: Indiana University Press, 1966), Figure 8. Reproduced by courtesy of the Trustees of the British Museum.

Figure 1–6. Javelin Thrower. Greek, Staatliche Museen, Berlin 2.

From H. A. Harris, *Greek Athletes and Athletics* (Bloomington and London: Indiana University Press, 1966), Figure 12A. Reproduced by courtesy of the Trustees of the British Museum.

Figure 1–7. Pankratiasts rolling on the ground. Greek, Metropolitan Museum of Art.

From H. A. Harris, *Greek Athletes and Athletics* (Bloomington and London: Indiana University Press, 1966), Figure 21. Reproduced by courtesy of the Trustees of the British Museum.

Figure 1–8. Two pairs of wrestlers. Greek, Staatliche Museen, Berlin 2.

From H. A. Harris, *Greek Athletes and Athletics* (Bloomington and London: Indiana University Press, 1966), Figure 13B. Reproduced by courtesy of the Trustees of the British Museum.

Figure 1-9. Runner awaiting the start. Greek, Metropolitan Museum of Art.

From: H. A. Harris, *Greek Athletes and Athletics* (Bloomington and London: Indiana University Press, 1966), Figure 5A. Reproduced by courtesy of the Trustees of the British Museum.

hoops, and board games. Hunting, fishing, and dancing were also common pursuits.

The Greeks' love of athletics originated in prehistoric times. As the invading Greek-speaking tribes gradually assimilated the Minoan-Mycenaean inhabitants, they took over many of their athletic practices as well; consequently, by Homeric times there developed in the Greek world an attitude toward and a style of athletics which combined the vigor of the northern invaders with the Minoan-Mycenaean love of rhythm, beauty, and music (Ridington, [n.d.], pp. 86–88).

The history of the Olympic Games must then be set against a background of athletic interest already prevalent in Homeric Greece. In both the *Iliad* and the *Odyssey* there is ample evidence that the Greeks enjoyed and participated in athletic contests. In the *Iliad,* the funeral games for Patroclus (Robinson, 1955, pp. 3–22) included a chariot race, a boxing match, a wrestling match, a footrace, a contest in armour, a discus throw, archery, and spear-throwing contests. A similar program of events is described in the *Odyssey.* When Ulysses visits the Phaeacians, he is invited to participate in their after-dinner games, which consist of footracing,

Figure 1-10. Pankratiast biting his opponent. Panathenaic amphora, British Museum.

wrestling, weight throwing, and boxing. It is evident, then, that there was, even in Homeric Greece, an interest in contests and athletics that was not apparent in previous civilizations.

Athletic contests and festivals became common from the ninth century on. Harris (1966, p. 27) lists 146 towns where athletic festivals of some kind are known to have been held in the prime days of Greek athletics. Of these many athletic contests, the Nemean, the Pythian, the Isthmian, and particularly the Olympic Games were outstanding.

Though there is disagreement regarding the date of the first reorganized games, all authors agree that from 776 B.C. the Olympic Games were held every fourth year until their abolition by the Roman Emperor Theodosius in A.D. 393.

Although the events in the program of the Olympic Games changed during the centuries, certain contests became standard. There were four races—the *stade* (approximately 200 yards), the *diaulos* (approximately 400 yards), the *hoplite* race (approximately 400 yards), and the *dolichos*, a long-distance race of uncertain length; the pentathlon, which included the long jump, the discus, the javelin, the footrace (stade), and wrestling; boxing, and the pankration. In addition, various types of chariot and horse races were also a regular feature of the festivities.

Although there are slight disagreements with respect to when some events were instituted (Gardiner, 1931, p. 35), most writers agree with the following chronological list of events as they were added to the Olympic Games:

Stade	776 B.C.
Diaulos	724 B.C.
Dolichos	720 B.C.
Pentathlon and Wrestling	708 B.C.
Boxing	688 B.C.
Pankration	648 B.C.
Boys: Stade and Wrestling	632 B.C.
Boys: Pentathlon	628 B.C. (Held once only)
Boys: Boxing	616 B.C.
Hoplite Race	520 B.C.
Two-Mule Chariot Race	492 B.C.
Horse Riding and Footrace Combination	488 B.C. (Discontinued in 436 B.C.)
Two-Horse Chariot Race	400 B.C.
Contests for Heralds and Trumpeters	388 B.C.
Four-Colt Chariot Race	376 B.C.
Two-Colt Chariot Race	260 B.C.
Colt Race (Riding)	248 B.C.
Pankration for Boys	200 B.C.

There is so much literary and archaeological evidence to support the events of the Olympic Games (Beck, 1964; Freeman, 1969; Gardiner, 1931; Harris, 1966; Hyde, 1921; Robinson, 1955; Rodenwaldt, 1936; Wright, 1925), that they will not be discussed here. It should be noted, however, that the origins of these Games go back to primitive religious festivals held at the shrine of Olympia well before 776 B.C. This religious association remained with the Olympic Games until they were discontinued. Sports were placed under the patronage of the gods, and the victorious athlete felt that he was pleasing to the gods and owed his success to them. That the athlete felt that any violation of the rules of the games was an act of sacrilege and displeasing to the gods undoubtedly helped to preserve the purity of the contests at Olympia, even when competition became fierce at other games (Gardiner, 1931; Kiernan and Daley, 1965).

The power that the Olympic Games held over the spirit of ancient Greece is well illustrated by the truce that prevailed between the warring city-states during the duration of the Games. The month in which the festival was held—falling sometime in August and September (Gardiner, 1910, p. 43)—was considered to be sacred, and a holy truce was proclaimed by the truce bearers of Zeus (Gardiner, 1910, p. 43). From the time the truce bearers began their truce trek, there was to be peace throughout the land and all competitors or visitors traveling to or from Olympia were under the direct protection of Zeus. The effect of this truce was at first purely local, but it spread with the growth of the festival to all the states taking part in it until the whole Greek world felt its influence. Any violation of the truce was punished by heavy fines to be paid to Zeus (Gardiner, 1910, p. 44). Thucydides mentions that when the Spartan forces entered Elean territory during the Olympic truce, they were fined 2,000 minas for each hoplite (Robinson, 1955). Even Philip of Macedon was obliged to apologize and make restitution to the Athenean Phyrron who had been robbed by his mercenaries while on his way to Olympia (Gardiner, 1931, p. 34). The observance of the Olympic truce was sometimes carried to extremes, as during the Persian Wars in 480 B.C., when on the very day the crucial battle of Thermopylae was fought between the Greeks and the invading Persians, the Spartans and their allies considered it more important to participate in the Olympic Games than to fight the invaders (Durant, 1969, p. 7).

For the first half century after the official beginning of the games in 776 B.C., the Olympic festival was confined mostly to the western Peloponnese. Only in the next fifty years did the influence of the festival spread to Sparta and then to the east to the Isthmus, Athens, Thebes, and even across the sea to Smyrna. For about 150 years, between 720 and 576 B.C., Sparta dominated the games (Wright, 1925, p. 17). Out of 81 victories recorded in this period, the Spartans won 46. When athletes began to specialize, Sparta disappeared from the games. Athens also gradually withdrew.

Despite the Spartan and Athenian loss of interest, the Olympic festival grew in popularity in other parts of Greece and also among the colonies. By the sixth century B.C., the Greek colonies, located in every part of the Mediterranean world from the Black Sea to the coast of Spain and Africa, began to dominate the games. In fact, they almost eclipsed the motherland, as evidenced by the fact that most of the so-called Treasures of Olympia were dedicated by colonies (Gardiner, 1931, p. 35).

The Greek civilization, then, made athletics popular, and spectators appeared to watch the athletes perform. Overspecialization and the increases in the value of prizes caused the Games to deteriorate, but not before a new concept toward athletics was apparent to the world. Stadia developed, and gymnasia spread throughout the land.

Professional performers were evident in other spheres of activity. There were, for example, the female acrobats who performed at the homes of the well-to-do. The difficult game of *cottabus* is one in which the professional acrobat is easily distinguished (Zachietzschmann, 1959,

p. 183). On vases, acrobats are also seen doing handstands, in one instance arching over the points of swords (Chapouthier, 1938a, Figure 31).

Besides the various athletic events seen at the festivals, there were games for all. What appears to be a team game, *episkyros*, is seen in one relief now in the National Museum (Zachietzschmann, 1959, p. 157). Another artifact shows a man with a ball in his hand, about to throw it to youths mounted on the shoulders of partners (Gardiner, 1931, Figure 209). One krater shows satyrs playing this game, while a boy stands nearby with a hoop. On two vases, girls (McClus, 1924, Figure 51) and boys (Klein, 1932, Plate xxi) are shown playing the game of passe-boule. One relief shows a youth bouncing a ball on his knee, and another more famous relief shows youths playing what appears to be shinny, with curved sticks and a ball (Gardiner, 1931, Figures 210 and 213).

Very few representations are seen of swimming, though it was considered part of the education of young boys. The "François Vase" depicts swimming, however (Boardman, 1964, Figure 76). A woman appears to be swimming in one amphora (Zachietzschmann, 1959, p. 170), and a diver is seen in a bronze statuette (Gardiner, 1931, Figure 64).

The children had still other games to play. As Palmer said:

> The games of the Greek children differed very little from the familiar range of activities which are enjoyed by children today. They apparently played various forms of blindman's bluff and pick-a-back, and made use of play things as swings, see-saws, hoops, skipping ropes, spinning tops, kites, wheel-barrows and hobby horses.
>
> They kept pets: rabbits, dogs and birds, and the young boys went fishing. Their toys consisted of model animals and dolls which were frequently made with movable arms and legs. While string games are not apparent, there is evidence of the spinning of a disc on a string to produce a humming noise.
>
> Both adults and children appear to have enjoyed a variety of amusements such as *Mora*, Knucklebones, and games similar to Draughts. (1967, p. 310)

ETRUSCAN CIVILIZATION

With the Greek civilization, then, evidence of games has been expanded. Athletics had become more a way of life of the people. The concept of Greek athletics spread throughout the Mediterranean world, and though no other society adopted the ideas completely, nevertheless many other civilizations were affected.

One civilization which was obviously affected by this Greek influence, though rarely mentioned in physical education literature, was the Etruscan civilization. The Etruscan civilization, or pre-Roman civilization, called "Tusci" or "Etrusci" by the Romans, Rasna by themselves, lasted from roughly 800 to 100 B.C., mainly in central Italy, between the Arno and Tiber rivers. There were twelve partially unified cities, the main one being Tarquinia, which is about twenty miles south of Rome. The language is largely undeciphered, so the literary evidence is lacking of this great civilization. A considerable amount of evidence is available from the underground tombs of the wealthier class of the Etruscans, where brilliant wall paintings depict the funeral games.

The following games are apparent from archaeological remains: music, dancing, discus throwing, javelin throwing, boxing contests, gladiatorial contests, wrestling contests, jumping contests, horse racing, chariot racing, hunting, fishing, acrobatics, exercises, board games, *ascolia* (trying to stand on a greasy vase made of goat skin), the game of Troy (maneuvers on horses moving in intricate patterns and movements), *kottobas* (flipping wine drops from a goblet into bronze cups or candelabra), *borsa* (a game in which a purse is played with), and the use of tops, balls, and dice.

A definitive study of the sports and games of the Etruscans by Sawula (1969), adequately presents evidence of the above activities. In addition, he cites the Greek influence in such contests as boxing, wrestling, running, jumping, discus throwing, and javelin throwing. The use of the amentum in the javelin and the halteres in the jump are two examples. We will not repeat Sawula's evidence for each of these activities because of its extensive nature and availability, but his conclusions are relevant in this section on ancient civilizations. His most notable observations and conclusions were (1969, pp. 172–74):

1. Most of the athletic events were held during funeral processions. The athletic events appear to be a means of honoring the deceased. However, there were, in all probability, athletic events other than those held at funerals. The festivals in honor of Voltumna seem to be of a national character similar to those held in Greece.

2. The Etruscans seem to be mostly spectator-oriented. Of the few activities they may have taken part in, horse and chariot racing, hunting, fishing, and dancing are the most apparent. The athletes appear to be slaves, although probably on a higher social level than other slaves.

3. The Etruscans erected wooden stands to seat the spectators. This idea seems to have passed down to the Romans through Tarquinius Priscus. Arenas of some kind, probably constructed of a wooden material, seem apparent, especially for chariot races, where a course seems to have been set out.

4. At athletic events both men and women were admitted. In many cases, as in *Tomba della Scimmia* and *Tomba della Bighe*, women appear to be the individuals in charge or at least those who are being honored.

5. Gladiatorial contests appear to have been initiated by the Etruscans, but not developed. This development occurred in other civilizations, for example,

the Roman and the Samnite. The "game of Phersu" is definitely different from the funeral rites of nearby civilizations.

6. Music and dancing played an important role in the life of an Etruscan. The flute was perhaps the most popular instrument. Acrobatic and armoured dancing also appeared.

7. Actors may have existed in Etruria but they were of a silent nature. The Romans probably developed actors following the Greek models.

8. Dice seem to have been popular among the ladies. Pawns of some sort may have been used in the board games. Other popular games included *kottobas, ascolia,* and *borsa.*

9. Boxing, as well as jumping, appear to have been aided by the music of a flute player.

10. There is no direct evidence of swimming, but diving was represented. Contact with the sea was a common occurrence for the Etruscans. Therefore, swimming of some sort must have been practiced.

11. Evidence of ball games is scanty but balls do appear. The context in which they were used is unknown.

12. Gymnastics seems to have had a place in the physical activities of the Etruscans.

13. The game of Troy was, most likely, an Etruscan game. The Etruscans probably passed it on in some form to the Romans.

ROMAN CIVILIZATION

Roman history is commonly divided into three parts: (1) the period of the Kings, from 753 to 510 B.C.; (2) the period of the Republic, from 509 to 27 B.C., in which Rome won her position in Italy and the Mediterranean and gained political and administrative experience; and (3) the period of the Empire, from 27 B.C. to 476 A.D., in which the greater part of Rome's Empire was acquired under the rule of the Emperors.

By 133 B.C. the Romans were undisputed masters of the Mediterranean, and much bounty flowed into Rome thereafter. Because of the considerable area of the Empire, it was natural that the influences of other countries would be felt. "The Roman roads were the arteries of the empire" and, literally, all roads led to Rome, but also the Mediterranean was *Mare Nostrum,* or "our sea" (Hardy, 1970, pp. 74, 75). By the first century of the Empire it has been estimated that in Rome alone there were some 400,000 slaves, the emperors themselves having households of 20,000 slaves (Hardy, 1970, pp. 86, 87). Roman luxury perhaps reached its peak from 31 B.C. to 68 A.D.; we hear of feasts costing $300,000 in present currency (Hardy, 1970, pp. 93, 94), and in 45 B.C. some 320,000 Roman citizens received free grain.

As Hardy says, however:

> Feeding the unemployed was not enough. They also had to be amused. This was done by free admission to the games. The games, or *ludi,* were originally religious celebrations. By the time of Augustus, sixty-four days in each year were occupied by the games. By the reign of Marcus Aurelius, their number had increased to 135 days in the year. These were the regular festivals. There were also extraordinary games. In 80 A.D., for example, Titus presented games for 100 days in succession and Trajan celebrated the conquest of Dacia by 123 days of continuous festivities. (1970, p. 96)

The Circus games had no parallel in the ancient world. They were for the entertainment of the masses, partly to keep the vast number of unemployed occupied. The Circus Maximus, with crowds up to 250,000, was the scene of the famous chariot and horse races. A day's racing generally consisted of 24 events. There was considerable betting, and the leading charioteers were heroes in Rome. The Spaniard Diocles, for example, drove chariots for 24 years and won 1,462 victories (Lindsay, 1967, p. 112). It was a rather serious business.

> (A.D. 39, Gaius Caligula.) Gaius poisoned horses and charioteers of rival factions; for he was strongly attached to the party that wore the frog-green, which from this colour was also called the party of the Leek. . . . One of the horses, which he named Incitatus, he used to invite to dinner, where he would offer him golden barley and drink his health in wine from golden goblets (Dio, [n.d.], p. 14).

During the Republic the Circus was used for gladiatorial and wild beast fights as well, and indeed the Christians were slaughtered there. After the building of the Colosseum, the "blood" sports were performed there. Admission was free to the Colosseum, all funds originally coming from the treasury, but more and more from private officials, often to gain votes. In A.D. 51 the treasury put out $85 million for such spectacles, in addition to the monies given by private individuals (Hardy, 1970, p. 99).

The gladiatorial contests possibly had Etruscan origins, the "game of Phersu," in particular, being considered a forerunner. But the Romans developed such activities to a hitherto unheard-of point. The training of the gladiators was highly systematized, as were the varying forms of combatant: the *Secutores,* the *Thraces,* the *Myrmillones,* the *Retiarii,* the *Hoplomachi,* the *Provocatores,* the *Dimachaeri,* the *Essedarii,* the *Andabatae,* the *Meridiani,* the *Bestiarii,* the *Fiscales, Caesariani* or *Postulati,* the *Catevarii,* and the *Samnites* (Lindsay, 1967, pp. 76–78).

Augustus, for one, remarked that he had given eight such exhibitions and that some 10,000 gladiators fought at them (Lindsay, 1967, p. 81). On the celebrations to commemorate Trajan's return—they lasted 123 days—some 11,000 animals were slain, and again 10,000 fought (Lindsay, 1967, p. 84; Dio [n.d.] p. 15).

The ability to die well became an honorable concern and appealed to the Roman personality. This difference in outlook between the Greeks and the Romans is summarized by Hardy:

Yet our legacy from each of these two great peoples is different. The Romans were the Marthas of Western civilization. The essence of our heritage from them is in practical things—engineering, for instance, and superior plumbing, as well as in a passion for order, discipline, law, and conformity; all of which are Latin words. The chief Greek contribution, however, is in art, literature, and ideas. It was the distinguished classicist, Mr. T. R. Glover, who once remarked: "Rome is famed for its drains: Greece for its brains." (1970, p. 1)

The influence of the Greeks was ever important, and gymnasia were attached to many of the homes of the well-to-do. But the overall attitude of the Greeks toward exercise was seemingly never adopted by the Romans. Galen, of course, was one who felt systematic exercise was important and necessary for health (Galen, 1951).

The Roman baths were for the poor as well as the rich, and these *thermae* "were actually grandiose adaptions of the Greek gymnasia, or palaestra . . ." (Lindsay, 1967, p. 33). The *thermae* were the largest establishments of the Empire, the simpler *balneae* being built during the Republic. The extent of these may be seen from the fact that there were 170 in Rome in 33 B.C., and 856 in the time of Constantine, some three hundred or more years later (Lindsay, 1967). As Cameron said: "In Italy, the gymnasium constituted a part of the Bath; in Greece, the Bath was looked upon as part of the gymnasium" (1772, p. 37). Not that they were all havens: "What bathing is when thou thinkest of it—oil, sweat, filth, greasy water, everything revolting—such is every part of life and every object we meet with" (Lindsay, 1967, p. 43).

Ball games also enjoyed considerable popularity in ancient Rome, particularly as they were often performed at the baths. Four different kinds of balls are mentioned by Martial: *pila paganica* (stuffed with feathers), *pila trigonalis* (used to play the game of trigon), the *follis* (balloon or bladder ball), and the *harpasta* (scrimmage balls) (Lindsay, 1967, p. 54).

Athletic contests were held in Rome, but they did not appeal in the manner in which they did to the Greeks. The Actian Games were held every four years at Nicopolis, and in 86 A.D. the quinquennial Capitoline Games were instituted, following the Greek system. During the later Empire, professionalism was rife, and some cities gave pensions to athletes. A union or guild of athletes was even formed (Lindsay, 1967, pp. 128–29). The events were similar to the Greek at such contests, though the boxing glove or *caestus* was more of a weapon. In any case, there is evidence of running, jumping, the pankration, wrestling, boxing, throwing the javelin, throwing the discus, weight lifting, gymnastics, and events for boys and girls.

Hunting and fishing were popular, and there is little doubt that the artificial fly was used (Lindsay, 1967, pp. 165–68). Nets, snares, and spears, dogs, and bow and arrow were used. Swimming was practiced, and it was recommended that every army recruit should be able to swim

(Lindsay, 1967, p. 188). Boating was believed to be likewise practiced (Lindsay, 1967, p. 190).

Of the other activities of the Romans, young and old, we see evidence of the following: acrobatics, juggling, tightrope walking, a form of bull leaping, a form of bull wrestling, cockfighting, hoop play, net games, *cottabos*, building toy houses, odd-and-even, riding a long stick, top spinning, knucklebones, and *buffet* (a game in which a player covered his face with his hands and guessed which other player hit him) (Lindsay, 1967, p. 207).

The Romans, then, performed a considerable range of physical activities, but their attitudes and proclivity for athletics could not be likened to those of the Greeks.

It is, of course, not possible to cover all ancient civilizations, but at least China and Japan should be mentioned. Gardiner (1910, pp. 14–17) notes that by 600 B.C. the Chinese were enthusiasts of sport. Boxing and wrestling were known and practiced, as well as jujitsu, which was readily adopted by the Japanese. A game of "butting" was played, and polo was introduced before A.D. 600 (Gardiner, 1910, p. 15). Gardiner quotes an old Chinese writer of the third century B.C.: "There were none among its inhabitants who did not perform with the pipes or some string instrument, fight cocks, race dogs or play football" (1910, p. 15). That football was relatively advanced may be seen from the following quote from the poet Lu Yu (A.D. 50–130):

> A round ball and a square wall,
> The ball flying across like the moon,
> While the teams stand opposed.
> Captains are appointed and take their places
> No allowances are made for relationship,
> According to unchanging regulations
> There must be no partiality.
> But there must be determination and coolness
> Without the slightest irritation at failure
> And if all this is necessary for football
> How much more for the business of life. (Gardiner, 1910, p. 16)

Culin's definitive work on the Orient (1958) covers the games of Korea, China, and Japan, but the origin of the activities he described are not established. The range of activities mentioned is considerable: toys and lanterns, snowmen, doll play, shadows, kites, kite fighting, playing house, rope-walker toy, windmill, the buzz, tops, spinning round, pop-guns, squash monkeys, turnip lanterns, cat's cradle, spiderweb (net) bat, ring puzzle, playing horse, nobleman play, hopping, jumping, leapfrog, jumping rope, seesaw, swinging, tug-of-war, wrestling, kicking, shuttlecock-kicking, water kicking, dam combat, fist striking, hand clapping, hide and find, drawing straws, tag, counting out, blind man's bluff, violent fighting, grass gaming, candy gaming, cherry gaming, apple gaming etc., clam-shell combat, ball batting, orange throwing, jackstones, metal striking, cash striking, eating all, measure taking, stone throwing, side or faction fights, shoe shooting, pitch pot, nyout (a gambling game) playing, promotion, dice, backgammon, chess, pebble game, games of *kono*, dominoes, playing cards, and so on.

OVERVIEW

The following generalizations have been offered by Howell (1971) with respect to research on sport and games in the ancient world.

First, the evidence in any one of the studies is never complete, but rather merely partial knowledge of the sports, games, and physical activities of that civilization. The majority of researchers are reluctant to generalize because of this fact alone. A new discovery, today or tomorrow, could reverse any present opinion drastically.

As Gottschalk put it:

> ... only a part of what was observed in the past was remembered by those who observed it; only a part of what was remembered was recorded; only a part of what was recorded has survived; only a part of what has survived has come to the historians' attention; only a part of what has come to their attention is credible; only a part of what is credible has been grasped; and only a part of what has been grasped can be expounded or narrated by the historian. (1950, p. 45)

Second, the games of certain classes have been emphasized and others de-emphasized. The games of the nobility and upper classes are generally the ones seen in archaeological and literary evidence from the early civilizations. The descriptions that tend to come down to us are the pursuits of kings and nobles and mythical godlike figures.

It is perhaps only natural that in general the games of the upper classes would be emphasized. All people will play, yet the poor and children are less likely to record or have recorded their activities, while those of a lord or king, his hunting prowess, for example, were naturally more frequently recorded. Literary evidence, in the main, is that of the upper classes, and we are often dependent solely on archaeological evidence for games of the poor or children—dolls, the game of "house," knucklebones, and so on.

As evidence increases in profusion, however—as in the case of the Greek and the Roman civilizations, for example—the more is the tendency for the evidence to be that of the total population. As Bishop put it in his study of the Romans:

> Undoubtedly the Romans' desire for public exhibitions and gladiatorial combats, of which an extensive literary and archaeological record has been preserved, has tended to obscure the less conspicuous evidence of individual delight in more informal activities. The study revealed the Romans' interest in all forms of physical activity, whether it be hunting, swimming, fishing, bull games or simply playing *latruneuli* after exercise in a bath. Indeed, with the establishment of the imperial *thermae,* games and physical exercise formed part of the daily agenda. This evidence supports the . . . hypothesis, that physical activities held a relevant position in the lives of Roman citizens, both rich and poor. (1970, p. 218)

Third, there has been continual difficulty in ascertaining if the evidence were indeed a game, and there is inconsistency in definition of terms. Various investigators have debated the merits of using the terms "sports" or "games" in their investigations. Some have preferred the term "physical activities." Perhaps "play" is a better term, as it is more encompassing. The fact is that lack of agreement in terminology is a factor that limits comparative analysis. The play theorists appear to agree to disagree, and each invents a new method of analysis. There are as many approaches as there are studies. Some researchers preclude dance in their analyses, others include it; hunting, fishing, and boating have occasioned similar difficulty, as have military pursuits.

Fourth, interpretations have been occasionally in error as one attaches one's own cultural attitudes and beliefs to the fragmentary findings of another culture. There is a constant danger of this occurring, and it must be continually guarded against. So often, the evidence is both unclear and sparse. There are innumerable examples of this. There is the bronze statuette of two wrestlers supporting vases, in the Sumerian civilization, and also the limestone votive plaque depicting either boxing or wrestling. The bull vaulting of the Minoans, which would seem to be clear in understanding, with a profusion of evidence, is not. Perhaps the best example is the Greek evidence of what has been interpreted by many authors as the forerunner of hockey and rugby, but certainly team games; various interpretations can and have been made.

Fifth, the amount of evidence of an activity is not necessarily related to the amount of that activity in a society. Literary evidence is emphatic that every Greek boy learned to swim, but archaeological evidence depicting this is rare; on the other hand, many activities that were not necessarily common appeared quite often in the evidence. As today, some sports are commonly used as subjects by artists; others are not. The great paintings by Brueghel are a rarity, in that they depict the games of the peasant and reflect hundreds of activities not normally recorded by the artist. The most common activity is often the least recorded.

Sixth, geographical grouping into ancient Western civilizations is traditional and convenient, but it is a limiting factor in the total understanding of the role of sports and games. Games do not recognize geographical barriers. What is missing to a large extent in this neat division is the influence of the ancient cultures situated in present-day India and China, Russia and the Ukraine, the movements of groups in and out of various tribes and the games they carried with them, the influence of the caravan routes, their prevalence and indeed their direction, the sea trade and its influence. Recent analysis of seal stones in the Ganges, for example, show bull games similar to those of the Minoans. Were these seal stones the products of the area and indeed representative of the activities there, or were they carried by traders, possibly from the island of Crete?

Seventh, games related to warfare occupied a large portion of the activities of certain cultures. Meikle, in his analysis of the Sumerians and the Hittites, had this to say:

> In an exploratory study of this nature in which a marked reliance is placed upon primitive art, it is only possible to draw tenuous conclusions. The evidence would tend to support the first hypothesis, that most physical activities of both civilizations were related directly or indirectly to the improvement of the efficiency of a fighting force in the field.
>
> In ancient societies, little control over the environment was possible; there was always a heavy reliance on the people to defend and preserve one's ecological niche, and in an area where the political situation was liable to erupt and the balance of power likely to change at any moment, it is not surprising that the physical activities assumed a highly practical nature, and that life should revolve around warfare and its related activities.
>
> Physical exercises tended to be associated with vocational training in the life of the farmer, the artisan, the hunter and the warrior, and to be of value only as they served practical aims. Activities such as chariotry, equestrianism, archery and swimming were first learned for the practical use in battle rather than for the pleasure they might give the participants. Certainly the members of the phalanx, infantry and chariot crews sought prowess in battle and in the chase, and practiced diligently to maintain this prowess when the need arose. However, the aims were basically utilitarian. (1971, pp. 187–88)

The warfare element appeared to be a dominating feature in such civilizations as the Sumerian, Hittite, and Assyrian, but this phenomenon could possibly have been a feature of the paucity of the evidence. Aspects of warfare were noticeable in each of the other civilizations, of course, but the evidence did not reflect such a dominant theme. In any case, activities such as gladiatorial combat, archery, boxing, wrestling, chariot racing, equestrian pursuits, and javelin throwing were common.

Eighth, games in general tended to be the mirror of the societies in which they occurred. This can be said to be true despite the meager evidence, particularly in relation to the physical pursuits of the lower classes. Let us take the Sumerians and Hittites as examples. As Meikle said:

> In support of the hypothesis that the physical evidence of the people were predominantly those of the upper-classes, the archaeological evidence unearthed to date

would seem to generally confirm this. It must be re-emphasized, however, that the evidence is incomplete. The physical activities strongly denoted a strict formality which was by no means evident for the lower classes, and in the majority of the chariot and hunting scenes one sees the image of the king constantly glorified as he led his troops into battle or rushed into the hunt. He is always shown at the table in banquet scenes and evidence of leisure time for him was implicit in the elaborate gaming boards found in the royal graves at Ur.

There was no evidence to support the contention that training in exercises existed for the masses of the people other than that developed in their daily work. Public celebrations such as those held on the triumphal return of a king gave some expression to a spirit of merriment in music, dancing and feasting, but generally speaking, opportunities for extensive recreation of the lower classes appeared to be quite rare.

Such is the impression gained from the surviving art forms, but this must not be taken to mean that those of the lower classes did not enjoy any recreation whatsoever. It is unfortunate that royalty at this period of history demanded such overwhelming attention. The activities related thereto were prevalent to the extreme and certainly such representation was to the exclusion of those pursued by the lower classes. . . . (1971, pp. 188–89)

In a sense, then, the games or physical activities of the Sumerian and Hittite, the Assyrian and Egyptian and Minoan and even the Etruscan civilization, which perhaps emphasized the games of the upper classes, were indeed a reflection of those societies in that they revealed the class differences and the magnitude of that difference. At the very least it is necessary to assert that a knowledge of the sports, games, and physical activities of a civilization afforded valuable insight into that civilization and one generally underplayed by classicists, historians, anthropologists, and so on. With respect to the Greek and Roman civilizations, the increased range of literary and archaeological evidence would allow one to generalize that the sports, games, and physical activities tended to be a microcosm of those societies.

Ninth, diffusion and acculturation are important factors in an analysis of games. Diffusion refers to the spread of an activity from a place of origin. The speed with which activities diffuse is a variable and is related to a great many factors. In our own time, we see how rapid diffusion can be with the spread and popularization of such activities as the use of the hula hoop and the frisbee, which clearly demonstrate the interrelationship of publicity, industrial production, and transportation, plus the influence of some undefinable concerns such as acceptance.

It is reasonably easy to study diffusion in the modern day, when we have knowledge of production and sales. In ancient times the information is unclear, as we are dependent on isolated finds, and so the subject of diffusion is one of academic conjecture. We are dependent on the very detailed studies of scholars to speculate on the origins and the spread of a single activity.

If dealt with simply, the archaeological evidence would imply that the beginnings of the board game were in Sumeria, diffusing to the Egyptian civilization, thence to the Hittites, and so on. However, it is not that simple, as the early board games were possibly of Chinese or Indian origin, finding their way to villages via caravans and trading vessels, being copied and modified by inventive locals. Moreover, earlier forms of the board game may not have survived, perhaps having been made of clay or some other general nonlasting material.

With respect to *acculturation,* which is taken here to mean the influencing of one culture by another culture, games afford an interesting examination point. Two civilizations in particular will be briefly examined to show the effect of acculturation insofar as games are concerned: the Etruscan and the Roman. The tomb paintings of the Etruscans show a marked Greek influence: the wrestling scenes, the discus, the running, the jumping, the javelin. It is true that there may have been Greek artisans painting these tombs, but the profusion of evidence indicates clearly that these activities were performed by the Etruscans and that there was an undoubted Greek influence in their adoption.

The influence of the Greeks on the Romans is not as well known, but a brilliant chapter by Bishop (1970), "Greek Athletic Games," develops evidence of acculturation. We are familiar with negative references, such as Cicero stating that Pompey admitted he had wasted "oil and toil" on games he sponsored (1928, p. 1), and Cicero writing to Atticus that "the attendance was small and I am not surprised. You know what I think of Greek games" (1965, p. 5). Lucan (1887, p. 279), for example, was emphatic: "You will meet an army enlisted from the Greek gymnasium, listless because of their palaestra course, and hardly able to bear arms." Martial (1927, p. 124) also stated: "Why waste the strength of the arms on stupid dumbells? A better exercise for one would be digging in the vineyard." Tacitus reported on this growing influence:

> Games ought to be conducted as of old, when the praetors presided with no compulsion on anyone to compete. Our fathers' manners, disused by degrees, were now being entirely thrown over by a license imported from abroad, whereby everything that was corrupt and corrupted was exhibited within the city. These foreign pursuits were ruining our young men, who were giving themselves up to the shameful practices of the gymnasium.

> ... it may be argued that agones were not as unpopular in Rome as most literary authorities would have us suppose. It must be remembered that the complaints of men like Cicero and Seneca were no doubt representing the protests of the intellectual and philosopher. However, they do not necessarily reflect the views of the populace. In fact, in a period when there was still a great deal of animosity towards the Greek culture, such remarks may have indicated, quite unintentionally, that the practice of a Greek style of athletic training was becoming alarmingly popular. (1937, p. 20)

Inscriptional and archaeological evidence is developed by Bishop (1970) to support this viewpoint. Evidence of boxing, of footraces, of competing in the nude is reasonably profuse. Augustus, in particular, established frequent and permanent athletic contests. The Actian Games were held every four years, modeled on the Panhellenic festivals, and included: footraces, wrestling, boxing, pankration and pentathlon, as well as contests for heralds, musicians, and poets. A wreath was given as a prize. These Actian Games, originally held at Nicopolis, near Actium, were founded in Rome in 25 B.C.

The Sebistia, or Augastolia, held at Naples, was another famous festival begun in the first century A.D. Strabo said of it:

> At the present time, a sacred contest is celebrated among them every four years in music as well as gymnastics; it lasts for several days and vies with the most famous of those celebrated in Greece. (1923, p. 7)

The program at these games was: the stade, diaulos, boxing, wrestling, pankration, pentathlon, and a race in armour, as well as equestrian events, including four-horse chariots. Music and dramatic events followed.

The games of the Greeks, then, influenced the Etruscans and Romans, and games provide evidence of this acculturation.

Tenth, certain games appear to be unique to a particular civilization. The uniqueness of certain games is an interesting phenomenon. There are, of course, many minor differences in board games and so on that a particular group has developed, but the fact that a game may have reasonably strong acceptance in one society and yet not appear in any other is worthy of analysis. The mock navy battles of the Romans, the stick fighting of the Egyptians, the game of "Phersu" of the Etruscans, the bull vaulting of the Minoans, are all examples of these. One must wonder, with trade and commerce bringing these nations into reasonably close contact, why these would not appear to have acceptance elsewhere. Two of the characteristics that these activities have in common are danger and difficulty in staging both of which would impede common acceptance.

Eleventh, certain activities may be classified as empty-categoried. That is, certain activities appear in nearly every civilization but are absent from one or two. Acrobatics, for example, does not appear among the Sumerians, ball games among the Sumerians and Hittites, chariot racing among the Minoans, equestrian pursuits among the Minoans, running among the Sumerians and Hittites, swimming among the Etruscans, and so on. Although it is possible that such activities did not appear in a certain civilization—for example, chariot racing among the Minoans because of the limitations of terrain—their absence in all probability is merely a function of the available evidence.

Twelfth, certain activities display commonality. Perhaps the most interesting phenomenon is the commonality of games: there are games that occur in each civilization, even considering the meagerness of evidence in some civilizations. Are these activities, then, the natural, the virtual inevitable activities of mankind? The main activities denoting commonality are boxing, wrestling, dancing, knucklebones, hunting, fishing, and board games.

Thirteenth, the theory of spontaneity and emergence would appear to be adequately confirmed. Even when taking into account the theories of diffusion and acculturation, there would appear to be sufficient basis to argue that certain games arise spontaneously. When a culture reaches a certain point in development, when certain geographical conditions prevail, when the mind of man seeks distraction—then certain games emerge, games of chance, such as knucklebones and the guessing games, board games, boxing, wrestling, dancing. There are sufficient variations within civilizations to show that even though there is commonality, there is evidence of spontaneity, certainly uniqueness.

Fourteenth, many activities have a magical or religious basis, but this significance appears to diminish as civilizations become increasingly complex. The religious or magical basis of many activities has been adequately explored by others. The excellent thesis by Simri (1965) on ball games is one such innovative study. Dance is another activity that might be looked at briefly. As Sachs said:

> On no occasion in the life of primitive peoples should the dance be dispensed with. Birth, circumcision, and the consecration of maidens, marriage and death, planting and harvest, the celebration of chieftains, hunting, war, and feasts, the changes of the moon and sickness—for all of these the dance is needed. (1937, pp. 4–5)

Kennedy has suggested that the religious aspect of dance generally had as its purpose communication with the unseen forces which provided food, promoted fertility, regulated the weather, gave good fortune in warfare, and thus controlled tribal warfare and human survival (Meikle, 1971, p. 63). But, as Meikle says:

> As Sumerian society became more complex and their world expanded, their dances probably no longer involved the simple telling of the hunt. Much more elaborate ideas had to be conveyed through gesture, and it is possible that as dancers appear on the majority of musical scenes, they too may have become a special class of performers. (1971, p. 63)

If this were the case, then there may have been a lessening of the religious or magical support of a particular dance, though indeed religion and magic may have served as the origin.

The May Day celebrations throughout the world, the swing, and the game of lacrosse are all examples of activities that originally had such a basis which, with the passing of time, is no longer recognized.

The game of "Phersu" of the Etruscans provides an example. It is believed to have a religious connection. As Sawula said:

> Richardson suggests that the man [Phersu] is acting out the scene in which Hercules comes to get Cereberus from the underworld; the blindfold ensures that the darkness of Hades is real to him. The masked actor wears a false beard, a cap with pointed ears, and a tight jerkin, a costume evidently of the underworld. The actor, who was supposed to be Hercules, was to free himself and capture the dog. . . .
>
> This rite owes its origin to earlier funeral occasions which offered sacrifices and offerings in order to comfort the deceased. (1969, p. 75)

The Etruscans probably initiated this type of gladiatorial contest and influenced the Romans, though of course it was at Campania and Lucania that gladiatorial combat was fully developed. When a gladiator was killed, he was taken out of the arena by a slave who was dressed as the Etruscan death demon Charon, and the term "lanista," believed to be of Etruscan origin, was the "superintendent of gladiators" (Bishop, 1970, p. 61). The main point is that the religious basis of such contests appeared to decline with the Romans.

Fifteenth, physical activities were occasionally used in antiquity as a political tool. This is a subject as relevant today as in ancient times. The Communist bloc, for example, provides a clear demonstration of the interrelationship of sport and politics, and in Canada, with increasing governmental involvement, we see the same trend. The best example was the Roman civilization. As Bishop put it:

> In support of the first hypotheses (i.e., that public amusements provided by the imperial government were used as a political tool to direct the activities of the populace and to direct the minds of the subjects from political affairs) the study revealed that through the provision of public spectacles, the imperial government was able to occupy and discipline the leisure hours of Rome's idle thousands. During the early years of the Republic such games were merely extensions of religious festivals held in honour of the gods. By the late Republic, however, public spectacles had become the best means of pursuing public favour and, under the Empire, of keeping the populace contented.
>
> The political significance of sponsoring and attending public amusements was witnessed by the attitudes and activities of the Emperors. Tiberius, for example, who disliked these diversions, was often present at the games, partly to do the entertainers honour but more important, to keep the populace in order by demonstrating his sympathy with their pleasure. Further, in spite of the fact that these entertainments were extraordinarily common, as early as the reign of Augustus private sponsors were allowed to give games only twice a year, and even then with a restricted program of events.
>
> During the Empire, the public spectacles had also supplied, to a large extent, the place that public assemblies had held under the Republic. Cicero said in 56 B.C.: "there are

three places where popular feelings find expression, at public meetings, at public assemblies and at games and fights." With the establishment of the Empire the public meetings and public assemblies were abolished while the games and gladiatorial fights remained under imperial monopoly. Finally, in a period of such political sterility, the division of popular passion into four factions in the Circus was useful to the government, and was encouraged by the Emperors.

If the spectacles were a political necessity, they served a far more important role as the amusement of an idle population. The popularity of these amusements was indicated by the increasing number of days on which they were given. In the last century of the Republic, such public holidays had taken place in fifty-nine days a year; they had doubled in number by the second century A.D., and in the third century occupied one hundred and seventy-five days. In addition, there were the extraordinary games that occurred very frequently, and which sometimes [were] prolonged an inordinate length of time. While those amusements were provided by the government as a political diversion, the increase in the number of days in which they were given was clearly in response to public demand. (1970, pp. 217–18)

Sports, then, even in antiquity, were occasionally used as a political tool.

Sixteenth, in an analysis of games of the ancient Western civilizations, each type of activity was evidenced. There was evidence of activities involving pursuit (the hunting of the Sumerians), chance (the game of "mora" and "atep" of the Egyptians), strategy (the chariot races of the Romans), dexterity (knucklebones of the Greeks), vertigo (the tumbling of the Etruscans), imitation ("house" of the Minoans), exultation (the Dionysiac dances of the Etruscans), and enigma (blindman's bluff of the Greeks).

Seventeenth, in an analysis of the ancient Western civilizations, games which were primarily related to a major aspect of society were evidenced. There was evidence of activities that could be classified as educational (the game of "house" of the Minoans), political (the gladiatorial contests of the Romans), economic (fishing of the Minoans), family (the board games of the Egyptians), ceremonial (the dances of the Minoans), socialization [i.e. social interaction] (ball games at the baths of the Romans).

Eighteenth, as civilizations rise and fall, so do sports and games. A continuous observation is that certain activities reach a peak in a civilization, and then decline. A level of acceptance or popularity does not seem to be maintained when a long time span is analyzed. The bull games of ancient Crete, the games at Olympia, the gladiatorial combat and chariot racing of the Romans, all reached their zenith and declined, never to attain that peak again. Other activities seem to ebb and flow in public acceptance, as we have seen in the last 150 years in Canada: the popularity of cricket in 1867, its decline, the upsurge in bicycling and baseball and subsequent declines, the professionalism of football and hockey, and so on. Who could predict what sports and games will hold a prominent position 300 years hence?

These, then, are some preliminary remarks endeavoring to sort out some generalizations with respect to the ancient Western world. The generalizations are tentative. What is needed is more information about other cultures, other civilizations, so that the jigsaw puzzle of games, their origin and diffusion, can be understood with more clarity. On one point there is a strong conviction—that games are a worthy academic study and can assist in revealing how people thought and acted in ages past.

GENERAL BIBLIOGRAPHY

AKURGAL, E. *The Art of the Hittites.* New York: Harry N. Abrams, 1962.

BECK, F. A. C. *Greek Education (450–350 B.C.).* New York: Barnes & Noble, 1964.

BENJAMIN, S. G. W. "Persia," *The Story of Nations.* London: Fisher Unwin, 1888.

BISHOP, H. WAYNE. "The Role of Physical Activities in Ancient Rome." M.A. Thesis, University of Alberta, 1970.

BOARDMAN, J. *Greek Art.* New York: Frederick A. Praeger, 1964.

BONOMI, J. *Nineveh and Its Palaces.* London: Office of Illustrated London Library, 1852.

BOSANQUET, R. C., and R. M. DAWKINS. *The Unpublished Objects from the Palaikastro Excavations 1902–1906, Part I.* London: Macmillan, 1923.

BOSSERT, H. T. *The Art of Ancient Crete.* London: Zwemmer, 1937.

BOYD, MARGARET. "Excavations at Kavousi, Crete, in 1900," *American School of Classical Studies at Athens,* [n.d.].

BREASTED, J. H. *The Battle of Kadesh.* Chicago: University of Chicago Press, 1903.

———. *Egyptian Servant Statues.* New York: Pantheon Books, 1948.

CAMERON, CHARLES. *Baths of the Romans.* London: George Scott, 1772.

CANTOR, NORMAN F. *Western Civilization: Its Genesis and Destiny.* Chicago: Scott, Foresman and Co., 1968.

CARTER, H. *The Tomb of Tut-Ankh-Amen.* New York: Cooper Square Publications, 1963.

CHAPOUTHIER, F. *Deux Epées D'Apparat au Palais de Mallia.* Paris: Libraire Orientaliste, 1938a.

———. *Études Crétoises V.* Paris: Libraire Orientaliste, 1938b.

CICERO. *Epistulae.* Trans. W. S. Watt. Oxford: Clarendon Press, 1965.

———. *Letters to His Friends.* Trans. W. Glynn Williams. London: William Heinemann Ltd., 1928.

CONTENAU, G. *Everyday Life in Babylon and Assyria.* London: Edward Arnold, 1954.

COTTRELL, LEONARD. *Life Under the Pharaohs.* New York: Holt, Rinehart & Winston, 1960.

———. *The Lost Pharaohs.* New York: Grosset & Dunlap, 1963.

CULIN, STEWART. *Games of the Orient.* Rutland, Vermont: Charles E. Tuttle Co., 1958.

DIEM, C. *Weltgeschichte des Sports und der Leibeserziehung.* Stuttgart: Im Cotta Verlag, 1960.

DIO. *Roman History.* [n.d.].

DURANT, J. *Highlights of the Olympics.* New York: Hastings House, 1969.

EVANS, A. J. "Mycenaean Tree and Pillar Cult," *Journal of Hellenic Studies,* 1901.

————. *The Palace of Minos at Knossos.* London: Macmillan, 1935.

EVANS, J. D. "Excavations in the Neolithic Settlement at Knossos, 1957–1960," *British School of Athens,* [n.d.].

FALKENER, EDWARD. *Games Ancient and Oriental and How to Play Them.* London: Longmans Ltd., 1892.

FREEMAN, K. J. *Schools of Hellas.* New York: Teacher's College Press, 1969.

FRIEDLANDER, LUDWIG. *Roman Life and Manners Under the Early Empire.* Trans. V. H. Freese and Leonard Magnus. New York: Barnes & Noble, 1968.

FRYE, R. N. *The Heritage of Persia.* Cleveland: World Publishing Co., 1963.

FURTWANGLER. *Antike Gemnen.* [n.d.].

GALEN. *De Sanitate Tuenda.* Trans. Robert Montraville Green. Springfield, Ill.: Charles C Thomas, 1951.

GARDINER, E. N. *Athletics of the Ancient World.* Oxford: Clarendon Press, 1931.

————. *Greek Athletic Sports and Festivals.* London: Macmillan, 1910.

GARSTANG, J. *The Hittite Empire.* London: Constable & Co., 1929.

GHIRSHMAN, R. *Persia from the Origins to Alexander the Great.* Trans. Stuart Gilbert and James Emmons. London: Thames & Hudson, 1964.

————. *Persian Art-The Parthian and Sassanian Dynasties.* New York: Golden Press, 1962.

————. *Persia From the Origins to Alexander the Great.* France: Thomas and Hudson, 1964.

GLOTZ, GUSTAVE. *The Aegean Civilization.* London: Kegan Paul, 1925.

GOTTSCHALK, LOUIS. *Understanding History.* New York: Knopf, 1950.

GRAHAM, J. W. *The Palaces of Crete.* Princeton, N.J.: Princeton University Press, 1962.

HALL, H. P. *Civilizations of Greece in the Bronze Age.* London: Methuen, 1928.

HARDY, W. G. *The Greek and Roman World.* Canada: McClelland & Stewart, 1962.

HARRIS, H. A. *Greek Athletes and Athletics.* London: Hutchinson, 1964.

HAZZIDAKIS, JOSEPH. *Tylissos: A L'Époque Minoenne.* Paris: Libraire Paul Geuthner, 1921.

HERODOTUS. *History.* Trans. by A. D. Godley, Loeb Classical Library, 4 vols. London: William Heinemann Ltd., 1946.

HITTI, P. K. *History of Syria.* New York: Macmillan, 1951.

HOGARTH, D. G. "Dictaen Cave," *Annals of the British School at Athens,* No. VI, 1899–1900.

HOWELL, MAXWELL L. "Toward a History of Sport," *Journal of Health, Physical Education and Recreation*, March 1969, pp. 77–79.

—. "An Historical Survey of the Role of Sport in Society, with Particular Reference to Canada Since 1900." Ph.D. Dissertation, University of Stellenbosch, South Africa, 1969.

—."Archaeological Evidence of Sports and Games in Ancient Civilizations: Part II, Interpretive Comments," *Procedings of the Second World Symposium on the History of Sport and Physical Education*. Alberta, Canada, 1971.

—. and DENISE PALMER. "Sports and Games in the Minoan Period," *Proceedings of the First International Symposium on the History of Sport and Physical Education*. Israel, 1968.

HOWELL, REET. "The Socio-Cultural Area," *Sport Sociology Bulletin*, Vol. IV, no. 1, Spring 1975.

HYDE, W. W. *Olympic Victor Monuments and Greek Athletic Art*. London: Paul Hamlyn, 1962.

KENNA, VICTOR. *Cretan Seals*. Oxford: Clarendon Press, 1960.

—. *Die Englischen Privatsammlungen*. Berlin: Verlag Gebr. Mann., 1966.

KIERNAN, J., and A. DALEY. *The Story of the Olympic Games*. Philadelphia and New York: Lippincott, 1965.

KLEIN, A. *Child Life in Greek Art*. New York: Columbia University Press, 1932.

KRAMER, S. N. *The Sumerians*. Chicago: University of Chicago Press, 1963.

LAYARD, A. H. *Discoveries in the Ruins of Nineveh and Babylon*. New York: Harper & Bros., 1853.

LINDSAY, PETER L. "Literary Evidence of Physical Education Among the Ancient Romans." M.A. Thesis, University of Alberta, 1967.

LLOYD, P. *Mesopotamia*. London: Lovat Dukson, 1936.

LUCAN. *Pharsalia*. Ed. C. E. Haskins. London: George Bell and Sons, 1887.

MALLOWAN, M. E. L. "A Copper Reen-Ring from Southern Iraq," *Iraq*, vol. X, Spring 1948.

MARINATOS, S. *Crete and Mycenae*. New York: Harry N. Abrams, [n.d.].

—. "The Swimmers: Dagger from the Tholos Tomb at Vapheio," *Essays in Aegean Archaeology*. Oxford: Clarendon Press, 1927.

MARTIAL. *Epigrams*. Trans. by W. C. A. Ker, Loeb Classical Library. 2 vols. London: William Heinemann Ltd., 1927.

MASPERO, G. *Art in Egypt*. New York: Charles Scribner's Sons, 1912.

—. *Life in Ancient Egypt and Assyria*. New York: D. Appleton & Co. 1908.

McCLUS, H. *The Daily Life of the Greeks and the Romans*. New York: Metropolitan Museum of Art, 1924.

MEHL, ERWIN. *Antike Schwimmkunst*. Munich, 1927.

MEIKLE, D. F. "Recreational and Physical Activities of the Sumerian and Hittite Civilizations." M.A. Thesis, University of Alberta, 1971.

MEKHITARIAN, A. *Egyptian Painting*. New York: Editions D'Art, 1954.

MONTETE, P. *Everyday Life in Egypt*. London: Edward Arnold, 1958.

MOSCATI, S. *Ancient Semitic Civilizations.* London: Eleck Books, 1957.

MOSSO, A. "Ceramic neolitica di Phaertes e vase dell 'epoca Manoica primitiva," *MA,* vol. XIX, 1908.

NAVILLE, E. *The Temple of Deir-el-Bahari.* London: Egyptian Exploration Fund, 1901.

NEWBERRY, P. E. *Beni Hasan* (two parts). London: Archaeological Survey of Egypt, 1893.

OESTERLEY, W. O. E. *The Sacred Dance: A Study in Comparative Folklore.* Cambridge, England: University of Cambridge Press, 1923.

OPPENHEIM, M. *Tell Halaf: A New Culture in Oldest Mesopotamia.* London: G. P. Putnam's Sons, 1933.

PALMER, DENISE. "Sport and Games in the Art of Early Civilization." M.A. Thesis, University of Alberta, 1967.

PARROT, A. *Sumer: The Dawn of Art.* Trans. S. Gilbert and J. Emmons. New York: Golden Press, 1961.

PHAIDON PRESS. *The Art of Ancient Egypt.* Vienna: Phaidon Press, 1936.

PORADA, E. *The Art of Ancient Iran.* New York: Crown Publishers, 1965.

PRITCHARD, J. B. *The Ancient Near East: An Anthology of Texts and Pictures.* Princeton, N.J.: Princeton University Press, 1959.

————. *The Ancient Near East in Pictures.* Princeton, N.J.: Princeton University Press, 1954.

RAWLINSON, G. *The Seven Great Monarchies of the Ancient Eastern World.* New York: J. W. Lovell Co., 1875.

RIDINGTON, W. R. "The Minoan, Mycenaean Background of Greek Athletics." Ph.D. Dissertation, University of Pennsylvania, Philadelphia, 1935.

ROBINSON, R. S. *Sources for the History of Greek Athletics.* Urbana: University of Illinois Press, 1955.

RODENWALDT, G. *Olympia.* London: Sedgewick and Jackson, 1936.

ROEBUCK, C. *The World of Ancient Times.* New York: Charles Scribner's Sons, 1966.

SACHS, C. *World History of the Dance.* New York: W. W. Norton and Co., 1937.

SAKELLARIOU, A. *Corpus der Minoischen and Mykenischen Siegel.* Berlin: Verlag Gebr. Mann., [n.d.].

SAVIGNONI, L. "Scavi e scoperte nella necropole di Phaestos," *Mon. Antiche,* vol. XIV, 1904.

SAWULA, L. W. "Physical Activities of the Etruscan Civilization." M.A. Thesis, University of Alberta, 1969.

———— and M. L. HOWELL. "Physical Activities as Depicted in Etruscan Tomb Paintings." Paper presented to Research Section of Canadian Association of Health, Physical Education and Recreation, Victoria, 1969.

SCHMIDT, E. F. *Persepolis II: Contents of the Treasury and Other Discoveries.* Chicago: University of Chicago Press, 1957.

SIMRI, U. "The Religious and Magical Functions of Ball Games in Various Cultures." Ed.D. Thesis, University of West Virginia, 1965.

SMITH, W. S. *The Art and Architecture of Ancient Egypt.* Baltimore: Penguin Books, 1958.

STRABO. *Geography.* Trans. Horace L. Jones. London: William Heinemann Ltd., 1923.

STROMMENGER, E. *5,000 Years of the Art of Mesopotamia.* New York: Harry N. Abrams, [n.d.].

TACITUS. *Histories and Annals.* Trans. C. H. Moore and J. Jackson. London: William Heinemann Ltd., 1937.

VILNAY, ZEV. "Sport in Ancient Israel," *Proceedings of the First International Seminar in the History of Physical Education and Sport,* 1968.

WARE, CAROLINE. *The Cultural Approach to History.* New York: Columbia University Press, 1940.

WILKINSON, J. G. *The Manners and Customs of the Ancient Egyptians.* London: John Murray, 1878.

WOLDERING, I. *The Art of Egypt: The Time of the Pharaohs.* New York: Crown Publishers, 1963.

WOODY, THOMAS. "Leisure in the Light of History," *The Annals of the American Academy of Political and Social Science,* 1957.

————. *Life and Education in Early Societies.* New York: The Macmillan Company, 1949.

WOOLLEY, L. *Mesopotamia and the Near East.* London: Methuen, 1961.

————. *Ur Excavations: The Royal Cemeteries.* Oxford: Oxford University Press, 1934.

WRIGHT, F. A. *Greek Athletics.* London: Jonathan, 1925.

ZACHIETZSCHMANN, W. *Hellas and Rome.* London: Zuemmer, 1959.

ZEIGLER, EARLE F. *Problems in the History and Philosophy of Physical Education and Sport.* Englewood Cliffs, N.J.: Prentice-Hall, 1968.

ZERVOS, C. *L'Art de la Crete.* Paris: Editions Cahiers d'Art, 1956.

Physical Education and Sport in the Middle Ages

Earle F. Zeigler

INTRODUCTION

A number of historians claim that the term "Middle Ages" for the period extending approximately from the sixth through the fifteenth centuries is a misnomer.[1] In the United States alone, hundreds of scholars are seeking new knowledge about this period through archeological investigation, the reading of unpublished texts (largely in the Vatican Archives), and other research techniques. It now appears that this period was indeed the "dawn" of a new civilization, that the Middle Ages were an outgrowth of antiquity just as our own civilization emerged from the so-called Dark Ages. This ties in with the theory that Rome declined more than it fell in exactly 496 A.D. We might, therefore, designate these particular centuries in the Western world as "Medieval Europe," or we might speak of the "Early" Middle Ages and the "Later" Middle Ages. Other historians include the Renaissance in the Middle Ages and offer three subdivisions: (1) Early Middle Ages, (2) Feudal Society, and (3) Renaissance. The important fact for us to remember is that there was a remarkable unity within Catholicism during this time and that such important modern institutions as our cities, our universities, and representative government developed from these origins. And yet there were many

[1]This is regarded as a preliminary survey of physical education and sport during the so-called Middle Ages. There has been relatively little reported in English about this topic - and presumably nothing of the quality of Woody's *Life and Education in Early Societies* (1949), which concludes with the Romans. There have been some good articles and chapters, however, and these will be reported.

Earle F. Zeigler is currently Professor of Physical Education, Faculty of Physical Education, The University of Western Ontario, London, Canada.

basic contradictions in this age and in this culture—a period during which the Roman Church and the Germanic peoples united to bring about the rise of the West.

Our plan in this essay is to subdivide the Middle Ages into the Early Middle Ages (sixth through thirteenth century) and the Later Middle Ages (fourteenth through seventeenth century). We will arbitrarily delimit our focus to what are loosely designated today as Western European countries. We will subdivide the Early Middle Ages further into the periods, "Formation of the West" and "Feudal Society." The Later Middle Ages will be subdivided into the periods, "The Renaissance" and "The Reformation."

EARLY MIDDLE AGES

Formation of the West

The political affairs of Greece and the eastern Mediterranean became quite separate from those of Western Europe after Constantinople became the center of the Holy Roman Empire. As indicated above, our concern will be with what is now known as Western Europe. Italy, for example, became a perennial battleground as various kings of the northern Germanic tribes invaded this territory successfully in the sixth century. For several centuries political authority in Italy was vested in many hands, such as the Ostrogoths, the Eastern Empire and the Papacy, the Franks, and the Lombards. While these developments were taking place in Western Europe, the Byzantine Empire to the south and east flourished. Constantinople, Baghdad, and Alexandria (in Africa) were great cities, and the names of such emperors as Constantine, Justinian, Leo, and Mauritius are known even today.

In Western Europe the political power gradually moved northward to the area of the Frankish kingdoms (modern France and Germany). Clovis, whose kingdom was eventually divided in 511 A.D., was a famous Merovingian (Frankish) king. Several hundred years later, when the so-called mayors of the palace assumed political power, the name of Charles Martel became important. Under his leadership the Franks defeated the Arabs at Tours in 732. Following this, a significant period of political and religious consolidation took place. Charlemagne became king in the late eighth century, extended the boundaries of his territory in all directions except the west, and was crowned Roman emperor by the Pope in 800. He became the most important political figure of this entire period.

Through his leadership, significant advancement was made in the political, economic, religious, social, and educational institutions of the time.

In the ninth century, after Charlemagne's death, a number of civil wars weakened the Empire. Attacks from every direction and eventual decentralization of political authority left the feudal lords in charge of local territories. This meant that the kings exercised lesser, relatively weak, nominal control. Hence, in both the eastern and western Frankish kingdoms, conflict and strife between the monarchs and their nobles brought about the breakdown of Charlemagne's Empire into a variety of feudal duchies and estates. In the meantime Otto I (or Otto the Great) took control and consolidated what was later to become Germany. In the process, responding to an urgent appeal from Pope John XII, he conquered Italy and thereby linked the future of Germany and Italy. In 962 A.D. he became the Holy Roman Emperor (of the West).

In England, invasions from the northeast by the Danes weakened most of the Saxon kingdoms greatly. Then Alfred the Great consolidated the defense against the enemy, gained a treaty, and permitted the invaders to settle northeast of the Thames River. These struggles continued after his death, however, and eventually the Saxon kingdoms were all defeated by William the Conqueror and his army from Normandy in 1066. In this way the English came considerably closer to the type of monarchy they finally achieved.

Feudal Society

In the period extending from the mid-eleventh to the thirteenth century, some European countries made greater progress than others in the development of centralized governments. England and France developed powerful centralized governments. Germany and Italy, however, were subject to continued struggles among the emperors, the nobility, and the Papacy, and, in fact, unification in these countries was not realized until the nineteenth and twentieth centuries.

And so it was during the period from the eleventh through the thirteenth century that feudalism characterized the political organization of this geographical area, a system that was marked by strong nobles, innumerable peasants, relatively weak kings, and a great deal of minor warfare. Warfare became so common that the Church found it necessary to inaugurate the so-called "Truce of God," a regulation that forbade conflicts on weekends and various holy days. This was the period when there were lords, kings, emperors, the Pope in Rome, knights, vassals, and serfs, not to mention archbishops, bishops, priests, and friars—a most difficult time for all men and women, and particularly trying for the lowly peasant at the bottom of the social scale. All nobles owed allegiance to the king. Some nobles were in vassalage to others, and they held land in fief to this overlord. The lines of authority steadily became extremely complicated. Despite these great difficulties, however, commerce was gradually extended, towns grew, the population increased, and extensive merchant and craft guilds developed. Situated "firmly in the middle" of all these developing social institutions characterized by steadily thriving economic organization, the Christian Church grew strongly in both political and economic power until the beginning of the Renaissance in the fourteenth and fifteenth centuries.

The Crusades were characteristic of this feudal period in the Middle Ages. These wars were started in 1095 at the urging of Pope Urban II because the Turks were hampering profitable trade between Europe and Asia, and threatened Constantinople. (As the center of the Byzantine Empire, Constantinople was ruled by Alexius I from 1081 to 1118). Because some Christian pilgrims had been persecuted, the Pope called upon the European countries for assistance. The First Crusade was much more successful than the later ones. The zeal for "crusading" eventually died out after approximately 150 years, and the Turkish enemy recaptured Jerusalem in 1244 A.D. It is difficult to assess the effects of the major and minor Crusades from the standpoint of the many social influences of the time. It is evident that the power of the Church was increased, while the power of the nobility most certainly declined. The so-called middle classes evidently could not help but prosper as well.

It may be postulated that the basic problem of this period was actually an intellectual one: how to reconcile medieval religious belief with the developing secular interests of a vigorous, young, and impressionable populace. The material world, a world of human beings with their sense experience, was very definitely subordinate to the spiritual realm of one God. During the twelfth and thirteenth centuries the influence of Aristotle and his scientific knowledge was again felt significantly, this time by the Christian world. It remained for St. Thomas Aquinas to develop a synthesis between natural and supernatural theology, a synthesis that today still provides the foundation for the Roman Catholic faith. The universal truths revealed through faith and revelation were based on the word and deed of God according to St. Thomas. Thomism, as it is often called, provided a solid core for the intellectual framework of the Church. It remained for Roger Bacon, William of Occam, Duns Scotus, and the subsequent humanism of the fourteenth and fifteenth centuries to challenge this strong position again.

Education in the Early Middle Ages

Because of meager evidence about the quality and quantity of the educational enterprise in the Middle Ages, the treatment of this era by educational historians has been insufficient in the past. However, a great deal more thoroughgoing historical research now taking place may correct earlier estimates of medieval education. Certainly there must have been some continuity from age to age; the "educational lights didn't suddenly go out" all over the Western world. It seems to be true also that the Church was not the only agency of education during this period. Royal and secular agencies did still take part in the education of selected groups of the population, although on a lesser scale.

In Italy, for example, secular education provided both by the towns and by private tutors continued throughout this entire period (from the fifth century on), despite the inroads made by the diverse raiders from the north. In fact, Lombard and Ostrogoth leaders seem to have encouraged such programs as soon as possible. Rhetoric, grammar, classics, law, and medicine are mentioned in the various curricula of the different types of schools. The evidence about similar efforts in northern Europe is slight, but there are indications that there was possibly more formal education available than has been realized previously.

Charlemagne has received historical recognition for his effort to extend educational opportunities. He stimulated the clergy to establish schools in all towns and on the many feudal manors. He also decreed that the palace school in his own court be started again, and then engaged the monk Alcuin to move from England to administer the program. In this way a pattern for subsequent rulers was established. Similar efforts were made in that part of the Empire that was German, although in this instance also, the main effort was in educating the children of the upper classes. Further, Alfred the Great in England is credited with the promotion of education for future leaders, as is Frederick II later in his court at Sicily.

The Church played the major role in formal education throughout the entire period from the sixth through the eleventh century by the inauguration of what have been called "monastic schools." The programs were designed fundamentally to prepare priests, but instruction was provided later for secular priests, monks, and nonclerics. In the late eleventh and twelfth centuries these monastic schools were superseded by the cathedral schools in the larger towns and communities. The various church councils with direction from the Pope made such schools a definite obligation. Thus, education was provided to meet a wide range of needs.

In the latter centuries of the Early Middle Ages, there were private educational efforts as well. A number of chantry schools were initiated by the wealthy. As the commercial guilds grew stronger and more influential in the larger communities, their leaders began schools in which priests were engaged to teach Latin to sons of the guild members.

In the first three or four centuries of the Early Middle Ages, monastic schools and cathedral schools were the agencies for what was called "higher education." Their function was gradually replaced by early types of university organization that developed as the teachers felt the need to organize guilds for their protection in dealing with secular or church authorities. Students found it necessary to organize in similar fashion to gain rights against what they considered to be possibly unreasonable demands made by teachers and/or townspeople. The typical teaching faculties in universities were theology, arts, medicine, and law. The University of Paris is generally considered to have been the leading such institution of the time, but was rivaled subsequently at Bologna in Italy and by the universities at Oxford and Cambridge in England.

The status of the teaching profession was at first generally quite low, especially at the elementary and secondary levels where the Church exerted such a strong influence. The status of university teachers increased gradually, however, until it ranked fairly close to that of political and church leaders—except for the amount of money earned. This stature remained only as long as the university teachers were involved with the great issues of the day that held import for the people (such as theological or political disputes).

Any discussion of education in the Middle Ages must include at least a brief discussion of the education of young nobles within the system of feudalism that prevailed. Almost all young knights were trained in chivalry, a system of customs (or ethics or usages) relating to manners, warfare, and religion. A young man had to learn to fight boldly and skillfully while on horseback, and yet had to display a variety of social graces to show that he was a gentleman too. In addition, because such a man lived at a time when the Christian church exerted an extremely strong influence, he was expected to be an example of the Christian virtues—loyalty, honor, mercy, and concern for the weak. Such an educational training encompassed a period of about fifteen years, which was typically divided into the following three periods: (1) ages 8 to 15: during this time he served as a page, was indentured to the ladies of the court, and learned the language rudiments and the ways of courtly life; (2) ages 15 to 21: he became a squire, served as an attendant to a knight, learned the warfare arts, and improved his social graces to an acceptable degree; and (3) from age 21 on: in this period he was inducted into knighthood after his valor and merit had been proved, and he began his service as a vassal to his liege. Such was the method whereby these young men became part of the upper class and entered into the well-established system of feudal aristocracy.

Physical Education and Sport in the Early Middle Ages

To gain some perspective on physical education and sport in what we have identified as the Early Middle Ages—the period extending from the fall of the Roman Empire and the subsequent "formation of the West" to the development of feudal society which fairly soon included the establishment of the larger communities into cities—it is important to comprehend how people at this time viewed their world and everything that had been, and was, taking place within it. Van Dalen spoke to this topic effectively when he stated:

> Medieval Man rejected the Graeco-Roman view that human events and achievements were a product of man's will and intellect. To him, the historical process was not the working out of the plans of man, but the unfolding of a plan that God had constructed and no man could alter: ... Medieval Man viewed history from a universalistic point of view. Because all men were equal in the sight of God and were engaged in working out his purposes, history could not be confined to a study of Greece, or Rome, or a chosen people, it had to embrace all mankind ... In a world where fear of death and dread of the last judgment were omnipresent, men were more concerned about their spiritual well-being than their physical well-being ... (in Zeigler, 1973, p. 217)

Even though Rome's glory and power were fast becoming a mere memory, Christianity continued to spread because of the energy, enthusiasm, and high moral standards of its followers. The Church managed to survive the invasion of the barbarians; it gradually became an important influence in that society as well, and its continued growth seemed a certainty.

The early Christians envisioned individual moral regeneration as the highest goal. They became most concerned about their souls and possible eternal happiness in God's Heaven. Thus, affairs of the soul were of God, so to speak, but matters of the body were felt to be of this world, and consequently of Satan. Often carried to the extreme by fanatics, this way of life was given the name of asceticism, the main idea being to subdue the desires of the flesh, even by means of torture if absolutely necessary.

A controversy has developed over the attitude of churchmen toward physical activity. The phrase "most churchmen were strongly opposed to physical education" during the early Christian period (Van Dalen et al., 1953, p. 98) has been called part of the "great Protestant legend." It does appear that further historical investigation is needed on this subject, however, as certain Catholic educational historians and others have stated that the Church has been unjustly maligned about this point.

Marrou asserts the opinion that physical education "simply died of old age" (1964, p. 185). He maintains that it was the "passion for athletics" that was criticized so sharply. This was so because Roman sports and games had led to many evils and excesses, and also because athletic festivals were often associated with earlier so-called pagan religions.

Ballou has investigated this topic most carefully, and the evidence he presents appears to corroborate the statement made above by Marrou. In a quotation from Tertullian, which he asserts could well "reflect the Christian approach to sport and physical activity," Tertullian wrote:

> Next let us consider the arts displayed in the circus games. In times past equestrian skill was simply a matter of riding on horseback, and certainly no guilt was involved in the ordinary use of the horse. But when this skill was pressed into the service of the games, it was changed from a gift of God into an instrument of the demons. (Tertullian, as quoted by Ballou, 1968, p. 162)

From this and other examinations of the literature, Ballou agrees that the presumed negative outlook of the Church against physical activity has been overemphasized. He concludes that "Christianity attempted to bring the relationship of it to sport into a more positive perspective compatible with a reverence for God, the dignity of man and the integrity of activity" (1968, p. 164).

For literally hundreds of years physical education found almost no place in what may be considered a very sterile period in the West. (We should keep in mind, however, that McNeill [1963, pp. 249–94] has designated this time as "Eurasian Cultural Balance"—a phase of man's development which he asserted began about 500 B.C. and extended to approximately 1500 A.D.) To keep this time period and locale in perspective, therefore, we need to understand that Hellenism, or the Hellenic civilization, was brought to a halt when the Roman Empire faltered. As McNeill explained:

> More than once, therefore, in the years from 500 B.C. to 1500 A.D., the ebb and flow of the frontiers between Middle Eastern, Indian, and Hellenic civilizations threatened to upset the fourfold cultural balance of Eurasia. Yet the dynamism first of Hellenism, then of Indian civilization, and finally of Islam never quite succeeded in destroying the balance; nor did the blending of elements derived from the separate but adjacent civilizations of Western Eurasia ever obscure the essential continuity of the three separate traditions. (1963, p. 250)

And somehow, probably due to their peripheral locations, China, Japan, Russia, and Western Europe managed not to become integrally involved with the major cultural centers. This is not to state that each did not develop to some extent culturally and geographically. The geographical area of our concern here, Western Europe, "moved eastward across the Elbe, northward to Scandinavia, westward to the Celtic fringes of Atlantic Europe, and southward into Spain and Italy" (McNeill, 1963, p. 251).

And what about these Germanic tribes whose warriors and families took part in great migrations that eventually brought about the disintegration of the Roman Empire? For information about them, we must turn to Tacitus' *Germania* and *Agricola* and later remnants from their early records as they became institutionalized. These people were evidently sturdy, powerful, and warlike. They were so imbued with the necessity for bearing arms that they typically conducted both public and private business in such a way that combat was possible at a moment's notice. A man bore arms after his ability to use them had been approved by his council of elders in the tribe to which he belonged. At such a time there was a formal investiture with a spear and javelin. The import of this ceremony was that the young man was moving from the status of household member of his father to that of a tribesman. There was evidently very little public spectacle, with the exception of periodic naked dancing accompanied by the brandishing of weapons.

Interestingly, women were highly regarded in this warlike society. There is evidence that their counsel was sought regularly. They attended their husbands and sons during and after battle, and occasionally they were known actually to engage in combat themselves when absolutely necessary. In such an environment, father and mother obviously saw to it that both boys and girls were raised in a hardy fashion. The young had to become self-dependent as soon as possible for the sake of sheer survival. Next to warfare, hunting is reported as a favorite occupation or avocation, as the occasion demanded. While the girls and young women mastered the rudiments of domestic life, the boys and young men were indoctrinated so that they typically became fierce warriors and hunters (Caesar in Book Six, Chapters 21–28, of the *Gallic War* is in essential agreement with Tacitus in *Germania* about basic points).

Similar statements about the men of the North, the Vikings, can be made, but it is generally agreed that their type of civilization was somewhat more advanced that that of the Germans. Various popular sports, games, and exercises included ball games, crude snowshoe racing, running, jumping, heavy stone throwing, spear hurling, and jumping for distance and height.

The chaotic and often miserable conditions that characterized the decline, fall, and aftermath of the Roman Empire were accompanied by the retrogression of practically all phases of the typical social institutions. This included public and private schools, which survived in only rare instances. As men and women turned to the monasteries and convents of the Christian Church for their general education and religious training, it was logical that the prevailing attitudes of the church toward sports, dancing, and physical activity other than manual labor would be reflected then and for a long time thereafter. At least the guidelines of daily manual labor resulted in the maintenance and development of farming, husbandry, elementary construction, development of crafts, and establishment of rudimentary hospitals. The time spent on reading and copying resulted in preservation of some of the learning of the past, along with an opportunity to master the basic fundamentals of education. There is some evidence that physical fitness was maintained in the West through vigorous activity, although the brothers in the monasteries of the East often carried their subjugation of the body to extremes with resultant unhealthy debility setting in. There is therefore no evidence that physical education was included in the curriculum embodying the so-called Seven Liberal Arts (the *trivium* and the *quadrivium*) offered to the monks or nuns (or indeed in the programs of study for the younger students aspiring to eventual higher learning). This seems to have been true also for the curriculum of the occasional "palace school" which appeared (for example, that developed by Alcuin for children of the nobles during the reign of Charlemagne). Fortunately, the irrepressible urges and instincts for play and movement could not be denied or totally eradicated. As appears to be the case (even today), the educational pendulum had swung too far in one direction.

Physical education (or what we today might call physical *training*) was revived to a considerable degree in what is often called the Age of Chivalry. Slowly but steadily, a type of governmental order extended throughout Western Europe. The period extending from the mid-eleventh to the thirteenth century has been called here the time of feudal society. This society or culture was divided into three classes: (1) the masses, who had to work very hard to support the other classes and eke out a bare existence for themselves; (2) the clergy, who carried on the affairs of the Church; and (3) the nobles, who were responsible for the government of certain lands or territories under a king, and who performed the necessary military duties.

An interesting insight into some of the changes that occurred in the eleventh century is presented by Horatio Smith:

> The Norman conquest effected two marked changes in the sports and pastimes prevalent at the close of the Saxon era, by restricting the privileges of the chase, and first establishing those barbarous game laws, the imposition of which was one of the greatest insults of tyranny, while their maintenance, in scarcely mitigated severity, at the present enlightened era, cannot be otherwise designated than as a monstrous oppression upon the lower orders, and a flagrant outrage offered to the spirit of the times. . . . (1831, pp. 114–15).

That the first of these "marked changes" was distressing could hardly be emphasized more. The second so-called marked change was reported much more enthusiastically:

> The second notable change in our pastimes, occasioned by the advent of the Normans, was the introduction of tournaments and jousts, together with all the pomps, gallantries and observances of chivalry, which, although they all bore the visible impress of war, were decidedly civilizing and even ennobling in their general tendency. (Smith, 1831, p. 115)

The curriculum during this period could be classified as training for social efficiency. Although there was an ideal, the emphasis on manners and social etiquette was greater than ever before. Along with this prescribed training in social conduct for the prospective knight—a man who was pledged to serve his feudal lord, the Church, and all women (as well as his own lady in particular)—a complex physical and military education of the most strenuous type was required for all aspirants to such status.

Interestingly enough, the emphasis shifted markedly in favor of a curriculum characterized by various activities, rather than one with extreme emphasis upon the person's intellectual development. As Wilds has explained, "At the earlier levels, the content consisted of health instruction, religious instruction, training in etiquette and obedience to superiors, playing the harp, singing, chess, and the development of skills in riding, jousting, boxing, and wrestling" (1936, p. 194). Included as well were the elements of reading and writing, but the so-called Seven Free Arts of the advanced curriculum involved strenuous physical involvement in jousting, falconing, swimming, horsemanship, and boxing —with time for the writing and singing of verse, along with the playing of chess, for the quiet, more relaxing times of day.

The ideal of social service was undoubtedly considerably better in theory than in practice, but there is no question that it did serve to set standards higher than those that existed previously. Dorsey reported, for example, that what was "a rich and cultured world lay helpless at the feet of warlike savages" and, referring to the entire era spanning some five hundred years, he concluded:

> Take it or leave it, the fact remains that the five centuries which saw Europe converted to Christianity also saw such a string of murders, parricides, fratricides, and poisonings, and such bestial, brutal, drunken licentiousness as cannot be found in five thousand years of Egyptian history; nor anywhere, says Gibbons, more vice and less virtue in the same space of time.... (1931, p. 576)

No matter what we may think of this period of man's history in the Western world, the ideals of chivalry still hold a fascination for many people. Broekhoff has reported interestingly on this topic. He explains that "brute physical force was elevated to a higher level by the principle of courtesy, which revealed itself not only as politeness in social relations, but also in the knight's attitude during battle" (in Zeigler, 1973, p. 226). In those days before the practical application of gunpowder had been discovered, the bow and arrow were quite naturally most important weapons, but as Broekhoff reports (from both Jusserand and Painter) French nobles found it distasteful to kill their enemies from a distance, thereby losing an opportunity to display their knightly skills and competencies (1973, p. 226). How can one "live on in memory" if he slays his enemy from a distance of 150 yards with a well-placed arrow? Broekhoff concludes that "a look at modern programs of physical education would only confirm the absence of a societal ideal or set of ideals"; however, he does find that "the activities in our modern arenas seem to lie closest to the ideals of chivalry" (1973, p. 232). (With this we find ourselves in complete agreement, and hasten to add that it is therefore most important that competitive sport be guided in such a way that educational benefits will result from a fine type of leadership. If sport is not a "socially useful servant," of what use is it?)

The aim of physical education or training, then, during this period of feudalism and manorialism (the political economy of the system that was local and agricultural) was certainly narrow, and health standards were usually frighteningly poor by present standards. The Greek ideal had been lost, and physical education once again served a most practical objective—that of producing a well-trained man in the art of hand-to-hand combat, possessing all of the necessary "physical and psychological" attributes. The aims and methodology of this type of training undoubtedly reflected the times most accurately.

In the latter part of the Early Middle Ages (as we have delimited them), there was a decline of feudalism as a correlative rise of an early type of nationalism (city-statism?) set in along with more vigorous trade and community growth. This resulted in a stronger middle class and an inevitable demand for an improved educational system designed to prepare the youth for a lifetime occupation. This vocational education was related to both commercial and trade interests (not mutually exclusive, of course). The intellectual training of the period at this level was elementary, and religious instruction was not neglected. In so-called trade training, the youth went through the stages of apprentice, journeyman, and master. The discipline was presumably severe, and teaching methodology involved example, imitation, and practice.

As mentioned above, the Christian world was marked further by the beginnings of an intellectual awakening at this time. The universities—embryonic by present-day standards—included higher education in law, theology, medicine, art, architecture, and literature. Monastic schools had given way to cathedral and parish schools. Scholasticism was designed to fortify the position of the Church through logic and theology.

We have already discussed the role of the knight in this society, but what about that of the other social classes? Further, what about the physical activity patterns of the farmers (peasants), the clergy, and the burghers in this somewhat more advanced society with a greater amount of role differentiation? Moolenijzer has provided some succinct characterizations of these groups who, along with the kings, nobles, and itinerant workers, made up this transitional society. Referring to the farmers, he characterizes their lot in life as being a difficult and lowly one in which "many lost their independence completely and sank to the level of domestic animals, dependent on the whims of their masters" (in Zeigler, 1973, p. 236). They were forbidden the use of arms, such regulation helping to curtail uprisings while preserving the game for the hunting pleasure of the lord of the manor. The usual indigenous games apparent in almost all cultures were present, of course, and Moolenijzer explained how the paintings and etchings of the period depicted such activities as wrestling, jumping, ball playing, stone casting, and running (1973, p. 236). A very interesting finding from the *Annales Lamberti,* a chronicle of 1075, complains about the typical lack of physical fitness among many farmers, a fact which discouraged the nobility from pressing them into service as foot soldiers in battle.

While knights and squires were involved in training for combat with such preparatory contests as quintaining—a device which consisted of a dummy with a shield attached placed on a swivel in such a way that the charging knight would be hit with a club if he didn't hit the dummy's shield dead center—inexpensive variations of such devices were developed at many levels of society. Thus, an inexpensive reproduction of this mechanism could well turn up at a village festival as a game for the amusement of farmers and others. Further, there were such seemingly ageless contests as footracing, tug-of-war matches, sack races, quarter-staff throwing, archery, caber tossing, and bowling with its many variations (1973, p. 236). Also, special mention was made of the popularity of dancing of all types (individual, dual, and group), including dance which could be classified as religious, esthetic, and competitive. Some of these dances became so frenzied and frantic that people's health was damaged (St. Vitus Dance, or the dance of death).

Moolenijzer reported that contrary to the impression held by many, the Christian Church—although officially violently opposed to sporting events and games presumably base—only "frowned on wasteful, nonutilitarian physical activity" (1973, p. 237), but "the clergy did not always enforce the rules and quite often interpreted them to their own liking." We can understand that monks and other clerics living apart from the populace might well preach strictures against certain types of physical recreation, while priests with active parishes might agree with the need for such activity and occasionally get involved themselves to a reasonable extent.

Last, we learn that the burghers "were able to erect their own *burhs* or walls" and, because of the service and money they could provide to both the rulers and the Church, they developed a living pattern of their own. Certain traditional games and activities were preserved, of course, but many of both old and new activities had to be modified for lack of space in the developing cities. Such physical recreation of an informal nature contributed to the social and recreational goals of the townspeople at festivals and fairs, on religious holidays (of which there were many), and during everyday life. However, the educational system did not provide regular physical education that might serve as a "physical fitness device" for subsequent military service (1973, p. 243).

Summary

How can we summarize this discussion on Physical Education and Sport in the Early Middle Ages? First, the four approaches to education during this period have been typically designated as (1) monasticism, (2) scholasticism, (3) chivalry, and (4) guild system. Monasticism was a type of moral-religious education including both literary and manual training. Scholasticism was a natural extension of monasticism, a religious-intellectual education which at the university level involved arts, medicine, law, and theology. Chivalry can be classified as social education of an aristocratic (as opposed to democratic) nature that included military, physical, and religious-moral training. The guild system of education was vocational in nature; it stressed either commercial training or trade training, and in both cases the intellectual training was elementary and religious instruction was not neglected.

Insofar as physical education and sport were concerned, the following points may be made:

1. The presumed negative outlook of the Church against *all* physical activity has been overemphasized. The Church was strongly against the violent excesses of later Roman sports and games.
2. There is some evidence that physical fitness was maintained in Western monasteries through manual labor. Physical education was not included in the Seven Liberal Arts.
3. Physical training was revived strongly during the Age of Chivalry. A complex physical and military education of the most strenuous type was required of all who aspired to become knights. The aim of physical education at this time was narrow, and health standards were very low.
4. Evidently the physical fitness of farmers was not high, and their physical recreation patterns were inadequate because of their low social status. Certain types of play and indigenous games could not be repressed at village fairs and festivals (nor at home).

5. Although the Church "frowned officially" on many sporting events and games, it was the truly wasteful types of physical activity that were sharply decried. There was some evidence that priests with active parishes might agree with the need for such activity, and occasionally would get involved themselves to a reasonable extent.

6. The educational system of the burghers in the developing towns and cities did not provide regular physical training, but did develop a pattern of modified (by space limitations) physical recreation which contributed to their overall social goals.

LATER MIDDLE AGES

The Renaissance Period

Social Institutions. The fourteenth, fifteenth, and early sixteenth centuries have become known as the Renaissance period in Europe in history. The word "renaissance" means "rebirth" in French, but it is now generally accepted that such an "awakening" as occurred was far from being a phenomenon that burst upon the world within a short period of time. McIntosh has stated:

> The preceding centuries had not been barren of knowledge of Greek life and thought. If the Greek language was not widely known, yet the works of many Greek authors had been available in Latin translations. The revival of Roman Law in the twelfth century was succeeded by an Aristotelian renaissance in the thirteenth. The views of Aristotle cannot have been unknown in the monasteries, schools, and universities of the twelfth, thirteenth, or fourteenth century. Plato's philosophy was also known at second hand. Some of the ancient theories of the cult of the body were doubtless rejected and others were adapted to the monastic and ascetic life. What was new in the fifteenth century was not the actual study of the classics but rather the attitude and approach of the "humanists" to them. (1957, pp. 60–61)

All of this leads to the conclusion that the roots of this development were indeed planted and nourished during earlier centuries, but it now appears that they came to fruition rapidly during this period and their growth was characterized by marked intellectual and commercial advancement. A secularism that began to take hold during the time of feudalism at the latter part of what we have called the Early Middle Ages now became a most powerful and dominating influence in this extremely interesting period of world history.

During this time the political development of France and England may be contrasted with that of the German, Slavic, and Italian states of central, eastern, and southern Europe, respectively. Through the employment of political monarchies, the growth of France and England was characterized by strong, centralized political authority. This early development could be considered an advantage because it enabled these countries to search out and gain control of vast colonial empires. In France, for example, Philip IV (the Fair) achieved supremacy over both the nobles and the Pope. Despite the long struggle with Edward I of England, known as the Hundred Years' War (1337–1453), each king was able to consolidate his own realm. Thus, Louis XI in France found at the end of this struggle that he could assess taxes directly upon the nobles *and* the middle class. Through this means France became a powerful force during this period. In England the speed of development within the political monarchy was perhaps even more rapid. Edward I was able to establish his own courts of law, and therefore the varied feudal laws soon gave way to early English common law. During this era the English Parliament made rapid strides as well and forced the rulers to pay considerable attention to the legislative power of a group destined to serve the welfare of the middle and lower classes of the country.

The developments that took place in the German, Slavic, and Italian states, as part of the so-called Holy Roman Empire, can hardly be compared with those of France and England. The "Empire" wasn't really an empire; it was a collection of states controlled by family dynasties. The emperor was chosen by the College of Electors composed of three Church and four secular rulers, and the numerous intrigues and coalitions that developed within this somewhat loosely formed confederation kept him relatively weak. The Germans made efforts to expand to the east in the thirteenth century, but they were stalled temporarily by a coalition of peoples. Through political maneuvering the Germans were able to regroup, and leadership provided by Maximilian I of the Austrian Hapsburgs enabled Emperor Charles V to marshal great power in Europe. This vast power was subsequently weakened, however, by attacks from various directions, as well as by the internal dissension created by the Lutheran Reformation.

The fortunes of various other states rose and fell during the Renaissance period. For example, Poland was quite powerful in the fifteenth century; later in the 1400s Sweden, Norway, and Denmark achieved strength through unity under the leadership of the Danes. The Russian Slavs, after considerable struggle with the Tartars, laid the groundwork for modern Russia about 1400. In 1453 the Ottoman Turks overran Constantinople and toppled the Byzantine Empire before invading Europe proper. Spain developed into a powerful state in European affairs in the late fifteenth century.

During the so-called Renaissance, Italy was a heterogeneous mixture of independent city-states. After the cities won their independence from the landed nobles, the rise of the mercantile class through the formation of guilds was quite rapid. In some cities such as Milan and Naples, the merchants were relatively weak, and efforts at more demo- cratic or republican government made little headway. Yet these city-states were very strong culturally and economically when France invaded Italy in 1494. Throughout this era the Papacy had great political influence, but this too eventually declined.

During this period, therefore, all sorts of new commerce and trade developed on both land and sea. The middle classes were gaining more political power, especially in England, France, and certain Italian city- states. Because of the harsh conditions under which the peasants typically lived, there were also many revolts in all parts of Europe. These con- tributed to the high death rate caused by wanton killing, disease, and famine. Even the strong Papacy's fortunes waxed and waned because of the persistent efforts of various kings and regional church councils. Even- tually, the national churches obtained enough influence to bring about the wars of the Protestant Reformation.

What rights did the state have in the struggle with the Church; what rights did the people have to determine their own governing regulations; what rights did the individual have as against the rights of the state and/or church over his person; and what rights did man have to deter- mine nature's moral order over the religious code established by the church? These were the questions to be answered as the humanists brought about a revival of classical learning during the period of the Renaissance.

Educational Institutions. A more serious struggle for the control of education took place during this period. Inroads were made into the almost complete monopoly that the Church had had in this sphere for a number of centuries because a strong relationship was recognized be- tween political control and the control of education of potential leaders of the future. With the rise of what has become known as the middle class through commercial growth, these citizens naturally demanded better education for their children because such training promoted their intel- lectual, business, *and* social advancement. Thus the foundation was grad- ually being laid for elementary and secondary schools that would later be part of national educational systems.

The efforts of the various secular authorities to play a greater role in the education of children and youth can be noted in several countries such as Italy, Germany, Scotland, and England. Yet the Church, under- standably, did not relinquish its almost total control readily and willingly; as students of the history of education appreciate, it is difficult to break with tradition. As inroads were gradually made, however, community governments, kings and nobles, voluntary endowed foundations, and private teachers' guilds were not to be denied. While this struggle was going on, the relatively new universities attempted to stay free from both secular and Church control. On occasion certain rulers, such as Louis XI in France in the fifteenth century, issued decrees and had laws passed to regulate the subject matter offered in these institutions.

Certain trends during this period should be mentioned. Democratization of education gradually became evident, although it by no means characterized the educational effort of the times. Teachers did gain increased status, especially at the upper levels. Those who taught at the lower levels were not so fortunate, and to a certain extent this distinction has continued down to the present day. Apprenticeship systems promoted by the guilds for the children of the middle and lower classes were a significant development.

An important advancement was the restoration of a balance among the various aspects of the educational curriculum. Renaissance leaders came to realize that the world had known a much better type of education for freemen at the height of the Greek and Roman civilizations. To glean the best from the literatures of these cultures, however, scholars had to comprehend Latin and Greek; fortunately for some at least, the growth of a leisured class meant that there would be time for an increased number to gain these skills. And the interests of many of these people were of this world, not of an intangible supernatural realm. Thus began a most diligent effort to regain these "fabled treasures" that very soon gave Latin and Greek, the so-called classics, a central place in a curriculum dominated by the humanities. This humanistic curriculum included intellectual, esthetic, moral, and physical aspects, and once again represented the ideal of a well-balanced education that included even the etiquette of the former era.

There were a variety of emphases within this "new approach." Esthetic aspects were stressed more in southern Europe, while moral education received greater attention in the north. Stylistic elegance counted for more in Italy than it did in Germany, where the development of a discriminating mind seemed more important than other aspects of the educational process. A famous humanist school in Italy was led by Vittorino da Feltre at the court of the Duke of Mantua, and the Dutch humanist Erasmus had a definite influence on European education after 1500.

Thus, although the humanistic ideal was eventually debased again, it did have an enormous influence on the education of the elite during the Renaissance period. The classics were firmly established in the curriculum, and they had to be mastered prior to university education. In the process, the educational aim was considerably broadened to the extent that preparation for service in life—whether as a nobleman, priest, merchant, or politician—received due emphasis.

The Reformation

Social Institutions The period known as the Reformation (in the sixteenth and seventeenth centuries) is a fascinating one to study. A variety of social forces were at work in differing degrees, dividing loyalties sharply. The Catholic Church was being attacked from many quarters; governments were centralizing their authority and becoming ever stronger; mercantilism was reaching unheard-of heights; the variations of humanism remained as strong influences; and scholars and scientists were achieving some proficiency in the use of the scientific method—the results of which increasingly shattered beliefs held for centuries.

Most significant in the seventeenth century were the various alliances made between kings and the rising business class against both the Catholic Church and the many nobles. Merchants and bankers respectively had either earned or were holding the capital necessary for kings to hire mercenaries to fight their wars, both large and small—and for better or worse, they often did supply it for these purposes. The split within the Church itself further weakened the hierarchical structure, as did the frequent plundering of the wealth that had been accumulated. Royal power was centralized most effectively in England, France, and Spain; whereas Germany and Italy did not enjoy comparable developments for a number of reasons. The concept of universal Christianity propounded so vigorously in the early and middle periods of the Middle Ages seemed destined to failure. The power of national states continued to grow—a political force of great magnitude that the world of the twentieth and twenty-first centuries will have to outgrow before it literally destroys itself.

A concomitant of this struggle for power was a fantastic rise in all types of commerce and trade. This development was especially notable in countries fronting on the Atlantic Ocean, principally England, France, Spain, and Portugal (and the Netherlands in the seventeenth century). The New World to the west was opened up, and soon the major trade routes were no longer solely in the Mediterranean. As a result the old economy was changed at its very roots. Towns grew into cities; inflation set in when the precious metals from the New World were converted into hard money; and the firm foundations of capitalistic society were laid with their basis tied to the strength of commerce and banking. The nation-states had to pursue the acquisition of new colonies vigorously, and accordingly found it necessary to regulate, while still encouraging, the interests of their business enterprises to guarantee the continuance of their newly found economic prosperity. In these ways the kings and merchants became richer and stronger, while the Church and the nobles with all their land and wealth became progressively poorer and weaker.

The end result was a completely altered class structure. The nobles became landed "country gentlemen" with much less influence; the rural gentry with their large parcels of land became stronger because the city dwellers (whose numbers were increasing) still had to eat; the merchants and the bankers of the middle class became infinitely more wealthy, and hence much more powerful; and the clergy, especially the higher clerics, still claimed respect but were basically much less powerful as their treasuries and holdings grew smaller.

Then came the religious revolts against the Catholic Church. Those who waged these struggles were backed by the wealth of the middle class and the newly won power of the centralized nation-states. Viewed superficially the religious attitudes of the people might be thought to be changing completely—a belief that a person living in the second half of the twentieth century might very easily attempt to transfer back to that earlier period. But this was not necessarily the case at all. In fact, this development could be classified as a type of internecine warfare. Many so-called Protestants simply rejected the authority of the Pope as the divine interpreter of God's word. They felt that it was the Bible that was God's instrument whereby he revealed truth to man. If a man "had the faith," so to speak, he "could be saved" without involvement in the Catholic Church's complex ritual. Furthermore, many of these dissenters were discouraged by what they felt to be the increasing secularism of the Church.

The name of Martin Luther is the one most closely associated with the Reformation. He stated the tenets of the Protestant position, refused on several occasions to recant, was promptly excommunicated by the Pope, received "protective custody" from the Elector of Saxony, and retired to the Wartburg Castle to translate the New Testament into the current vernacular language of the Germans. All of this took place in the early part of the third decade of the sixteenth century. The Protestant position of Lutheranism became identified with the civil authorities, and the struggle between Church and state went on. At the same time, a number of uprisings by the peasants themselves took place. It wasn't until 1555 at Augsburg that the states won the right to decide what religion their subjects would follow. It can hardly be argued, however, that the terms of this peace treaty represented any great advancement for individual freedom, since by law the ruler of a particular country (nation-state, so to speak) could then decide whether his subjects would be Catholic or Lutheran.

Equally significant developments were taking place in other countries. In Switzerland, for example, Zwingli and Calvin led the forces of religious revolt. What was eventually called Calvinism can be considered the sharpest break with the Catholic Church. In Calvin's *Institutes of the*

Christian Religion, written in 1536, he placed great stress on retaining only those concepts for which the Bible gave authority. John Calvin's theocracy restored the political supremacy of the Church. His religious subjects were forced to adopt his theory of predestination. If they wished to be saved—and they couldn't know in advance whether God had predestined them to be saints or sinners—there wasn't much choice but to live a life that would be considered correct in His eyes. This movement developed great power eventually and spread from Switzerland to Germany, to France, to The Netherlands, to England and Scotland, and eventually to America.

Some mention should be made in passing of the beginnings of the Reformation in England, when John Wycliffe made strong attacks from 1377 on against orthodox Church doctrines. In the sixteenth century a succession of rulers, beginning with Henry VIII, took turns at efforts to either strengthen or weaken the power of the Church. The Church of England, established in 1534, really did not include any significant doctrinal changes and later contested with the Calvinist Puritans on the subject of reform away from Roman Catholicism.

And finally, in Germany, the devastating Thirty Years' War (from 1618 to 1648) broke out as the Bohemian Calvins strove to wrest themselves from the control of the Catholic Church. Before this struggle finally ended with the Peace of Westphalia in 1648, the Swedes, the Danes, and the French became embroiled as well. The end result was that the developing nation-states became sovereign and no longer subject to the Holy Roman Empire. It is generally recognized that the treaty signed in 1648 was extremely important, and that it had a great deal to do with the nationalistic struggles waged in Europe quite regularly ever since that time.

Although there is no doubt that the Catholic Church did gradually become less of an influence during these centuries, it cannot be proposed that the blows struck by the various reformers should be considered mortal ones. There was what can be correctly called a Catholic Counter-Reformation, and The Church (as it had been called) remained stronger than any other single religious group in the West. Indeed reforms were made to correct a number of the abuses that had brought about the Protestant Reformation, but the Inquisition and various council meetings gave ground slowly and tended to maintain the status of the traditional doctrines within the Church. Further, the establishment of a number of educational agencies, such as the Society of Jesus under Ignatius de Loyola, was most effective as an agent of preservation of the status quo.

The religious influence on the Renaissance culture had been great indeed. Moreover, we cannot underestimate the subsequent influence of the nationalistic seeds that were being sown during this period of approximately two centuries. But despite the authority of religion and its leaders, who functioned with the firm belief that theirs was fixed and revealed truth, and despite the additional fact that many rulers believed that they too were endowed with certain knowledge, ability, and power by their Creator, it was during this period that some of the basic foundations of modern science were being established by a limited few individuals. Scientists like Francis Bacon, Galileo, Kepler, Copernicus, and others were gradually altering rational man's conception of himself and his place in the universe. Many of these men were made to suffer greatly for their radical beliefs. For example, Giordano Bruno was burned at the stake.

A type of materialism did develop, however, which was in sharp contrast to the metaphysical positions held by both Catholic and Protestant theologians. As so often happens, a compromise developed between two hostile positions. In this case the dualistic position postulated by Descartes represented a means whereby a reasonable degree of compatibility could be achieved. He offered the theory that the universe was actually composed of mind and matter, and, most important, that these two substances were separate and distinct. Theologians were quick to seize upon the concept of an independent mind as their domain, and matter was left for the scientists to investigate almost at will. This type of dualism left man divided into two parts, so to speak, and educators—especially physical educators!—have been plagued in their work ever since by the remnants of this belief (or theological—philosophical position). Even today, when the unity of the human organism seems to be quite generally accepted by scientists, this underlying, pervasive dualistic position still causes great difficulty for those seeking to function according to scientific principle.

Educational Institutions. Social influences within the culture during this period of turmoil undoubtedly affected the educational organizations greatly. Although a few educators felt a need for education as a formal institution to join forces with the prevailing social institutions in the shaping of the world to come, the strongest influences on society were exerted by the Church, the state, the developing economic structure, and the scientific humanism that was catching the imagination of some.

As might be expected, the religious wars wreaked great havoc with the educational system extant. Although some progress was made during intervening periods of peace, it wasn't until after 1648 that any new outline of educational organization emerged. Some efforts were made to extend educational opportunities downward, but the traditional class structure of Europe was very strong. The final result was merely to distinguish between one type of basic education for the masses and a vastly superior system of classically humanistic education for those who had the wealth, power, and leisure to take advantage of such offerings. Essentially, then, the educational reformers were presenting theories about universal and democratic educational systems, but such theories and reforms were a very long way from realization. Interestingly enough, there was even some organized effort to educate girls and young women, a step forward unheard of during the entire Middle Ages.

Most significant during the period of the Reformation was the increasing amount of civil control of education at a time when there was strife between the warring religious groups. In Germany, to cite an instance, the Protestant religious leaders allied themselves with the Protestant heads of state. In this way the schools were transformed along with the churches. Civil codes for schools were developed that provided elementary education for all in the towns and villages. In Switzerland and The Netherlands, where Calvinism prevailed, the Protestant Church was even stronger and brought about free education including, as might be expected, religious instruction for all. The situation in France differed because of the power of the Catholic Church. Actually, the state asked the Church to organize compulsory education for all, and it was only at the university level that Louis XIV superimposed any educational requirements. The Huguenots eventually (in 1598) did win the right to conduct their own schools, when the Edict of Nantes also provided some financial support for this purpose.

In the British Isles the Church of England retained its control over education, but difficulty arose since the Protestant rulers claimed that they were the technical heads of the church and acted accordingly with the conduct of education. The Puritans sought to establish a system of schools under the state, but their plan was thwarted by the Restoration toward the end of the seventeenth century. Thus it may be concluded that educational control continued to be vested with the church in France, Italy, England, and Spain, despite intermittent efforts to place it under civil control, but that greater civil control was achieved in those countries where the influence of Luther and Calvin was the greatest (notably Germany, Switzerland, and The Netherlands).

Certain other aspects of educational change may be noted during this last of the four periods we have arbitrarily included under the heading of the Middle Ages. First, the status of the teacher was elevated to a degree, with improved professional preparation in some instances and early efforts at standardization and certification. With the greatly increased number of vernacular schools (and secondary schools also), it should be stressed also that the rate of illiteracy decreased markedly. Third, the opportunity to develop personal libraries, because of the availability of printed books for the first time, represented a highly important educational advancement, especially for the wealthier classes. Fourth, the family was urged to play a greater educational role, particularly those adhering to the Protestant faith, Last, although the overarching influence of the church still dominated education, scientific and humanistic educational theory was gradually broadening and deepening educational aims and objectives.

In summary, therefore, vernacular curricula were developing all over Europe; the classical curriculum prevailed generally for the preparation of future leaders; vocational training was introduced in many quarters for children of the poor; improved academies were begun for those of the upper classes who desired a more practical education, although they were sons of nobility; and the universities typically retained their emphasis on theology and the classics.

Physical Education and Sport in the Later Middle Ages

There are many ways we can approach this topic, considering the varying emphases during this era. Wilds, in his educational history (1936, pp. 249–377) developed "assimilation charts" that designate the influences as: individual humanism, social humanism, Protestant Reformation, Catholic Reformation, verbal realism, social realism, sense realism, disciplinarianism, and rationalism (the latter term describing the eighteenth-century influence). Wilds' classification was employed generally by Van Dalen and Bennett (1971), and it certainly proves helpful to the person seeking some understanding of what happened in the past.

Although it would be convenient to follow a similar approach—one for which there is most certainly some justification—we instead shall construct our definitely imperfect tale according to the relatively flimsy evidence available through the pronouncements, strictures, and recommendations of those who were writing and speaking on the topic of education during this period. The words of Dorsey inclined us in this direction:

> Divisions—epochs, eras, dynasties, reigns, etc.—which serve book purposes are not necessarily rational or sharp divisions; they are conveniences, like punctuation marks on the printed page or milestones on a pike. As every naturalist presumably rebels against the necessity of dividing plants and animals into orders, species, genera, etc., so the historian of human behavior must regret the implications that seem justified from cutting history into slices that can be consumed at one sitting. This observation seems especially applicable to the history of civilization. (1931, p. 638)

Exactly how the intellectual awakening of Western Europe blossomed into a full-scale cultural revival or renaissance cannot be delineated to the satisfaction of all. The prevailing religious and political formulas were steadily causing the breakdown of the feudal order, but they had not produced a seemingly viable alternative until certain individuals decided to examine the bases for the relatively long life and vitality of the Classical Age of Greece and Rome. It was hoped that a return to an age that seemed more advanced and civilized than the prevailing medieval culture could prevent a collapse of the society, while at the same time the humanism of the classical period would transform a didactic, decaying era into a period marked by vitality and strength. It is notable that a significant number of scholars decided that the best information was to be obtained from the original classics themselves, and not from the Christian evaluation of the ideological base of this civilization. Owen explains further:

> . . . the Humanists instead looked to the ancients for guidance. They became critical rather than pious in their approach to the evidence of the past; and they endeavored to evaluate it by relying on practical experience and good sense rather than canonical tradition and syllogistic pseudo-logic, that is, to assess it rationally rather than dogmatically. By doing so, they began to give the classical heritage they were so assiduously studying an air of both historical validity and contemporary relevance, at once redefining its details and reevaluating its purport in terms the ancients themselves might have used and understood. (1974, pp. 111–12)

Francesco Petrarca (better known as Petrarch) was undoubtedly one of the first to realize that classical Greek thought could be employed to provide a new cultural framework for the decadent period in which he lived. He is credited with the discovery of certain Latin manuscripts which furthered the new development. His poetry, literature, and other intellectual thoughts have stamped him as one of the great humanists of the time —a man who struggled with the conflict that he felt between the asceticism of medieval times and the newer possibilities for individual expression and fulfillment. Petrarch lived between 1304 and 1374, and today we date the beginning of the humanist movement in Italy somewhere during these years.

The educational aims and methods of these humanistic scholars, and especially their ideas about the role of physical activity in the education of youth, may best be gleaned from an examination of the writings of such men as Petrus Paulus Vergerius (1349–1420), Vittorino da Feltre (1378–1446), Guarino Guarini da Verone (1370–1461), Leone Battista Alberti (1404–1472), Aeneas Sylvius Piccolomini (later Pope Pius II) (1405–1464), Mapheus Vegius (1405–1458), Matteo Palmieri (1406– ?), Baldassare Conte Castiglione (1478–1529), Girolamo Cardano (1501–1576), and Hieronymus Mercurialis (1530–1606). Before looking at these individuals' views about physical activity, let us briefly review the educational aims and methods of early humanism. An outstanding treatment of this topic was that by William Harrison Woodward at the turn of the twentieth century (1905, pp. 179–250). Woodward makes it clear that the

"Humanists as a body were profoundly convinced of the *practical* character of Classical studies" (p. 182). They hearkened back to the Aristotelean ideal that stressed the perfection of man as a citizen. It is perfectly understandable, therefore, that the educational process was to involve complete training for everyday life as a citizen, with special emphasis on the need for practical judgment in public affairs.

During this fifteenth century, however, a gradual shift took place so that "the conception of the 'perfect citizen' involved as a necessary condition that of the full development of the individual" (p. 185). Some were uneasy about this transition, and it can be understood that there was a necessity for a reasonable amount of consensus on the concept of "the ideal education" among the Church, the state, and the "innovative" leaders of humanistic thought. It was undoubtedly true that excellence and a high level of proficiency in one area brought immediate attention and acclaim, but the highest degree of recognition was reserved for those who pursued "a wide range of studies, which will have for their result both knowledge and a full, dignified life" (p. 187).

Woodward identifies a "nobler type of Christian individuality" as a leading aim of humanistic education. Along with the so-called "active virtues," such traits as courage, restraint, patriotism, and self-sacrifice were admired greatly (p. 188), while "distinction in social life was marked by power of conversation, and by personal carriage, by resourceful leisure and dignified old age" (p. 189).

Not only did the humanist educator demonstrate great care in the selection of the subject matter to be included in the curriculum at the several educational levels, but he gave considerable attention as well to the selection of the teacher or tutor for the young. This person needed to possess most of the knowledge, competencies, and skills which he wished to develop in his charges. In addition to possessing ability in the several areas of concern, he had to have personal character of the highest caliber. As Woodward explains (based on the writings of Aeneas Sylvius), "his responsibility is that of the father of their moral and intellectual nature; and by this presumption he will be determined in his devotion to his work in the discipline which he enforces, and in the example which he himself sets forth" (p. 202). It is evident that Vittorino, about whom Woodward is writing, truly excelled in his methodology: "Hence he sought out that subject and that method of instruction which he believed to be best adapted to each individual intelligence. Upon the dullest he would bestow infinite pains, that by devising simple tasks or some special form of training he might meet the needs even of the least promising scholars" (p. 203).

What then did these various Italian humanists have to say about the role of sport, physical training, and physical activity generally in the education of youth? Space does not permit a detailed discussion of each educator, but we must consider the significant recommendations because of their great importance. First, we must keep in mind that the training of the previous centuries still prevailed directed toward courtly and military pursuits. It was a question, therefore, of gradual infiltration by the humanistic educational spirit. The Court where such an ideal was approximated to the highest degree was probably that of the Duke of Mantua (the Gonzaga family), or perhaps the Ferrara Court (where Guarino was the tutor).

Vergerius' treatise *De Ingenuis Moribus* was published in perhaps fifty editions commencing in about 1472, although it may have been written as early as 1404 for use by the son of Francesco Carrara, the lord of Padua. In it he includes such topics as (1) character and its discipline, (2) liberal studies, (3) the manner of study, (4) bodily exercises and training in the art of war, and (5) recreation. It is truly significant that under the heading of "liberal studies" he lists prominently "that education which calls forth, trains and develops those highest gifts of body and of mind which ennoble men, and which are rightly judged to rank next in dignity to virtue only" (in letter to Ubertinus of Carrara; reported in Woodward, 1905, p. 102). In this important document Vergerius includes what might be considered to be the essence of the professional responsibilities of the three allied professions of health, physical education, and recreation: health knowledge, vigorous bodily exercise, and a broadly based pattern of recreational activities. As soon as the boy can use his limbs, he should be trained in arms. Concurrently, as soon as he can "rightly speak," his training in letters should begin. These are the two main liberal arts for Vergerius and, as he states, "in choice of bodily exercises those should be adopted which serve to maintain the body in good health and to strengthen the limbs: and thus it will be necessary to consider to some extent the case of each individual boy" (Woodward, 1905, p. 114). Then, stressing the traditional dichotomous view of the nature of the concepts of "work" and "play," Vergerius affirms that "we are not so constituted that we are able to bestow ourselves all day long upon our ordered tasks," and encourages "the sharp exertion of ball-play"; "recreation in hunting, hawking, or fishing"; "gentle riding, or in pleasant walks"; "recourse to music and to song"; or even "absolutely nothing for a while" (pp. 116–17). However, the playing of dice for money, dancing to music, and the watching of dancing girls were looked upon with disfavor (pp. 116–17).

When physical educators on this continent think about which man had the greatest influence on physical education, Vittorino da Feltre's name is undoubtedly the first that comes to mind. Woodward reports that "there is little doubt that, next to his intercourse with Barzizza, the treatise of Vergerius, enforced by its writer's life and example, served mainly to determine Vittorino in the great decision of his life" (1905, p. 16). That decision was to accept the invitation from Gianfrancesco Gonzaga, the Marquis and head of the family that controlled the Lordship of Mantua. This turned out to be a most successful arrangement, and Vittorino remained in the service of the Marquis Gonzaga and his wife, Paola di Malatesta, until his death in 1446 at the age of 68.

Exercise and sport occupied a very important place in Vittorino's overall educational scheme. Following the example of Greece and Rome, he combined the educational ideal of the committed humanist with the Christian influence of the times and the need to prepare the young males under his supervision to follow a career of arms. Any given day's educational training was not complete unless "the full personality had received a cultivation duly proportioned to the three sides of human nature" (p. 65). He placed special emphasis on certain ball games, leaping, and fencing. It is noteworthy that Vittorino appears to have "taken generally a wider view of physical training than that of Vergerius, Castiglione, and Milton, who laid special emphasis on partial exercises, aiming rather at strengthening the frame, inducing habits of hardiness and power of bearing fatigue, than at any special athletic skill" (p. 66). Truly, as Bazzano stated in his study on "The Contributions of the Italian Renaissance to Physical Education," "Vittorino has been acclaimed the first teacher of the Renaissance because the program which he implemented at La Giocosa encompassed a balance between the physical, intellectual, and moral aspects of education" (1973, p. 87).

The following list summarizes the educational goals in regard to health, physical education, sport and games, and other types of recreation, of those men who are considered leaders in Italy's humanist movement of the fourteenth, fifteenth, and sixteenth centuries:[2]

1. Petrus Paulus Vergerius (1349–1420)—discussed above.
2. Vittorino da Feltre (1378–1446)—discussed above.
3. Guarino Guarini da Verone (1370–1461)
   Stressed an education involving both physical and intellectual aspects; recommended games, dances, and hunting; stressed benefits of physical education in areas of physical fitness, combat training, provision of esthetic experience, and wholesome use of leisure; and viewed dance as legitimate phase of physical training curriculum. (A keen scholar of Greek, Guarino understood the important role of dancing in Greek culture. This position was not held by many of his contemporaries who were strongly influenced by the attitude of the Church in this matter.)
4. Leone Battista Alberti (1404–1472)
   Possessed outstanding all-round ability; affirmed physical education's con-

---

[2]The detailed material in this list was gleaned from Bazzano, 1973; Woodward, 1905; McIntosh in McIntosh et al., 1957; and Gerber, 1971.

tribution to the development of a virtuous man through opportunities to prove courage and to display honesty, and took the position that education took place *through* the agent of the body, while concurrently education *of* the body was a result.

5. Aeneas Sylvius Piccolomini (later Pope Pius II) (1405–1464)
   Argued that the organism was indivisible; reasoned that active involvement in physical training helped to develop total fitness in addition to an esthetically pleasing body, resulted in a person capable of bearing arms in a manly fashion, and developed vigorous health.

6. Mapheus Vegius (1405–1458)
   Believed that education should develop all aspects of a man—the physical, the mental, and the spiritual; viewed physical education as a phase of overall liberal education in a balanced perspective; stressed that healthful habits were important; reasoned that physical fitness should not be developed to the extreme, but should also involve a recreational approach.

7. Matteo Palmieri (1406– ?)
   Urged that education be practical and contribute to a productive life; believed that a citizen should be fully able to meet the physical and other emergencies of life; argued that participation in physical activities contributed to the vigor of the soul; and stressed especially the need for a balanced education resulting in the universal man ("L'uomo universale").

8. Baldassare Conte Castiglione (1478–1529)
   Recommended an education of the whole man for the courtier; included training for arms and activities of a similar nature (including even "tenyse"); urged physical training that would develop grace and ease of performance; and preferred men of medium height for such an educational pattern.

9. Girolamo Cardano (1501–1576)
   Patterned his recommendations after Galen's *De Sanitate Tuenda* stressing the healthful results of exercise and the division of exercises into classifications.

10. Hieronymus Mercurialis (1530–1606)
    Recommended physical activity as contributing to health; was not in favor of athletics involving extreme specialization; stressed that a body which possessed health and dexterity was needed for a cultivated mind; classified gymnastics into preventive and therapeutic activities; believed in physical training as an integral part of a liberal education, but stressed its function in preventing bodily degeneration while maintaining health.

It is not a simple matter to trace the spread of the humanistic educational influence into other parts of Europe at this time, and we will not attempt to do so in detail. Graves does point out that certain changes took place as the aims and methodology of this approach spread in a number of different directions (1910, p. 141). In Germany, for example, the emphasis was less on "a desire for personal development, self-realization, and individual achievement, and took on more of a social and moral color" (p. 141). Reisner discussed what he called "the development of a new educational clientele in Northern Europe," as follows:

As one views the historical development of the revival of humanistic learning over a period of three centuries, the Italian phase of that revival seems almost like a trial performance on a small stage of a drama which eventually absorbed the attention of all of Europe. The new interest in the whole range of classical literature began to make its way north of the Alps early in the second half of the fifteenth century, and before the end of that century the influence of the new learning was strong in many German and Lowland schools. The campaigns of the French kings in an effort to conquer portions of Italy, which began in 1494, operated powerfully in bringing the rich Italian culture into the intellectual and artistic life of France. During the first half of the sixteenth century the progress of the new learning was rapid, and long before the end of that century its conquest of secondary education in all of Europe was complete. (1927, p. 390)

There appears to be no doubt that great changes had taken place in Europe since the twelfth and thirteenth centuries—in education, in government, in business, and in social organization. Developing science and maritime discoveries increased the world of commerce greatly; the system of industrial production developed to the point where the next major change was the addition of power in manufacturing in the late 1700s; vast changes took place in rural life which fomented great unrest, while laws of apprenticeship and laws for the poor were instituted to keep many from starvation and destitution; and the educational status of the masses was maintained at an extremely low level. Concurrently, the power of the nobility declined, and new forms of military units were developed which served the kings as paid armies. Sea power assumed military importance, and the practical use of gunpowder forced the former professional at arms to assume status as a courtier and "gentleman" in the king's court. At the same time, his intellectual learning was enhanced greatly by the invention of the printing press, which made literally millions of books available. Thus, from both the middle class and the nobility—the status of both of which had changed markedly—emerged what Reisner has identified as a "new clientele" throughout Europe (1927, pp. 408–10).

As might be expected, the educational ideas emanating from the humanism of Italy were interpreted differently in each country to which they spread; such interpretation depended, of course, upon the interplay of various social forces in the particular country. In Germany, a most important figure in the educational diffusion of classicism and the so-called new learning was Rudolph Agricola, a Dutch humanist whose real name was Roelof Huysman. He took up a post in Heidelberg University after study in Italy and is credited largely with the spread of the concept of the "whole man" in Germany, an idea in opposition to the prevailing scholasticism of the time. The social climate of Germany, however, was not yet ready, for a type of humanism similar to that which evolved in Italy. Some groundwork had been laid earlier by others in the nonmonastic order known as the Hieronymians ("Brethren of the Common Life"), a group that had started in Holland in 1376 whose efforts were extended into both Germany and northern France. Because of their desire to improve both content and method in the prevailing educational pattern, and the fact that a number of schools had been established in which this newer influence had been introduced, a spirit of readiness and enthusiasm was present when the humanistic influence began to spread north from Italy. Thus, it has been stated that the "social piety" of the north combined with the "broad literary spirit" of Italy to form a unique brand of humanism possessing both pious and humanitarian qualities (Wilds, 1936, pp. 262–63).

Desiderius Erasmus (1466?–1536) was affiliated with the "Brethren" as were such other educational leaders as Philip Melanchthon and Johann Sturm. Erasmus, who Durant has designated as "the greatest of the humanists," undoubtedly exerted a strong influence in many countries (Durant, 1957, pp. 271*ff.*). He showed some enthusiasm for physical exercise as a part of the education of children, but neither in his writings nor in his personal life (pp. 271*ff.*) did he show any interest in or appreciation of the Greek ideal in physical culture. He did advocate a certain level of fitness, however, so that men could conduct their lives effectively. Yet he decried overemphasis in this regard and was not concerned with the development of athletes (Erasmus, trans. Woodward, 1904, p. 202).

Among the educational and religious leaders who influenced physical activity and sport in various countries during this era, the influence of Martin Luther (1483–1546) was truly significant. Whereas the ideas emanating from Italy have been identified as "individually humanistic," and later became designated as "socially humanistic" when they crossed the Alps and infiltrated the social thought of many countries to the north, other, often countervailing, religious and educational thought was occurring within the prevailing religious structure of the European culture. Of course, in 1521 at Wurms it was impossible to appreciate the enormous impact that the anger of one monk—as expressed in the 95 theses he fastened to the door of Wittenberg Church in 1517—would have on the Western world in the centuries to come. So many changes had taken place in the culture of the time that Luther's challenge was more or less the culmination of a series of lesser attacks that occurred in various forms. The Protestant Reformation and the subsequent Catholic Counter-Reformation are very important to this discussion, of course, because they influenced European education during the sixteenth and seventeenth centuries at the very time that the early North American development was taking place. Whether or not there can be full authentication of Luther's famous words, "*Hier stehe Ich, Ich kann nicht anders*" ("Here I stand, I can do no other"), the impact of such a truly courageous response to those present at The Diet at Wurms was tremendous for the history of the Western world.

Martin Luther himself was enthusiastic about the place that sport and physical activity could fulfill in the educational pattern of youth. He appeared to be fully imbued with the concept of what was eventually called "muscular Christianity" some three centuries later. The underlying thought was that health and physical fitness enabled a man to work profitably for himself and his family, for others less fortunate than himself, and for the greater glory of God (Luther, trans. Wace and Buchheim, 1896, pp. 279–80). Eby reported further that Luther viewed wholesome recreational pursuits as important means whereby young people's energies could be directed into desirable educational channels. He recommended music as one beneficial activity, and listed fencing and wrestling as further useful and healthful types of physical activity (Eby, 1931, p. 176).

It must be kept in mind, though, that even though elements of the newer classical theory of education gradually took hold, the Church controlled almost all education through its cathedral schools. Luther wished the people to have an opportunity to read and write the vernacular so that they could truly understand the Bible and its message of Christianity, which he believed that the Catholic Church had distorted through its agents. Thus, even though he was in favor of certain types of sport and physical activity, his great concern was for religious and concurrent social reform. Further, "physical education was increasingly relegated to an inferior position while the Protestant sects were intensifying their endeavors to curb worldly pleasures" (Van Dalen, Mitchell, and Bennett, 1953, p. 155).

During approximately the same years that Luther had an effect on ecclesiastical and educational affairs in the German states (along with Philip Melanchthon, Johannes Bugenhagen and others), educational and religious reformers like Ulrich Zwingli (1484–1531) and John Calvin (1509–1564) in Switzerland were causing great changes to take place in the educational system there. Although Calvin's influence in his native land and elsewhere, including North America, was great, Zwingli's education had a humanistic bent that gave it a breadth significantly dissimilar to that of both Luther and Calvin. He led a reformation against the Church that ended in war, and he himself subsequently died in battle at the age of 47 on October 11, 1531. In a treatise on "The Christian Education of Youth," Zwingli wrote favorably about the inclusion of games and sports in the educational curriculum; his concern was that they involve a degree of skill and that they be directed to worthwhile ends in the effective training of the body (Zwingli, trans. Reichenback, 1899, p. 90).

Whereas Zwingli, with his humanistic background, saw some value in physical training, John Calvin, his theological successor, soon promulgated religious and educational doctrines that were highly restrictive concerning the role of physical activity and amusements. It is difficult for the modern mind to comprehend how much difference there was between the ideas of a Vittorino da Feltre and those of a religious zealot like Calvin. Instead of viewing human nature as at least neutral, if not basically good, Calvin was undoubtedly one of the most extreme persons in history in this regard. For him, "Original sin, therefore, appears to be an hereditary pravity and corruption of our nature, diffused through all the parts of the soul, rendering us obnoxious to the Divine wrath . . ." (Calvin, in Eby, 1931, p. 236). It is no wonder, therefore, that Calvin and his followers in both Europe and later in the New World were loath to provide opportunities for sinful humans to become even more depraved through involvement in idle play and types of recreation that placed emphasis on the flesh and men's and women's sensuous appetites. In Leon's translation of the "By-laws of the Academy of Geneva," we can comprehend most vividly the strict regimen outlined for students and faculty. The only evidence of opportunity for physical activity in the program is Wednesdays from noon until three P.M.: "Then recreation shall be allowed till three o'clock, but in such a way that all silly sport be avoided." At one other point during the week, on Saturday, "recess from lessons shall be given till three" (Eby, 1931, pp. 258–59).

Turning our attention now to England, we find that the humanistic emphasis in education did not really begin to catch on there until late in the fifteenth century. Certain foreign visitors had made sporadic attempts to broaden the educational base of the English prior to that time. At various times scholars from England had made pilgrimages to Italy, bringing a number of scholarly manuscripts back to university libraries such as Oxford's. It is interesting to note that, because certain similar societal changes were taking place in these two countries at approximately the same time, the newer idea of reverting to classical educational ideals was embraced with considerable enthusiasm, especially by members of the upper classes (Weiss, 1941, pp. 11*ff.*). However, again we find the influence of Erasmus to be considerable in England because of the extended period of time he spent there. McIntosh verifies the relatively low esteem in which the body was held by Erasmus by quoting from his essay "On the Contempt of the Word," in which he states, "The body is earthly, wild, slow, mortal, diseased, ignoble; the soul on the other hand is heavenly, subtle, divine, immortal, noble" (McIntosh, 1957, p. 73). Another example of his belief that "the physical" in education should be played down is the statement that, "Personally I venture to regard the mental advantages gained as outweighing some slight risks in the matter of physical vigour" (Erasmus, trans. Woodward, 1904, p. 202).

Undoubtedly a number of the essays and books from Italy carried the message of humanism (for example, Castiglione's *Il Cortegiano* as translated by Hoby in 1561). Fortunately, some thirty years earlier Sir Thomas Elyot had begun the spread of "humanistic gospel" in England by recommending exercise and recreation as part of the youth's educational program during the time of Henry the VIII. He recognized that hours of intensive study should be interrupted by play and healthful exercise. Activities recommended by Elyot included archery, fencing, dancing, tennis, running, riding, wrestling, swimming, dumbbell exercises, and other types of weight lifting. These types of physical activity were similar to those recommended in the Golden Age of Greece. Further, as McIntosh clarifies for us: "Elyot was, in fact, concerned with the three main objectives of physical education, enrichment of personality, social success, and physiological efficiency. His was the first book in English to pay equal attention to each of these objectives" (1957, p. 75).

Roger Ascham was another significant educational writer of the sixteenth century in England. His book *Toxophilus*, appearing in 1545, some fourteen years after Elyot's *The Governor*, explained the intricacies of shooting with the long bow. It was his publication *The Schoolmaster*, however, which devoted a considerable amount of space to physical education and its teaching methods (1898, Vol. XXXII). This material appeared originally in 1570 and therefore supplemented the earlier statements of Thomas Elyot. Both of these men had special interest in the educational development of the youthful courtier who eventually was expected to emerge as a leader and/or statesman in society, and who could be expected to bear arms in the service of the king. Thus Ascham used phrases such as "courtly exercises" and "gentlemanly pastimes." His courtiers, once grown up, needed to be sharp-witted statesmen and gentlemen ready to do battle at a moment's notice.

Let us next take a brief look at both the religious and secular leaders who had resisted the Protestant religions strongly. These are the people who had been attempting to rectify the practices of the Church from within even before the revolts had set in, as well as those who saw their interests threatened by the Reformation Movement and who sought to bring vitality back to the mother Church. The reforms that took place during this time were within the context of the Church as the strongest religious group in the West; but there were other social forces at work (such as developing science) that signaled the continuation of a conflict which still has not been resolved in the twentieth century.

A number of different Catholic orders (the Jesuits, for example) sprang up because many recognized the wisdom of combining religious instruction with general education for improved social living. Fortunately, the Jesuits emphasized training for life on this earth, while at the same time maintaining that the relationship of man to his God was the leading educational aim of the program being espoused. Thus, a reasonably good balance was attained in the educational process, because the body was supposed to be kept as physically fit as possible. In this way God could be served best.

Noted churchmen who made an effort to carry on the humanistic tradition in physical activity were Cardinal Jacopo Sadoleto (1477–1547) and Cardinal Silvio Antoniano. Antoniano's volume, published in 1584, stressed the desirability of including exercises and games in the child's school experiences to promote the development of a strong and healthy body (Zanfagna, 1940, in Van Dalen et al., 1953, p. 168). Similarly, Sadoleto's treatise, published much earlier, was in accord with the humanistic tradition and perceived the physical fitness, health, and recreational objectives possible through a broadly based educational program designed to equip man to serve both God and his fellow man in everyday life.

In passing we should mention also the contribution of François Fénelon, the Archbishop of Cambrai, who lived almost a century later (1651–1715). As a Roman Catholic, he made a significant contribution to the education of both men *and* women with his treatise on *The Education of Girls* in 1687 and his *Télémaque* in 1699, in which he recommended following the example of Ulysses in the education of a young prince. Fénelon is purported to have advocated healthful exercise and play for young children, and this advice was followed by Madame de Maintenon in her educational syllabus at the Convent of St. Cyr.

The Late Renaissance Period

Having discussed the attitudes and beliefs toward exercise, sport, play, dance, and health on the part of the many humanists and of the religious reformers, we can now move ahead to a review of the physical activity and sport patterns of the third phase of this era of awakening: a movement that has been identified as a period when the interest in science continued unabated and there was renewed concern as well for the everyday realities of life—the post-Renaissance realism. Keep in mind that these three phases did not necessarily follow sequentially one after the other. They were most certainly synchronous to a considerable degree, and yet it can be said that the emphasis on realism increased as a result of the developing narrowing educational objectives of the humanists and the typical narrowness in emphasis of the religious reformers. In these latter instances, it might be stated that the Protestant reformers were even more harsh in their condemnation of "bodily desires and impulses" than their Catholic brethren (the Calvinists as opposed to the Jesuits). Our concern, then, will be the educational ideas expressed by educational theorists functioning in several countries of Western Europe late in that period termed the Renaissance and the Reformation (actually the opening years of what has also been called Early Modern Times).

In England, Richard Mulcaster (c. 1531–1611) was an outstanding teacher and educational theorist of the Elizabethan Age (1558–1603). An Etonian educational background in the classic civilizations of the Hebrews and Greeks undoubtedly influenced his interest in sport and physical training after his appointment as the first Headmaster of the Merchant Taylors' School in 1561. The extent of physical training included in the educational curriculum of young men, as presented in his *Positions* (for the Training up of Children) in 1581 and in the first part of the *Elementarie* in 1582, was certainly not typical of the time. In this pioneer effort on school gymnastics, which we hope he was able to put into practice to a reasonable extent, Mulcaster borrowed extensively from ancient authors, such as Galen and Hippocrates. However, the originality he introduced reflects great credit upon him. He sought to classify exercises into various categories (that is those related to sports, those with application for martial training, and those of a strenuous physical nature which he believed to contribute to the person's health). Further, he classified exercises as being preparatory, main, or recuperative in nature. Then he determined those that should be employed primarily indoors, as well as those to be used outdoors (for example, wrestling and ball playing, respectively). Finally, he designated six different circumstances which the exercise leader must keep in mind to carry out his task most effectively —type of exercise, person being exercised, where taking place, when it is occurring, how much of it is involved, and the way in which it is being carried out (Mulcaster, 1581). Brailsford discusses the contribution of Mulcaster at length and finally concludes: "Thus, even Mulcaster's staunch advocacy appears to have made little impact on attitudes towards physical education in Elizabethan schools" (1969, p. 51; pp. 44–51 are based on R. E. Quick's 1888 edition of *Positions*). McIntosh stresses that Mulcaster rather than Comenius should be given credit for "pioneer work in the use of the vernacular, in teaching first those subjects which give scope for activity, and in teaching examples before rules" (1957, p. 76). He makes note further of Mulcaster's "departure somewhat from the Courtier tradition in making a definite attempt to relate physical education to school life rather than to the life of the court" (1957, p. 77).

Other British writers of this period who made some reference to the role of physical culture in the education of the young were Francis Bacon

(1561–1626) and John Milton (1608–1674). Bacon is best known for his contribution to the discipline of philosophy by his careful efforts to apply science's inductive methodology to his investigations. Even though he has been criticized in several ways because of inadequacies in his application of this approach, he nevertheless contributed significantly to scientific method through this improvement over scholasticism's typical method of *a priori* reasoning. It cannot be claimed that Bacon argued consistently for the inclusion of physical training in the curriculum, but he at least sensed that a direct relationship existed between mind and body. He maintained the need for exercise as part of a healthful existence and declared further that excessive specialization should not be practiced in the average person's daily life (Wright, 1900, p. 216).

John Milton was a poet, author, and political figure of the seventeenth century in England. *Paradise Lost,* his blank-verse poem in twelve books, published in 1667, is generally regarded as one of the English language's greatest epic poems. Milton was a highly controversial figure of his time. He argued for improvement of the educational system through broadening its highly intellectualistic aims to include a more classical outlook that stressed service to fellow man with the goal of improving the quality of life, both public and private (Milton, 1911, p. 9). His classical view did not extend to "equal partnership" in the educational curriculum for physical training, however, being limited to a position that could be described as naturalistically realistic. Vigorous exercise could be employed to produce a strong, healthy, fit body capable of performing effectively and gallantly in battle (1911, p. 125). Consistent with this position, he postulated a sharp dichotomy between work and play. In the imaginary Academy he devised in his *Tractate of Education* (1928), Milton included an hour and a half before lunch for exercise and rest. Prominent in this program he recommended wrestling, a sport in which Englishmen were "wont to excel."

Two important French writers of the fifteenth and sixteenth centuries must be mentioned during this period for their contribution to the history of physical education and sport: François Rabelais (c. 1483–1553) and Michel de Montaigne (1533–1592). Rabelais, both a writer and physician, could be called a classical realist with a humanistic orientation. He is best known for his writing about a giant known as Gargantua and his son Pantagruel. Some five books about this duo appeared between 1523 and 1562. This tale has received worldwide recognition as a masterpiece of literature. Of particular concern to us are Rabelais' thoughts about education, and especially his views on physical education (which are said to have exerted some influence on Montaigne, and somewhat later on both Locke and Rousseau). In the educational program of the fictional Gargantua, Rabelais included periods of strenuous physical training in addition to lessons in the Seven Liberal Arts. These activities included wrestling, various track and field events of running and jumping, archery, horseback riding, and all types of military arts. It was presumed that such exercise would promote vigorous health, and that games and sports should be employed often for recreational diversion. Rabelais even went so far as to describe indoor activities that could be pursued when the weather did not permit regular outdoor physical training (1849, Book I).

Michel Eyquem Montaigne is reputed to have been one of the world's finest essayists, whose works present his own judgment on subjects relating to man and nature. He wrote, for example, on such topics as pain, death, friendship, the possibility of knowledge, human fallibility, the goodness of life, and so on. His ideas about education have been described as being humanistic in nature with a social or utilitarian orientation. Many of his thoughts about education appear in two essays entitled "On Pedantry" and "On the Education of Children." His educational aim included all of those attributes that go to make up a well-rounded, culturally oriented individual. Evidently Montaigne's father excelled in all types of physical activity, but Michel unfortunately did not inherit such ability. Nevertheless—or perhaps because of this deficiency in his own makeup—he stressed that physical education, including a wide variety of activities, should be important aspects of the young gentleman's training. Thus, the young person's "physical adapability" would be developed "at the same time with his soul" in such pursuits as "running, wrestling, music, dancing, hunting, handling horses and weapons" (Montaigne, 1948, p. 122). It is obvious that Montaigne was influenced heavily in his educational thought by his study of the classical literature available to him. Certainly he was ahead of his time—or was recommending a return to the "good old days"—in believing that the body and soul should be equals in the educational process. His writing had an influence on many who followed—one that is difficult to assess. John Dewey believed in "learning by doing"; how far from this most important dictum is Montaigne's famous quotation "To know by heart only is not to know at all"? Finally, although his program was designed for education of the male in the upper classes, he should be remembered for his promotion of an education that fostered a fundamentally "comprehensive and stable philosophy of life" (Reisner, 1927, p. 488).

OVERVIEW

To summarize this analysis of sport and physical activity in the later Middle Ages, seven approaches to education during this period have been alluded to, *but not followed precisely* in our presentation (Wilds, 1936):

(1) individual humanism; (2) social humanism; (3) Protestant Reformation; (4) Catholic Reformation; (5) verbal realism; (6) social realism; and (7) sense realism.

The educational aim of so-called individual humanism was for a full and abundant life for the individual, whereas the emphasis of social humanism inclined somewhat more in the direction of improving society as a whole as well. With the revolt against the Catholic hierarchy by Luther and others, the aim in education was to maintain a Christian influence by allowing the person to interpret the Scriptures individually. The ideals of intelligence, social virtue, and individual piety were to be integrated with "the best ideals of the past" (Wilds, p. 284). The counter-Reformation within the Catholic Church corrected many abuses while restoring considerable energy and power to the movement. The long range aims of the Protestants and Catholics were quite similar in education, the main difference being in the latter's efforts to preserve the authority of the Church through indoctrination within the educational system. The various realistic movements mentioned above meshed quite naturally with many of the trends previously described. Those with a strong humanistic orientation were more concerned with an individual's all-round development, while most of the reformers were concerned with the introduction of a more social orientation into the educational system. The religious reformers, of course, placed the greatest emphasis upon the person's relationship with the Creator.

Insofar as physical education and sport were concerned, the following points may be made:

1. The leading educational theorists of the Renaissance were essentially in agreement about the need for a broadly based curriculum that afforded a prominent role to physical education and sport.
2. Although there was not complete unanimity, a number of these educators appeared to have embraced a concept of education *through* the medium of physical activity (as opposed to what might be designated as a more limited concept of education *of* the physical).
3. As the Renaissance movement spread from Italy to other European countries, the inclusion of physical activity and sport in the curriculum became evident to a greater extent than previously. It is not possible to claim, however, that conditions approximated the ideal except in a few educational institutions.
4. It should not be forgotten that many of these educational theorists were espousing programs for upper-class children, and that the children of the masses were not able typically to take advantage of these improved, imaginative programs that included a variety of physical activities designed to train the young man for warfare, for improved health, and for recreational diversion from rigorous intellectual and religious training.
5. Some educational theorists stressed the importance of rigorous physical activity for youth, but then took a stand against particular athletic games and sports.

6. The more strictly moralistic reformers took a stand against dance in the curriculum, while those with a better understanding of the Classical Period urged that it be included from the standpoint of desirable esthetic experience and appreciation.

What sound conclusions may we draw from this brief survey? It is immediately obvious that many of our cherished modern institutions may be traced to their beginnings during this period—for example, the structure of our cities and the desirability of representative government. Our universities became recognizable entities for the first time during this era through the establishment of such institutions at Bologna, Paris, and Oxford.

Reflection about the status of physical education and sport in any particular country, or culture for that matter, leads one time and again to the realistic, but dreary, conclusion that progress in social affairs has never been a straight-line affair—"onward and upward" to an ideal educational program in which all boys and girls receive a broadly based and conceived human movement experience in sport, dance, play, and exercise as an integral part of the entire educational experience.

With notable exceptions, such as the opportunities afforded to youth under the supervision of Vittorino da Feltre at La Giocosa in Renaissance Italy, this period of approximately four hundred years was not a time that future sport historians will be able to praise. The leading values of the society were reflected in the several educational systems of the Middle Ages. The political environment governed how much education of what type would be made available. Also, the state of the economy was such that only a favored few, with the possible exception of those in religious orders, received what might be called a good education. The strong religious emphasis of the time may have condoned bodily exercise associated with manual labor, but sport and dance were often viewed with disfavor. Certainly the state of medical knowledge was not yet sufficient to make even rudimentary health education knowledge available. Leisure time for active and creative recreational pursuits was similarly unavailable to the large majority of the populace. Those who worked hard to earn their daily bread achieved a modicum of physical fitness, as did others preparing for service at arms. Whether men could play at sport often depended upon the natural environment or the availability of space. Often unorganized games and sports were permitted, but definitely not encouraged. And there were restrictions established against the activities of the students enrolled at universities in overcrowded cities.

Although the Later Middle Ages cannot be identified as a "golden age" of sport and physical activity, a few men had a vision of what it might be under ideal circumstances. For those dedicated, inspired men we should be grateful. The human community of West European civilization has played a remarkable and revolutionary role in the world since 1500 A.D. McNeill tells us that this rapid advancement may be attributed to (1) the ease with which this society was able to appropriate the alien inheritance "of the classical, Moslem, and Byzantine worlds relatively uninhibited by their own past"; and (2) provision of the opportunity for "popular participation in economic, cultural, and political life" (1963, p. 558).

If we take a long-range view, we can possibly take heart from these conclusions about the remarkable development of the Western world. As sport and physical activity historians, we have a professional duty to tell how sport, dance, play, and exercise have been related to people's development in the past. Nevertheless, we must in conclusion express the hope that better times lie ahead for all people everywhere in the realm of sport and physical activity.

GENERAL BIBLIOGRAPHY

ADAMS, GEORGE B. *Civilization During the Middle Ages.* New York: Charles Scribner's Sons, 1922.

ADAMSON, J. W. "Education," *The Legacy of the Middle Ages.* Ed. C. G. Crump and E. F. Jacob. Oxford: Clarendon Press, 1951.

ARTZ, FREDERICK B. *Renaissance Humanism (1300–1500).* Kent, Ohio: Kent State University Press, 1966.

ASCHAM, ROGER. *The Scholemaster.* Ed. Edward Arber. Boston: Heath's Pedagogical Library, 1898. See Vol. XXXII. (Ascham's volume *Toxophilus,* 1545, is included in *The Whole Works of Roger Ascham;* see Vol. II. *The Scholemaster* is Vol. III. Trans. the Rev. Dr. Giles. London: John R. Smith, 1864).

BAGLEY, J. J. *Life in Medieval England.* London: B. T. Batsford, 1961.

BALLOU, RALPH. "Early Christian Society and Its Relationship to Sport," *Proceedings of the 71st Annual Meeting of the National College Physical Education Association for Men,* Houston, January 11–13, 1968. Ed. C. E. Mueller. Minneapolis: NCPEAM, 1968, pp. 159–164.

BARON, HANS. *The Crisis of the Early Renaissance.* Princeton, N.J.: Princeton University Press, 1955.

BAZZANO, CARMELO. "The Contributions of the Italian Renaissance to Physical Education." Ph.D. Thesis, Boston University, 1973.

BELL, DORA M. *L'Ideal Ethique de la Royauté en France au Moyen Age.* Paris: Librairie Minard, 1962.

BLUNDEL, JOHN W. F. *The Muscles and Their Story, from the Earliest Times.* London: Chapman & Hall, 1864. (This is a translation of *De Arte Gymnastica* by Hieronymous Mercurialis.)

BOORDE, ANDREW. *A Compendious Regyment or Dyetary of Health,* 1542.

BOYD, WILLIAM. *The History of Western Education.* New York: Barnes & Noble, 1966.

BOYKIN, JAMES C., "Physical Training," *Report of the Commissioner of Education (1891–92),* I, 451–594. Washington, D.C.: Government Printing Office, 1894.

BRAILSFORD, DENNIS. *Sport and Society: Elizabeth to Anne.* London: Routledge & Kegan Paul, 1969.

BROEKHOFF, JAN. "Chivalric Education in the Middle Ages," *A History of Sport and Physical Education to 1900.* Ed. E. F. Zeigler. Champaign, Ill.: Stipes Publishing Company, 1973. (This article was published originally in Monograph XI of *Quest,* December 1968, pp. 24–31.)

BRUBACHER, J. S. *A History of the Problems of Education* (2nd ed.). Englewood Cliffs, N.J.: Prentice-Hall, 1966.

BURCKHARDT, JACOB. *The Civilization of the Renaissance in Italy.* New York: Oxford University Press, 1965.

BUTTS, R. F. *A Cultural History of Education.* New York: McGraw-Hill Book Company, 1947.

CAESAR. *Gallic War.* See Book Six, chapters 21–28.

CASTIGLIONE, BALDESAR. *The Book of the Courtier.* Trans. C. S. Singleton. New York: Doubleday, 1959. (*Il Cortegiano* appeared also trans. L. E. Opdycke. New York: Charles Scribner's Sons, 1903).

COATES, DONALD T. "Sports and Pastimes of the Middle Ages." M.A. Thesis, University of Idaho, 1938.

CORNISH, F. W. *Chivalry.* New York: The Macmillan Company, 1901.

DIEM, CARL. *Weltgeschichte des Sports und der Leibeserziehung.* Stuttgart: Cotta, 1960.

DORSEY, GEORGE A. *Man's Own Show: Civilization.* New York: Blue Ribbon Books, 1931.

DURANT, WILL. *The Age of Faith.* New York: Simon and Schuster, 1950.

———. *The Renaissance.* New York: Simon and Schuster, 1953.

———. *The Reformation.* New York: Simon and Schuster, 1957.

EBY, FREDERICK. *Early Protestant Educators.* New York: McGraw-Hill Book Company, 1931.

ELYOT, SIR THOMAS. *The Boke Named the Govuernour.* London: Everyman's Library, 1885. See Book I, Sections 16–20 on exercise and dancing; also see Book III, Section 22 on diet. (This work was published originally in 1531. Other pertinent chapters in Book I are 21, 22, 26, and 27. The book was published in 1883 also in London by Kegan Paul, Trench and Co.)

ERASMUS, DESIDERIUS. *De Pueris Instituendis* in *D. Erasmus Concerning the Aim and Method in Education.* Trans. and ed. W. H. Woodward. Cambridge: University Press, 1904.

EYLER, MARVIN. "Origins of Some Modern Sports." Ph.D. Dissertation, University of Illinois, Urbana, 1956.

FERGUSON, WALLACE K. *The Renaissance.* New York: Holt, Rinehart & Winston, 1940.

———. *The Renaissance in Historical Thought.* Cambridge: The Riverside Press, 1948.

FREEHILL, ALPHONSE M. "Physical Culture and Recreation in the Middle Ages." M.A. Thesis, Catholic University of America, 1931.

FROISSART, JOHN. *Chronicles of England, France, Spain, and the Adjoining Countries,* 2 Vols. Trans. T. Johnes. London: Smith, 1842.

GAUTIER, LEON. *La Chevalerie.* Ed. Jacques Levron. Ain: Arthaud, 1960.

GENST, H. DE. *Histoire de l'Education Physique: Temps Ancien et Moyen Age.* Brussels: A. de Moeck, 1947.

GERBER, ELLEN W. *Innovators and Institutions in Physical Education.* Philadelphia: Lea & Febiger, 1971.

GERVASE, M. "Ideals of Knighthood in Late Fourteenth Century England," *Studies in Medieval History.* Ed. R. W. Hunt *et al.* Oxford: Oxford University Press, 1948.

GRAVES, F. P. *A History of Education During the Middle Ages.* New York: The Macmillan Company, 1910.

GRISAR, HARTMANN. *Martin Luther.* London: B. Herder Book Company, 1935. (This was adapted from the Second German edition by Frank J. Eble.)

GUNDERSHEIMER, WERNER L., Ed. *The Italian Renaissance.* Englewood Cliffs, N.J.: Prentice-Hall, 1963.

HACKENSMITH, C. W. *History of Physical Education.* New York: Harper & Row, 1966.

HAYS, DENYS. Ed. *The Age of the Renaissance.* New York: McGraw-Hill Book Company, 1967.

HOLE, CHRISTINA. *English Sports and Pastimes.* London: B. T. Batsford, 1949.

HUIZINGA, J. *The Waning of the Middle Ages.* Garden City, N.Y.: Doubleday, 1956.

HUNT, R. W., *et al.*, Eds. *Studies in Medieval History.* Oxford: Oxford University Press, 1948.

JOSEPH, LUDWIG H. "Gymnastics from the Middle Ages to the Eighteenth Century," *Ciba Symposia,* X (1949), 3–5.

JUSSERAND, J. J. *Les Sport et Jeux d'Exercice dans l'Ancienne France.* Paris: Librairie Plon, 1901.

KILGOUR, RAYMOND L. *The Decline of Chivalry.* Cambridge, Mass.: Harvard University Press, 1937.

KRISTELLER, PAUL O. *Renaissance Thought.* New York: Harper Torchbook, 1961.

LOCKE, JOHN. "Essay Concerning Human Understanding," *Philosophers Speak for Themselves: From Descartes to Locke.* Ed. T. V. Smith and Marjorie Grene. Chicago: University of Chicago Press, 1957.

———. *Some Thoughts Concerning Education.* London: Cambridge University Press, 1902. The introduction and notes are by R. H. Quick. (The first edition of this work cited by Quick was in 1880.)

LOPEX, ROBERT S. *The Three Ages of the Italian Renaissance.* Charlottesville: University of Virginia Press, 1970.

LUCAS-DUBRETON, J. *Daily Life in Florence, in the Time of the Medici.* New York: The Macmillan Company, 1961.

LUCKI, EMILY. *History of the Renaissance, V: Politics and Political Theory.* Salt Lake City: University of Utah Press, 1964.

LUTHER, MARTIN. "Concerning Christian Liberty," *Luther's Primary Works.* Trans. Henry Wace and C. A. Buchheim. London: Hodder and Stoughton, 1896.

————. "Letters to the Mayors and Aldermen," *Classics in Education.* Ed. Wade Baskin. New York: Philosophical Library, 1966.

MARIQUE, P. *History of Christian Education,* vols. I–III. New York: Fordham University Press, 1924–1932.

MARROU, HENRI I. *Histoire de l'Education dans l'Antiquité.* Paris: Editions du Seuil, 1958. (This has been published also as *A History of Education in Antiquity.* Trans. G. Lamb. New York: The New American Library of World Literature, 1964.)

MAZZEO, JOSEPH A. *Renaissance and Revolution.* New York: Pantheon Books, 1965.

McINTOSH, PETER C. "Physical Education in Renaissance Italy and Tudor England," *Landmarks in the History of Physical Education,* pp. 60–80. Ed. P. C. McIntosh *et al.* London: Routledge & Kegan Paul, 1957.

McNEILL, WILLIAM H. *The Rise of the West.* Chicago: University of Chicago Press, 1963.

MEHL, ERWIN. *Grundrisz des Deutschen Turnens.* Vienna: Deutschen Turnbunden, 1923.

MERCURIALIS, H. *De Arte Gymnastica.* Libri Sex. Amstelodami: Andreae Frisii, 1672.

MILTON, JOHN. *Of Education, Areopagitica the Commonwealth.* Boston: Houghton Mifflin Co., 1911.

————. *Tractate on Education.* New Haven: Yale University Press, 1928. (This is also Volume 13 of *The Harvard Classics.*)

MONROE, PAUL. *Source Book of the History of Education.* New York: The Macmillan Company, 1921.

————. *A Textbook in the History of Education,* pp. 243–313. New York: The Macmillan Company, 1916.

MONTAIGNE, MICHEL DE. *The Complete Essays.* Trans. D. M. Frame. Stanford, Cal.: Stanford University Press, 1948.

————. *The Education of Children.* New York: G. P. Putnam's Sons, 1910. (This is also Volume 32 of *The Harvard Classics.*)

MOOLENIJZER, NICOLAAS J. "The Legacy from the Middle Ages," *A History of Sport and Physical Education to 1900.* Ed. E. F. Zeigler. Champaign, Ill.: Stipes Publishing Company, 1973. (Published originally in Monograph XI of *Quest,* December 1968, pp. 32–43.)

MULCASTER, RICHARD. *Elementarie.* Ed. E. T. Campagnac. Oxford: Clarendon Press, 1925.

————. *Positions* London: T. Vautrollier, 1581.

MULLER, HERBERT J. *The Uses of the Past.* London: Oxford University Press, 1952. (This is available in paperback. New York: The New American Library of World Literature, 1954.)

OLIPHANT, JAMES. *The Educational Writings of Richard Mulcaster.* Glasgow: James Maclehose & Sons, 1903.

OWEN, G. L. *The Betterment of Man: A Rational History of Western Civilization.* New York: G. P. Putnam's Sons, 1974.

PAINTER, SIDNEY. *French Chivalry.* Baltimore: John Hopkins Press, 1940.

PICCOLOMINI, AENEAS SYLVIUS. "De Liberorum Educatione," *Vittorino da Feltre and Other Humanist Educators.* Ed. W. H. Woodward. Cambridge: Cambridge University Press, 1897.

RABELAIS, FRANCOIS. *The Works of Francois Rabelais.* Trans. Sir Thomas Urquhart and Motteux. London: H. G. Bohn, 1849, Book I.

RANDALL, JOHN H. *Making of the Modern Mind,* pp. 58–107. Boston: Houghton Mifflin Co., 1926.

REISNER, EDWARD H. *Historical Foundations of Modern Education.* New York: The Macmillan Company, 1927.

RICE, E. A., J. L. HUTCHINSON, and M. LEE. *A Brief History of Physical Education* (4th ed.). New York: The Ronald Press, 1958.

ROTHE, JOHANNES. *Der Ritterspiel.* Ed. Hans Neumann. Halle: Max Niemeyer, 1936.

SALUSBURY, JOHN. *Certain Necessary Observations for Health,* 1603.

SANTAYANA, S. G. *Two Renaissance Educators: Alberti and Piccolomini.* Boston: Meador Publishing Company, 1930.

SAURBIER, BRUNO. *Geschichte der Leibesübungen.* Frankfurt a.M.: Limpert, 1963.

SCHMIDT, ALBERT-MARIE. *John Calvin and the Calvinist Tradition.* Trans. Ronald Wallace. New York: Harper & Row, 1960.

SCHOELEN, EUGEN. *Erziehung und Unterricht im Mittelalter.* Paderborn: Ferdinant Schöningh, 1965.

SELLERY, GEORGE C. *The Renaissance.* Madison: University of Wisconsin Press, 1965.

SETTON, KENNETH M. "A New Look at Medieval Europe," *National Geographic,* 122, no. 6 (December 1962), 798–859.

SHAW, CHARLES GRAY. *Trends of Civilization and Culture,* pp. 212–58. New York: American Book Company, 1932.

SMITH, HORATIO. *Festivals, Games, and Amusements, Ancient and Modern.* London: Henry Colburn and Richard Bentley, 1831.

SYMONDS, JOHN A. *The Revival of Learning.* New York: G. P. Putnam's Sons, 1960.

TACITUS. *Agricola.*

——. *Germania.*

THOMSON, HARRISON S. *Europe in Renaissance and Reformation.* New York: Harcourt, Brace & World, 1963.

TOWNSEND, WILLIAM J. *Great Schoolmen of the Middle Ages.* New York: G. E. Stechert & Co., 1905. (Published originally by Hodder and Stoughton, London, 1881).

VAN DALEN, D. B. "The Idea of History of Physical Education During the Middle Ages and Renaissance," *A History of Sport and Physical Education to 1900,* pp. 217–33. Ed. E. F. Zeigler. Champaign, Ill.: Stipes Publishing Co., 1973.

——, E. D. MITCHELL, and B. L. BENNETT. *A World History of Physical Education* (1st ed.): Englewood Cliffs, N.J.: Prentice-Hall, 1953.

——, and B. L. BENNETT. *A World History of Physical Education* (2nd ed.). Englewood Cliffs, N.J.: Prentice-Hall, 1971.

VAN NIEKERK. GERT. "Evidence of Physical Activities, Play Games, and Pastimes of the Vikings, 700 to 1200 A.D." M. A. Thesis, University of Alberta, 1971.

VERGERIUS. P. P., "De Ingenuis Moribus" (1404), W. H. Woodward, *Vittorino da Feltre and Other Humanist Educators.* Cambridge: Cambridge University Press, 1897. (2nd printing, 1905.)

WATKINS. GLENN G. "The Law and Games in Sixteenth Century England." M. A. Thesis, University of Alberta, 1969.

WEISS. R. *Humanism in England.* Oxford: Oxford University Press, 1941.

WILDS. E. H. *The Foundations of Modern Education.* New York: Farrar & Rinehart, 1936.

WILDT. KLEMENS C. *Daten zur Sportgeschichte* (Teil I: "Die Alte Welt und Europa bis 1750"). Schorndorf: Verlag Karl Hofmann, 1970.

————. *Leibesübungen im Deutschen Mittelalter.* Frankfurt a.M.: Limpert, 1957.

WILLIAMS. SAMUEL G. *A History of Medieval Education.* Syracuse, N.Y.: C. W. Bardeen Company, 1903.

WINTER. MILDRED E. "Sport Games in Germany in the Middle Ages." M.A. Thesis, Columbia University, 1931.

WOODWARD. W. H. *Education During the Renaissance.* Cambridge: Cambridge University Press, 1904.

————. *Vittorino da Feltre and Other Humanist Educators.* Cambridge: University Press, 1905 (reprinted from 1897 ed.).

WRIGHT. W. A. *Bacon, The Advancement of Learning.* Oxford: Clarendon Press, 1900.

YOUNG. N. D., "The Tournament in the Thirteenth Century," *Studies in Medieval History.* Ed., R. W. Hunt *et al.* Oxford: Oxford University Press, 1948.

ZEIGLER. EARLE F., Ed. *A History of Sport and Physical Education to 1900.* Champaign, Ill.: Stipes Publishing Company, 1973.

ZWINGLI. ULRICH. *The Christian Education of Youth.* Trans. A. Reichenback, from a reprint of original Swiss edition of 1526 (1899).

BIBLIOGRAPHIC ADDENDUM

Since the chapter was written, an interesting and scholarly monograph entitled *Sports and Pastimes of The Middle Ages* written by John Marshall Carter of Georgia Southern College, Statesboro, has appeared (Columbus, Georgia 31906: Brentwood University Edition, 1984). Professor Carter is also under contract with Greenwood Press, Westport, CT, U.S.A. for a volume to be called *Sports in the Middle Ages.*

Also, for people with a reading knowledge of German, I can commend another publication entitled *Die Anfaenge des modern Sports in der Renaissance* (A. Krueger & John McClelland, Eds.). London: Arena Publications, 1984.

Further, working with Professor Dr. Arnd Krueger, Institut fuer Sportwissenschaften, Georg-August-Universitaet Goettingen, Sprangerweg 2, 3400 Goettingen, Federal Republic of Germany (who has excellent fluency with the English language), we have developed an address list of some 20 scholars in Europe and North America who have written on this topic. Professor Carter has agreed to coordinate the development of an "exchange pattern" and other interesting materials on this topic. Anyone interested in this list should write to Prof. E.F. Zeigler, Thames Hall, The Univ. of Western Ontario, London, Ont., Canada N6A 3K7.

Physical Education and Sport in Modern Times

Robert G. Glassford
Gerald Redmond

INTRODUCTION

Time is an interesting phenomenon, encompassing as it does a geological time, an inner time which is an expression of changes in the body over a life span, and an abstract or mathematical time which is tied to a solar rhythm. This latter time has permitted man to link events and changes to a very precise scale, and consequently it has become a useful gauge for historians. By using this scale, man is able to plot social, economic, and political development, to trace the patterns of change. And the rate of change has accelerated steadily during recorded history, particularly during the period 1800 to the present. In 1850 there were only four cities in the world with a population of over one million, but by 1960 the number exceeded 140 (Toffler, 1970, p. 23). This rapid growth in world population has had parallels in technology, production of goods, and development of knowledge. "Discovery. Application. Impact. Discovery" (Toffler, 1970, p. 31). Caught in this sweep of change were the fields of sport and physical education. The purpose of this chapter is to encapsulate something of the history of that change and the directions of development. This task cannot be properly accomplished in the pages which we have devoted to it, but we hope that at least doors will be opened to a number of areas, and we encourage all readers to consult the sources listed in order to develop a base of knowledge in the areas of sport and physical education. The list is far from exhaustive, but it encompasses a number of key sources which, in turn, will open new horizons.

Robert G. Glassford and Gerald Redmond are both currently professors of physical education at the University of Alberta, Edmonton, Canada.

As the history of sport and physical education in North America is dealt with in another chapter, only limited mention of this geographical area is made here. Since so much of the accelerative thrust toward change has emerged in North America, this has had a limiting effect on "pulling the threads" of development together as tightly as might be desirable. To bridge the resultant gaps, the reader is encouraged to use these two chapters in concert.

WORLD PHYSICAL EDUCATION SINCE 1800

The study of men and women shows that they are conditioned by their heritage, by their social environment, by the ideologies they share, as well as by universal history, the historical place and moment, and by each one's own personal history. It is small wonder, then, that significant differences have occurred in the development of physical education throughout the world since 1800. What is more surprising is that there has also been a great deal of similarity among the systems of physical education that have emerged in the world's nation-states. This may be due in large part to the high degree of similarity in the problems that physical educators have always attempted to solve through their programs. Leonard and Affleck have succinctly noted this phenomenon: "Man's earliest endeavor to perfect the body, discipline the mind and mold the character of the young by means of selected forms of physical activity and special regimen could doubtless be traced back to a prehistoric age" (1947, p. 17).

Physical education has been an aggregate of assembled procedures hinged upon a series of guiding principles, ideas, or a base philosophy. At various points in history, imaginative men and women have created "systems" or "methods" of physical education which have in turn been built upon and elaborated by disciples of these innovators,[1] and the details of application have been handed on as prescriptions to those who followed. For most of us the terms "Ling system" (Swedish), "Turnen (or Jahn) system," "athleticism," "Danish system," "French system," conjure up in our minds some concept of the generalized physical activities and procedures incorporated in the method. Knowledge of the ideas and principles that gave rise to such systems is less clear, although such knowledge would, doubtless, enable us to understand more completely the interplay among the social, economic, political, military, and intellec-

[1]For an excellent review and analysis of the impact that these individuals have had upon the field of physical education, the reader is referred to Ellen W. Gerber, *Innovators and Institutions in Physical Education* (Philadelphia: Lea and Febiger, 1971).

tual developments that form the reality in which the various syste found. The ideas and principles that produced the new systems of physical education in the 1800s were generated extensively in the preceding century.

Out of the seventeenth and eighteenth centuries there emerged at least five significant revolutions: scientific, agricultural, commercial or economic, industrial, and democratic.[2] Changes in these broad fields gradually undermined the *Ancien Régime*[3] and formed the foundations upon which a new regime was built. To trace these revolutions in detail is beyond the scope of this chapter, but it is important to identify a number of the key shifts which had implications for changes in physical education and sport both in Europe and throughout the world.

The roots of the Agricultural Revolution extend back into the 1600s but it became a significant and expansive force in England during the mid 1700s when the old three-field fallow system (which required the fields lie fallow every third year) gave way to a new system based upon crop rotation whereby nitrogen-fixing crops were grown every second year. This practice, coupled with the use of artificial fertilizers, increased the productivity of the land and, along with the Enclosures Acts of England, served to force small farmers and farm laborers off the farms and into the growing towns. This freeing of men from the land assisted the growth of the Industrial Revolution (Brinton *et al.*, 1973, pp. 389–90). The resultant rural-urban shift led to the need for new adaptive strategies within society, strategies that reshaped sport, recreation, and physical education.

The Industrial Revolution, which was typified by a shift from energy sources of a human or animal nature to energy sources based on nonliving mechanisms (fossil fuels and internal combustion engines), produced many changes that have had far-reaching effects on physical education programs. The laboring class increased in size, as did the size of the towns. A population boom began about this period as a result of such advances as smallpox vaccination, the work of Pasteur and Lister in the discovery of germ infection and its control through antiseptics, and improvement in surgical techniques. The base was developed for the emer-

---

[2]This study, like most histories of physical education written by Euro-North Americans, commences with Europe and then moves on to other political and geographical areas of the world. However, it is important to recognize that various types of programs of physical education and sport existed in many other areas. It is significant, though, that programs in these other areas were affected negatively and positively by the developments that occurred in Europe during the 1800s.

[3]The term *Ancien Régime* was used by the French to describe the religious, legal, socio-cultural, and economic institutions which were prevalent in Western Europe in the late seventeenth and eighteenth centuries. It contrasted with the new regime which arose from the revolution of 1789 (Brinton *et al.*, 1973, p. 385).

gence of a leisure-time problem. Large populations of young children in confined areas with little to do helped to stimulate the development of public school systems (this development being augmented by the invention of the high-speed printing press).

The Danes and the Prussians were among the first to respond. The Danish Great School Commission recommended the creation of a national system of schools in 1799, and by 1809 an ordinance had been introduced which strongly recommended that gymnastics be a part of the program. A critical step for physical education was taken by the Danes in 1814, when they made elementary school education compulsory and within it a compulsory gymnastic component. In Prussia, August Francke's education plan had caught the imagination of Friedrich Wilhelm I, who enacted school laws which preceded those of the Danes. Friedrich II, influenced by Johann Hecker, built upon these. As a consequence, by 1763 Prussia's elementary education program emerged with education standards, compulsory attendance, and supervisory regulations (Zeigler, 1973, p. 268).

The Transportation Revolution, a component of the Industrial Revolution, produced improvement of road and canal systems, invention of the steam engine (which in turn lead to the creation of the railroad and steamships), and ultimately the automobile. The combined effect of these shifts produced yet another in the organization of businesses (Quigley, 1961, p. 251). The demand for capital monies for investment exceeded the capabilities of individuals or small partnerships to respond. The result was that a corporate form of enterprise emerged which mobilized the savings of large numbers of the population under the control of a few key individuals. Better, safer, faster transportation, *laissez-faire* economics,[4] and corporate enterprises produced a world trade fair and with it an exchange of ideas and new principles. The world was shrinking! The need for new markets for the sale of goods and new sources of raw materials sent the entrepreneurs to all parts of the globe. New social systems emerged to integrate the complex of changes. Within these changes were embedded programs of physical education and sport.

But their emergence was not due solely to the shift of the dominant social group from bureaucracy to bourgeoisie, nor to a change in agrarian patterns, nor to the transformation of the economic organizational pattern from commercial capitalism to industrial capitalism. There were two other significant shifts which were to affect the principles upon which

---

[4]This doctrine is set out in *The Wealth of Nations,* wherein Adam Smith attacked attempts on the part of merchants to protect home industries through high tariffs. He maintained that if a foreign country could supply the commodity more cheaply than the home nation, then it should be bought from that nation, and in turn there should be sold to that nation what could be best produced in the home industry.

physical education programs were built: one was in political structure and another in organization of the military.

The political organization of European nations had long been based upon dynastic monarchy, a situation which could be maintained only as long as the best weapon available was restricted in use to a minority of the population. When the gun became available to the majority, it became impossible for any minority to enforce unpopular laws, and so the days of the dynastic monarch were limited. As Quigley has noted, the reorganization had a dual impact: "On the one hand it became necessary to shift from minority rule to majority rule, and on the other hand it became necessary to find a new political organization that could place its appeal to allegiance on a basis that could be used for the majority of the society" (1961, p. 255). Thus emerged the *national state* and *nationalism.* This shift reduced the importance of the mercenary soldier and yielded a new form of military organization which was based more upon a patriotic national army. As a direct consequence, the fitness of the citizen for labor and defense emerged as a key principle which was to shape the methods and systems of physical education for the next 150 years. These developments created the social environment in which the programs of Ling, Nachtegall, and Jahn were nurtured and later exported to the world.

In education, too, the *Ancien Régime* failed the tests of reason and natural law. Writers during the Age of Enlightenment attacked both the strong ecclesiastical control of education and the dominant emphasis upon the study of ancient history, theology, Greek, and Latin. These philosophers advocated greater stress upon modern history, modern languages, science, and, for some, physical activity. Notable among these authors was John Locke (1632–1704), one of England's greatest philosophers, whose *Essay Concerning Human Understanding* and *Some Thoughts Concerning Education* profoundly influenced the thinking of many educators and political theorists. A proponent of Descartes' dualistic philosophy, Locke opened his famous treatise on education with the words: "A Sound Mind in a Sound Body, is a short, but full Description of a Happy State in this World" (1913, p. 1). Perhaps it was not unexpected that Locke, educated in the field of medicine, clearly enunciated theories pertinent to physical fitness and to the education of the child. He labeled the mind of the newborn child a *tabula rasa,* a blank slate, upon which was gradually encoded the knowledge which the child acquired through experience and his reflections on those experiences. Influenced by the writings of Locke, others began to view children not as truncated adults, but as growing, maturing beings who required vast ranges of experiences in order to mature and grow intellectually and physically.

Another of the scholars of the Age of Enlightenment who attacked the prevailing system was Swiss-born Jean Jacques Rousseau (1712–

1788), whose plea for progressive education was contained in *Emile,* half treatise and half romance. The educational procedures that Rousseau prescribed departed in every particular from eighteenth-century practice: "Life is the trade I would teach him. When he leaves me, I grant you, he will be neither a magistrate, a soldier, nor a priest; he will be a man" (1911, p. 9). Rousseau's theories had obvious shortcomings, but his principles and ideas became the base for many new educational programs in the late 1700s and early 1800s.

Building upon the concepts formulated by Galileo, Copernicus, Kepler, and Newton that natural laws control the physical world, these writers had surmised that natural laws must operate and be given recognition in social domains such as government and education. But concepts and theories must be put to the test of the real world, and at the critical point in history during the latter part of the eighteenth century it was the Swiss Pestalozzi, de Fellenberg, and Wehrli, and the German Basedow who were instrumental in putting into operation the principles of education advocated by Rousseau and Locke (Van Dalen and Bennett, 1971, p. 357).

Brevity seriously restricts the development of a sound understanding of the subtle and dramatic, direct and indirect effects of the scientific, commercial-economic, democratic, agricultural, and industrial revolutions on the resurgence of physical education and sport as important elements in the cultures of virtually every nation of the world. Such, however, was the case. To summarize some of the value shifts, we can look at a series of ethics that have existed from 1800 onward that have served as guiding principles for sport and physical education programs. These are the ethnocentric, biocentric, egocentric, and, more recently, the anthropocentric ethics (Valaskakis and Sindell, 1976, p. 13).

Ethnocentric Ethic. Advocates of this ethic place the interests of the *national state* above those of the individual or any other group. Sport and physical education are viewed as mechanisms for enhancing the nation and are typified by the systems of Jahn, Ling, Nachtegall, those of the contemporary socialist nations such as the U.S.S.R., Hungary, and Czechoslovakia, as well by the special programs that emerge in the democratic nations during time of war.

Biocentric Ethic. Systems which place man as a part of nature rather than masters apart from it were created by followers of Rousseau. Notable among these were Basedow, Pestalozzi, Salzmann, Guts Muths, and more recently Gaulhofer, Streicher, Laban, Dalcroze, and Montessori. Programs which evolved from this ethic are pupil-oriented, developed in accordance with the natural developmental stages and learning readiness of the individual. Laban's "expression-gymnastics," which built upon the natural desire of the child for movement and spontaneous play, reflect this ethic as does the subsequent movement education which grew from Laban's work. Outdoor education programs, snow schools, and school camps are a part of the systems of physical education based upon this ethic.

Egocentric Ethic. Early Athenian physical education was based upon beauty, harmony, excellence, and the development of mind and body. The egocentric ethic emphasizes these virtues as well as the principles of honesty, fair play, sportsmanship, effort, interest, initiative, and courage. The individual is of primary importance. "Muscular Christianity," the essence of which was captured and nurtured in Charles Kingsley's *Westward Ho* and Thomas Hughes' *Tom Brown's Schooldays,* was a fundamental force in propounding the values of the egocentric ethic. The games programs of the great public schools of England formed the basis of the school and university curricula that emphasized games and athleticism, a system of physical education and sport that was eventually to affect large segments of the total world's population through international sports festivals such as the Olympic Games.

Anthropocentric Ethic. The emphasis of this ethic shifts the focus away from any particular group, region, or nation and up to the global or species-wide level. The values held by such groups as the Club of Rome, which stress the necessity of conservation and the *equal concern* maxim, form the base of the ethic. No system of physical education has yet emerged which uses the principles and ideas of anthropocentrism as the hinges upon which a program is built, although traces of concern can be seen in programs of outdoor education in Scandinavian countries, Canada, and the United States. As a consequence this ethic will not be further elaborated in this chapter.

ETHNOCENTRISM: THE NATION-STATE

During the latter stages of the 1700s massive changes were occurring at all levels of society, and internal as well as international conflicts were inevitable. In many ways the Napoleonic Wars represented a struggle between the old and the new. Nations which had once held economic and political sway were losing prestige as well as their holdings to powerful new states. The era of the professional soldier had drawn to an end, and the need for a physically fit, mass citizen army to protect national boundaries became the new order.

Denmark, quick to adopt new economic, educational, agricultural, and commercial policies, found herself in a situation of conflict with England and an emerging German nation. Largely because of this external threat, the field of physical education experienced rapid growth under the guiding hand of Franz Nachtegall (1777–1847). He built the first private outdoor gymnasium to be found in Europe, created and directed the Military Gymnastic Institute (1804), and was largely responsible for having school physical education incorporated as a compulsory subject for Danish youth 7 to 14 years, in 1814, and for all prospective teachers, in 1818 (Van Dalen and Bennett, 1971, p. 257). By 1839 it was estimated that 2,500 of approximately 2,600 public schools ". . . were making at least some provision for systematic bodily exercise" (Leonard and Affleck, 1947, p. 183).

Nachtegall's work was not proceeding in isolation. In Sweden a contemporary, Per Henrik Ling (1776–1839), was formulating a new system of gymnastics that was to influence our field well into the twentieth century.[5] Like those of Denmark, Sweden's borders had been seriously threatened for decades, and in 1805, when Sweden entered into a pact with Russia, England, and Austria, Napoleon seized her remaining Baltic holdings and Swedish Pomerania. Because citizen armies now significantly supplemented the professional armies, programs which had as their object the development of physical fitness of large segments of the population were assured the support of Swedish royalty. Ling was quick to respond, and by 1814 he had built, under royal sponsorship, *The Royal Central Gymnastics Institute* (RCGI). Calling upon his knowledge of anatomy and physiology, his extensive reading, and his practical experience in the fledgling field, Ling created a systematic program of exercises which utilized free-standing movement as well as apparatus-based drills. An innovator of importance, Ling was responsible for the development of a wide range of apparatus including the vaulting box, stall bars, the Swedish boom, the window ladder, and the oblique rope (Gerber, 1971, p. 159). His programs of gymnastics extended beyond the ethnocentric objective into the fields of medical, esthetic and pedagogical gymnastics —evidence of the breadth of this pioneer's philosophical base. The triumvirate of military, pedagogical, and medical gymnastics, built upon by Lars Branting, Hjalmar Ling, and others, was to endure for decades and

[5]There are some historians who suggest that Ling was influenced by the work of Nachtegall; however Van Dalen and Bennett (1971, p. 237) point out that it is by no means clear that Ling was strongly influenced by this pioneer. It is known that he spent five years in Copenhagen (1799–1804) and while there he took up fencing and spent time at Nachtegall's gymnasium. Whether or not Nachtegall's programs were instrumental in shaping Ling's thinking has not been finally determined, but upon his return to Stockholm he immediately set about establishing physical activity programs.

Figure 3–1. Per Henrik Ling (Swedish System)

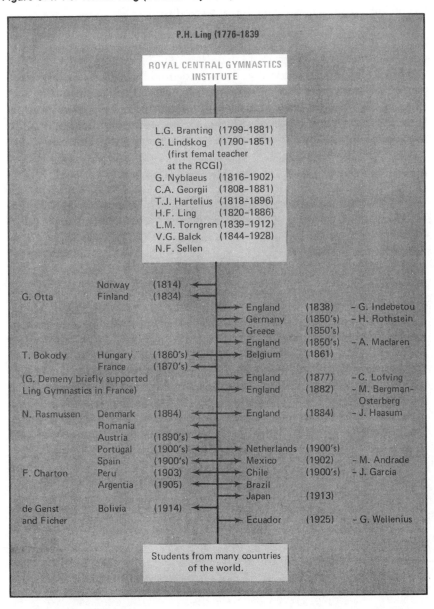

P.H. Ling (1776-1839

ROYAL CENTRAL GYMNASTICS INSTITUTE

L.G. Branting (1799-1881)
G. Lindskog (1790-1851)
(first femal teacher at the RCGI)
G. Nyblaeus (1816-1902)
C.A. Georgii (1808-1881)
T.J. Hartelius (1818-1896)
H.F. Ling (1820-1886)
L.M. Torngren (1839-1912)
V.G. Balck (1844-1928)
N.F. Sellen

	Norway	(1814)	
G. Otta	Finland	(1834)	
	England	(1838)	– G. Indebetou
	Germany	(1850's)	– H. Rothstein
	Greece	(1850's)	
	England	(1850's)	– A. Maclaren
T. Bokody	Hungary (1860's) Belgium	(1861)	
	France (1870's)		
(G. Demeny briefly supported	England	(1877)	– C. Lofving
Ling Gymnastics in France)	England	(1882)	– M. Bergman-Osterberg
N. Rasmussen	Denmark (1884) England	(1884)	– J. Haasum
	Romania		
	Austria (1890's)		
	Portugal (1900's) Netherlands	(1900's)	
	Spain (1900's) Mexico	(1902)	– M. Andrade
F. Charton	Peru (1903) Chile	(1900's)	– J. Garcia
	Argentina (1905) Brazil		
	Japan	(1913)	
de Genst	Bolivia (1914)		
and Ficher	Ecuador	(1925)	– G. Wellenius

Students from many countries of the world.

to influence the youth of the nations of the world who even today can attend the Royal Central Gymnastics Institute.[6]

There was a third person who subscribed to the belief that gymnastics could positively affect the nation-state, a German whose work was to influence millions—Friedrich Ludwig Jahn (1778–1852). When, on November 18, 1799, Napoleon Bonaparte executed his *coup d'état* and seized power in France, the lives of many people were changed, including that of Jahn. As a youth, Jahn witnessed the defeat of the Prussian forces at Jena and this event, coupled with his strong sense of a national spirit, instilled in him a drive to help create a strong, vigorous German youth.

Figure 3–2. Friedrich Ludwig Jahn (The Art of Gymnastics)

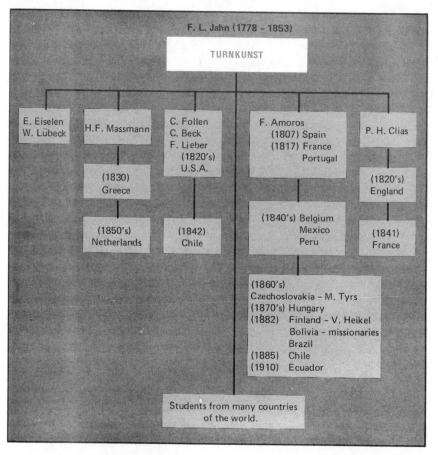

[6]Since 1967 the Royal Central Gymnastics Institute has been called the Institute for Gymnastics and Sports.

Jahn's *Turnen* system, which borrowed heavily from that created by Guts Muths, included the natural activities of running, jumping, climbing, and hanging, to which he added low organization games, wrestling, and exercises on apparatus. To the equipment recommended by Guts Muths he added the horizontal bar and special activity uniforms made of unbleached linen. By building the first *Turnplatz* (a special area where exercises were conducted) near Berlin in 1811, Jahn hoped to instill in his students a spirit of nationalism. The concept spread rapidly, and between 1814 and 1818 *Turnplatz* were developed in 52 cities (Leonard, 1905, p. 5). But Jahn's outspoken attacks against the Austrian chancellor, Metternich, lead to his arrest in 1819 on a charge of treason and to a *Turn-Sperre* (a prohibition of *Turnen*) which lasted until 1842. This restriction caused an important change in the character of *Turnen* exercises, since participants were forced to conduct their programs in secrecy, mostly within the confines of houses. Many of the activities which required large spaces were lost and those which utilized apparatus and limited space, and which were easy to discipline and control, grew in importance. As a consequence, there emerged activities which were later to be introduced into schools and housed in school gymnasia.

During the period of the *Turn-Sperre*, politically suspect supporters of Jahn's *Turnen* fled Germany and sought sanctuary in other nations. Karl Beck (Round Hill School), Karl Follen (Harvard and Boston gymnasia), and Francis Lieber (Boston gymnasium) were three such *Turners* who, along with other students of Jahn, carried gymnastics throughout the world. The nationalistic base was lost in most cases, but the Jahn "system," along with the systems of Ling and to a lesser extent that of Nachtegall, became a significant part of physical education development in many nations of the world.

Unlike sport, the diffusion patterns of which are blurred with passing time, the starting points of the ethnocentric-based systems of physical education are sharply fixed and the patterns of spread reasonably clear. Initially restricted to the nations of Europe, the programs gained intercontinental acclaim through the work of migrant disciples such as Beck, Follen, and Lieber, and through military personnel, physically active businessmen, missionaries, and students of other nations who came to study at the Royal Central Gymnastics Institute in Stockholm or the Military Gymnastics Institute in Copenhagen. In many cases the attendance of such scholars was motivated by the rapid spread of compulsory education, a component of which was compulsory physical education. The emergence of a strong middle class, a burgeoning urban population, wars, and threats of wars provided continuing impetus for required physical education programs in the new schools. The strong sense of nationalism coupled with real or perceived external threats were to remain key

Figure3–3. Franz Nachtegall (Father of Danish Gymnastics)

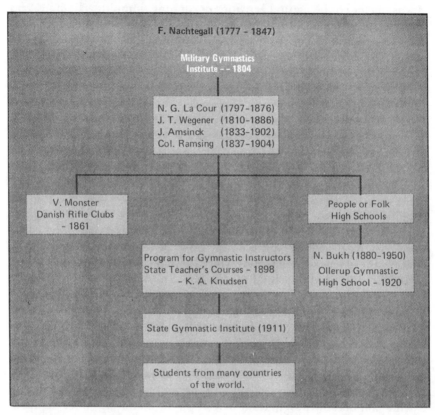

factors in the perpetuation of programs of physical education tied to the ethnocentric ethic. Over time the individual "systems" blended into each other, were augmented by segments of other programs or by newly developed systems, but the underlying *raison d'être* for this type of physical education program remained throughout the period from 1800 to today. Physical educators around the world have marched school children, drilled them on fixed routines, lined them up for stunts on apparatus, and double-timed them around a field or a rectangular room. And physical preparedness was developed, or so it was hoped. During this period several other key programs emerged throughout the world that require brief mention.

In 1862, Czechoslovakian Miroslav Tyrs created the *Sokol* (Falcon) movement, an organization open to all classes and both sexes but based upon national freedom and brotherhood. *Sokol* was basically a system of gymnastic exercises divided into four groups: (1) individual exercises

Table 3–1. Dates for Commencement of Compulsory School Physical Education (Incomplete Listing)

NATION	ELEMENTARY LEVEL	SECONDARY LEVEL
Argentina		1898
Austria	1869	1869
Belgium	1842	
Bolivia	1928	1928
Brazil[1]	1851	1855
Chile	1920	
Columbia	1904	1904
Czechoslovakia	1869	1874
Denmark[2]	1814	1814
Ecuador	1922	1922
England[3]	1870	1870
Ethiopia[4]	1900	1900
Finland	1843	1843
France[5]	1872	1872
Germany	1860	1860
Greece	1834	
Hungary[6]	1868	
Italy[7]	1859	1859
Japan	1872	1872
Lebanon	1928	1928
Netherlands	1890	1863
New Zealand	1877	1877
Norway[8]	1848	1869
Philippines	1937	1937
Poland	1919	1919
Portugal	1901	1901
Republic of China[9]	1929	1929
South Africa		1874
Sweden[10]	1824	1820
Switzerland	1874	
Thailand	1898	1899

[1] Law 630, passed in 1851, required that elementary school boys have physical education. Both this date and the 1855 date for secondary schools are somewhat misleading in that few people attended schools in Brazil at this time. A more appropriate date might be 1930, when decrees were passed making attendance (and physical education) compulsory for all Brazilian youth.

[2] Not until 1904 was a law enacted in Denmark which required that gymnastics be a part of all elementary school programs for *girls* as well as boys.

[3] The Education Act of 1870 made a concession to physical education by stating that ". . . 'attendance at drill under a competent instructor for not more than two hours per week and twenty weeks in the year may be counted as school attendance'—for purposes of financial grant from the government" (McIntosh, 1963, pp. 108–9). It was not obligatory and it was for boys only, but it was a gesture of recognition of the emerging field. It should be noted that even yet England does not have compulsory physical education.

[4] No data were found to indicate that there was a planned program of instruction for physical education at that time.

[5] Boys' physical education was made compulsory in public schools in 1872. A series of laws in 1880, 1887 and 1905 reemphasized the requirement by requiring physical education in girls' programs, private and church schools (Van Dalen and Bennett, 1971, p. 273).

[6] Law Number 37 introduced compulsory elementary education, but the provisions of the law were not enforced and compulsory education remained more theory than practice. Physical education did not become firmly entrenched until the Socialist government gained control of the country in 1945.

[7] Established by the Casati Law.

[8] These dates indicate compulsory programs for boys only. Dates were not found which designated that physical education had become compulsory for girls.

[9] Established by the National Physical Education Law of that year.

[10] Sweden's first laws requiring physical education pertained to boys only.

with no assists and no apparatus; (2) apparatus-based gymnastics; (3) exercises demanding personal assists from another individual; and (4) combative exercises. Although subsequently suppressed by Germany and by the Soviet Union, *Sokol* units still exist in many parts of the world. Poland borrowed the *Sokol* program in 1867 and Hungary based its nationalistic *Levente* (Young Hero) movement of the 1920s on it as well. Variations of this nationalistic theme have emerged in several countries under the broad heading of "labor and defense." Although Sweden's early (1907) National Sports Badge system could not be placed in this category, the idea caught on and grew through the German Sports Badge program (1913) to the GTO (*Gotov k trudu i oborone*—"Be Ready for Labor and Defense") and BGTO ("Will Be Ready for Labor and Defense") badge program of the U.S.S.R. in 1931, to the "Labor and Defense of the Fatherland" program of China (1951), the MHK badges of Hungary (1949), as well as Hungary's subsequent *Kilian* Physical Exercises Movement (1961). Within the past few decades many other nations throughout the world have incorporated physical fitness badge schemes into their physical education programs, although few have overtly stated the "labor and defense" rationale.

The physical education of millions of young people was shaped by the Politburo of the U.S.S.R. through its *Massovast* (mass participation),

Figure 3–4. The Epitome of the Ethnocentric Ethic: the GTO (*Gotov k trudu i Oborone*—Be ready for Labor and Defense) Badge of the U.S.S.R.

СДАВАЙТЕ

НОРМЫ

КОМПЛЕКСА

ГТО

Masterstvo (proficiency) programs, by Hitler and the National Socialist Party through the Hitler *Jugend* and other state-related programs, by Mao Tse-tung through his national defense concept of physical culture, to a lesser extent by Benito Mussolini through the *Opera Nazionale Balilla,* and by the Portuguese Youth Fitness and Military Preparedness. Such programs, which frequently included activities such as shooting, grenade throwing, forced marches, and obstacle course work, met with criticism by physical educators from democratic nations. Notwithstanding this fact, the history of physical education development throughout the nations of the world has been interwoven with military-oriented programs and leadership training.

Within France the programs created by Amoros (1817) and Clias (1841) were designed to develop the military capabilities of youth. Indeed, in the 1820s the Swiss-born Clias had been invited to England, where he organized programs for the English military after having served Switzerland in this way. The work of Clias and Amoros produced a number of direct and indirect consequences. In France their work led to the establishment of the Military Normal School of Gymnastics at Joinville, the graduates of which served both military and schools alike and thereby shaped the development and content of physical education programs.

England's Archibald Maclaren's *A Military System of Gymnastic Exercises for the Use of Instructors* was an important document within that nation's emerging physical education. Although the material had a military focus, Maclaren was not interested solely in the training of soldiers; he was concerned about civilian health and educational gymnastics. In these latter areas he set out his theories in *A System of Physical Education.* Maclaren's development of progressive exercises and overload routines, his use of anthropometric measures, his new teaching methodologies, his concern for individual differences, and his campaigns for physical education in the schools mark him as an important figure in the field (Gerber, 1971, pp. 215–19).

Other great pioneers blended together work on military programs with broader-based, generic programs of physical education to the benefit of both areas. P. F. Lesgaft (1837–1909), the founder of the scientific system of physical education in the U.S.S.R. and a teacher of Pavlov, was one such person. His holistic theories of physical education are little known outside the Soviet Union but his philosophy, concepts, and theories are central to the U.S.S.R.'s scientific approach to physical culture (Riordan, [n.d.], p. 11) and have earned him the unofficial title of "Father of Russian Physical Education."

One other phenomenon found in a number of nations requires brief consideration. This is the sports school concept, which includes two basic types: the spare-time sports school and the specialized sports school.

These unique schools predominate in the Socialist countries, but the Federal German Republic, Italy, Finland, and Austria have also developed highly specialized programs and facilities for the athletically gifted youngster. These individuals are identified by coaches and physical educators at an early age (generally in the range of 6 to 10 years) as a result of their participation in regular school activity programs. In the case of the spare-time sports school, selected students are enrolled in carefully developed training programs while they continue to take part in classes at their regular school (although their school day is often reduced in length). The specialized sports schools are somewhat different, as students who attend these schools are the elite. They live in residence, take their regular program of studies at this school, and participate in comprehensive athletic programs. Those nations which have fostered the development of these schools consider international sport to be an important "window" through which the world views their social, political, and economic structure. Specialized sports schools help to ensure that nation a favorable representation as well as an opportunity for the gifted to reach their full potential.

Today a number of nations require premilitary training as a part of their secondary school physical education programs. Notable among these are the Philippines, the People's Republic of China, Israel, the United Arab Republic, the People's Republic of Korea, and Taiwan. Nations which are threatened or perceive a threat continue to be strong subscribers to the ethnocentric ethic. International conflict often results in the passage of government legislation aimed at improving the fitness level of the people, the creation of or increased emphasis upon national sports or fitness badges, and an increased budgetary appropriation for the construction of fitness facilities. An analysis of martial arts programs in Japan, Thailand, Taiwan, Malaysia, and other nations would provide additional insight into the nature and depth historically of the ethnocentric ethic. Of the four ethics noted, it is, perhaps, the one which has the deepest and most widespread root system. It draws strength from man's territorial nature and gains its shape through a nation's economic and political structure. When these are threatened, programs or systems of physical education which foster physical fitness and military preparedness will flourish.

The programs themselves have undergone significant changes since the work of Nachtegall, Ling, and Jahn early in the 1800s. Physical education programs of today which have as their reason for being the need to prepare the people of the nation for "labor and defense" currently use sophisticated ergometers to assess individual cardiovascular fitness, reliable and valid anthropometric measurements to assess changes as a result of scientifically designed progressive exercise regimens,[7] motivational devices such as the badge systems, specialized sports schools to enhance and to reshape physical education. The underlying rationale for the program itself, however, has continued to be derived from social, political, and economic forces.

BIOCENTRISM:
THE DEVELOPMENT OF NATURAL MOVEMENTS

> ... the natural inclination of youth to play about in the open air to compensate for that which was neglected in school cannot be curbed. The young individual is polished like a rock in the stream. It is always better to have this happen sooner than later if only the stream is not entirely polluted and muddy. (Guts Muths, 1796)
>
> Games should, therefore, be exercises for youth (for adults too) which are beneficial in some way. They should move the body more or less and promote its health; this occurs only through running, jumping, etc. or through happy laughter and softer movements. They should bring speed, power and flexibility in the limbs, harden the body either accidently or purposely against pain, and activate this or the other sense vividly. (Guts Muths, 1796)
>
> (Cited by Moolenijzer, 1973, pp. 301–3)

The concept that man responds to natural movement impulses, a need to play; that man discovers himself and his world through experience (both sensation and reflection); that there is value in free, voluntary, and natural physical activity, is not a new one. But it received new and vital emphasis during the Age of Enlightenment through the writings of authors such as Locke and Rousseau. Spurred by changes envisioned or occurring within the *Ancien Régime,* by their own concerns for inequities within society, and by the writings of others, both men set out treatises on education that were to have far-reaching effects on physical education. Their ideas were taken up and advanced by men such as Pestalozzi, Basedow, Guts Muths, Froebel and later Gaulhofer, Streicher, Laban, and Morison.

Johann Heinrich Pestalozzi (1746–1827), a Swiss educator, sought to provide an educational experience for children which included a strong program of physical activities, particularly the natural activities of running, jumping and climbing, low-organization games, and self-discovery movements. Much of Pestalozzi's later recognition as an educational pioneer came as a result of his books *Leonard and Gertrude* and *How*

[7]Men such as England's Archibald Maclaren, France's Georges Demeny and Georges Hébert, Germany's Carl Diem, America's Dudley Allen Sargent, Denmark's Johannes Lindhard, and more recently scholars like Sweden's Per-Olaf Astrand, Japan's Ikai, and America's Cureton have been instrumental in providing a sound base upon which improved exercise programs have been developed.

Gertrude Teaches Her Children, which were based on his practical experiences.

Like Pestalozzi, German-born Johann Basedow (1723-1790) was a staunch believer in man's natural rights and in the education of youth in accordance with natural laws. He recommended that all strata of the population participate in vigorous physical activity, and when in 1774 he opened the Dessau *Philanthropinum,* a private academy and the first neo-humanist school, the curriculum included three hours of physical activity per day. Initially these activities included the knightly and martial exercises of horseback riding, fencing, and dancing, but such activities ran contrary to Basedow's philosophy of education. The situation changed markedly with the appointment of J. F. Simon (and later J. J. DuToit) to the position of physical activity director. Under their leadership, guided by Basedow's philosophy, a new system of exercises based on a more natural form gradually emerged (Leonard and Affleck, 1947, p. 69).

There followed a series of academic institutions based upon the *Philanthropinum* model, but only one had a significant impact on the emergence of physical education programs based on the biocentric ethic. This was the *Schnepfenthal Educational Institute* founded in 1784 by C. G. Salzmann, a former teacher at Basedow's *Philanthropinum.* From the outset a strong physical activity program was instituted based upon the work carried out at Basedow's academy and upon principles set down by Rousseau. This program was initially organized by C. C. André, but in 1786 the position was given over to a man who was to become a giant in this emerging field, Johann Christoph Friedrich Guts Muths (1759-1839). A meticulous scholar, Guts Muths kept personal records on the growth rates and levels of performance of each of his students, and from this data base he developed individualized exercise programs so that his pupils could progress according to their needs. He was perhaps the first physical educator to operate a pupil-oriented program wherein the activities were prescribed according to the natural developmental stages and the learning readiness of the individual. As outstanding as he was as a teacher, it was Guts Muths' literary ability coupled with his excellent documentation of childrens' responses to exercise and activity that mark him as the "Grandfather of Physical Education" (Gerber, 1971, p. 115). He wrote and published extensively, but it was his book *Gymnastics for the Young (Gymnastik für die Jugend)* which led to his fame and which, in many ways, concluded "a process of development which led from knightly exercises to a system of physical exercises seen as a means of education on the basis of a philanthropic way of thinking" (Wildt, 1971, p. 2).

Guts Muths' programs and his publications were to influence a number of physical educators including men such as Nachtegall, Clias, Amoros, Spiess (the father of German school gymnastics), Jahn, Eiselen,

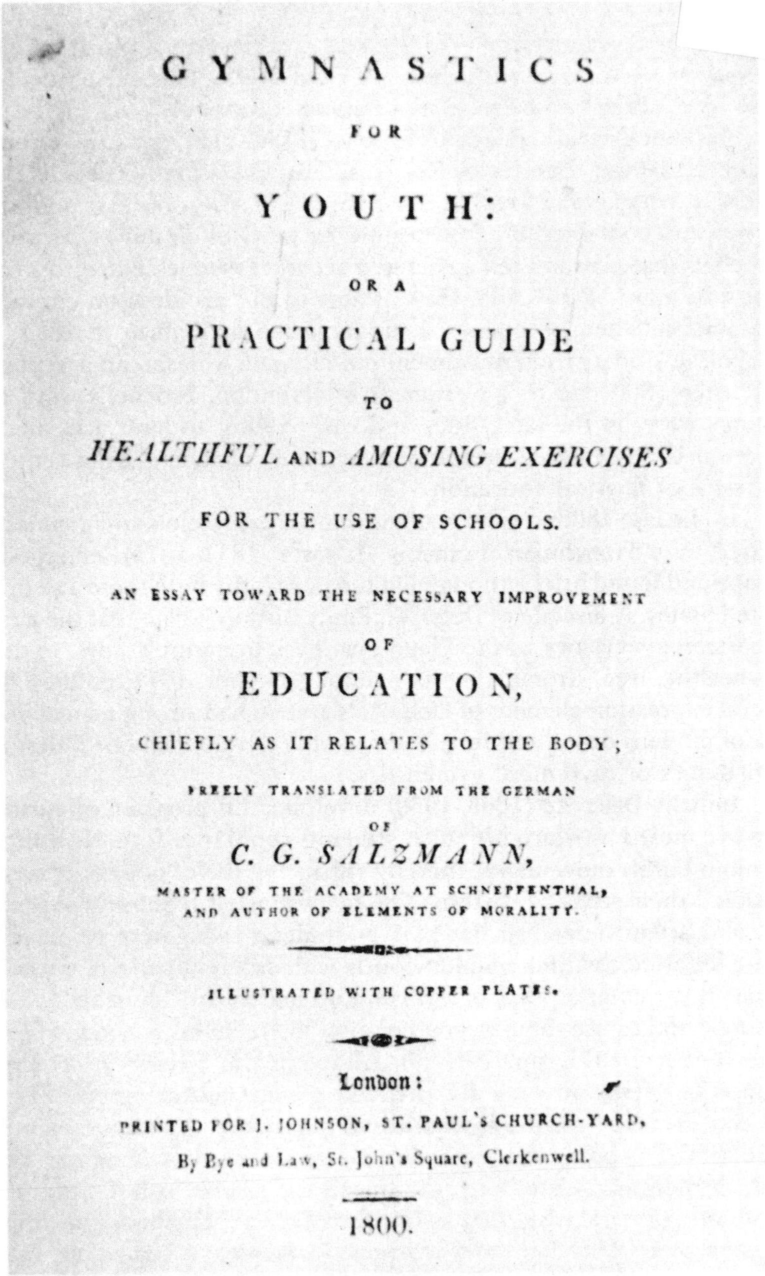

GYMNASTICS

FOR

YOUTH:

OR A

PRACTICAL GUIDE

TO

HEALTHFUL AND *AMUSING EXERCISES*

FOR THE USE OF SCHOOLS.

AN ESSAY TOWARD THE NECESSARY IMPROVEMENT

OF

EDUCATION,

CHIEFLY AS IT RELATES TO THE BODY;

FREELY TRANSLATED FROM THE GERMAN

OF

C. G. SALZMANN,

MASTER OF THE ACADEMY AT SCHNEPFENTHAL,
AND AUTHOR OF ELEMENTS OF MORALITY.

————————

ILLUSTRATED WITH COPPER PLATES.

————————

London:

PRINTED FOR J. JOHNSON, ST. PAUL's CHURCH-YARD,

By Bye and Law, St. John's Square, Clerkenwell.

1800.

Figure 3–5. The title page of the first English edition of Guts Muths' *Gymnastik für die Jugend,* which was wrongly attributed to C. G. Salzmann.

and Ling, but his material was to be used to achieve ends which were not necessarily coextensive with those of Guts Muths himself, particularly those aims which had political and military overtones.

Another German, Friedrich Froebel (1782–1852), was also strongly influenced by the theories of Rousseau and Pestalozzi. Froebel's most important educational treatise, *The Education of Man,* was first published in 1826 and contained his theories on the unity of all things, as well as his beliefs that play and self-generated activities were essential to a complete education of the child. He was able to put his ideas on education into practice when he opened a kindergarten in Keilhau in 1837. Although the kindergarten movement did not gain widespread acceptance until after 1860 due to government intervention, Froebel's work and writings were, in the late 1800s and early 1900s, to have a significant effect on child-centered educational systems, including child-centered programs of physical education.

In the late 1800s a system of movement expression and gymnastics devised by a Frenchman, François Delsarte (1811–1871), emerged in Europe and found brief although limited popularity both there and in the United States. A disciple of Delsarte, Emily Bishop, wrote that the aim of Delsartean gymnastics was to "lead man back to nature's ways, to make him healthy, free, strong, simple, natural" (Gerber, 1971, p. 203). The natural expression element of Delsarte's system had strong appeal in the area of modern dance and foreshadowed the development of Dalcroze's eurhythmics or rhythmical gymnastics.

Initially Dalcroze (1865–1950) developed his program of eurhythmics as a means by which his music students could transform rhythm and beat into bodily movements, thereby enhancing their "powers of apperception," their sense of rhythm. The method itself required concentration and attentiveness on the part of students, who were required to create different rhythms simultaneously with different parts of the body, to march the counterpoint of a rhythm, to master an "alphabet" of arm gestures, and to use them in combination to create expressions of emotions (Gerber, 1971, pp. 195–99). Although the Swiss-born Dalcroze claimed a widespread value for rhythmic gymnastics for schoolchildren, the system never gained international popularity. Its importance lies more in the people who were directly or indirectly influenced by it. Madame Bergman-Österberg introduced the system in her curriculum for women physical educators at Dartford College, England, thus touching thousands of students and teachers. Rudolph von Laban, the father of movement education, studied the method, and although he discarded it as a totality, some elements of Dalcroze's eurhythmics remained. The area of natural and modern dance was significantly affected by eurhythmics through Mary Wigman, Hanya Holm, and Kurt Joos.

Another of those touched by Dalcroze was the German, Rudolf Bode, who studied eurhythmics under the originator and then produced his own system of *Ausdrucks-gymnastik* or expression-gymnastics based on the natural movement patterns of children and the belief that " . . . all movement must be of the whole body and must originate at the centre and flow to the extremities" (McIntosh, 1971, p. 124). Bode's methods, in turn, influenced Finnish physical education programs. For years the Finnish Women's Physical Education Association had opposed organized athletic competition, and leaders like Elin Kallio, Elli Bjorksten, and Hilma Jalkanen borrowed from the movement principles of Bode, Laban, Delsarte, and modern dancers such as Hinrich Medau in order to create a new program of gymnastics for women. The program which they created remains a significant component of the syllabus for female physical education teachers in Finland (Herron, 1966, p. 20).

Just as Bode's *Ausdrucks-gymnastik* was in part a rebellion against the rigid Jahn *Turnen*, so also was the *Natürliches Turnen* or natural gymnastics program developed by the Austrians Karl Gaulhofer and Margarete Streicher during the early 1900s. The underlying principle of this system was that programs of activities should be adapted to the nature of man, to spontaneous activity and movement patterns. The implications can be summarized in the following:

> (1) it was an approach, a manner of performance, rather than a system or a group of particular exercises; (2) it was attentive to biological principles; (3) as applied to movement, it connoted a process of moving from one status of balance to another with a minimum expenditure of energy; (4) it assumed that a natural movement is an integrated mental-physical concept and an expression of a personality which reflects the person's individual style of performance. (Gerber, 1971, p. 239)

Gaulhofer and Streicher included in their child-centered program a wide range of natural movements including labor movements, hiking, swimming, skating, as well as games. No detailed curriculum was ever prepared, but the originators of the "Austrian School" worked from a basis of "exercise intention" which were formulated into four groups: "normalizing exercises, forming exercises, performance exercises, and exercises leading to complete and artistic control of movement" (Broekhoff, 1968, p. 47). The Gaulhofer-Streicher system was well accepted in Austria and gained some popularity in parts of Germany, but it had very limited influence in the rest of the world. Its greatest importance, perhaps, was not in the area of program development per se, but in the liberalizing influence on the more rigid systems of gymnastics. It had its most significant impact on physical education programs in the Netherlands after Gaulhofer was appointed Rector of the Amsterdam Academy of Physical Education in 1932. Since 1945 the Austrian system used in the

Netherlands was gradually transformed. Ultimately it was replaced by a new program entitled the "Basic Teaching Plan," devised by Groenman, Gordijn, Rijsdorp. This plan sets out stages of movement development designed to provide students with movement experiences, self-assurance, body control eventually leading to optimum personal performance, and an awareness of individual potential and limitations (Broekhoff, 1968, p. 48). Within this system the teacher's task is to select from a variety of exercises or movement forms those that will best fit the needs or stages of development of the children and also satisfy the intentions or objectives of the exercise.

Another system which built extensively upon the biocentric ethic has become popularized under the generic title of "movement education."[8] The emergence of movement education can be traced back to the theories and practical work of the German-born professional dancer, Rudolph von Laban, who emigrated to England in 1936. The Austrian system of Gaulhofer and Streicher had been introduced to several of the teacher training colleges of England, as had the expression-gymnastics of Bode and the modern dance techniques of Mary Wigman. After exposure to these as well as other programs, and because of shifts in educational administration within physical education, England was ready for change. And changes occurred! The passage of the 1944 Education Act required that local education authorities provide facilities for physical education; unfortunately there was no stipulation that anyone was required to use them. But two other changes were to have a significant impact on English physical education and subsequently physical education in many parts of the world. One of these changes was in the content of physical education and the second was in the introduction of the "discovery" concept (McIntosh, 1971, p. 130). In his books *Effort* and *Modern Education Dance,* Laban had specified four aspects of motion (flow, time, space, and weight), eight combinations of these ranging from slashing to floating, and " . . . sixteen movement themes ranging from themes concerned with awareness of space through the themes concerned with the awakening of group feeling and themes concerned with expressive qualities or moods of movements" (McIntosh, 1971, p. 130).

The term "movement" became of prime importance for advocates of Laban's concepts, and phrases such as "the art of movement," "movement gymnastics," and "movement education" became a part of physical

[8]An excellent analysis of the development of the movement education programs of England can be found in a paper by Peter McIntosh presented at the Big Ten Symposium on the History of Physical Education and Sport in 1971. The author sets out the social changes that were occurring in England during the period of growth of this system, their impact on changes in the educational environment, and the background of the title "movement education."

education vocabulary. As with the Austrian system, proponents of movement education believe that children learn most effectively and efficiently when they are given the opportunity to search for and "discover" the movement sequence which is best for them. No uniform standards of performance are established. Instead generalized tasks are assigned and the child finds a solution within his own level of understanding, his physical limits, and his movement repertoire. Skills are refined through coaching and individualized suggestions as to how the movement quality might be improved.

The key to movement education was to wed this "discovery" element to the factors of movement as identified by Laban. Advocates of the system believe that the principles involved are applicable to generalized physical tasks in physical education and to dance movements, and that it has transfer potential to games as well. The questions of generality versus specificity of skill acquisition and transfer of training provided the foci of debate. Female teachers strongly advocated the merits of the movement education approach whereas male teachers were more reticent to accept the approach in its entirety. "A serious rift developed within the physical education profession and it was sex-linked, as the geneticists say" (McIntosh, 1971, p. 131).

Through the 1950s and 1960s movement education continued to grow, but a metamorphosis also occurred. Many of Laban's movement themes were discarded and new concepts generated—body shape, direction of movement, and so forth. Three branches emerged as well: basic movement leading to games; basic movement leading to gymnastics; and basic movement leading to dance. The program became an integral part of primary/elementary school physical education in England and an important part of the program for girls at the secondary level. For the older males the more traditional sport-based programs persisted, although altered to an extent by the impact of movement education philosophy and content at the lower grade levels.

But movement education was not restricted to the British Isles. Through teacher training programs, exchange programs, and emigration patterns it was carried to many parts of the world. Physical education programs in Canada and the United States have been significantly affected by the Laban approach, as have the programs of the Federal Republic of Germany, Israel, Spain, Italy, Norway, Austria, and to a lesser extent those of New Zealand and Australia. It had a strong ground swell in the mid-1970s, but its future shape and the extent to which it will "run" is still uncertain.

Another program of physical education which stresses one's place in nature and as well as one's natural movements is the one generically titled "outdoor education." The utilization of the natural environment for physical activity is not new. Indeed, aboriginal peoples throughout the world used the "natural" gymnasium to prepare their young people for adulthood. Tests for strength, skill, endurance, and patience were part of the *rites de passage* of thousands of native groups, and these abilities were developed and honed in what were fundamentally outdoor education programs. Since the early 1950s physical education teachers in many nations have created special programs encompassing skiing, camping, hiking, canoeing-kayaking, rock scrambling, and numerous other outdoor skills.

Physical education programs in Australia, under the direction of men such as Gordon Young and Fritz Duras, were in the vanguard of the outdoor education movement. New South Wales, for example, as early as 1906 established special school camps staffed by trained personnel (James, 1969, p. 21). In recent years every child in that state between the ages of 10 and 12 has been transported from school to the camp for a ten-day session (Bennett *et al.*, 1975, p. 62).

Although all outdoor education programs are not as advanced as those of New South Wales, in the last three decades countries like New Zealand, Norway, Sweden, England, U.S.S.R., Czechoslovakia, Hungary, Japan, France, and Switzerland have all created special school camps for students. A possible reason for the growth in this dimension of physical education is that it utilizes techniques based on a philosophy of first-hand experiences— learning through direct contact with the natural environment. Through this contact a nonconscious ideology of respect for the natural world and people's place in it can be fostered, these will be the forerunner programs stressing the anthropocentric ethic already alluded to. In many ways this thinking returns physical education to the fundamental principles set out by Rousseau, Basedow, Guts Muths, and Pestalozzi and Froebel which focused upon people as a part of nature and upon people's natural movements.

EGOCENTRISM: SPORT AND SPORTSMANSHIP

During the nineteenth century, while systems of gymnastics were being developed into programmes of physical education in Germany and Scandinavia, English "Public Schools" evolved their own peculiar physical education which was no less comprehensive and just as highly organized as its continental counterparts. (McIntosh *et al.*, 1969, p. 177)

The English "system" took the form of games and sports which had been pursued by the boys of the English public schools for generations.

It grew, however, to great importance in the early to middle 1800s,[9] and by the end of the century the games phenomenon had been carried to the corners of the British Empire which, at that time, essentially meant the corners of the world. The activities varied but the stress was on the virtues of honesty, fair play, sportsmanship, individual effort, initiative, and courage. The essence of this ethic was informally codified in the movement labeled "Muscular Christianity" which was evangelized in Hughes *Tom Brown's Schooldays* and Kingsley's *Westward Ho.*

The games of the English public schools (particularly rugby, cricket, rowing, soccer, and athletics) spread rapidly throughout the world, principally because the schools that spawned them also produced the leaders of the English business world and government. In short, "they became a most important cultural export" (Ellis, 1966, p. 3) and had such a far-reaching effect on world physical education that it is difficult to exaggerate their impact.

But the egocentric ethic as developed through the sport and games model was not spread solely by the English themselves. Visitors to England from other nations were often impressed by the social qualities and many virtues which could seemingly be traced to the school playgrounds. A German gymnastic teacher, August Hermann (1835–1906), spent considerable time in England, became convinced of the value of the game structure, and was directly responsible for introducing rugby to German schoolboys in 1874 (Leonard and Affleck, 1947, p. 134). The introduction of this game was followed closely by the introduction of American baseball (1875) and cricket (1876).

Under the leadership of men like Koch (1846–1911), von Schenckendorff (1837–1915), and Hartwich (1843–1886), the German playground movement boomed, eventually leading to a *spielfeste* (games festival), to the establishment of a special teacher training program centered upon games (the Gorlitz Plan), and to the creation of a Central Committee for the Promotion of Games. Denmark's playground movement developed as well. Bardenflith, the Danish minister of Church and School Affairs, issued a proclamation in 1896 which stated that games were to be introduced and regularly used in the physical education programs of the public schools. Torngren, the director of Sweden's Royal Central Gymnastics Institute, was so impressed when he visited England in 1877 that he wrote a book on English games, and his colleague, Viktor

[9]An interesting and comprehensive study of the organized games phenomenon of the English Public Schools and particularly the impact that Dr. Thomas Arnold had on them can be found in Brian T. P. Mutimer, "Arnold and Organized Games in the English Public Schools of the Nineteenth Century," unpublished Ph.D. Dissertation, University of Alberta, 1971.

Balck, actively set about establishing a games component in the Swedish physical education program.

But it may well have been the visit to England by Baron Pierre de Coubertin in 1884 that has had the greatest single impact not only on the games-sport concept for school physical education but on world sport (there will be more on this in the second part of this chapter, on sport). Convinced by what he saw in England, Coubertin returned to France imbued with the ideal of revitalizing the youth of his nation.

> When he began formulating his ideas for educational reform into a theory of pedagogical sport, much wider advantages were incorporated. They were almost entirely based on what Coubertin estimated to be the steadfast merits of the English sports system. He was firmly convinced that the English young men learned fair play, honesty, and integrity from sport experiences. He was sure that such worthy moral characteristics were not confined to the school playing fields but penetrated the individual's total personality if organized opportunities were presented. Another attitude that Coubertin was certain developed from school sports encounters was loyalty. He deemed this virtue to be the highest requirement of citizenship and one that was at a low ebb in the France of the 1880's. (Leiper, 1976, p. 25)

At the outset, Coubertin was basically concerned with the game structure as a pedagogical device, but the French, never quick to embrace British ways, were not likely to readily accept British games. It is likely that Coubertin, long an admirer of the ancient Greeks, saw the potential linkage to the early Olympic Games.

It is possible to trace, country by country, the emergence of physical education programs and program objectives based on the English game and sports movement, but that is beyond the scope of this chapter. Perhaps the widespread influence is most clearly highlighted in the later section on sport, for the seeds of this phenomenal structure were germinated on the playing fields of the English public schools before the turn of the nineteenth century. Today there is not a single program of physical education in the world that has not been influenced in some way by the egocentric ethic as it is embodied in games and sports.

CONTEMPORARY SCHOOL PHYSICAL EDUCATION

It is interesting to note the degree to which the three major ethics identified for this chapter have been fused into contemporary school physical education. Based upon a recent survey of 81 nations, the following is a list of generally agreed-upon objectives for such programs:

1. Development of physical fitness and health.
2. Enhancement of social development.

3. Improved knowledge and skill level in sports and games.
4. Development of leadership ability and enhanced ability to cooperate others.
5. Development of broad-based recreational skills, particularly for leisure time beyond the school years. (ICHPER, Part I, 1969, p. 1)

In 1967 physical education was a required subject for males and females at one or more levels of formal education in 72 of 73 countries surveyed by ICHPER. Over 90 percent of the respondents indicated that it was required in all three levels of their programs (elementary/primary, intermediate, secondary). While the majority (approximately 80 percent) of the physical education programs at the elementary level are taught by the regular classroom teacher, qualified physical educators conduct these courses at the intermediate level in 55 percent of the cases. At the secondary level the number has risen to 82 percent (ICHPER, Part I, 1969, pp. 1–2). These figures may be somewhat misleading in instances where the questionnaire was completed with ideal rather than actual structures in mind. The reality of specific situations might reduce the above percentages somewhat, given that qualified teachers are not always available in every community. This factor notwithstanding, it is clear that older children receive physical education instruction from better qualified professionals than do the elementary/primary aged children.

Early in the period under examination in this chapter, physical education programs based on the ethnocentric ethic (particularly the systems of Ling, Jahn, and Nachtegall) had a tremendous worldwide impact on the field as a whole. Significant elements of the "labor and defense" objectives remain a part of many programs, but contemporary curricula through the nations which were influenced by Western democratic countries in the 1800s and early 1900s reflect a strong emphasis on the egocentric ethic. The sport and game environment, based extensively on the virtue of effort, individual initiative, courage, and sportsmanship, and fired by the popularization of sport through the numerous well-publicized sports festivals, dominates the curriculum at the intermediate and secondary levels. The ICHPER questionnaire revealed that dance, some form of gymnastics, games of low organization, and aquatics dominated the curricular elements at the elementary/primary level. By the intermediate and secondary levels the game or team sport orientation was widespread. The most frequently named activities were soccer, football, basketball, volleyball, track and field (athletics), gymnastics, and swimming. In recent decades the tendency has been for secondary school programs to cover an expanded range of activities with a greater emphasis upon individual as opposed to team sports.

It was noted, in response to an inquiry as to the major problems impeding program development in physical education, that limited and poor-quality facilities and equipment are major constraining factors. This is particularly true among the emerging nations which have modelled themselves after the Western industrialized society with its highly differentiated organization. Education, and to a great extent physical education, has suffered due to restricted budgets. Many nations simply cannot afford large, expensive complexes that are used only six hours per day. In an effort to overcome this problem, more than 50 percent of the nations who responded to the ICHPER questionnaire noted that community facilities were being used for their physical education programs. This was especially true of aquatic centers. The community-school concept (related in many ways to the Danish folk school) appears to be a wave of the future (Shuttleworth, 1975).

The Professionalization of Physical Education

Between 1800 and the present time a wide range of changes have occurred within the field of physical education. Initially programs tended to emerge as a result of the enthusiasm, the concern, and the beliefs of a few key individuals. This fact notwithstanding, the underlying rationale and the structure of the programs themselves were significantly shaped by the social, economic, political, military, and intellectual developments within the various geographical areas, principally in Europe. Other nations of the world (China, Japan, Thailand, and so forth) had programs based upon their own cultural heritage, but with the exception of the martial arts of Japan and China, few had any impact on the emerging field.

Governments, initially concerned about the problems of "labor and defense," began to legislate compulsory participation in physical education (Table 3–1) and to provide the necessary funding to ensure facilities and staff for preparation programs for physical education teachers (Table 3–2). Today excellent programs, with a curriculum span of three to five years, are offered in most nations of the world, but recognized degree programs in the field are far from universally found (Bennett *et al.*, 1975, pp. 90–91). The ICHPER survey of 1967–1968 reveals a high level of similarity among the professional preparation programs. Most prospective physical educators are required to study teaching methods, hygiene, physiology/exercise physiology, anatomy, psychology, the history of physical education (education), and kinesiology. There is also a high level of consistency throughout the nations surveyed as to the activity areas studied (Table 3–3).

Beginning in 1889, when the first congress on physical education was held under the chairmanship of Baron Pierre de Coubertin, through to the present, thousands of national and international congresses or meetings have been held for the purpose of sharing ideas and new developments. Concurrently national councils, associations, or alliances of physical education have been created, the aims of which are to solidify the field, to lobby with a strong common voice at government level, to develop standards and codes of ethics, to regularize the annual or biennial meetings, and to act as a clearinghouse (often through a journal) for new information in the field of physical education. These councils and congresses have been instrumental in the generation of a scientific approach to the field. In an attempt to find answers to recurrent problems, research centers have sprung up around the world, with the Socialist countries in the vanguard. Centers such as the *Deutsche Hochschule für Körperkultur* in Leipzig, the *Deutsche Sporthochschule* in Köln, and the University of Turku Sports Research Unit in Finland often use a team or integrated approach in problem solving. Physical education researchers in the Western nations are more inclined to carry out specialized and individual research projects. Each approach has advantages but within the world of international sport competitions the integrated approach is currently proving to be a powerful tool.

Although not yet widespread, there have been a number of important experimental programs in physical education that may have a major impact on the field. Notable among these is the Vanves study. In 1950 the small satellite community of Paris was selected by the medical and physical education professions of France for a long-term experiment. The purpose of the study was to try to reduce the long periods of enforced inactivity which both groups believed to be detrimental to the well-being of the students. The proportion of time given to physical education was increased from 8 to 22 percent. After 22 years of research the data strongly indicate that the experimental group who receive the enriched physical education programs not only are more physically fit, they tend to do better on the French national academic examinations (*Sport in France*, [n.d.], pp. 9–11). The results of this and other research, coupled with present work in adapted and medical physical education, are creating many changes in the field. Specialization is becoming more prevalent; greater demands are being placed on the academic preparation of physical educators; new teaching methods are being generated based on improved communications media. Even the name is changing. Today programs in human kinetics, human movement studies, kinesiology, kinanthropology, leisure studies, replace the more traditional physical education/physical culture labels. But are the ethics underlying the programs really so different? Are the guiding principles, ideas, and base philosophies greatly changed? History has a way of revealing to us a high degree of similarity in our endeavors "to perfect the body, discipline the mind and mold the character of the young" (Leonard and Affleck, 1947, p. 17).

Table 3–2. Institution of Professional Programs for Physical Education Teachers

NATION	YEAR	NAME
Argentina	1901	Physical education teacher training program.
	1906	National Institute of Physical Education.
Austria	1871	Institute of Physical Education, University of Vienna.
Belgium	1908	Higher Institute of Physical Education, University of Ghent.
Bolivia	1914	Teachers trained in Ling gymnastics by De Genst and Ficher.
	1926	Division of Physical Education, University of La Paz.
	1931	Normal Superior Institute of Physical Education.
Brazil	1909	Physical Education School of the Police Force.
	1933	School of Physical Education of the Army.
	1937	School of Physical Education, University of Brazil.
	1939	National School of Physical Education and Sport.
Bulgaria	1944	Higher Institute of Physical Culture.
Chile	1906	Institute of Physical and Manual Education.
	1918	Institute of Physical and Technical Education, University of Chile.
Czechoslovakia	1891	Division of Physical Education, Charles University, Prague.
Denmark	1804	Military Gymnastics Institute.
	1808	Civil Gymnastic Institute (lasted for 6 years).
	1828	Normal School of Male Physical Education Teachers, Military Gymnastics Institute.
	1839	Above school extended to females.
Ecuador	1936	Institute of Physical Education, Central University, Quito.
England	1885	Training College for Teachers—became the Dartford Program of Physical Education for Women (Madame Bergman Österberg) in 1895.
	1908	South Western Polytechnic (Physical Education Program for Men).
Finland	1882	Institute of Physical Education, University of Helsinki.
Germany	1848	Central Training School for Teachers of Gymnastics.
	1851	Royal Central Institute of Gymnastics.
Greece	1939	National Academy of Physical Education.
Hungary	1925	Royal Hungarian College of Physical Education.
India	1920	College of Physical Education.
Israel	1944	One-year program in Tel Aviv (in 1960 this became the Physical Education Teachers' College at the Wingate Institute).
	1953	Wingate Institute of Physical Education.
Italy	1928	Academy of Physical Education.
Japan	1878	Gymnastic Training Center.
Mexico	1936	National School of Physical Education.
New Zealand	1948	School of Physical Education, University of Otago.
Norway	1870	Central Gymnastics Institute (became the State College of Physical Education in 1915).
Peru	1905	Teacher Normal School for Men (French Gymnastic System).
	1932	Carlos Carceres Alvarez National Institute of Physical Education.
Poland	1913	Faculty of Physical Education, University of Cracaw (lasted only one year but was reestablished in 1927).

Table 3–2. (Continued)

NATION	YEAR	NAME
	1919	Faculty of Physical Education, University of Poznan.
	1925	State Institute of Physical Education, Warsaw
Republic of China	1916	Nanking Teachers College.
Republic of South Africa	1921	Cape Town Training College.
Romania	1922	Institute of Physical Education, Bucharest.
Russia	1896	Physical Training Center (established by the Minister of Education for men and women, under the direction of P. F. Lesgaft).
Spain	1807	Royal Pestalozzian Institute of Madrid.
	1919	Central School of Gymnastics of Toledo.
Sweden	1814	Royal Central Gymnastics Institute.
U.S.S.R. (see Russia)	1919	P. F. Lesgaft Institute for Physical Culture and Sport, Leningrad.
	1920	State Institute for Physical Culture and Sport, Moscow.
United Arab Republic	1937	Division of Physical Education in the Higher Institute of Education, Cairo.
Venezuela	1936	League of Physical Education (later to become the National Institute of Physical Education).

Data for this table were obtained principally from Van Dalen and Bennett (1971) and from the Phi Epsilon Kappa Monographs 1–6 edited by William Johnson.

SPORT SINCE 1800

A consensus now exists that sport reflects the society in which it occurs, that people at play reveal significant things about themselves and their culture or civilization. This was as true in the past as it is now. The fundamental changes which have occurred in the world between 1800 and today have greatly affected sport, perhaps the most telling social mirror of a society. At the beginning of the nineteenth century, sport was emerging from medieval inhibitions, but it was still largely local and rural, informal and unstructured, lacking codification or mass direction, and rigidly based upon class distinctions. There were exceptions to this general classification, but sport was certainly not considered to be of great consequence in an era dominated by the transformation of Western civilization through the industrial and democratic revolutions. By the mid-1970s, however, sport was definitely a world concern. It was now international and urban, a highly organized and complex social phenomenon of epic proportions which was increasingly demonstrating its unique ability to harness and focus the attention and energies of millions of diverse citizens through its various spectacles. For most of the 890 million inhabitants of the world around 1800, sport was an occasional pastime or luxury; at present, sport intrudes far more consistently upon the lives of earth's five billion people. The present status of sport in the world is

Table 3–3. Frequency Rate of Activity and Theory Courses in Physical Education Teacher Training Programs

SUBJECT	FREQUENCY						TOTAL
	Primary		Intermediate		Secondary		
	Men	Women	Men	Women	Men	Women	
Activity							
Basketball	29	29	42	34	46	47	227
Athletics (Track and Field)	30	29	41	42	41	43	226
Swimming	31	33	35	35	47	40	221
Folk Dance	28	36	30	38	39	48	219
Apparatus	27	25	33	30	47	43	205
Gymnastics	29	33	25	30	34	39	190
Volleyball	24	22	33	30	36	36	181
Rhythmics	19	29	19	31	20	45	163
Camping	19	17	23	21	27	27	134
Soccer	30	1	39	1	45	1	117

Theory	
Methods (Pedagogy)	48
Hygiene, First Aid and Diet	42
Physiology (and Physiology of Exercise)	37
Anatomy	35
Psychology (including Child and Educational Psychology)	32
History of Physical Education (and Education)	31
Kinesiology and Biomechanics	27
Practice Teaching	16
Organization and Administration of Physical Education	15
Tests and Measurements (including Statistics)	13

These data are summarized and modified from the International Council on Health, Physical Education and Recreation, *Teacher Training for Physical Education*, Questionnaire Report, Part II, 1967–68 (Washington: ICHPER, n.d.), pp. 107–10. A total of 63 countries responded to the activities questionnaire and 44 to the theoretical courses questionnaire.

indeed awesome, and its impressive dimensions may be discerned in the arts and sciences, in education, politics, religion and elsewhere. Although sport has an enduring pedigree since the earliest civilizations, it can be fairly argued that the phenomenon of "modern sport" was born of the Industrial Revolution and developed mainly in the nineteenth and twentieth centuries (Goulstone, 1974).

Since the Industrial Revolution had its origins and most significant early developments in Britain, the United Kingdom seems a logical starting point for any investigation of modern sport. England has been termed "The Mother of Sport," but as Arlott and Daley have pointed out:

There is a tendency to suggest that England invented a number of games, but that is not strictly true . . . England's contribution to sports is that it developed many of them to a high standard and formulated them so that they might be played competitively in orderly fashion. (1968, p. 13)

Figure 3–6. Playground games in a Peking, China, junior high school.

Actually, the popularity of Scottish "formulas" such as golf, curling, and even Highland Games around the world suggests that the term "Britain" may be more appropriate than "England" (Fittis, 1891). According to the late H.A. Harris, consideration of the place of sport in modern society need begin only at the point where games became national; that depended upon agreement throughout the country on a code of rules for each game. In his view: "In this development, Britain led the world" (Ueberhorst, 1972, p. 136). McIntosh had agreed with such sentiments earlier and added another vital factor:

> The panorama of World Sport in the middle of the twentieth century shows games and sports from many different countries of origin . . . . Nevertheless, the majority of sports in current practice, and the very great majority of the more popular, were exported from Britain. (1963, p. 80)

In essence, therefore, the great British contributions to sport in the nineteenth century concerned the transformation to orderliness, the development of organizations, and export to other lands. Such elements were not completely absent beforehand — one can find organized sport on the Britain pattern outside of the United Kingdom in the eighteenth century, for example — but the comprehensive nature of British contributions during this period is undeniable. They were part of historical processes for which it is notoriously difficult to establish exact reference points (when did the Industrial Revolution "begin," or the Middle Ages "end"?) but whose main force was experienced in the nineteenth century.

One particular sport provides a pertinent example here. The word "football" connotes Association football (or soccer) in most countries as the most popular team ball-sport in the world today, but in New Zealand, South Africa, or Wales, "football" really represents rugby football, and in North America, American and Canadian football are the dominant forms. Gaelic football, Australian Rules football and Rugby League football reflect significant cultural differences, also. Varieties of football have been noted since earliest times, in Ancient China and Rome, for example, and it was a violent pastime for centuries in medieval Europe. As early as 1586, exploring British seamen and Eskimos took part in the "first recorded international football match" (Morison, 1971, p. 597), and subsequent contests of sorts followed in the New World during the seventeenth and eighteenth centuries. Yet it was in Britain during the nineteenth century, mainly through experimentation and trial in the public schools, that the two major forms of modern football, rugby and soccer, developed. The Football Association (Soccer) was formed in 1863 and the Rugby Union in 1871. Although the American universities of Princeton and Rutgers played each other in a game closely resembling soccer in 1869, and a team of Old Etonians voyaged to compete against Yale in a similar contest four years later, American football and Canadian football are actually more akin to rugby and stemmed largely from another intercollegiate (and international) contest between Harvard and McGill universities in 1874. All these forms of football now have millions of devotees in all five continents (although soccer remains the only form in Olympic competition) (Marples, 1954).

Therefore, although it may be inaccurate to describe Britain as the cradle of sport, it may be regarded as the main crucible in which modern sport was forged for mass production and worldwide distribution. Every sport has its own story of development and inherent peculiarities; nevertheless, the pattern mentioned for football was repeated so often that experts have readily acknowledged the trend. Sports with debatable origins and pedigree — from badminton, billiards, and boxing to cricket, croquet, and curling; from golf and field hockey and football to lawn bowling and squash; table tennis, tennis, and water polo, among others — largely established their place in the modern world via Britain through a formative Georgian, Victorian, or Edwardian experience. The Industrial Revolution created irrevocable social changes which in turn served to mold modern sport, and export was easily accommodated through the international network of Empire (now Commonwealth).

The difficulty of determining starting points for processes of change has already been mentioned, and the "export" of sport is a case in point. Sports are diffused by people. In the evolution of modern sport, explorers preceded the colonists and made the first social contacts in new lands. After settlement, these territories were often maintained or expanded by military means, and soldiers joined merchants, missionaries, and other settlers in leisure-time pursuits. The off-duty British garrison and its environs around the globe often became a social center, and there sport began to develop. Evidence is plentiful from many countries (see, for example, the analysis of the impact of the British military garrisons on sport in Canada, in Lindsay, 1969, pp. 351-64), but the following example from India will suffice to illustrate the arrogance, panache, and joie de vivre of the international British ruling and sporting elite:

> The great pastime of the British in India was sport. A love of cricket, tennis, squash and field hockey would be, with the English language, the most enduring heritage they would eventually leave behind. Golf was introduced in Calcutta in 1829, thirty years before it reached New York, and the world's highest course was laid out in the Himalayas at 11,000 feet. No golf bag was considered more elegant on those courses than one made of an elephant's penis — providing, of course, that its owner had shot the beast himself.
>
> Every major city had its hunt, its hounds imported from England. Regularly its members went galloping off in their pink coats and white breeches chasing over the hot and dusty plains after the best substitute India offered for a fox — a jackal. The most dangerous sport was pigsticking, riding down wild boar with steel-tipped wooden lances. The foolhardy, it was claimed, even went after jackals, panthers and, on occasion, a tiger that way. The Indian national game, polo, was avidly taken up by the British and became a British institution.

The indication that a love of sport, besides the English language, was "the most enduring heritage" of the British is obviously of significant import (Collins and Lapierre, 1975, p. 15). Most people might have imagined it to be parliamentary government, educational or legal systems, or even the most pragmatic legacy of builders and engineers. Consistent civilian immigration to the various colonies in succeeding years, allied with gradual military reductions as these colonies progressed toward nationhood, further ensured the dynamic growth of nineteenth-century sport. Old familiar sports became a means of enabling immigrants to retain their old world identity in a strange new environment; later on in the century the development of new sports in that environment (often deliberate adaptations of other familiar activities) contributed toward the assimilation process, too, as immigrants and their descendants eventually became citizens of their adopted country.

Before attempting to discuss in some detail the "irrevocable social changes" which served to create modern sport, we might note further examples of the "dynamic growth" of sport at that time. Harris has made the point that in three decades after 1855.

. . .practically every sport of importance in the modern world had been organized in Britain with an accepted code of rules, the first international matches had been played, and — a matter of great social significance — women had begun to take part in games. (Ueberhorst, 1972, p. 177)

These points were also substantiated by McIntosh (1963) and well-illustrated by appropriate tables. Table 3-4 depicted here is a partial further elaboration, giving dates of the formation of sports governing bodies in a few countries.

Despite the incompleteness of Table 3-4 it does bear out the prominent status of Britain as a pioneer of modern sport, while at the same

Table 3-4. Dates of the Formation of Sports Governing Bodies in Selected Countries

SPORT	AUSTRALIA	GREAT BRITAIN	CANADA	GERMANY
Archery	1948	1861	c. 1932	
Association Football	1962	1863	1912	1900
Athletics	1927	1880	1889	1898
Badminton	1935	1893	1921	
Baseball			1920[4]	
Basketball		1936	1922	
Boxing		1880	1969[8]	
Cricket	1905	1788	1911	
Curling		1838[10]	1935	
Cycling	1901[11]	1878	1894	1884
Equestrianism		1923	1930s	
Fencing	1947	1898[12]	1914	
Field Hockey		1886	1962	
Football (Amer./Can.)			1882	
Golf	1898	1754	c. 1895	
Gymnastics		1890	1899	
Horse Racing	1842	c. 1750	1926	
Ice Hockey		1914	1886	
Indoor Bowling		1961	1907	
Lacrosse		1880	1867	
Lawn Bowling	1911	1892	1927	
Lawn Tennis	1904	1888	1890	1902
Rowing		1879	1880	1883
Rugby Football	1875[17]	1871	1929	
Shooting	1887	1860	c. 1869	
Skating		1879	1887?	1888
Skiing		1903	1921	1904
Swimming	1909	1869	1909	1886
Table Tennis	1937	1927	1930s	
Volleyball		1955	1953	

[1] Dates for the formation of sports governing bodies in the U.S.S.R. are not available; dates given here are for the first national championships (All-Union) following the 1917 Revolution (Riordan, 1976).
[2] Prerevolution Russia; these are clubs and societies, not national organizations.
[3] National Association of Amateur Athletes of America.
[4] Amateur.
[5] National League was formed in 1876.
[6] Professional.
[7] Women; the men's championship started in 1924.
[8] Part of the AAU of C since c. 1920.

time indicating some significant exceptions to this role. Obviously other "important" and popular sports were developed outside of Britain, such as the martial arts of the Far East and skiing from Scandinavia. In fact, some sports were specifically developed away from British precedents and were utilized in a spirit of emergent nationalism, such as ice hockey and lacrosse in Canada, and baseball and American football in the United States. These and other, similarly developed sports, like basketball and volleyball were in turn exported to Britain and other countries. (Arlott, 1975; Boyle, 1963; Howell and Howell, 1969; Menke, 1953; Weaver, 1968).

Table 3-4. (Continued)

SPORT	NEW ZEALAND	SWEDEN	U.S.A.	U.S.S.R.[1]	RUSSIA[2]
Archery	1943		1879	1964	1879
Association Football	1890	1904	1913	1922	1894
Athletics	1887	1895	1879[3]	1922	1886
Badminton	1927		1936	1963	
Baseball			1871[5]		
Basketball	1946		1898[6]	1923[7]	
Boxing	1902			1937[9]	1895
Cricket	1894		1878		1868
Curling	1873	1916	1867		
Cycling	1932	1900	1880	1923	1880
Equestrianism	1950s				
Fencing	1937		1891	1928	1857
Field Hockey	1902		1922	1935[13]	
Football (Amer./Can.)			1876[14]		
Golf	1910		1894		
Gymnastics	1956			1928	1863
Horse Racing	1876?		1894	1938	1826
Ice Hockey	1963		1896	1947	1898
Indoor Bowling	1949		1875		
Lacrosse			1879		
Lawn Bowling	1886		1937		
Lawn Tennis	1886	1906	1881	1924	1860[15]
Rowing	1887	1904	1872	1913[16]	
Rugby Football	1892			1968	
Shooting	1924		1871	1924	c. 1800
Skating	1937	1904	1888	1918	1864
Skiing	1933	1908	1904	1919	1895
Swimming	1890	1904	1878	1921	1834
Table Tennis	1933		1930	1951	
Volleyball			1928	1933	

[9] Not the date of an All-Union championship; Morton (1963, p. 130) states that there was a call for an All-Union team in this year.
[10] Royal Caledonian Club.
[11] Professional.
[12] *Oxford Companion to Sports and Games* cites 1902.
[13] Women; the men's championship started in 1971.
[14] Intercollegiate.
[15] Date given by Riordan; a pre-Wingate form of tennis played in England in the 1860's, and Russia-England sports contacts were common during this period.
[16] First Russian Olympiad included rowing (Morton, 1963, p. 160).
[17] South Australia RFU, predecessor to the Australian RFU.

Another identifiable aspect from Table 3-4 is the importance of the second half of the nineteenth century in modern sports. When historians are in doubt regarding the suitable naming of an era or period under investigation, it frequently is referred to as a time of "transition." Perhaps such a label could be applied to the first half of the nineteenth century, when various activities were being brought together in the shape of modern sport. Then as many experts have noted, the latter part of the century witnessed a sports explosion, described most often under the term "the rise in sports." The nineteenth century has often been depicted as "the age of progress," mainly because of the advance of technology, and the progress of sport in its last three or four decades was phenomenal. Then the international foundation was truly laid for the gigantic proportions of sport today (Arlott and Daley, 1968; Betts, 1974; Harris, 1975; McIntosh, 1963).

Much of this progress was due to the inventions of the period. The steamboat (1788), railway (1830), bicycle (1839), vulcanized rubber (1841), pneumatic tire (1889), steam turbine and motor car (1884-1885) all improved transportation and thus facilitated greater social contact and mobility. Such technology aided the usual development of individual sport clubs, fostering interclub competition, and then interregional sporting contacts, the formation of national sports governing bodies, and an increase in international sport bodies and competition. Indeed, the tendency for inventions of utilitarian purpose being put to recreational use was very evident in the nineteenth century. Thus, soon after they were available, bicycles and cars became recreational vehicles and were raced in sport competition (and even the drivers of steam boats and railway engines were not immune from this urge at times!). This pattern was of course continued in the twentieth century with, for example, the appearance of the airplane (1905, and the jet engine in 1939), and the subsequent common use of flying as a means of transport and/or sport. New sports were born of the technological explosion also. The first human parachute drop was made by Jacques Garnerin on October 22, 1797, from a hydrogen balloon at about 3,000 feet. Since then we have progressed through stages to the current popular sport of skydiving from airplanes. The perfection of the aqualung in 1943 "put man back into the sea with all the freedom of a fish" and so increased his mobility and pleasure in another dimension. Thus, within a relatively short space of time, the somewhat confined play-forms of man within his environment at the dawn of the nineteenth century were dramatically transformed, through inventive genius, into the numerous new sports of men and women on land, on sea, and in the air. So these products of the modern world at play — seen in scuba diving, moto-cross, snowmobiling, water skiing, and so on — have taken their place besides the older, traditional sports (London: *The Sunday Times*, 1970).

All sport, old and new, was inevitably affected also by other inventions which eventually became essential elements within modern society. Such developments as the steam press (1814), camera (1826), dynamo/ transformer (1831), electric telegraph (1837-1839), typewriter (1873), gramophone/telephone (1876), electric lamp (1881), cinematograph (1895), and radio (1901) were representative of profound changes which contributed to the evolution of modern sport. Again, the process was continuous, until a combination of scientific endeavors led in the 1930's, to the appearance of television — the medium which has altered contemporary social habits, sport included, as much as any other. Among the many and perhaps obvious examples which could be given to illustrate the consistent interaction between invention and sport, the fact that "the first flickering, commercial motion picture was a four-minute film of a boxing match shown in New York City in 1895," and that the first test of Marconi's wireless was to report on an international yacht race in 1899, are both interesting landmarks (Bennett et al., 1975, p. 249). The relationship between sport and technology in the modern world is a vast and complex one, and readers are therefore encouraged to refer to the specialized, in-depth studies of this topic (Betts, 1951; Jobling, 1970).

One very identifiable aspect of the developments referred to has been the inexorable emergence of a huge, international mass-production recreation-and-sport industry, replete with specialized paraphernalia, catering to the ever-expanding leisure market (Vickerman, 1975). The process of urbanization was an integral feature of the development of this industry. Cities have existed for thousands of years but only recently have they accommodated a significant proportion of the world's population. In 1800, urban dwellers in cities of 20,000 or more made up only 2.4 percent of the world total by 1950 this percentage had increased ninefold. The change has been particularly dramatic in Western societies, again as an inescapable facet of the Industrial Revolution (Girouard, 1985). For example, today no less than three-quarters of Americans are estimated to live in places officially defined as urban (DeFleur, et al., 1973, p. 279). To a very large extent, therefore, modern sport is urban sport. The city has become the natural nerve center of the international sport complex, the home of the masses of participants and spectators, and the site of huge stadia and other facilities.

When Joseph Strutt produced his comprehensive *The Sports and Pastimes of the People of England in 1801,* Book III was entitled, "Pastimes Usually Exercised in Towns or Cities, or Places Adjoining to Them." Books I and II were devoted to Rural Exercises "by Persons of Rank" and "Generally Practised," indicating the important class distinction. At that time the "urban" content of Book III was devoted mainly to the tournament, drama plays, minstrels, and dancing, and some cruel animal sports (bull baiting and cock fighting). By the end of the nineteenth century the literature reflected the changes which had occurred in sport since Strutt's single-handed contribution. This from the preface to *The Encyclopaedia of Sport,* published in 1897, for example, is significant:

> Lovers of Sport cannot complain that in recent years their interests have been neglected by English publishers; but, although books devoted to the consideration of Sport continue to multiply apace, no serious effort has been made to produce a national Encyclopaedia of Sport.
>
> Many editions of Blaine's *Encyclopaedia of Rural Sports,* which first appeared in 1840, were published down to 1870. Blaine announced that he proposed to describe "the progress of each sport to its present state of perfection," and he acquitted himself creditably. The book was very useful in its day, but its day is past.
>
> Football was so slightly regarded when Blaine's work appeared that he actually makes no mention of a game which is now among the most popular of our recreations. Some sports, Cricket for example, have been completely revolutionized during the last fifty years; and others, Badger-baiting and the like, described by Blaine, have disappeared from the catalogue of national amusements, and are here relegated to the article on Obsolete Sport. (Suffolk and Berkshire et al, 1897)

In their attempt to cover the whole range of sport, the editors enlisted the services of "the leading authorities on every branch of sport" as contributors. The hunting connotation lingered on in obvious fashion — chronologically the Encyclopaedia proceeds from "Aardvark" to "Zebra"! — with such references as "Aurochs," "Coursing," "Pig-sticking," "Taxidermy." and "Woodcock". But the work also had sections on the "America Cup," "Badminton," "Croquet," "Cycle-Racing," "Football" (four classifications), "Lacrosse," "Lawn Tennis" (and "Tennis"), "Ski," and "Yachting," among other innovations not touched upon by the authors of previous surveys of sport. Coming forward to contemporary sport literature, now quite gigantic in its scope (this whole chapter could be devoted to "Sport and Literature since 1800" and remain an inadequate survey), it is certain that Strutt's classification, understandable in 1801, would require radical revision today. To stay with encyclopedias as an example, not only have there been a large number of general encyclopedias of sport produced in the twentieth century, but the explosion of sport literature in more recent years has included a proliferation of highly specific encyclopedic tomes undreamed of by our sporting ancestors — for example, *The Encyclopaedia of Football Drills* (1954). *The Encyclopaedic Dictionary of Mountaineering* (1969), or *The United States Lawn Tennis Association Official Encyclopaedia of Tennis* (1972). Over the years, too, in encyclopedias of general knowledge the space devoted to sport has steadily increased. A recent significant literary landmark in sport history was the addition of sport to the famous "Oxford Companion" cultural series, when *The Oxford Companion to Sports and Games* was published in 1975. The brief description on the jacket is illuminating:

> 1152 pages and over 5000 alphabetical entries — 100 expert contributors — Main entries for more than 200 active sports and games played throughout the world — Biographies of leading players and performers — individual entries for important sports events, clubs, organizations and venues — 200 line drawings and diagrams of playing surfaces — 400 action photographs. (Arlott, 1975)

Impressive as this sounds, editor Arlott points out in the preface that blood sports were excluded, as well as board and table games, and most street, folk, and children's games. Yet coursing was included "since the Waterloo Cup is a national Competition"; and bullfighting also "because it is likely to be watched — as a public spectacle or on television or film — by people who wish to be informed about it." Clearly, if one were now allowed only two books to place in a time capsule for posterity to understand the evolution of sport in the nineteenth century and twentieth centuries, Strutt's individual masterpiece of 1801 and Arlott's compilation of 1975 might well provide the most thoughtful comparison. Side by side, they vividly represent two different worlds of sport; pre- and post-Industrial Revolution. (And if a third book were allowed, *"The Encyclopedia of Sport* of 1897 would provide a useful perspective of the transitional process at approximately the midway point.)

Although *homo ludens* may now be classified as mainly an urban species, especially in the mass assemblies, people's habitat has been dramatically extended to worldwide proportions. The technology of the modern world, allied with increased affluence and leisure time, has enabled its citizens to "sport" anywhere. Hence the world can now be viewed as an international sporting playground, the raison d etre for the "mass-production recreation-and-sport industry" referred to earlier. Tourists-at-play can now cross oceans and continents with ease to indulge their physical pleasures: surfing at Hawaii, skiing in Austria, trout fishing on New Zealand lakes, or whatever. Others involved in more "serious" sport can do likewise as individuals or teams crisscross the world to compete. Sheer distance is no longer a deterrent for any kind of sport, in a world which seems to qualify in so many ways as Shangri-la of sporting opportunity.

Yet this is to paint too rosy a picture, for this international playground as it developed has been the scene of many conflicts, also. If sport is a constant of history, so too is war. And the rise in sophisticated technology since 1800 has been reflected in the terrible conflagrations and pogroms which have occurred since then. Two global conflicts have been labeled as "World Wars," and a future nuclear holocaust, should it occur as

World War III, is the ultimate horror. Throughout history mankind at play has often practiced for war, just as behavior in battle has often revealed gamelike qualities (Huizinga, 1955, pp. 89-118). For some, sport is the panacea, the viable alternative to war; for others, sport contributes significantly to aggression, prejudice, and eventual conflict.

Baron Pierre de Coubertin (1863-1937), whose lifetime spanned 37 years of each century in our period, was convinced that sport could be used to increase goodwill among the nations of the world (as well as invigorate his own country of France). This belief led him to create the largest sports festival ever, the modern Olympic Games. It may also be regarded as the greatest experiment in sport and physical education ever conducted, for ironically Coubertin's aim was to use the Olympic Games in order to popularize on an international level, the educational role of sport — "to ennoble and strengthen sports, in order to assure their independence and duration and thus to set them better to fill the educational role which devolves upon them in the modern world" (Killanin and Rodda, 1976, p. 139). Underlying Coubertin's concept of "pedagogical sport" was his philosophy of Olympism, a philosophy that embraced four essential factors: (a) amateurism, (b) the development of health and (moral) character, (c) international sport competition as instrumental toward peace, and (d) sport as an integral part of culture.

Coubertin was influenced by two main sources: The Olympic Games of Ancient Greece, and the contemporary ideal of "Muscular Christianity" in England, epitomized in Thomas Hughes' fictional novel *Tom Brown's Schooldays* (1857). Coubertin interpreted these ancient and modern forms of athleticism as significant contributions to the glory of Ancient Greece and the foundation of the British Empire. Despite some opposition, his grandiose dream was realized in Paris on June 23, 1894, when 79 delegates from twelve countries unanimously endorsed a modern cycle of Olympic Games. This must rank as probably the most important single act in the history of sport; this vote subsequently touched "the lives of millions of people . . . and changed the face of competitive sport for ensuing generations" (Leiper, 1976, p. 1). Certainly Olympic celebration has dominated sport in the modern era (Chester, 1975; Coote, 1972; Kamper, 1975; Kieran and Daley, 1973; Killanin and Rodda, 1976; Leiper, 1976; MacAloon, 1981).

The development of the modern Olympics has been somewhat erratic (see Table 3-5) and plagued by political problems. Until the 1964 Tokyo Games, the steady growth in the number of nations and athletes participating faltered each time the Games were held outside Europe. From the 295 athletes representing 13 nations who took part in the first modern Olympic Games in 1896 at Athens, the numbers increased to nearly 8,000 athletes representing 123 nations at Munich in 1972. There were 9 sports with 42 events in 1896, compared with 21 sports and 193 events at the 1972 Games. But the Munich Olympics will be forever remembered for the invasion of the Olympic Village by Palestinian terrorists, who held Israeli athletes hostage and demanded the release of 200 Arab political prisoners. By next day, 11 Israeli athletes and coaches had been assassinated, and 5 of the terrorists and a West German policeman were slain in a shootout at the local airport. Despite this tragedy, the Games went on, albeit a day behind schedule. Less awful, but still real as problems for the Olympic Movement, were the political and financial problems of the 1976 Montreal Games, and the boycotts of the 1980 Moscow Games and the 1984 Los Angeles Games. The International Olympic Committee (IOC), as arbiter of the modern Olympic Games in a troubled world, faces the biggest challenge in modern sport (Hoberman, 1984).

It would seem fitting that the modern Olympics should begin in Greece, in a stadium built over an athletic site of antiquity; and that the four-year period between the celebration of the Games should be called an Olympiad in the ancient Greek fashion. There were other similarities, too, such as the procession of athletes into the stadium. But there were important differences as well, as might be expected in such a revival across centuries. Coubertin's main innovations were: the Olympic Motto (borrowed from Didon) of Citius, Altius, Fortius! meaning "Ever faster, higher, stronger!"; the Olympic flag (five rings of blue, yellow, black, green and red on a white background representing all continents and nations); and the modern Olympic Oath, first used at the 1920 Games in Antwerp. The Olympic Torch Relay was initiated by Carl Diem for the 1936 Berlin Games; and the Olympic Village evolved from the Games of 1924 (Paris), 1928 (Amsterdam), and 1932 (Los Angeles), although such a facility was not mandatory in Olympic rules until 1949. By the year 1921 these rules necessarily included comprehensive details regarding the opening and closing ceremonies. These innovations can be regarded, by and large, as the "symbols and traditions of Olympism" (Leiper, 1976, pp. 53-65). Other aspects of the modern Olympic Games which differed from their ancient pedigree, although perhaps less symbolic, had profound repercussions in the modern world.

The steadfast location at Olympia of the ancient Games was a unifying factor within Greek civilization; yet the site of the modern Olympics has been rotated among the major cities of the world. Diplomacy made this practice seem desirable and modern technology rendered it easily possible. However, there were attempts to locate them permanently in various modern sites, and voices are now being raised anew for a permanent center for the celebration of the modern Olympic Games, in light of the many problems encountered to date.

Table 3-5. Dates, Places, and Numbers of Olympic Games (Summer)

OLYMPIAD NUMBER	OLYMPIAD DATES	OLYMPIC GAMES NUMBER	OLYMPIC GAMES DATES	PLACE	NUMBER OF COUNTRIES	NUMBER OF ATHLETES Men	Women
I	Jan. 1, 1896-Dec. 31, 1899	1	Apr. 6,-Apr. 15, 1896	Athens, Greece	1 3	295	
II	Jan. 1, 1900-Dec. 31, 1903	2	May 15,-Oct. 28, 1900	Paris, France	2 1	1,066	8
III	Jan. 1, 1904-Dec. 31, 1907	3	July 1.-Oct. 29, 1904	St. Louis, U.S.A.	2 1	548	8
IV	Jan. 1, 1908-Dec. 31, 1911	4	Aug. 27,-Oct. 29, 1908	London, England	2 2	1,998	36
V	Jan. 1, 1912-Dec. 31, 1915	5	May 5,-July 22, 1912	Stockholm, Sweden	2 8	2,447	57
VI	Jan. 1, 1916-Dec. 31, 1919	Not celebrated — granted to Berlin					
VII	Jan. 1, 1920-Dec. 31, 1923	6	Apr. 20,-Sept. 12, 1920	Antwerp, Belgium	2 9	2,527	64
VIII	Jan. 1, 1924-Dec. 31, 1927	7	May 3,-July 27, 1924	Paris, France	4 4	2,939	136
IX	Jan. 1, 1928-Dec. 31, 1931	8	July 28,-Aug. 12, 1928	Amsterdam, Holland	4 6	2,708	263
X	Jan. 1, 1932-Dec. 31, 1935	9	July 31,-Aug. 7, 1932	Los Angeles, U.S.A.	3 8	1,296	35
XI	Jan. 1, 1936-Dec. 31, 1939	10	Aug. 1,-Aug. 16, 1936	Berlin, Germany	4 9	3,652	328
XII	Jan. 1, 1940-Dec. 31, 1943	Not celebrated — granted to Tokyo, then to Helsinki					
XIII	Jan. 1, 1944-Dec. 31, 1947	Not celebrated — granted to London					
XIV	Jan. 1, 1948-Dec. 31, 1951	11	July 29-Aug. 14, 1948	London, England	5 8	3,677	385
XV	Jan. 1, 1952-Dec. 31, 1955	12	July 19,-Aug. 3, 1952	Helsinki, Finland	6 9	5,349	518
XVI	Jan. 1, 1956-Dec. 31, 1959	13	Nov. 22,-Dec. 8, 1956	Melbourne, Australia	6 7	2,813	371
			June 10,-June 17, 1956	Stockholm, Sweden (equestrian only)	2 9	145	13
XVII	Jan. 1, 1960-Dec. 31, 1963	14	Aug. 25,-Sept. 11, 1960	Rome, Italy	8 4	4,859	537
XVIII	Jan. 1, 1964-Dec. 31, 1967	15	Oct. 10,-Oct. 24, 1964	Tokyo, Japan	9 4	4,854	732
XIX	Jan. 1, 1968-Dec. 31, 1971	16	Oct. 12,-Oct. 27, 1968	Mexico City, Mexico	1 2 5	5,782	844
XX	Jan. 1, 1972-Dec. 31, 1975	17	Aug. 26,-Sept. 10, 1972	Munich, Germany	1 2 1	6,659	1,171
XXI	Jan. 1, 1976-Dec. 31, 1979	18	July 17,-Aug. 1, 1976	Montreal, Canada	1 2 8	5,845	1,470
XXII	July 19 - Aug. 3, 1980	19	July 19,-Aug. 3, 1980	Moscow, USSR	8 1	4,265	1,088
XIII	July 28 - Aug. 12, 1984	20	July 28,-Aug. 12, 1984	Los Angeles	1 4 0	(7,800)	

Most scholars agree that women were excluded from participation in the ancient Olympic Games, but they have competed with outstanding success on a regular and increasing basis in the modern Olympics since 1900. This fact reflects the evolving status of women in the modern world, particularly in Western industrialized societies, where their role is obviously very different from that in ancient Greece; women have been gradually emancipated during the nineteenth and twentieth centuries from their expected role as admiring spectators to participants in their own right.

The Olympics of antiquity were based upon individual competition, whereas the modern Olympics include team sports: football (soccer) since 1900; basketball in 1904 as a demonstration sport, then as an integral competition since 1936; field hockey since 1908 (except for the 1912 and 1924 Games); water polo since 1900; and volleyball since 1964. Field handball was included in the 1936 Olympics, and indoor handball since 1972. In addition, many of the individual sports have introduced team events over the years (Kamper, 1975).

The most radical departure of all from ancient Olympic tradition, of course, was the establishment of the modern Winter Olympic Games, the first of which were held at Chamonix, France, in 1924. These have also steadily grown since their inception, again faltering only when taken outside Europe to the United States in 1932 and to a lesser extent in 1960. At Chamonix in 1924, 291 men and 13 women from 16 nations participated, whereas 1,065 men and 228 women from 37 nations were competitors in 1968 in the Xth Winter Olympics at Grenoble (also in France). Skiing, skating, bobsledding, tobogganing, and ice hockey are the sports of the Winter Olympics, and "ice hockey and skiing, particularly, have had a long history of difficulties with the application of the amateur def-

Table 3-6. Olympic Winter Games

OLYMPIC GAMES NUMBER	OLYMPIC GAMES DATES	PLACE	NUMBER OF COUNTRIES	NUMBER OF ATHLETES	
				Men	Women
1	Jan. 25,-Feb. 5, 1924	Chamonix, France	16	291	13
2	Feb. 11,-Feb. 19, 1928	St. Moritz, Switzerland	25	336	27
3	Feb. 4,-Feb. 13, 1932	Lake Placid, U.S.A.	17	257	21
4	Feb. 6,-Feb. 16, 1926	Garmisch-Partenkirchen, Germany	28	675	81
	Games of 1940 and 1944 not celebrated				
5	Jan. 30,-Feb. 9, 1948	St. Moritz, Switzerland	28	801	77
6	Feb. 14,-Feb. 25, 1952	Oslo, Norway	30	624	108
7	Jan. 16,-Feb. 5, 1956	Cortina d'Ampezzo, Italy	32	791	132
8	Feb. 18,-Feb. 28, 1960	Squaw Valley, U.S.A.	30	502	146
9	Jan. 29,-Feb. 9, 1964	Innsbruck, Austria	36	758	175
10	Feb. 6,-Feb. 18, 1968	Grenoble, France	37	1,065	228
11	Feb. 3,-Feb. 13, 1972	Sapporo, Japan	35	910	215
12	Feb. 4,-Feb. 15, 1976	Innsbruck, Austria	37	1,600 men and women	
13	Feb. 14,-Feb. 23, 1980	Lake Placid, U.S.A.	37	833	234
14	Feb. 7,-Feb. 19, 1984	Sarafero, Yugoslavia	49	1,181	409

inition to individual performers and sometimes to whole teams'' (Leiper, 1976, p. 13).

At this point perhaps it should be pointed out that Coubertin's Olympic concept was not entirely an original one in the modern world. Early in the seventeenth century, for example, Robert Dover established his "Olympick Games" in the Cotswolds; and it seems that other athletic festivals in seventeenth-century England were termed as "Olympics." The traditional Highland Games of Scotland, too, were similar in many respects, although E.N. Gardiner preferred to compare them to Homeric sports: "The nearest parallel to them is to be found in the sports of the Highland Clans, but it is probable that, if we knew more, other parallels might be found wherever a similar state of society has existed" (Gardiner, 1967, p. 27). During the nineteenth century there were several "Olympic" counterparts before Coubertin's brainchild. From 1849, for more than forty years, "Olympic Games" were staged by a Dr. W. P. Brookes near the town of Wenlock, in Shropshire, England. J. Astley Cooper was the promoter of a scheme for an "Anglo-Saxon Olympiad" during the 1890's. In Greece itself, one Evangelios Lappas offered the King of Greece an endowment "for the restoration of the Olympic Games, to be celebrated every four years, following the precepts of the ancient Greeks, our ancestors". Subsequently such Games were held in Greece irregularly but with some success, in 1859, 1870, 1875 and 1888 (Mandell, 1976, pp. 26-35; Redmond, 1981).

Strangely, one of the most significant of the nineteenth-century pre-Coubertin Olympics took place far away from Europe, and before the efforts of Brookes and Lappas, in British North America. In 1844 an "Olympic Games" meeting was held in Montreal. Scottish associations had held their versions of the traditional Highland Games in parts of North America before 1844 (Redmond, 1982, pp. 159-167) but these Montreal Olympics were certainly an auspicious occasion. They extended over two days with 29 events on the program, including 5 lacrosse matches. They were given unprecedented patronage and support by the Governor-General and the city corporation. Two authorities were certainly not reticent in their recent evaluation of the modern significance of these Montreal Olympic Games of 1884, an occasion they also termed "an epoch-making event":

> Neither in Britain nor in the United States had anything quite like these games yet been held. Toronto, a few years earlier, had held a number of field days; so had some American cities. But in their size, organization, variety, and social and cultural diversity, Montreal's Olympics were unique; on the basis of them Montreal has a strong claim to be considered one of the birthplaces of modern organized sport. (Wise and Fisher, 1974, p. 13).

This claim is greatly strengthened by additional consideration of Montreal as "the Cradle of Canadian Sport," since it was also a focal point for significant developments in such sports as curling, ice hockey, football, and lacrosse during the nineteenth century, as well as a fertile ground for the formation of local, provincial, and national sports organizations (Wise and Fisher, 1974, pp. 13-25).

Brief tribute should be paid to these Scottish Highland Games as one of the lasting international highlights in the growth of sport since 1800. They continue to be held, with great pageantry, in literally hundreds of places around the world outside of their birthplaces (and of course within Scotland itself), especially in Canada, Australia, New Zealand, and South Africa. But they are also still celebrated with great enthusiasm in many parts of the United States, i.e., outside of what was the British Empire (Webster, 1973). A letter from reader J.L. Lea in *The Canadian* of January 3, 1976 (p. 27), complimented this Scottish "World festival," while decrying the "huge debt" and fanfare surrounding the Montreal Olympic Games of 1976. While comparisons may be odious at times, any survey of world sport since 1800 would be remiss if it did not include reference to the spectacular international success enjoyed by the Scottish Highland Games, a phenomenon which shows no sign of decline at present (Donaldson, 1986).

Since the first "Great International Caledonian Games" were held in New York City in 1867 and the Olympic Games began at Athens in 1896, however, there has been a steady growth of what might be termed other "major international multi-sport events," involving several sports and many countries. This development has been of the most significant features of twentieth-century sport. Most of these modern sport festivals are organized along geographical/regional lines, but some have racial or religious connotations, and still others are for "special populations" such as students or disabled persons.

The first of the regional Games after the inauguration of the modern Olympics were the Far Eastern Championship Games. The charter members, China, Japan, and the Philippines, assited by the Young Men's Christian Association (YMCA), organized the first competition in 1913. Siam (Thailand) and Malaya also participated the following year and these Games continued for about twenty years (Bennett et al., 1975, pp. 149-50). Elsewhere, in Central America:

> Early in the 1920s, sports enthusiasts in Puerto Rico, Cuba, Mexico and other Latin-American countries decided to have an Olympics of their own, feeling that such contests would enhance goodwill among the nations, as well as develop the athletic skills of their young men and women. (Menke, 1953, p. 814)

Later the first of the Central American Caribbean Athletic Games —

"Juegos Deportivos De Los Centro-Americans Y Del Caribe" — were started in Mexico City in 1926, under rules similar to those of the Olympic Games. Their success led to a permanent quadrennial festival involving more than a dozen countries.

The First British Empire Games were held in Canada at Hamilton, Ontario, in 1930 (although efforts for such a celebration can be traced back to Englishman J. Astley Cooper's 1891 proposal for a "Pan-Britannic [Sports] Festival"). There were 400 athletes representing 11 countries at Hamilton, and these Games have since become a permanent fixture among the British family of nations (Agbogun, 1970). At the XI Commonwealth Games (so re-named) at Edmonton, Canada, in 1978, there were 46 countries participating, with a total of nearly 1500 athletes.

Two years after the successful launching of the British Empire Games, the Maccabiah Games took place for the first time in Palestine in 1932. These are now held in Israel each year following the Olympic Games. The first Balkan Games, in which Bulgaria, Greece, Romania, and Yugoslavia compete annually, were begun in 1932 also. Two years later the international sporting spotlight switched to India, where the West Asiatic Games were held, only once, with Afghanistan, Ceylon, and Palestine taking part. Then in 1951 the first Asian Games were celebrated in New Delhi, attended by representatives from 14 countries (Bennett and Van Dalen, 1971, pp. 611-12). These Games increased in stature over the years, until, in 1963, the Games of the New Emerging Forces (GANEFO) were begun at Djakarta, Indonesia, and these have also occurred with irregular frequency since then. In 1959 twelve sports were included on the program of the first Southeast Asia Peninsula Games, held at Bangkok, Thailand. A political motivation could be discerned in the beginnings of all these Games, and of course it is implicit in GANEFO's title. This had obviously been the case in Bogota, South American in 1938, when the Bolivarian Games were first held; these are Games in which countries liberated by Simon Bolivar take part.

In the same year of the first Asian Games in 1951, two other major sport festivals were begun in other continents. In South America the Pan-American Games were first staged in Buenos Aires. They have since been held one year prior to the Olympic Games, at Mexico City (1955 and 1975), Chicago (1959), Sao Paulo (1963), Winnipeg (1967), Cali (1971), and in other cities. Also in 1951, the IOC permitted Egypt to organize the first Mediterranean Games. Two years later the Pan-Arab Games were initiated in Egypt as well, sponsored by the Arab League of Nations.

Such festivals were not limited to countries situated on large land masses adjoining oceans; in 1963, in the capital city of Suva on the small second Games were held three years later, at New Caledonia, a $5 million sport complex was used and 14 territories participated. The first African Games took place in 1965 at Brazzaville (the Congo) with about 30 nations represented; but these were not held again until 1973 in Lagos, Nigeria, because of economic and political reasons. Yet another addition was made in South America in 1969 when the South American Games began at Ecuador.

International Student Games were first held in 1924 and renamed Universiade in 1959. The International Federation for Sports at Universities (FISU), organized in 1947, sponsors these World University Games held every two years. The 1973 Games in Moscow attracted 3,500 male and female athletes from 67 countries. Since 1960, physically disabled and handicapped people from many countries have had the opportunity to compete in the Paralympics, which are held immediately after the Olympics in the same host country. (These Paralympics were born of the previous stimulation over many years provided by the International Stoke Mandeville Games in England). In 1976 at Toronto this event was advertised as the Olympiad for the Physically Disabled.

Even the "workers" of the World have enjoyed their own specific international competition, since the forming of the International Workers Sport Federation (CSIT) in 1913. This is but one of a whole host of such international organizations which are involved in various ways in physical education, recreation and/or sport. Some others are the International Sporting Press Association (AIPS), 1924; the International Union of Students Council (IUSSC), 1946; the International Military Sports Council (CISM), 1948; the International Recreation Association (IRA), 1956; the International Playground Association (IPA), 1961; the European School Sport Federation, which was created in 1963 "to develop international competition" and was replaced in 1972 by the International School Sport Federation (ISSF); and many others.

Surveying this growing list of major international multi-sport festivals, it seems that in less than a hundred years the modern editions of the Funeral Games and Olympic Games of the Ancient Greeks have been transformed into many gigantic, worldwide modern counterparts. And those mentioned but briefly are just a few examples of this contemporary phenomenon in history. There are also similar international Games on a smaller scale. Of these, the Havlanta Games and the CANUSA Games are interesting examples. The Havlanta Games, from 1949 to 1959, featured annual competition in a variety of sports for the citizens of Havana, Cuba, and Atlanta, Georgia (U.S.A.). This experiment was the inspiration behind the CANUSA Games, begun in 1958 between people in Flint, Michigan (U.S.A.), and Hamilton, Ontario (Canada), now an annual summer event (Bennet and Van Dalen, 1961; Bennet et al., 1975).

In fact, it is hardly an exaggeration to claim that, in many ways, the "sporting calendar" with its regular daily, weekly, monthly, annual, biennial, and quadrennial events now dominates the modern world's timetable. This is not to suggest, of course, that such events are more important than, say, sessions of the United Nations or Disarmament Conferences. And certainly wars and natural disasters affecting the lives of millions are always too frequently on the international agenda. But while such things occur consistently, they tend to come suddenly and irregularly and they are difficult to forecast. Contrast this with the modern curriculum of world sport, which — although it is sometimes necessarily rearranged and interrupted, usually due to political factors — has become synchronized with an international modern lifestyle. As Alvin Toffler has stated in *Future Shock,* we are no longer at the mercy of the elements as we once were, e.g., darkness at night, frost in the morning, and no longer enslaved by an unchanging physical environment, so that we can now orient ourselves in space and time by social instead of natural irregularities:

> In the United States the arrival of spring is marked for most urban dwellers not by a sudden greenness . . . but by the opening of the baseball season . . . Similarly, the end of summer is marked as much by the World Series as by any natural symbol. (1970, p. 395)

Toffler also points out that even those who ignore sports cannot but be aware of these "large and pleasantly predictable events." Radio and television take sport into most homes, newspapers and magazines galore are filled with sport news, and individuals and teams play their part so that sports leagues everywhere fulfill their destinies each season, and "the drama plays itself out within a set of reassuringly rigid and durable rules" (Toffler, 1970, p. 350).

If machinery is considered as "anti-natural," then the clock is the archetypal machine, and some have regarded its invention as marking the real birth of the mechanical and technical age (there had been machines such as the drill and sources of power such as the watermill, but these lacked regular consistency and depended upon a river in spate or the worker being fresh). The clock "working its way inhumanly through day and night, changed life radically" and led to the idea of time in the abstract. Indeed, Lewis Mumford has claimed that the clock, not the steam engine, is the key machine of the modern industrial age (London: *The Sunday Times,* 1970; Mumford, 1962, pp. 12-18). Thus Toffler's timely analysis of the status of sport as a sort of "social clock" in modern times is highly significant, reflecting the way in which it orders our lives with increasing regularity. Even its regular events which are held inconsistently and have no set timetable — world championship boxing matches, for example, or challenges for the America's Cup in yachting — are crucial to this position and readily accommodated when necessary, i.e., when actual dates have been confirmed. Often it seems, in fact, that there is even a special kind of ritual enjoyment attached to the rigmarole of arranging such fixtures. The necessary amount of reassuring predictability in sport time is balanced by a certain amount of suspense and variety.

The America's Cup race took place from 1930 to 1983 off Newport, Rhode Island, U.S.A. Before then it was sailed off New York. (By contrast, world boxing championships have been held and will continue to take place in a variety of places, even Zaire and Phillipines, usually wherever the most lucrative television contract can be obtained). Since the schooner *America* first won the cup in 1851 by decisively beating the best yachts of the Royal Yacht Squadron in a race around the Isle of Wight (Heaton, 1973), the Americans then held off 23 challenges in what is generally regarded to be the oldest surviving "World Championship" in a single-sport, until 1983. Then an Australian 12-metre yacht pulled off what many consider to be the greatest upset in sporting competition, winning the final series 4-3 (after trailing 3-1) and taking the trophy which the Americans had held for 132 years back to Australia. But the American skipper who endured that loss, Dennis Conner, subsequently provided a dramatic comeback by winning the final series 4-0 sailed off Freemantle, Western Australia in 1987, when the American yacht *Stars and Stripes* defeated the Australian defender *Kookaburra III*, and the America's Cup returned to the United States.

The America's Cup is but one exotic example of many such international competitions in various sports. For besides the growth of multi-sport festivals, such as the Commonwealth, Olympic, and Pan-American Games, there has also been a parallel development in the growth of single-sport competitions involving several nations. One of the most prominent features of modern sport, alluded to earlier, is the repetition of a pattern, i.e., a single sport is codified and exported, and becomes international in character, accompanied by the formation of clubs and associations from local through national to worlwide status, for which processes modern technology provides the means of international communication and competition.

An examination of the mushrooming of what might be termed "single-sport world championships" since the first America's Cup race in 1851 lends further credence to the immense role of sport within our modern "concepts based on experience of sequence and change." Toffler's example of the World Series in baseball as marking the end of summer is understandable in view of the fact that this annual event now easily captures the attention of millions (Toffler, 1970). The Series and the Super Bowl (for American football) rank as the greatest American sports spectacles of modern times. Despite the fantastic amount of interest and income generated, the term "World Series" is a misnomer since it is really a competition between two American baseball clubs representing different leagues (Smithells and Cameron, 1962, pp. 441-42). The supreme example of a genuine World Championship for a single sport is that of Association Football (soccer). Although international soccer contests of various sorts were common in the nineteenth century, as we have seen, the World Cup for soccer was begun in 1930 at Montevideo in Uruguay, to coincide with that country's one hundredth year of independence. The huge Centenario Stadium was built for this event. Its location there, however, considerably reduced the number of possible entrants and only 13 nations took part, 9 of them from the American continent. Happily for the host nation, Uruguay defeated Argentina by 4 goals to 2 in the final game. From this relatively modest beginning, this festival has expanded to the point where more than 100 nations from all five continents compete, and it ranks second only to the Olympic Games as a sports spectacle in terms of the worldwide television audience attracted. (Barrett, 1973).

There are now too many world championships in various sports to account for them all — from archery through frisbee throwing and even "tiddlywinks" to yachting (and to this may now be added the Admiral's Cup as well) — but a brief survey of the dates and places for several gives some indication of their comprehensive diversity. Not all of them are officially labeled as "World Championships" but unofficially they have been recognized as such. For example, the sport of tennis has many international competitions, such as the All-England Championships at Wimbledon (1877), the Davis Cup (1900), the Wightman Cup (1923), the Federation Cup (1963), and recently spawned "World Team Tennis" as well. Golf has also produced many international competitions, such as the Walker Cup (U.S.A., 1922), the Curtis Cup (England, 1932), the World Amateur Team Championships (for men, Scotland, 1958; for women, France, 1964), the I.G.A. World Cup (Canada, 1953) and others. Before Wimbledon in the nineteenth century there came a Racquets Championship (1838) in London, and afterwards we find a World Road Racing Cycling Championship (1893) in Chicago, a World Championship for Speed Skating (1893) in Holland, for figure Skating (1896) in the U.S.S.R., and the All-England Championships for Badminton (1899) in London again.

It should be mentioned here to avoid possible confusion that some sports other than soccer also have an international trophy designated as a "World Cup." These include: the World Cup for Golf (1953), the Field Hockey World Cup (1971 for men; 1973 for women), the Rugby League World Cup (1954), the World Cup for Alpine Skiing (1967), and the World Cup for Volleyball (1965), among others. And, of course, many other competitions besides the golf and tennis examples already given have individually named trophies, such as the Thomas Cup (1948-1949) and the Uber Cup (1956) in badminton, the President's Cup (1965) in equestrianism, and the Schneider Trophy (1913 to 1931) in flying. Proceeding alphabetically by sport, other prominent examples of single-sport world championships in the twentieth century could include: archery (Poland, 1931); basketball (Argentine, 1950); bobsledding (Switzerland, 1927); curling (Canada, 1959); fencing (Belgium, 1930); gliding (Germany, 1937); ice hockey (Belgium, 1920); judo, karate, and kendo (Japan, 1956 and 1970); lacrosse (Canada, 1967); lawn bowling (Austria, 1930); netball (England, 1963); parachuting (Yugoslavia, 1951); pelota (Spain, 1952); roller skating (Italy, 1937); ski flying (Yugoslavia, 1972); softball (for men, Australia, 1965; for women, Mexico 1966); squash (Australia, 1967); swimming (Yugoslavia, 1973); table tennis (England, 1926); and trampolining (England, 1964); (Arlott, 1975).

In addition to there being separate championships for men and for women in various sports, plus quite a number of Junior World Championships, the picture is further complicated by the fact that many sports break down into world championships for different categories. A world championship for Graeco-Roman wrestling was instituted in 1921, for example, whereas a freestyle wrestling world championship did not begin until thirty years later. Ice-skating has male and female categories in speed skating and figure skating, as well as joint events in pairs and in dancing. Shooting is represented by many different types, e.g., air rifle, air pistol, skeet, service calibre, small bore, trapshooting, etc.

Even this incomplete survey shows that sport is now truly international and that countries everywhere, from all continents, have contributed to this status. As well as being symbolic in terms of time, therefore, it may also be considered so in terms of communication or a kind of international language (just as music, painting, and other arts are so considered). Thus skiers or skaters, soccer or ice hockey players, can communicate through an appreciation and understanding of each others' skills, even when they do not comprehend each others' language. This is part of the argument in favor of sport as an international friendship agent, i.e., more sport contact leads to greater international understanding. Unfortunately, this is not guaranteed in practice, where often the contact, especially in the form of intense competition, has led to bad feelings between nations.

We have seen that the greatest international sports arena of all time, the Olympic Games, was resurrected toward the end of the nineteenth century in the hope that greater worldwide amity would result. And no one could deny that since that time these Games have provided excitement and pleasure to millions of people from all over the world, and that often people of various nations have interacted positively and respectfully. The Games have produced athletic heroes from every participating country; some of their exploits will not be forgotten as long as sport history is recorded. Their standards of performance, the "records" of the Olympics, have seemingly reached nearly to the limits of human capability, just as they have in other "World Championships" mentioned. (In the previous century, who could have imagined, for example, athletes high jumping over 7 feet, pole vaulting over 18 feet, long jumping nearly 30 feet, or running the mile regularly in under 4 minutes?) (Benagh, 1970; Hart, 1974). The modern Olympics have contributed much toward excellence in modern sport and in many ways have been worthy of the noblest ancient Greek ideals. Yet the ancient Games lasted over a thousand years while their modern counterpart may not survive a century. Why? Whatever the precise answer, it must be associated with the new environment of the world, its complex technology, and its concomitant condition of "future shock" mentioned earlier. While the evolution of the modern Olympic Games may be regarded as the most significant aspect of the modern era, their ultimate fate is now the biggest question in sport. And many of the problems of the Olympics, e.g., exorbitant costs, political wrangling, definitions of the term "amateur," have been reflected in other international sport competition as well.

It will be recalled that Coubertin won the prize for literature at Stockholm in 1912 with an entry entitled Ode to Sport, entered anonymously under two German pseudonyms. This eulogy consisted of nine verses praising sport in turn as "the delight of the Gods," Beauty, Justice, Daring, Honor, Joy, Fecundity, Progress; it ended as follows:

O Sport, you are Peace! You forge happy bonds between the peoples by drawing them together in reverence for strength which is controlled, organized and self-disciplined. Through you the young of all the World learn to respect one another, and thus the diversity of national traits becomes a source of generous and peaceful emulation. (Killanin and Rodda, 1976, pp. 161-62)

These are noble sentiments and all such qualities have been demonstrated in modern sport. Yet Coubertin knew his Ode portrayed an ideal to be strived for rather than reflecting the absolute reality of sport. As Marie Therese Eyquem has pointed out, he was aware that "sport could indeed be the best or the worst of things," for to Coubertin:

Athleticism can occasion the most noble passions or the most vile; it can develop impartiality and the feeling of honour as can love of winning; it can be chivalrous or corrupt, vile, bestial; one can use it to consolidate peace or to prepare for war. (Killanin and Rodda, 1976, p. 139)

Thus even the Baron would probably concede the validity of a more cynical "Ode to Modern Sport," such as: "O Sport, you are Ugliness!" relating it in other verses to Cruelty, Hypocrisy, Profiteering, and a few other maladies. Indeed, there have been distinguished critics of athletes and sport in the modern era, contemporary counterparts to Diogenes and Xenophanes, from the anti-Muscular Christianity writers of the nineteenth century (McIntosh, 1968, pp. 57-79) to the radical authors of more recent years. Even to eminent Canadian historian A.R.M. Lower,

Figure 3-7. The Peoples Stadium, Budapest, Hungary. A tribute of the Hungarian people to their love affair with sport.

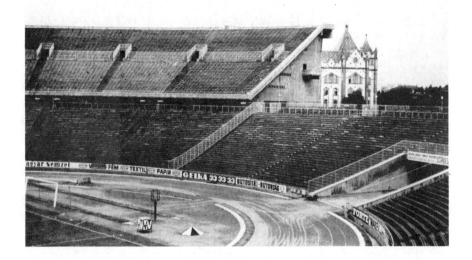

for example, the modern emphasis on sport represented a "historical retrocession" from "puritan to pagan" (Heick and Graham, 1974, p. 95). But just as American writers have dominated the genre of sports fiction (Umphlett, 1975), so the radical sports book has been mainly an American creation. Such titles as *The Athletic Revolution* (Scott, 1971); *The Jock Empire: Its Rise and Deserved Fall* (Dickey, 1974); *The Sports Factory: An Investigation into College Sports* (Durso, 1975); *A Long Way, Baby: The Inside Story of the Women in Pro Tennis* (Lichtenstein, 1975); and the ultimate in protest inscriptions, *Rip off the Big Game: The Exploitation of Sports by the Power Elite* (Hoch, 1972), are but a few representative samples of such works. Similar literary objections could be cited from other countries, such as the Canadian publication, *The Death of Hockey* (Kidd and Macfarlane, 1972).

Perhaps the most disturbing critic of all was George Orwell, the prophetic author of *Animal Farm* and *1984,* who was entirely opposed to international sport, calling it "war minus the shooting" (Orwell, 1945, p. 153). This provided the title for a realistic yet optimistic appraisal of (subtitle): "The rise of mass sport in the twentieth century and its effects on men and nations" under the title of *War Without Weapons,* which included a chapter entitled "The Olympic Frankenstein." This again argued the hypothesis of sport as a safety valve for the aggressive instincts that lurk below the surface of our civilization (Goodhart and Chataway, 1968).

The debate literally rages on today as the pros and cons of sport everywhere occupy the media and therefore our minds. It illustrates vividly the most dominant factor in the evolution of sport since 1800, i.e., that sport has become utterly serious. This seriousness is manifest in more ways than can be adequately discussed here, but the international competitions that have been briefly discussed are central examples; behind these endeavors are the serious actions of thousands of concerned and involved individuals and institutions: athletes, churches, coaches, commercial firms, governments, and spectators. The evolution and status of coaches in the modern world, for all amateur and professional sports and for all age groups and both sexes, is another supreme indicator. The increasing involvement of national governments in sport is another crucial revelation in this respect (see, for example, Morton, 1963; Kolatch, 1972; Noll, 1974; Lapchick, 1975; and Redmond, 1986). *A Declaration on Sport* (ICSPE, 1964) was issued after the 1964 Olympic Games by the United Nations Educational, Scientific, and Cultural Organization (UNESCO), and it was stated on the first page by Director-General Rene Maheu that the State, trade unions, political parties, and churches are all taking an increasingly active interest in sport "to serve it, naturally, but also to use it for their own purposes." One example only, from the Western world, of the complex involvement of "the State" and other agencies in sport is given here in the diagram of the sectors and components of the sport system in Canada (Figure 3-8). Canada was but one of the challenging nations in the latest America's Cup competition, a championship which points up the seriousness of modern international sport, when all syndicates involved spend literally millions of dollars on equipment and weather data in their attempts to be successful.

Like all other modern institutions, the Church had to adapt to the challenges of the times, including the Industrial Revolution and global warfare. One of the most dramatic and obvious results of this shock was the rapid completion of the transition from asceticism to athleticism. The Church quickly became a patron of sport and found moral benefit in its practice — a convenient stance to say the least, since by the twentieth century most of its clergy and congregation were sport participants, or spectators, or both. Church leagues in various sports arose on either side of the Atlantic, and the Sabbath was gradually assimilated into the sporting calendar. Some of the most famous clubs in British professional soccer today, such as Aston Villa, Bolton Wanderers, Everton, Fulham, Queen's Park Rangers, and others, were born as Church social clubs (Betts 1974, pp. 210-31, 352-55; Marples, 1954, pp. 167-68). The Young Men's Christian Association, begun in 1841 in a back street of London serving tea and bible readings as an antidote to the vices of the city, very quickly expanded into an international association, complete

Figure 3-8. Diagram of the Sections and Components Comprising the Sport System in Canada

PUBLIC SECTOR

NATIONAL

FEDERAL GOVERNMENT

1. Department of National Defense — Primary Agencies Responsible for Sport
2. Other federal agencies — Department of National Health and Welfare Fitness and Amateur Sport Branch Sport Canada

Provincial Director's Council on Fitness and Amateur Sport

PROVINCIAL

PROVINCIAL GOVERNMENTS

1. Department of Education — Primary Agencies Responsible for Sport (e.g. Ontario)
2. Attorney General's Office — 1. Ontario Ministry of Culture and Recreation
3. Other provincial agencies — Sport and Fitness Division

Provincial Government Regional Sport and Recreation Branches

REGIONAL/LOCAL

REGIONAL/MUNICIPAL GOVERNMENTS

1. Parks and Recreation Department
2. Recreation Commissions

SHARED SECTOR*

National Sport and Recreation Centre Inc.

Sport Participation Canada PARTICIPaction

Canada Games Council

Provincial Sport Administration Bodies and Federations
1. Sport Ontario
2. Manitoba Sports Federation etc.

Provincial Sport Affiliated Organizations
1. Action B.C.
2. SHAPE-UP Alberta etc.

Universities and Colleges
1. Faculties, Departments, etc. of Physical Education Recreation and Athletics
2. Intramurals, Sport Clubs

Regional/Community Sports Councils

Regional/Local Boards of Education and Schools
1. Physical Education Courses
2. Interschool Athletic Program
3. Intramural Programs

Games Societies (Temporary Structures)
1. Canada Games Societies
2. C.O.J.O.
3. Commonwealth Games Foundation etc.

PRIVATE SECTOR

National Advisory Council of the Fitness and Amateur Sport Program

Sports Governing Bodies, Organizations and Associations
National — 1. Sports Governing Bodies
Provincial — 2. Multiple Sports Agencies
Regional/Local — 3. Multiple Games Associations
4. Sport Affiliated Organizations

Provincial Advisory Councils of Fitness and Amateur Sport
1. Alta. Advisory Committee on Physical Fitness

Professional Associations
National — 1. C.A.H.P.E.R.
Provincial — 2. Coaching Associations of Canada etc.
Regional/Local

Service Agencies and Service Clubs
1. Y.W.C.A. & Y.M.C.A.
2. Royal Canadian Legion etc.

Business and Industry
1. Industrial Sports Leagues
2. Commercial Sponsorship of Amateur and Professional Sport

Commercial Sporting Interests
1. Sports Clubs and Facilities
2. Sporting Goods Manufacturers and Distributors
3. Sport Consultants etc.

Professional Sport
1. Football
2. Hockey etc.

Media
1. Television
2. Radio
3. Newspapers etc.

Miscellaneous Sector
1. Churches
2. Private Schools etc.

* Councils, federations and organizations falling within this sector vary in their degree of shared sector status with some naturally leaning more toward the public side and others more toward the private.

159

with gymnasia, colleges, and its own sports, before the end of the century (Leonard and Affleck, 1947, pp. 515-28). Today the YMCA is perhaps better known as an Athletic Association (and as an inexpensive accommodation chain) than as a Christian institution. Certainly, sport now dominates its programs. However, for people who equate Christianity with sport, and vice versa, the distinction is perhaps unimportant. Perhaps the crux was really "Muscular Christianity," a phrase invented during the 1850s to describe succinctly the widely held belief that games contributed toward a moral character and fostered patriotism, which was in turn transferable to other situations and later life; this doctrine was espoused most successfully in the novels of Reverend Charles Kingsley and Thomas Hughes. Here was the necessary formula to blend Christian thought with Victorian concepts of competition and progress, often manifest upon imperial battlefields. Despite its intelligent and vocal critics — from Wilkie Collins and Rudyard Kipling to George Orwell, among others — the triumph of the Muscular Christian gospel was assured. Beyond fictional novels, in recent studies Mangan has shown how the ideology of athleticism pervaded the Victorian and Edwardian Public School in the United Kingdom, and spread to the outposts of Empire (Mangan 1981 and 1986).

In ancient Greece successful athletes sometimes gave the implements of their victory, discuses and halteres, even their strigils, as thank offerings to the Gods, to be housed in appropriate temples. Today the modern counterpart is seen on every continent as each culture honors its sporting heroes and heroines in literally hundreds of "halls of fame" and museums which revere their memory while preserving their artifacts (Lewis and Redmond, 1974). Many such facilities cost millions of dollars, have stained-glass windows, churchlike columns and spires, and even conduct prayer meetings on their premises. In many ways they can be regarded as the Churches of Modern Sport, to which the mass of disciples attend Worship. In an article in *Sports Illustrated,* June 28, 1971 (pp. 62-74), Jerry Kirshenbaum described a 10,000 mile tour of these institutions in the United States as an "irreverent pilgrimage" to "holy places." One is vividly reminded of Henry Lawson's cynical doggerel:

> In a Land where sport is sacred,
> Where the Laborer is God,
> You must pander to the people,
> Make a hero of a clod. (Dunstan, 1973, p. 2)

Obviously not all athletes are clods, but where is there a country now where sport is not sacred? It is a sobering fact that a serious scholar like William Kilbourn should begin his *Religion in Canada* with the reflection that "if I were asked by some stranger to North American culture to show him the most important religious building in Canada, I would take him to Toronto's Maple Leaf Gardens'' (1968, p. 6) or that Keith Dunstan should write five years later "Sport is the ultimate Australian Supereligion" (1973, p. 7).

Sport is now an integral part of Sunday as never before, the norm rather than the exception. Frank Deford (1976) coined the term "Sportianity" in analyzing the appearance and growth of such groups as Athletes in Action and the Fellowship of Christian Athletes, as well as the growing popularity of locker-room prayers and team chaplains. He suggested a strong economic motive, just as Foster Dulies had a dozen years previously before such comtemporary phenomena, when he wrote, "Play had to be considered a virtue for the sake of the nation's prosperity" (1965, p. 393). Voices from other nations would echo "Amen!"

"Religion and Sport" is now "in" as never before; it is perhaps rivaled only by the attention given to "Politics and Sport" today (Rogers, 1972). For example, the Spring 1975 issue of the *Sport Sociology Bulletin* contained articles entitled: "Karate and Christianity: Parallels on Different Planes," "The Places of Athletics in the Life of the Christian," and "The Cohesive Function of Religion and Sport at a Sectarian University." The Joint Working Group of the Canadian Catholic Conference and the Canadian Council of Churches produced its "Pastoral Reflections on the Occasion of '76 Olympics entitled *A Christian View of Sports.* Many more examples could be given of this trend. But none of the more recent hypotheses or opinions in the area rival the assertion of Robert Henderson in 1947, perhaps the most significant in sport history: that all modern games played with bat and ball descend from one common source: an ancient fertility rite observed by Priest Kings in the Egypt of the Pyramids. Therefore, for Henderson, such popular activities as baseball, cricket, and tennis are "merely vestigial remains of religious rites of ancient times" (1947, pp. 3-7). It would be difficult to find a more thought-provoking analysis of the transformation from (religious) "holy days" to (sport) "holidays" in all of sport literature.

Henderson is but one of many scholars who have pointed up the seriousness of sport by devoting their attentions to it. Since his book was published in 1947, the academic study of sport has rapidly increased and gained some respect and influence, so that there are now national and international associations and societies concerned with such aspects as the history, philosophy, psychology, and sociology of sport, as well as exercise physiology and sports medicine, replete with their associated professional journals and texts, conferences and congresses, and supported by an increasing number of related courses in academic institutions. A common interest in the phenomenal social significance of sport has brought about this international inquiry. Readers are invited to peruse three volumes as pertinent examples only (literally hundreds could be given) of this worldwide endeavor: *Research in the History, Philosophy and International Aspects of Physical Education and Sport: Bibliographies and Techniques* (Zeigler, Howell and Trekell, 1971); *Sport in the Modern World: Chances and Problems,* published on behalf of the Organizing Committee for the Games of the XXth Olympiad at Munich, 1972 (Grupe, 1973) and *Sports: A Reference Guide* (Higgs, 1982). Another attempt "to study in some depth sport and physical education in 35 selected countries" entitled *Comparative Physical Education and Sport* is also highly recommended. In this book in such chapters as "Sport Facilities and Equipment," "Amateurism and Professionalism," "Sports for Girls and Women," "Sport and Race," "Sport and Economics," "Sport and Mass Media," etc. readers will find more details than are possible in this chapter (Bennett, Howell, and Simri, 1975).

Although the status of sport in the modern world has made such attention inevitable, not everybody has agreed with it or welcomed it. While himself contributing to the trend in yet another recent book subtitled "Sport and American Life," Paul Gardner regretted that "we seem to be entering a period of overkill, and a formidably serious subject entitled The Sociology of Sport has descended upon us, replete with pretentious terminology, unreadable theses, and various other trappings of pseudo-learning" (1975, Foreword footnote, n.n.).

More unfortunate than any possible academic "overkill" created through modern sport, however, are the number of real deaths which have occurred in connection with sport. Violence among spectators is a worrisome trend, particularly where association football (soccer) is concerned, a sport which has a peculiar capacity to arouse its supporters. So much so that in recent years there have been a disturbing number of soccer riots resulting in the deaths of spectators in Africa, Asia, Europe and South America. Many deaths have been due to the inherent dangers of sport itself, such as are evident in high-speed motor racing, and others due to the violent physical contact involved in so many sports. Fatal injuries have also come about as athletes have driven themselves beyond safe limits, usually under conditions of intense competition. In 1800, when James Parkinson wrote his little moral tale for children entitled: *Dangerous Sports,* dedicated to "Parents and Schoolmasters" and "Warning them against wanton, careless, or mischievous Exposure to Situations, from which alarming injuries do often proceed," he could have had no conception whatsoever of the implications of such a title today, where the field of sports medicine has necessarily become an international undertaking. And if such glimpses into the future of sport provided by recent films like *Rollerball* or *Death Race 2000* are really prophetic, then it will be a "growth industry" for some time. The seriousness of modern sport is truly epitomized by the injuries within its arenas, large and small, amateur and professional, around the world.

Perhaps the most worrisome trend of all in modern sport, however, and one which again can be attributed to its seriousness and status in the modern world, is the use of these arenas for political protests. The disputes between people and nations *within* sport itself have been troubling enough. Even the late Harold Harris was moved to suggest that perhaps "a quiet death and seemly burial" might be the "best and kindest solution" for the Olympic Games (1975, p. 190). When sport is used to continue and/or justify conflict between different ideologies, or serve economic purposes primarily, then its nature is rapidly altered and its very existence threatened. Alex Natan gave a timely warning in 1958:

> Never has a state risen so swiftly to world power as has sport. It has within sixty years hurried through a development for which empires have needed five centuries. At the same time no other power has ever shown such considerable symptoms of decay in so short a span as has the sporting movement. (1958, p. 47)

The challenges of this "decay" present enormous difficulties which may or may not be surmountable. But when the sporting arena is also used as a vehicle for political protest by parties outside of sport, because of the phenomenal publicity gained for a cause, then even greater problems surround sport.

Miss Emily Davison, a member of the Women's Social and Political Union, chose the English Derby for her protest when on June 4, 1913, she threw herself in front of the King's horse, Amner, which was in the lead. The horse and jockey survived the impact and fall, but Miss Davison died from her injuries "and the Women's movement had its martyr" (Dobbs, 1973, p. 178). Some years later, on September 5, 1972, at Munich, the Olympic Games became the scene of a far more violent act, as already mentioned. Despite the "Munich massacre," the Games went on. Since then, the sites of other Olympics at Innsbruck and Montreal have resembled armed fortresses, with the host nations having to spend millions of dollars on security precautions. As Dobbs asked after Munich: "And so long as sport continues to attract a major share of our attention, who can know what the future has in store?" (1973, p. 178).

The first sentence of this section on "Sport Since 1800" maintains that "sport reflects the society in which it occurs, that people at play reveal significant things about themselves and their culture or civilization." Strutt himself said as much in 1801, in his Preface: "In order to form a just estimation of the character of any particular people it is absolutely necessary to investigate the Sports and Pastimes most generally prevalent among them" (1801, p. 2). Since then, events and other writers have confirmed this view many times over. However, a "just estimation" of our civilization from an examination of world sport is an elusive task. Strutt's thesis remains valid, and therefore sport *must* be examined, but the data are much more comprehensive and complex now. In a world threatened by nuclear war, a depletion of material resources, overpopulation and starvation, new diseases, and increasing terrorism, the significance of sport often seems incomprehensible. In fact, sport since 1800 has developed to a state of quandary, eloquently and precisely stated several years ago by one of its greatest scholars, Peter McIntosh:

> The enormous growth of sport as a World-wide phenomenon may herald the birth of a new Olympic ideal and a new asceticism, an asceticism which looks to achievement and prowess in play as an end in itself. The final conclusion then is a paradox; sport, if it is pursued as an end in itself, may bring benefits to man which will elude his grasp if he treats it as little more than a clinical, a social or a political instrument to fashion those very benefits. (McIntosh, 1968, p. 203)

Sport was not considered a paradox as the nineteenth-century dawned; but as the twentieth-century moves towards its close it is nothing less than a bewildering social phenomenon of gigantic proportions, and always a necessary fact of human existence in our modern world.

GENERAL BIBLIOGRAPHY

AGBOGUN, J.D. "A History of the British Commonwealth Games, 1930-1966." M.A. Thesis, University of Alberta, 1970.

ARLOTT, JOHN, Ed. *The Oxford Companion to Sports and Games.* London: Oxford University Press, 1975.

ARLOTT, J., and A. DALEY. *Pageantry of Sport: From the Age of Chivalry to the Age of Victoria.* New York: Hawthorn Books, 1968.

AVAKIAN, LINDY. "Physical Education and Athletics in Japan." *The Physical Educator,* vol. 17, no. 4, December 1960.

BAKER, WILLIAM J. *Sports in the Western World.* Totowa, N.J.: Rowman and Littlefield, 1982.

BALZ, FRITZ. "Some Remarks About Physical Education and Sport of Handicapped Children," *Gymnasion,* VIII (Autumn-Winter 1971), 16-18.

BARRETT, N., Ed. *World Soccer from A to Z.* London: Pan Books, Ltd., 1973.

BENAGH, J. *Incredible Athletic Feats.* New York: Bantam Books, 1970.

BENNET, B.L., M.L. HOWELL and U. SIMRI. *Comparative Physical Education and Sport.* Philadelphia: Lee and Febiger, 1975.

BENNETT, B.L., and DEOBOLD B. VAN DALEN. *A World History of Physical Education.* Englewood Cliffs, N.J.: Prentice Hall, 1971.

BETTS, JOHN RICHARDS. *America's Sporting Heritage: 1850-1950.* Reading, Mass.: Addison-Wesley Publishing Company, 1974.

————. "Organized Sport in Industrial America." Ph.D. Dissertation, University of Michigan, 1951.

BISQUERTT, LUIS, and CLYDE KNAPP. "Physical Education in Chile," *Physical Education Around the World,* pp. 1-17. Ed. William Johnson. Monograph No. 5. Indianapolis: Phi Epsilon Kappa, 1971.

BOUCHARD, CLAUDE. "The Physical Activity Sciences: A Basis Concept for the Organization of the Discipline and the Profession," *International Journal of Physical Education,* VIII no. 3 (Fall 1976), 9-15.

BOYLE, ROBERT H. *Sport: Mirror of American Life.* Boston: Little, Brown and Company, 1963.

BRASCH, R. *How Did Sport Begin?* New York: David McKay, 1970.

BRINTON, CRANE, JOHN B. CHRISTOPHER, and ROBERT LEE WOLFE. *Civilization in the West* (3rd ed.). Englewood Cliffs, N.J.: Prentice-Hall, 1973.h

BROEKHOFF, JAN. "Physical Education in the Netherlands," *Physical Education Around the World,* pp. 46-53. Ed. William Johnson. Monograph No. 2. Indianapolis: Phi. Epsilon Kappa, 1968.

BURCHELL, S.C., *et al. Great Ages of Man: A History of the World's Cultures: Age of Progress, 1850-1914.* New York: Time-Life Books, 1966.

CANTELON, HARTFORD A. "The Political Involvement in Sport in the Soviet Union." Unpublished M.A. Thesis, University of Alberta, 1972.

CHESTER, D. *The Olympic Games Handbook.* New York: Charles Scribner's Sons, 1975.

CISZEK, RAYMOND A. "Health, Physical Education and Recreation: Columbia," *The World Today in Health, Physical Education, and Recreation,* Ed. C.L. Vendien and J.E. Nixon, Englewood Cliffs, N.J.: Prentice-Hall, 1968.

CLAY, MAURICE A. "Physical Education in Columbia," *Physical Education Around the World,* pp. 31-45. Ed. William Johnson. Monograph No. 3. Indianapolis: Phi Epsilon Kappa, 1969.

COLLINS, LARRY, and DOMINIQUE LAPIERRE. *Freedom at Midnight.* New York: Simon and Schuster, 1975.

COOTE, J. *History of the Olympics in Pictures.* London: Tom Stacy Ltd., 1972.

Declaration on Sport. Paris: International Council of Sport and Physical Education, 1964.

DEFLEUR, M.L., W.V. D'ANTONIO, and L.B. DEFLEUR. *Sociology: Human Society.* Glenview, Ill.: Scott, Foresman, 1973.

DEFORD, FRANK. "Religion in Sport," *Sports Illustrated,* April 19, 26, May 3, 1976.

DICKEY, GLENN. *The Jock Empire: Its Rise and Deserved Fall.* Radnor, Penn.: Chilton Book Company, 1974.

DOBBS, BRIAN. *Edwardians at Play: Sport 1890-1914.* London: Pelham Books, 1973.

DONALDSON, EMILY ANN. *The Scotish Highland Games in America.* Gretna: Pelican, 1986.

DULLES, F.R. *A History of Recreation: America Learns to Play.* Englewood Cliffs, N.J.: Prentice-Hall, 1965.

DUNSTAN, KEITH. *Sports.* Australia: Cassell, 1973.

DURSO, JOSEPH. *The Sports Factory: An Investigation into College Sports.* New York: Quadrangle, 1975.

ELLIS, M. "Physical Education in England," in *Physical Education Around the World,* pp. 1-16. Ed. William Johnson. Monograph No. 1. Indianapolis: Phi Epsilon Kappa, 1966.

Eureka!: The Sunday Times Magazine History of Invention. London: The Sunday Times, 1970.

FIELD, W.G. "F. L. Jahn, Father of Gymnastics," *Gentlemen's Magazine* (New Series), LXVIII, 155-67.

FITTIS, ROBERT SCOTT. *Sports and Pastimes of Scotland.* Paisley: Alexander Gardner, 1891.

FOURESTIER, MAX. "Les Experiences Scholaires de Vanves," *International Review of Education,* VII (1962-63), 81-85.

FROYSTAD, E. *Program for Physical Education.* Oslo: Royal Ministry of Church and Education, 1963.

GARDINER, E.N. *Athletics of the Ancient World.* Oxford: Clarendon Press, 1967.

GARDNER, PAUL. *Nice Guys Finish Last: Sport and American Life.* New York: Universe Books, 1975.

GERBER, ELLEN W. *Innovators and Institutions in Physical Education.* Philadelphia: Lea and Febiger, 1971.

GERMAN SPORTS FEDERATION (Deutsches Sportbund). *Recommendations for the Promotion of Physical Education in Schools.* Frankfurt: Main, 1959.

GIROUARD, MARK. *Cities and People: A Social and Architectual History.* New Haven and London: Yale University Press, 1985.

GOODHART, P., and C. CHATAWAY. *War Without Weapons.* London: W.H. Allen, 1968.

GOULSTONE, J. *Modern Sport: Its Origin and Development through Two Centuries.* Bexleyheath, Kent: Published by the author, 1974.

GRUPE, OMMO, Ed. *Sport in the Modern World: Chances and Problems.* Berlin: Springer-Valag, 1973.

GUTTMANN, ALLEN. *From Ritual to Record: The Nature of Modern Sports.* New York: Columbia University Press, 1978.

HARRIS, H.A. *Sport in Britain: Its Origins and Development.* London: Stanley Paul, 1975.

HART, H.H. *Physical Feats that Made History.* New York: Hart Publishing Company, 1974.

HEATON, PETER. *Yachting: A Pictorial History.* New York: The Viking Press, 1973.

HEICK, W.H., and ROGER GRAHAM. *His Own Man.* Montreal: McGill-Queen's University Press, 1974.

HENDERSON, ROBERT W. *Ball, Bat and Bishop.* New York: Rockport Press, 1947.

HENRY, FRANKLIN M. "Physical Education: An Academic Discipline," *Journal of Health, Physical Education and Recreation,* 35 (September 1964), 32-33, 69.

HERRON, ROBIN, E. "Physical Education in Finland," *Physical Education Around the World,* pp. 17-22. Ed. William Johnson. Monograph No. 1 Indianapolis: Phi Epsilon Kappa, 1966.

HOBERMAN, J.M. *The Olympic Crisis: From its origins to the Moscow Games.* Austin: University of Texas Press, 1984.

HIGGS, ROBERT J. Sports: *A Reference Guide.* Westport, Connecticut: Greenwood Press, 1982.

HOCH, PAUL. *Rip Off the Big Game: The Exploitation of Sports by The Power Elite.* New York: Doubleday and Company, Inc., 1972.

HOWELL, MAXWELL L., and NANCY HOWELL. *Sports and Games in Canadian Life: 1700 to the Present.* Toronto: Macmillan of Canada, 1969.

HUIZINGA, JOHAN. *Homo Ludens: A Study of the Play Element in Culture.* Boston: Beacon Press, 1955.

INTERNATIONAL COUNCIL ON HEALTH, PHYSICAL EDUCATION, AND RECREATION. *Physical Education in the School Curriculum. ICHPER International Questionnaire Report, Part I, 1967-68 Revision.* Washington, D.C.: ICHPER, 1969.

_____. *Physical Education and Games in the Curriculum. ICHPER Questionnaire Report, Part 1.* Washington, D.C.: ICHPER, c. 1963.

JAMES, JANICE. "An Interdisciplinary Approach to Outdoor Education and Selected Program Implications for Alberta Grade Six Pupils." Unpublished M.A. Thesis, University of Alberta, 1969.

JOBLING, IAN F. "Sport in Nineteenth-Century Canada: The Effects of Technological Changes on its Development." Ph.D. Dissertation, University of Alberta, 1970.

JOHNSON, WILLIAM. (ed.). *Physical Education Around the World.* Monograph No. 1. Indianapolis: Phi Epsilon Kappa, 1966.

_____. *Physical Education Around the World.* Monograph No. 2. Indianapolis: Phi Epsilon Kappa, 1968.

_____. *Physical Education Around the World.* Monograph No. 3. Indianapolis: Phi Epsilon Kappa, 1968.

_____. *Physical Education Around the World.* Monograph No. 4. Indianapolis: Phi Epsilon Kappa, 1970.

_____. *Physical Education Around the World.* Monograph No. 5 Indianapolis: Phi Epsilon Kappa, 1971.

_____. *Physical Education Around the World.* Monograph No. 6. Indianapolis: Phi Epsilon Kappa, 1972.

JUDD, GERRIT P. *The History of Civilization.* New York: The Macmillan Company, 1966.

KAMPER, E. *Who's Who at the Olympics.* Graz, Austria: Leykan-Verlag, 1975.

KERESTES, ALEXANDER. "A Report on Physical Education and Sport in Hungary." Unpublished report, University of Alberta, Edmonton, March 1966.

KIDD, B., and J. MACFARLANE. *The Death of Hockey.* Toronto: New Press, 1972.

KIERAN, J., and A. DALEY. *The Story of the Olympic Games, 776 B.C. to 1972.* Philadelphia: J.B. Lippincott Company, 1973.

KILBOURN, W. *Religion in Canada: The Spiritual Development of a Nation.* Toronto: McClelland and Stewart Limited, 1968.

KILLANIN, LORD, and J. RODDA, Eds. *The Olympic Games*. Don Mills, Ontario: Collier-Macmillan Canada, 1976.

KOLATCH, JONATHAN. *Sports, Politics and Ideology in China*. New York: Jonathan David, 1972.

LAGISQUET, MAURICE. "Health, Physical Education, and Recreation: France," *The World Today in Health, Physical Education, and Recreation*. Ed. C.L. Vendien and J.E. Nixon. Englewood Cliffs, N.J.: Prentice-Hall, 1968.

LAPCHICK, RICHARD E. *The Politics of Race and International Sport: The Case of South Africa*. London: Greenwood Press, 1975.

LARCHER, CLAUDE PIERRE. "Physical Education in France," *Physical Education Around the World*, pp. 18-22. Ed. William Johnson. Monograph No. 5. Indianapolis: Phi Epsilon Kappa, 1971.

LEIPER, JEAN M. "The International Olympic Committee: The Pursuit of Olympism, 1894-1970." Ph.D. Dissertation, University of Alberta, 1976.

LEONARD, FRED. "F. L. Jahn and the Development of Popular Gymnastics in Germany, Part I," *American Physical Education Review*, V (1904), 18-39.

———. "F. L. Jahn and the Development of Popular Gymnastics in Germany, Part II," *American Physical Education Review*, X (1905), 1-19.

———. and G.B. AFFLECK. *A Guide to the History of Physical Education*. London: Henry Krimpton, 1947.

LEWIS G., and G. REDMOND. *Sporting Heritage: A Guide to Halls of Fame, Special Collections and Museums in the United States and Canada*. New York: A.S. Barnes and Company, 1974.

LICHTENSTEIN, G. *A Long Way, Baby*. Greenwich, Conn.: Fawcett Publications, 1975.

LINDSAY, PETER L. "German Gymnastics under Jahn." Unpublished paper, University of Alberta, Edmonton, 1969.

———. "A History of Sport in Canada, 1807-1867." Ph.D. Dissertation, University of Alberta, 1969.

LOCKE, JOHN. *Some Thoughts Concerning Education*. Introduction and notes by R.H. Quick. Cambridge: University Press, 1913. (1st ed. 1880).

LOWE, BENJAMIN. *The Beauty of Sport*. Englewood-Cliffe, N.J.: Prentice-Hall, 1977.

LUDWIG, ELIZABETH A. "Basic Movement Education in England," *Journal of Health, Physical Education and Recreation*, December 1961, pp. 18-19.

MACALOON, JOHN J. *This Great Symbol: Pierre de Coubertin and the Origin of the Modern Olympic Games*. Chicago: University of Chicago Press, 1981.

MANDELL, RICHARD D. *The First Modern Olympics*. University of California Press, 1976.

MANDELL, RICHARD D. *Sport: A Cultural History*. New York: Columbia University Press, 1984.

MANGAN, J.A. *Athleticism in the Victorian and Edwardian Public School*. London: Cambridge University Press, 1981.

MANGAN, J.A. *The Games Ethic and Imperialism*. Harmondsworth: Viking, 1986.

MARPLES, MORRIS. *A History of Football*. London: Secker and Warburg, 1954.

McIntosh, Peter C. "The Recent History of Physical Education in England with Particular Reference to the Development of Movement Education," *The History of Physical Education and Sport,* pp. 121-33. Ed. Bruce L. Bennett. Proceedings of the Big Ten Symposium on the History of Physical Education and Sport. Chicago: The Athletic Institute, 1971.

————. *Sport in Society.* London: C.A. Watts and Co., 1963.

————. J.G. Dixon, A.D. Munrow, and R.F. Willetts. *Landmarks in the History of Physical Education.* London: Routledge and Kegan Paul, 1969.

McNair, David. "Physical Education in the Elementary Schools of Scotland before 1900." Paper presented at the Second World Symposium on the History of Sport and Physical Education, Banff, Canada, 1971.

Menke, Frank G. *The Encyclopedia of Sports.* New York: A.S. Barnes and Company, 1953.

Moolenijzer, Nicolaas J. "The Concept of 'Natural' in Physical Education (Johann Guts Muths - Margarete Streicher)," *A History of Sport and Physical Education to 1900,* pp. 289-307. Ed. Earle F. Zeigler. Champaign, Ill.: Stipes Publishing Company, 1973.

Morison, Samuel, Eliot, *The European Discovery of America.* New York: Oxford University Press, 1971.

Morton, Henry W. *Soviet Sport: Mirror of Soviet Society.* New York: Collier Books, 1963.

Mumford, Lewis. *Technics and Civilization.* New York: Harcourt, Brace and World, 1962.

Mutimer, Brian T.P. "Arnold and Organized Games in the English Public Schools of the Nineteenth Century." Ph.D. Dissertation, University of Alberta, 1971.

Natan, Alex. Ed. *Sport and Society.* London: Bowes and Bowes, 1958.

Noll, Roger G., Ed. *Government and the Sports Business.* Washington, D.C.: The Brookings Institution, 1974.

Orwell, George. *Shooting an Elephant and Other Essays.* New York: Harcourt, Brace and World, 1945.

Parkinson, James. *Dangerous Sports.* London: F.G. Barnard, 1800.

Quigley, Carroll. *The Evolution of Civilizations.* New York: The Macmillan Company, 1961.

Redmond, Gerald. *The Caledonian Games in Nineteenth-Century America.* Rutherford, N.J.: Fairleigh Dickinson University Press, 1971.

Redmond, Gerald. "Prologue and Transition: The 'Psendo-Olympics' of the Nineteenth-Century", *Olympism,* pp. 7-21. Eds. Jeffrey Segrave and Donald Chu. Champaign, Illinois: Human Kinetics, 1981.

Redmond, Gerald. (ed.) *Sport and Politics.* Champaign, Illinois: Human Kinetics, 1986.

Redmond, Gerald. *The Sporting Scots in Nineteenth-Century Canada.* London and Toronto: Associated University Press, 1982.

Rice, Emmett A., John L. Hutchinson and Mabel Lee. *A Brief History of Physical Education* (5th ed.). New York: The Ronald Press Company, 1969.

RIORDAN, JAMES. "Pyotr Franzevich Lesgaft (1837-1909): The Father of Russian Physical Education." Unpublished paper, Bradford University, England, n.d.

RIORDAN, JAMES. *Sport in Soviet Society.* London: Cambridge University Press, 1977.

ROBERTS, GLYN C. "The Rise of European Nationalism and Its Effect on the Pattern of Physical Education and Sport." *A History of Sport and Physical Education to 1900.* Ed. Earle F. Zeigler. Champaign, Ill.: Stipes Publishing Company, 1973.

ROGERS, C. "Sports, Religion and Politics: The Renewal of an Alliance," *The Christian Century,* April 5, 1972, pp. 392-94.

ROUSSEAU, JEAN JACQUES. *Emile or Education.* Trans B. Foxley. London: J.M. Dent and Sons, 1911.

SANBORN, MARION ALICE and BETTY G. HARTMAN. *Issues in Physical Education* (2nd ed.). Philadelphia: Lea and Febiger, 1970.

SCOTT, JACK. *The Athletic Revolution.* New York: The Free Press, 1971.

SHUTTLEWORTH, JAMES JOHN. "Community Education and Recreation in England and Wales: The Derivation of a General Approach." Ph.D. Dissertation, University of Alberta, 1975.

SMITHELLS, P.A., and P.E. CAMERON. *Principles of Evaluation in Physical Education.* New York: Harper and Brothers, 1962.

Sport in France. Published by the Ambassade de France, Service de Presse et d'information (n.d.).

STRUTT, JOSEPH. *The Sports and Pastimes of the People of England.* 1801.

[The Earl of] Suffolk and Berkshire, H. PEEK, and F.G. AFLALO. *The Encyclopedia of Sport,* 2 vols. London: Lawrence and Bullen, 1897.

TOFFLER, ALVIN. *Future Shock.* New York: Random House, 1970.

UEBERHORST, H. *Geschichte der Leibesubungen.* Verlag Bartels and Wernitz KG. Vol. 4, 1972.

UMPHLETT, W.L. *The Sporting Myth and the American Experience.* London: Associated University Presses, 1975.

VALASKAKIS, KIMON, and PETER SINDELL. "A Blueprint for a Conserver Society for Canada." Unpublished paper presented at the University of Alberta, May, 1976.

VAN DALEN, DEOBOLD B., and BRUCE L. BENNET. *A World History of Physical Education: Cultural Philosophical, Comparative* (2nd ed.). Englewood Cliffs, N.J.: Prentice-Hall, 1971.

VENDIEN, C. LYNN, and JOHN NIXON. *The World Today in Health, Physical Education, and Recreation.* Englewood Cliffs, N.J.: Prentice-Hall, 1968.

VETO, J. *Sports in Hungary.* Budapest: Corvina, 1965.

VICKERMAN, R.W. *The Economics of Leisure and Recreation.* London: The Macmillan Press, 1975.

WEAVER, ROBERT B. *Amusements and Sports in American Life.* New York: Greenwood Press, 1968.

WEBSTER, DAVID F. *Scottish Highland Games.* Edinburgh, Reprographia, 1973.

WILDT, K.C. "Physical Education and Sports in the Federal Republic of Germany: A Review of their Development and Present Status." Paper presented at the Second World Symposium on the History of Physical Education and Sport, Banff, Canada, 1971.

WISE, S.F., and D. FISHER. *Canada's Sporting Heroes: Their Lives and Times.* Don Mills, Ontario: General Publishing Company, 1974.

ZEIGLER, EARLE F. "Historical Foundations: Social and Educational," *A History of Sport and Physical Education to 1900,* pp. 267-76. Ed. Earle F. Zeigler. Champaign, Ill.: Stipes Publishing Company, 1973.

_____. M.L. HOWELL, and M. TREKELL. *Research in the History, Philosophy and International Aspects of Physical Education and Sport: Bibliographies and Techniques.* Champaign, Ill.: Stipes Publishing Company. 1971.

Section Four
Physical Education and Sport in the United States

Robert Knight Barney

Most survey histories are conspicuous for what they leave unsaid, rather than for what they report. The historian, in attempting to reconstruct the past, is prone toward oversimplification. He or she selects a miniscule number of facts and faces out of a crowd of events so complex as to be almost incomprehensible, and then attempts to paint a landscape of history as clear as any image reflected from a looking glass. Sadly, the results of such representation are opaque in quality. However, if an insight into the highlights of history prods one to pursue the deeper facets of "that left unsaid," then the survey history becomes a useful tool in learning. With that in mind, the author has attempted to "stride to the highground" and to leave the morass of deeper details to the investigative inquiry of those readers whose interest might be motivated in such a direction.

The following survey examines the physical exercise heritage of the United States of America. Viewed in collective fashion, the sport and physical education experiences of the United States have formed a mosaic which, more than any other of the world's cultures, most closely resembles that vivid contribution made to man's sporting heritage by Classical Greece and Rome; many feel that that contribution represents a cycle in sport history which is tending to be repeated now in North America.

Robert Knight Barney is currently Professor of Physical Education, The University of Western Ontario, London, Canada.

THE UNITED STATES OF AMERICA

America's European Heritage: Ascetic Ideal and Work Ethic

It has long been held by numerous social historians that the American way of life has been little more than an extension of the Old World customs and traditions of those people who settled and developed the nation which rose from the embers of British mercantilism to become the United States of America. Irrespective of the contributions made to the broad landscape of American life by later Southern European immigrants, and by the black African, whose descendants are finally merging into mainstream America, the people whose influence was the greatest in framing America's cultural heritage were from Northern Europe. Their well-established traits, combined with an instinctive desire to forge a better life for themselves in a new land, provided the chief ingredients in the recipe for America's unfolding culture, including developments in sport and physical education.

An analysis of the legacy transferred to America by Northern Europeans exposes a common prescription for human thought and deed which contributed in both negative and positive ways toward shaping the watershed of physical education and sport history. That commonality of European "thought and deed" lay vested in the ascetic ideal, or, as it came to be expressed in America, the Protestant work ethic. Seldom in the history of mankind has a human ideal so affected the consequence of sport and physical education.

Asceticism, an ideal rooted in Hebrew, Greek, and early Christian cultures, espoused the doctrines of self-denial and restriction of worldly pleasures in favor of strict obedience to God and pursuit of a simple and spiritually rewarding life. Asceticism became the steadfast core of early Christian creed and was most vividly expressed in Roman Catholicism. Modifications to the Catholic expression of asceticism made by developing Protestant religions during the fourteenth, fifteenth, and sixteenth centuries of Northern Europe's Reformation Period were of particular importance to the physical exercise heritage of America. Protestant alteration of Medieval asceticism underscored the importance of thrift and economic assertion cast in the spirit of individual and group capitalism. To make money through one's personal industry and business acumen was also to serve the Lord. The Almighty favored those who helped themselves (Griswold, 1934, p. 24).

Attendant to the Protestant ethic's accent on strict religious observance and dedication to one's personal industry was the curtailment of activities which might encroach on carrying out the ethic's goals. In respect to sport and physical exercise in early America, the ethic of the ascetic ideal often reflected a detestation of idleness, an abhorrence of frivolity and play, as well as an avoidance of recreation and sport (Dulles, 1965, pp. 5–10).

The seeds of Medieval European asceticism were planted and nurtured in the furrows of a scarcity economy, that is, an economy with a severe deficiency of material goods for consumption and enjoyment (Fairs, 1976, pp. 16–18). America mirrored a similar economy from the outset of its history until well into the second half of the nineteenth century. However, as the profile of America's economy gradually changed from one of scarcity to one of established surplus, a natural relaxation of ascetic restraints occurred concurrently (Fairs, 1976, pp. 20–25). As a result, Americans began to turn their attention to more worldly and pleasurable pursuits, including large-scale indulgence in sport and physical exercise activities, as both participants and spectators.

Customs and lifestyles are arrived at only after slow evolution of social processes. So, too, is lengthy passage of time necessary for change to occur in patterns which have become well established (Rostow, 1960, p. 52). The first two and a half centuries of American history demonstrated only slight alteration in an agrarian-based scarcity economy. An explosion of technology and a commensurate rise of a distinct surplus economy following the Civil War provided the first in a series of events which gently but firmly separated America from the inherited European ethos of piety, thrift, and attention to business as service to God. The slow disintegration of American Protestant ethic shifted sport and physical exercise from a supernumerary to a center-stage role in American life.

Colonial and Young Republic America: Tavern, Town, and Trespass Sport

The term *sport* is an interesting word to contemplate. Certainly it has connoted different meanings at various times in history. For instance, an English dictionary published in the late eighteenth century described sport as: "play, diversion, game, frolic, and tumultuous merriment; mock contemptuous mirth, that with which one plays; play, idle gingle; diversion of the field, as of fowling, hunting, fishing" (Sheridan, 1789). Such a definition might give the impression that the term being defined is *recreation* instead of sport. But to have such an impression would be to superimpose modern values on an era two centuries passed, and that would be unfair. Yet the definition does project two general themes applicable to the first two centuries of American sporting history: first, that sporting and leisure exercise was generally undertaken in a spontaneous manner, and, second, that such activity was more often than not devoid of any but the most simple types of organization. In fact, simplicity might be the best word to characterize early America's sporting experience.

Beyond that, however, our adopted definition give us no clue as to what was the most distinguishing characteristic of the period's sporting atmosphere, that being a firm link between sport and practical events, particularly those that helped to meet the demands of a marginal economic environment or that served the interests of religious creed and class status.

The development of early American sport, though negatively affected at certain times and in particular places by churchly posture on the subject, reflected a framework of activity featuring both diversity and distinctiveness: *diversity* in the variety of activities present in colonial and young Republic society, and *distinctiveness* in the types of sports peculiar to each geographical area of the emerging nation. For sport history purposes, early America can be partitioned into three distinct areas: New England, the Middle Atlantic and South, and the Frontier. The sporting character of each was dependent on its own social and economic character.

New England. Benjamin Franklin once proclaimed: "America's recreation is business," an utterance which probably bespoke the ethic of New England more than any other area of early America. While a printer's apprentice in Boston, long before his ascendance to fame as a man of literature, science, and international diplomacy, Franklin constructed a moral code and scored himself daily on his progress. His list of moral virtues included temperance, silence, order, resolution, frugality, industry, sincerity, justice, moderation, cleanliness, tranquility, chastity and humility. How like New England Puritan Franklin to chart the virtues of life necessary for both priestly and material satisfaction! In his aphorisms for the common man, Poor Richard sang his loudest praise for industry and "the wasting not of time." "Diligence is the mother of good luck," he said, "and God gives all things to industry" (Reid, 1896, p. 194). Franklin's espousal, pure Calvinistic doctrine in its best form, conveyed the idea that idleness was to be abhorred, particularly idleness that was ungainfully employed in pursuit of "frolic, merriment, mirth, and idle gingle diversion."

In general, New England's colonial society experienced no really severe class distinctions. Most people were hard working and pious, either by direct dedication to the tenets of Puritanism, or by emulation of those who were. The wealthy and influential, although not set apart in social class distinction in the normal sense of the term, nevertheless were rarely "not of the faith" and thus consciously existed as conduct models in society. Their predilection toward work and their general denial of idle enjoyment, at least publicly, served to stymie the rapid growth of sports and games in New England (Dulles, 1965, pp. 12–13).

But even in this bastion of American Puritanism, sporting indulgence existed in various forms. Though restricted, sport was nevertheless visible enough to make a modest contribution to early America's sporting mosaic (Jable, 1976, pp. 35-38). And what were the activities of leisure existing as a result of church oversight, condoned in small measure by religious authority, or carried out in trespass of such dictates? As might be imagined in an area where climatic conditions were not favorable to subsistence efforts, leisure activities were channeled toward self-preservation or cooperative pursuits, such as hunting, fishing, fowling, house and barn raisings, corn huskings, activities related to harvest festivals, and the impromptu contests and social interaction associated with Thanksgiving, militia days, and town meeting gatherings. Many of these were given at least tacit endorsement by the Puritan leaders for both practical and emotional reasons (Davis, 1972, p. 2).

At other times, New England Yankees pursued frivolity that neither served a practical need nor gained approval from the church. Most vivid of these were activities associated with the tavern—a landmark in early American society fully as popular in its day as the neighborhood bar or lounge of the twentieth century. The tavern existed as a journey stop-off point and as a meeting place for expressions of conviviality and camaraderie. Naturally, the great "enhancer" of such social interplay was the bottle and tankard, normally frowned on by Puritan code. In his efforts to increase business, the tavern owner often arranged for entertainments in the form of shooting contests, gambling games, matches of skill and endurance such as wrestling and boxing, blood contests including bear-baiting, cockfighting, and other animal confrontations, and theatrical plays and interludes. It might be said that early America's tavern keepers were the nation's first sport promoters.

New England contributed in two ways to the formation of America's sport—in one sense, activities given sanction by religious concurrence and, in another, "trespass sport," that is, pastime activity beyond the boundaries of Puritan mandate. Segments of New England society championing each sport form jousted with each other. Puritanism, with its deeply embedded work ethic, exhibited vast endurance; its final demise to the counterforce of social relaxation was greatly prolonged but, nevertheless, quite distinct.

Middle Atlantic and Southern States. Outside of New England, except perhaps in Pennsylvania, the impact of religion and the work ethic was less restraining in the evolution of American sport and recreational pastime. Part of the reason was that the milder climate of the Middle Atlantic and Southern regions was more accommodating to a relaxation of the self-preserving, dawn-to-dark need to work. Then too, in the South, as well as in New York, distinct class societies evolved wherein a laboring lower-class population of Indians, indentured servants and later black African slaves carried out society's work tasks while a leisured governing aristocracy developed a tendency toward play and recreation. Such a phenomenon has been a constant of history to greater or lesser degree in all civilizations.

Unhampered by the restrictions of Puritanism, at least in long-term force, New Yorkers, Virginians, and Carolinians pursued various types of play activity to fill their leisure time. In New York, an area first settled by the Dutch but subject to British rule from the early 1700s, sport activity was pronounced. The Dutch were active participants in recreational pastimes transferred to the New World from Holland. Dutch tradition, coupled with the English penchant for recreational sport when the fetters of religion were relaxed, created a formidable amount of leisure pastime, particularly in the form of winter activities. Skating, sleigh riding, coasting, gala winter carnivals, and a primitive form of ice hockey or shinny were standard outdoor recreational fare. The ingenious Dutch were not long in finding means whereby skittles, the colony's favorite leisure activity, could be played during the winter months. Indoor surfaces were contrived in the 1600s and skittles, a form of bowling, became a simple extension of the popular outdoor game played on grass. Ninepins so captivated the attention of the Dutch, as well as the English residents of nearby Connecticut, that attempts were made by church leaders to place restrictions on its pursuit in favor of more dedicated application to religious observance. With an abundance of wild game and aquatic life in forest and waterway, it was natural for New Yorkers to indulge regularly in hunting, fowling, and fishing. Under English influence, horse racing developed firm traditions in New York, initially at Salisbury Plain on Long Island, and later at various sites in what eventually became New York City (Robertson, 1964, pp. 9–11). The stratification of New York society prompted the evolution of balls, dances, and social extravaganzas among the wealthy.

In Virginia and the Carolinas, where class structure became even more pronounced than in New York and where the region's economy was firmly wedded to agriculture, a planter aristocracy evolved that managed and played while slave underlings toiled in tobacco field and rice tidewater. The core of recreation for the leisured aristocracy in the South became field sports—fox hunting, horse racing, hunting, and fowling. Cockfighting developed into a highly popular leisure activity which gathered a spectator following of both planters and slaves (Dulles, 1965, p.

35). Often enamored by things from France, Southern ladies and gentlemen gave festive parties and gala balls featuring the latest dances of French origin. Theatrical interludes and plays also became a part of Southern America's leisure habit. In general, the Middle Atlantic areas of Maryland and New Jersey followed the leisure patterns established in Virginia and New York, respectively.

A study of events in early Pennsylvania provides an interesting model for measuring religious constraints imposed on certain frivolous pursuits against the inherent need to play. In 1681, when William Penn was granted title to the land in British America which became known as Pennsylvania, the noble English statesman had every intention of establishing a New World colony that would become a utopia for Quaker religious practice. Penn being a dedicated convert to the religious mission of the Society of Friends, his translation of Quakerism was reflected in the form of Blue Laws (so called because they were written on pieces of blue paper), which sharply curtailed leisure activities on the Sabbath as well as during the week. In his enunciations on such diversions as cockfighting, bull baits, dice, cards, masques, balls, and plays, Penn scornfully characterized them as activities "breeding immorality and vice, exciting people to rudeness, cruelty, looseness and irreligion" (Beatty, 1939, p. 291). Even though Pennsylvania Quakers did not attempt to impose their zealously held religious beliefs on non-Quaker settlers, they did expect that all residents of the colony would behave "in the Quaker way" and practice the standards of morality and virtue held sacred. At the close of the seventeenth and throughout much of the eighteenth century, immigration into Pennsylvania by significantly large groups of Anglicans and Presbyterians exercised an influence on the lifestyle of the Friends. Exemplifying a more liberal and worldly approach to life than Quakers, Anglican and Presbyterian practices slowly eroded Penn's "Holy experiment." Philadelphia, the center of Quaker culture in Pennsylvania, rapidly became a city of relaxed social atmosphere. Confronted by such "ungodly intrusion," Quakers sought to preserve their ways by retreating to the hinterland areas of Pennsylvania. The result was that Blue Laws restricting all types of "rude and riotous sports" began to have diminishing influence (Jable, 1974, pp. 108–120).

Another factor in the disintegration of Blue Law doctrine was the development of the tavern, a consistent nemesis to religious influence on idle diversion. In Pennsylvania, leisure and sporting activities associated with the tavern were censured by the Society of Friends. Diversions such as cockfighting, turkey shooting, bear baiting, horse racing, gambling and lottery-type games, dancing, musical concerts, and forms of primitive drama were all carried out in the tavern atmosphere. Pennsylvania's colonial inn rapidly became the social center for the common man—a center for his leisure recreation and a forum for his reproach of the domineering Quakers. In the tavern he received the type of relief from his demanding lifestyle that a Quaker conversely found in his meeting house.

The Frontier. In the Piedmont beyond tidewater and tobacco fields and in the lands west of the Alleghany Mountain barrier settled young America's most adventurous and individualistic people—people whose lifestyles were largely unhampered by population density, religious censure, and governmental restriction. During the colonial and young Republic periods of American history, the frontier signified the western portions of the original British colonies and the broad expanses of forest and plain west of the Alleghenies along the Mississippi River Valley. Living on small farms, homesteads, and occasionally in small settlement towns, the frontiersman led a life in direct contrast to that of his brethren in the East. The frontiersman's isolation offered him a unique opportunity to pursue leisure-time activity as he pursued other facets of life—with a spontaneity and rambunctiousness that would become the embodying spirit and personality trademark of Americans in general.

The sporting and leisure activities of the frontier exemplified both the cooperative instinct needed to survive the exacting hardships of an environment devoid of luxury, and the individualism of people who recognized little authority but their own in the pursuit of their destiny. Accompanied by the ubiquitous earthen jug of homemade spirits, frontierspeople took part in such help-thy-neighbor activities as barn and cabin raisings, harvesting of crops, and corn huskings, their toil lightened by the prospect of the festive celebrations that followed. Physical strength and skill at activities indigenous to frontier life were important. Contests in log rolling, rough and tumble wrestling, bareknuckle boxing, shooting at marks for prizes, jumping contests, and racing one's horses became common. For men and women of America's hinterland areas, one of the most popular forms of recreational pastime was dancing. Jigs, reels, square and folk dances of Old Country origin were rapidly adapted to the "fiddle, flute and flagon" of the frontier. As frontier society became more developed, the country fair became an important recreational event, as did the camp meeting featuring attempts by various religious sects to rejuvenate the often ignored churchly instincts of the unenlightened. On the frontier, as in every other section of young America, gambling and sporting activities and the "barroom and bedroom bedevilment" of the tavern formed important aspects of leisure time.

Despite the negative influence of the Puritan ethic on the sporting pastimes of America's colonial forefathers and young Republic citizens, the semblance of a leisure portrait began to come into focus; it reflected sport and recreation taking place in both cooperative and competitive circumstance, in both worldly and unworldly social atmospheres economic environments of both scarcity and semi-surplus. The Co and young Republic periods reflected the dominance of New W asceticism and its work ideal over social relaxation; but conversely, the two periods also demonstrated the well-tested thesis that human nature reflects a strong and inherent need to play, and that such a need must, at some time and in some form, be satisfied (Huizinga, 1948). Participation in sports and games during America's early history provided that necessary safety valve for expression of such need, an expression which in time gained Americans a reputation as avid and energetic participants in sport.

Federal, Antebellum and Civil War America:
Taproot of Organized Sport and Physical Education

The span of years marking the Federal, Antebellum, and Civil War periods of American history (1820–1865) marked a change in America's character that led to its acknowledged position today as the most urban and industrial country in the world. That distinction, both envied and despised by the modern world, can be traced to the triumph of Hamiltonian Federalist economic and political aspiration in the form of manufacturing and strong federal government over Thomas Jefferson's dreams of America as a rural, agrarian nation ruled by powerful state governments and a laissez-faire federal body.

The nation's developing industrial expansion and concomitant expansion of urban areas gave fresh impetus to opening the American frontier. With free or "dirt cheap" land "there for the taking," the western frontier was ready for the arrival of those straining against the Allegheny waistband of populous eastern America. For several decades, however, the expected mass movement was instead a gradual westward migration of trappers, land speculators, traders, miners, and prospective farmers. To go West one needed a stake, and the way to gain it was to go first to the city, labor in the growing manufacturing industry, accumulate some capital, and then move West to pursue a new life in a new land, free from the negative effects of urban surroundings. For the most part, however, history records that the era's would-be western migrants, whether native American or newly arrived European immigrant, became instead imprisoned in growing cities, caught in the web of their failure to gain and preserve the capital needed for westward emigration (Shannon, 1945, pp. 31-37). Contemporary America is no different. A significant portion of America's urban migrants of the past fifty years have been people who were intent on "gaining a stake" in a city job so that a fresh start might be made elsewhere.

By 1850 America's chief cities—Boston, New York, Philadelphia,

Baltimore, Washington, Charleston, Savannah, and Columbus, Georgia —showed population figures that had accelerated rapidly. Such population density constituted an ominous potential for social unrest. Although the subject even now remains in debate, there is enough evidence to support a thesis that recreation in the nineteenth-century cities served as a social safety valve that relieved the pressure of frustrated hopes for living in the West (Paxton, 1917, p. 145). Sport, to the confined urbanite, became a "here and now" solution to a pitifully frustrating "when and how" problem. To the city dweller, watching a horse race, a ball game, the theater, oarsmen, pugilists, or pedestrian performers provided compensation for his obliterated dream of leaving the city.

It can be argued that sport in some form has always been present in the lives of mankind, regardless of environmental conditions. But it can also be supposed that certain environmental conditions are more receptive than others to the rise of sport. The city environment lent itself to the sporting movement in America. The informal, rural sporting pastimes of early America, however, could hardly be expected to fulfill the leisure recreation needs of a growing urban society. Prodded by the efforts of individuals bent on profitting through the commercialization of spectator sports, thousands were led into a passive role. Thus in pre-Civil War America, the genesis of an "audience habit" evolved (Dulles, 1965, p. 147). People themselves were rarely participants in the sporting action, but most were caught up with the impending crisis of who would win.

The role of creating and maintaining interest in sport was played by the sporting entrepreneur or promoter. More often than not, he was accompanied in his efforts by the newspapers. Aside from being financially rewarded, the promoter was crucial in helping to embellish America's sporting heritage. His stage became the racetrack, theater, tent, river, fairgrounds, and forest clearing; his audience, a growing American middle class, excited by the prospect of contest.

Between 1820 and 1865 some of the nation's major sporting events took place on the racetrack. The country's long-established tradition of matching carefully bred horses in contests of speed and endurance continued in even more dedicated fashion than ever. During that period four components of horse racing were greatly enhanced: (1) the number of meetings, (2) proliferation of gambling, (3) increase in public attendance, and (4) the phenomenon of winners' purses (Adelman, pp. 31-52). Race courses could be found in all areas of the East, with the exception of New England. The South and West were well represented, with established tracks in New Orleans, Louisville, Cincinnati, and San Francisco. In 1823 an estimated throng of almost 60,000 people witnessed the epic thoroughbred contest between American Eclipse and Sir Henry, turf representatives of the North and South, respectively, and in 1845 Peytona, an Alabama-bred thoroughbred, bested Fashion before a crowd of over 70,000 (Robertson, 1964, pp. 52–64). The activities of the turf were reported regularly to a receptive public by two of America's oldest sporting publications, the *Spirit of the Times* and the *American Turf Register*.

Racing of another kind also captivated the attention of Americans. The English pastime of long-distance running and walking, often referred to as pedestrianism, gained wide public acclaim and was particularly suited to the flair and advertising genius of sport promoters. Storied confrontations between American and British "go as you please" performers made for ideal spectator events. In 1835 Henry Stannard ushered in organized pedestrianism in America by becoming the first person to cover ten miles in less than an hour, an accomplishment which won him a purse of $1,000 and thrilled a crowd of over 40,000 people assembled on Long Island for the event (Lucas, 1968, p. 587). During the next two decades American pedestrian performers competed in international races in their own country and abroad with systematic regularity. As the era waned, American pedestrian history noted the beginning of Edward Payson Weston's competitive career, an odyssey which saw him cover over 100,000 miles in pedestrian "tramps" held between 1861 and 1913 (Lucas, 1968, pp. 587–88).

Few sports activities during the period captured the public's imagination and satisfied their lust for excitement more than did the affairs of the prize ring. Prohibited by law in most cities, pugilistic matches were carried out under an aura of secrecy and illegality. The type of boxing representative of the time was far removed from that of the modern era and, in fact, was but a modification of the frontier's rough and tumble, head-butting, eye-gouging brawls. There were no weight divisions and no limit of rounds; the bout went on until one fighter or the other succumbed or acknowledged defeat. The crowds at such contests were seldom large, because bouts had to be staged away from population centers in order to escape the authority of the law. For Americans the concept of a world boxing championship evolved when Tom Hyer defeated James "Yankee" Sullivan in 1849. In October 1858, between 3,000 and 4,000 people, some of them from as far away as New Orleans, steamboated across Lake Erie to Canada's Long Point Island to witness John Morrisey's knockout victory over John "Benecia Boy" Heenan (Lardner, 1972, p. 33). In 1860 an international match held in England between Heenan and Britain's Tom Sayers for the championship left vacant by Morrisey's retirement ended in confusion when the match was halted by the crowd in the forty-third round. Sayers was later awarded a controversial victory, while Heenan returned home to be welcomed by 12,000 boisterous greeters (Dulles, 1965, p. 146). Capitalizing on his fame, Heenan boxed a series of public exhibition matches, luring to such occasions the huge crowds normally precluded by the need for secrecy and isolation. Two of the nation's leading newspapers, the *New York Times* and the *New York Herald,* regularly registered outrage at the brutality of the prize ring, but at the same time graphically described the pugilistic events. The gory details of boxing were of intense interest to sport-minded Americans, a fact which did not escape circulation-conscious newspapers.

Sailing ships and river craft played a primary role in the discovery, settlement, and expansion of America. What could be more natural than for Americans to develop interest in contests held on the water? From Plymouth to Jamestown, early settlers had matched their small coastal craft in some of America's earliest sailing and rowing competitions. To the nineteenth century must be accorded the distinction, "America's age of sail and oar." Promoted by newspapers, journals, and the activities of the sports entrepreneur, regatta contests developed a rich international and domestic flavor. The period's first event of note occurred in 1824, when the American barge *Whitehall* defeated a British craft in a rowing contest in New York Harbor. An estimated crowd of 50,000 witnessed the competition, "cheering themselves hoarse" as the winning crew pocketed a prize of $1,000 (Dulles, 1965, p. 142). Rowing regattas spread throughout America as boat clubs were formed in populated and hinterland area alike. Those in Boston, New York, Philadelphia, and Detroit became the most established.

Yale formed a rowing club in 1843, followed by Harvard in 1844. In 1852 America recorded its first intercollegiate athletic competition, an event which, even then, was undermined by commercial exploitation. Railroad promoters matched the Harvard and Yale crews in a rowing contest on the waters of Lake Winnipesaukee off Center Harbor, New Hampshire, for the purpose of advertising the area as a vacation spot (Lewis, 1967, pp. 637–48). By the end of the Antebellum period, Pennsylvania, Brown, Dartmouth, and Trinity had joined with Harvard and Yale in college regatta competition.

The sport of yacht racing was of particular interest to nineteenth-century Americans. The New York Yacht Club was formed in 1844 and rapidly became America's symbolic representative in international racing. In 1851, under the leadership of Commodore John C. Stevens, the New York Yacht Club's sloop *America* took part in the initial episode of the storied America's Cup competitions. Basking in the glow of *America*'s victory over a British racing fleet marshalled on the waters off southern England near the Isle of Wight, the American minister to Paris congratulated the winning crew by stating: " . . . And what a victory! . . . beat in her own native seas . . . contending against a fleet of seventeen sail of her picked models of naval architecture . . . is something that may well encourage us in the race of maritime competition which is set before us" (Betts, 1974, p. 38). Minister William C. Rives' words were indeed well inaugural in 1851, except during periods of war. The United States, represented by the New York Yacht Club, defended the championship cup for well over a century, until Australia won it in the America's Cup challenge held off Newport, Rhode Island in 1983. In 1987 Dennis Conner of the San Diego Yacht Club returned the cherished cup to United States custody. Yachting clubs developed steadily along America's eastern and western seacoasts, with those at Marblehead and Nahant, Massachusetts, achieving particular distinction in racing competition.

When noting the country's predilection for racing water craft, steamboat racing on the nation's inland waterways should not be ignored. Contests generating feverish excitement and frenzied gambling were common events along the rivers of the Mississippi Valley. Those races which took place on the Mississippi River itself, especially on the run from St. Louis to New Orleans, formed a colorful chapter in American sport history.

Jacques Barzun, noted scholar and frequent critic on the customs and idiosyncrasies of Americans, once wrote: "Whoever wants to know the heart and mind of America had better learn baseball" (Wallop, 1969, p. 22). There is little doubt at this writing that baseball has captivated the sporting minds of more Americans, for a longer period of time, with greater intensity than any other single activity in the nation's sporting history.

The now discredited myth that Abner Doubleday invented the game at Cooperstown, New York, in the late 1830s has yielded to the firm substantiation that baseball evolved from forms of English children's sport transferred to America in the seventeenth century (Henderson, 1947, pp. 170–96). Ball games, known in various areas of England as rounders, feeder, baseball, and stoopball, claimed the attention of American youngsters as early as the seventeenth century. Baseball took on various names in its early American experience: Massachusetts ball, cricket, town ball, "one old cat," "two old cat," and others. Each form was distinctive, but all had batsmen, bases, fielders, and a ball. The most significant architect in the nineteenth-century development of baseball was Alexander Cartwright, a professional surveyor in New York City. In the early 1840s Cartwright experimented with modifications of the various forms of baseball in America. The results of his efforts gave to the game such enduring characteristics as: foul lines, four bases arranged in diamond form, 90-foot distances between each base, nine men per side, three strikes per batsman, and three outs per half inning.

Enlivened by Cartwright's zeal for baseball, fellow colleagues of a New York social group called the Knickerbocker Club formed a team and challenged members of a rival club to a contest. On June 19, 1846, the two groups retired to a Hoboken, New Jersey site called Elysian Fields and played America's first recorded game of baseball, a four-inning affair won by the Knickerbocker Club's opponents, 23–1 (Wallop, 1969, p. 30).

Baseball expanded throughout the East as an amateur game for gentlemen. The representative teams of several clubs became important missionaries in the diffusion of baseball. By 1858 the Olympics of Philadelphia, the Gothams and Mutuals of New York, and the Knickerbocker Club, fully recovered from its history-making drubbing, were all among the East's strongest nines. Baseball was carried west on the crest of railroad development and transferred to the South largely by the Civil War aftermath of Confederate troops returning home from Union prisoner of war camps, where they had learned to play the game. Prodded by civic pride and a desire to win, keen rivalries developed between cities. The sporting attention of the American public began to focus on baseball in significantly increasing fashion, arousing the curiosity and intuitive reaction of promoters who sensed very quickly that the professionalization of the game could be financially rewarding. The period of American history succeeding the Civil War would only too well demonstrate the wisdom of such intuition.

Complementing the emerging American preoccupation with sport and amusement, attention was directed toward other types of pastimes. The theater developed and achieved greater popularity, enlisting the enthusiasm of thousands. Legitimate drama, burlesque, Shakespeare farce and variety, the minstrel show, opera, ballet, and musical concert gave eager consumers a variety of opportunites from which to choose. The rise of the circus and museum, both partially the product of the imaginative genius of America's premier amusement entrepreneur, Phineas T. Barnum, provided the public with still other forms of leisure recreation. America experienced a cultural awakening during the 1840s and 1850s, a phenomenon resulting in large audiences at Lyceum lectures held the country over. Dancing emerged from the limited invitation parties held by the affluent to become a popularly received public social expression. A fancy for salt water bathing attracted residents of the East Coast to the waters of the Atlantic, and thousands found it great sport as well to gape at ladies and gentlemen clad in the colorful but often bizarre bathing attire of the period. A *New York Herald* reporter in 1853 was moved to exclaim: "I noticed several ladies of admirable shapes . . . Oh! ye happy waves, what a blissful destiny is yours, when you can enclasp and kiss such lovely forms" (*New York Herald,* July 19, 1853). Most of the leisure and sporting activities prevalent in the East were also pursued "out West," perhaps in less sophisticated form, but certainly with no less enthusiasm. The chief theme of western amusement was gambling, and the variety of "games of chance" at one's disposal was almost inexhaustible.

America's Federal, Antebellum and Civil War periods, for the most part, were characterized by a transition from largely pre-modern forms of sport to modernization character. Such modernization was in turn characterized by development of sporting clubs, written rules, newspaper coverage, inter-city and intercollegiate competition, and, of course, growing public attention. All of these characteristics would proliferate after the Civil War's temporary distraction was spent.

Physical Education Programs. An analysis of the growth of sport during the period would not be complete without at least a survey portrayal of those contributions made by physical education. Physical education as a genuine school curricular entity would not become widespread until the early twentieth century. However, the fundamental bases for the discipline's emergence into the mainstream of American education were laid during the nineteenth century.

The curriculum of America's dame schools, Latin grammar institutions, private academies, and theology-oriented colleges of the Colonial and Young Republic periods reflected little or no attention to physical education experiences for students. The achievement of mind and body fitness through physical exercise was not likely to be appreciated fully by a society whose core ethic was wedded to the pursuit of the materialistic and utilitarian. Isolated events of the early nineteenth century, however, created interest in physical well-being resulting from systematic exercise. Such interest was enhanced by the efforts of a small group of concerned Americans and the influence of foreign exercise systems transferred to America by Northern Europeans.

Perhaps the first American to focus public attention on the health values of exercise was Benjamin Franklin. As early as 1749 Franklin expressed the "value of exercise in hardening the constitution" (Franklin, 1749, p. 10). A half century later Noah Webster observed the value of exercise, particularly for youth, when he stated that it should be "the bizziness of yung persons to assist nature, and strengthen the growing frame by athletic exercise" (Webster, 1790, p. 388). Neither Franklin's nor Webster's messages had much impact during their time. By 1820 a concern over the lack of fitness in American youth moved Captain Alden Partridge, a former superintendent of West Point, to set about the task of establishing schools in New England whose curricula were to be highlighted by vigorous physical outdoor activities. Using the military school model as his beacon, Partridge was only moderately successful (notably at Norwich University in Vermont), but he found a richer reception in the American South (Leonard and Affleck, 1947, p. 268).

In 1824 the arrival in America of Karl Beck and Karl Follen, two disciples of the gymnastic and Republican political expression of Friedrich Jahn, signaled the beginning of German gymnastics in America. Beck found employment at the Round Hill School in Northampton, Massachusetts, where a portion of his duties were devoted to the development of physical education programs in the form of German gymnastics (Bennett, 1965, pp. 58–59). Thus, Beck's appointment and a recognition of the place of physical exercise in the school day became a landmark episode in the history of American physical education. Karl Follen won an appointment to the Harvard faculty as an instructor of German, but within a year he, too, had begun to teach German gymnastics to Harvard students and interested Boston townspeople (Leonard and Affleck, 1947, pp. 231–42). What had been but a small influx of German immigrants to America prior to the 1840s became an avalanche-like flow as a result of the failure of the Revolution of 1848 in Germany. From that point the German-American ethic of physical exercise reached formidable proportions for the remainder of the century, particularly as it was expressed in the various *Turnvereine* (gymnastics clubs) which blossomed wherever Germans settled in their adopted land.

History notes also the important contributions made to America's pioneer physical education processes by Dioclesian Lewis and Catharine Beecher. Lewis, the innovator of "musical gymnastics," is perhaps better known in history as the creator of the first school in America for the preparation of physical education teachers. Lewis's Boston Normal School of Physical Education, though it had a short life (1861–1868), had far-reaching impact on American awareness of body health and fitness (Barney, 1974, pp. 63–73). Joining Dio Lewis as an important figure in the evolution of physical education in America was Catharine Beecher, member of the historic Beecher family, well known for its enlightened stances on the subjects of theology, slavery, education, and women's suffrage. Between 1830 and the time of her death in 1878, Catharine Beecher carried on a crusade dedicated to improvement in the health and physical well-being of American women. Like Lewis, she had an active pen and is responsible for some of America's earliest physical education literature (Gerber, 1971, pp. 252–55).

The close of the period marked the origin of formal physical education programs in American colleges. By 1860 gymnasia had been erected at Harvard, Yale, and Amherst. Under the leadership of Edward Hitchcock, a pioneer program of physical education based on physiological principles and scientific measurement was developed at Amherst in 1860 and continued there for the remainder of the century under Dr. Hitchcock's direction. In general, colleges and universities throughout the eastern United States, as well as developing institutions in the Midwest, began to become sensitive to a growing interest in health-related physical exercise shown by members of the medical profession. Such sensitivity resulted in the building of limited facilities and the appointment of supervisory staff.

As colorful as the events linked to sport, recreation, leisure amu.
ment, athletics and, to some extent, even physical education, were during
the Federal, Antebellum, and Civil War periods, they were but a pale
prelude to what would follow in America's post-Civil War era, aptly
described by sport historians as the era during which the rise of sport and
physical education quite distinctly manifested itself in the social fabric of
American life.

America's Gilded Age: Exercise Systems and the Rise of College Sport

America's post-Civil War period, a major portion of which has been
referred to as the "Gilded Age," proved to be unrivaled in the nation's
history in the scope and significance of changes in the American lifestyle.
The tragic war between the Union and the Confederacy, uncontested as
the most crucial event in the domestic history of the United States (Rostow, 1971, p. 186), nevertheless resulted in national progress of an
unprecedented nature. The nation took the first giant step toward resolv-
ing the social dilemma of slavery and embarked on a Civil Rights path
more representative of the word "democracy". Also, the Civil War, as no
other event, spurred advances in technological and industrial development. In extraordinarily rapid fashion the economic destiny of the United
States became wedded to industry rather than to agriculture.

The expansion of the nation's railroad system and such later nineteenth-century inventions as the incandescent light bulb, electrification,
the trolley car, the Atlantic cable, the wireless, and many others, had a
phenomenal impact on American life. Developments in transportation
and communication, in particular, were of crucial importance in the rise
of sport and its subsequent diffusion to every segment of the nation.
Finally, and perhaps most important, the social and economic posture of
America's Gilded Age provided the first really significant force in the
disintegration of the Puritan ethic of restraint which had pervaded the
lives of most Americans in one way or another. In the years between the
end of the Civil War and the opening of the twentieth century, the
economy of the United States changed from one of deficit to one of
surplus. That fact, by itself, served to prod the nation's population toward
a relaxation of the sun-up to sun-down work ethic inherited from its
ancestors and an adoption of a slower pace of personal productivity
augmented by a growing penchant to be entertained. The process of
sport, in all its various late nineteenth-century ramifications, whetted that
appetite for entertainment.

As far as sport and physical education were concerned, the landmark developments of the Gilded Age were in the rise of college sport
and the clash of various exercise systems for supremacy as the single
system best suited for the physical education needs of America's schools.

College sport rose from obscure and infrequent regatta gatherings
and baseball contests to entrenched fixtures of athletic participation and

observation. Football rapidly developed into the sport form which commanded the largest share of public attention. Only college basketball would be able to muster a challenge to football's continual command of the college sports scene, but that challenge would not really begin to materialize until at least fifty years after the first interuniversity football contest was played.

The evolutionary process of American college football began in 1869 when students from Princeton and Rutgers contested in a football game more resembling soccer than today's football (Parke Davis, 1911, pp. 44–50). The critical event which moved the game toward the form we know today was an 1874 meeting between American and Canadian universities. In the spring of that year the football club of McGill University in Montreal journeyed to Cambridge, Massachusetts to compete with Harvard in two football games. The first contest was played under the Harvard rules (similar to those of soccer), but the second introduced to the United States the rules of English rugby union adapted to the Canadian football scene by McGill (Lewis, 1970, p. 8). Developed initially at Rugby School in England, the rules of rugby football allowed running with the ball, tackling, and lateral passing. Harvard students became infatuated with the "new game," and its football club took it up in earnest. Other American universities seeking to compete against Harvard under the old rules were rebuffed. Finally acceding to the Crimson's terms, a rugby-type football format soon became the standard. At the turn of the century America's captivation with the rough contact sport spilled from college campuses to sandlot play and quasi semiprofessional competition. From its primitive beginnings in the late 1890s in western Pennsylvania, professional football spread eastward to Philadelphia and westward into Ohio, where it found a fertile field of interest (Claassen, 1963, p. 4).

A noted sport historian has stated that college sport in America would not have achieved its present status without the impact of football (Lewis, 1970, p. 9). Those who argue that basketball has had at least an equal impact might debate the point, but can do so only from the basis of a contemporary setting. From its organizational beginnings in the 1860s, football, in all of its levels of play, has graphically portrayed the American craze for contact sport.

College athletics other than football also contributed to the rise of sport in America. Rowing, the oldest intercollegiate sport, continued its rich history. In 1876 Harvard and Yale, the most established crews in college rowing, became concerned over the unwieldiness of college regattas. A sharp increase in the numbers of crews wishing to participate had led to the necessity of qualifying heats. Such an odious formality led Harvard and Yale to retire from the large regatta gatherings to race against each other annually on the Thames River near New London,

Connecticut (Krout, 1929, pp. 81–82). During the next two decades Cornell University dominated college rowing in the absence of Harvard and Yale. Like football, rowing became a national sporting fixture. Crews from Wisconsin, Stanford, California, and Washington competed regularly in intersectional regattas, the most important of which was the annual championship meeting held initially at Saratoga and later on the Hudson River near Poughkeepsie, New York. College rowing during the Gilded Age became the first college sport with participation in international competition. Harvard in 1869 and Cornell in 1887 sent their crews across the Atlantic to compete against England's best oarsmen (Krout, 1929, p. 84).

Rowing regattas organized outside college competition gained momentum during the period, with enthusiastic and successful amateur rowing clubs being developed in Detroit, Duluth, Philadelphia, Boston, New York, San Francisco, and Jacksonville, Florida.

Partly the result of Scottish Caledonian influence, and in part spawned from amateur sporting clubs in America, track and field activity found its niche in college sport in the early 1870s. Running, jumping, and throwing competitions, though present in obscure form in America before the Civil War, blossomed fully during the immediate post-Civil War period (Redmond, 1971, pp. 15-16). In 1873 D. E. Bowie, a Canadian Scot and student at McGill University in Montreal, bested Cornell and Amherst runners in a two-mile race which marked Amercia's first collegiate track and field event (Redmond, 1971, p. 82). Attendant to the 1874 edition of the prestigious Saratoga regatta, which featured the finest college crews in the East, America's first intercollegiate track and field meet was held with athletes from various northeastern universities competing (Krout, 1929, p. 188). The initial meeting proved so successful that college track and field emerged on its own as a genuine competitor to rowing for the "favor and fancy" of college sporting adherents, spectator and participant alike.

From its modest beginning in 1859, college baseball continued its evolution with keen competition among Harvard, Yale, Dartmouth, Princeton, and Brown. College baseball, however, soon succumbed to America's penchant for the professional game. College tennis, ice hockey, and basketball evolved late in the century and once again the initial sites of development can be traced to the northeastern United States. The original concept of basketball, sparked by James A. Naismith's constructive genius, developed in December 1891 at the YMCA Training School in Springfield, Massachusetts. Initially designed as an indoor activity for YMCA winter programming, basketball demonstrated early evidence of being just the activity the nation's "sporting instinct" needed to sustain interest from the cessation of football in the late autumn until the start of baseball in the spring.

No portrait of amateur sport during this period would be complete without at least cursory mention of America's role in the first modern Olympic Games. A testimony to the dedication of the Frenchman Pierre Coubertin, the first edition of the modern Games was held in Athens, Greece in 1896. As far as America was concerned, the Games were one of the world's best kept sport secrets. Word of them being held reached a limited number of the many amateur athletes in the United States, the result being that four Princeton track team members were joined by five athletes from the Boston Athletic Association to form the nucleus of America's scanty representation (Mandell, 1976, p. 114). After an ocean voyage and amid the splendor of Hellenic arrangements in Athens, the Americans, particularly the Boston men, acquitted themselves excellently, winning most of the track and field events (Mandell, 1976, pp. 123–51). If little had been known in America about the impending Olympics, the news of her athletes' victories at the Games brought some newspaper coverage and renewal of enthusiasm among track and field followers.

For many Americans of this era there were numerous opportunities to participate in a variety of sports—old favorites as well as newcomers. Hunting, fishing, skating, winter coasting, boating, and hiking had wide appeal for people of all social classes. Factions of the wealthy were drawn toward playing tennis, riding to hounds, yachting, and attending celebrated horse race meetings. A craze for cycling developed in the late 1870s and early 1880s, stimulated in part by British development of an easy-to-ride bicycle which rapidly made the curious and ungainly velocipede extinct. The evolution of the golf and country club in the late 1880s spurred interest in golf, although for many decades to come the activity would remain the province of the affluent.

The development of professional sport, particularly in the last quarter of the century, found a ready market among middle-class Americans. The professional sports receiving the most public attention were baseball, pugilism and, for a time, pedestrianism.

Isolated instances of paid performers playing on amateur baseball clubs were noted prior to and immediately following the Civil War. Then in 1869 a team representing Cincinnati became the first all-professional baseball team. And what a team it was! Throughout the spring, summer, and early autumn, Cincinnati's Red Stockings coursed through the East, Midwest, and even to the Pacific Coast, earning 69 victories and one tie in 70 contests against the best competition that America could offer (Stern, 1969, pp. 36–37). The attention that was focused on Cincinnati as a result of the 1869 season justified many times over the Red Stockings' $9,500 payroll for that year (Stern, 1969, p. 31).

A firm commitment to the concept of professional baseball developed from the Cincinnati experience of 1869 (Barney, 1978, pp. 61-70). In

1876 a zealous Chicago businessman, William Hulbert, persuaded baseball representatives of St. Louis, Louisville, Cincinnati, Philadelphia,
New York, Hartford, and Boston to join with his Chicago team to form a
National League (Voigt, 1966, pp. 61-64). The league flourished through
the next decade, but faced a stiff challenge to its survival in 1889 as a
result of what has been popularly referred to as baseball's reserve clause.
Militant players became incensed over the jurisdiction that club owners
exercised over them as a result of owning their contracts. The National
League plodded through the 1890s, leaving in the wake of its struggle a
number of dismembered franchises. The effects of the Spanish-American
War brought about a decline in baseball attendance near the end of the
century. Added to the National League's attendance dilemma was the
looming spectre of a rival league being formed. Springing from the imaginative mind and industrious effort of Ban Johnson (Voigt, 1966, p. 241),
the creation of the American League in 1902 produced a format for
"major league" play which led to one of sport's most enduring and cap-
tivating classics—the World Series.

  With the aid of the *National Police Gazette*, America's most widely
read nineteenth-century sport publication, boxing achieved wide interest. History's best-known pugilists of the Gilded Age were two Americans
of first-generation Irish descent: John L. Sullivan, Boston's celebrated
"Strongboy," and James J. Corbett, product of San Francisco's notorious
Barbary Coast. Sullivan gained the world's heavyweight championship in
1882 by defeating Paddy Ryan in a bareknuckle bout purposely staged at
an isolated resort site in Mississippi (Lardner, 1972, p. 49). Police intrusion was a constant threat and often occurred at prizefight meetings.
Given to overeating, overdrinking, and personal public acclaim of his
considerable fighting talents, Sullivan nevertheless defeated all challeng-
ers to his throne during the decade following his defeat of Ryan. In one
of sport history's epic events, the scientific, crafty, and gentlemanly Jim
Corbett gained the championship from Sullivan by knocking out the
Bostonian in the twenty-first round of a title fight held at the Olympic
Club in New Orleans in 1892. The Corbett-Sullivan fight ushered in a
new era of boxing: the Queensberry Rules took effect, and boxing was
legalized because gloves were worn by the combatants (Lardner, 1972 p.
82). The transfer of prizefighting from secluded, woodland clearings,
waterbound barges, and other locations of secrecy and inaccessibility to
the large, brightly lit public halls and auditoriums of the late nineteenth
century placed the sport among the most attractive and entertaining to
the American public.

  Pedestrian contests reached the pinnacle of their importance on the
American sports scene during this period, particularly before 1870. In
few professional sports were entrepreneurial forces at work more than in

the popular "go as you please" contests. Trials for the Sir John Astley Belt, emblematic of pedestrian supremacy, were a focus of sporting attention on both sides of the Atlantic, in the United States and Great Britain (Lucas, 1968, pp. 588–93). The champions of both countries vied in some of sport history's most stirring athletic confrontations. Especially appealing to the urban dweller (and made so by the exhortations of promoters), excited, overflow crowds congregated in the halls when the contests were held. A graphic testimony to the public's interest in the sport was the fact that in 1879 *The Boston Globe* published 1,415 articles dealing with pedestrian activity. In 1885, when interest in the once-acclaimed spectacle had waned, only 46 pedestrian articles appeared in the *Globe* (Lewis, Jan. 1969, p. 143). The same phenomenon can be noted in other newspapers of the period.

As the century waned, a distinct middle class arose, becoming a distinguishing factor in the nation's commitment to urban industrial growth. In a short time urban dwellers found themselves contemplating several of the positive dimensions of American industrial capitalism: (1) increased productivity, (2) distribution of goods, (3) increased leisure time, and (4) an appreciable amount of dollars to spend on richer fulfillment of time away from work. The avenue of sport, from both a participant and viewing standpoint, became an important factor in America's leisure legacy.

Pre-Civil War messages railing on the subject of America's deteriorating national health, spoken and published by alarmists such as Christian physiologist Sylvester Graham (of Graham Cracker fame), prodded the nation's population to think more seriously of their health and bodily fitness. Though the Gilded Age proved to be a quiescent period in health reform, it was a period reflecting vigorous activity and growth in institutional physical education (Whorton, pp. 132-167). American physical education history between 1860 and 1890 reflected a number of approaches aimed at solving problems associated with health and fitness, no particular one of which could be said to have emerged as singularly dominant.

Of significant impact on the direction of physical education during the early part of the period were the effects of the Civil War. Chiefly because of concern by military officers over the general state of unfitness prevalent among Union soldiers, attempts were made by government officials to train school-aged boys in the methods of military drill (Weston, 1962, p. 32). The military drill concept of physical education, enhanced by the passing of the Morrill Land Act in 1862 (Leonard and Affleck, 1947, pp. 280–81), rose to the peak of its influence toward the end of the Civil War. Following the war, the practice of military drill in educational settings came under sharp attack from educators in general, and even more specifically from physical educators espousing the values of calisthenic and apparatus exercise (Barney, 1987, pp. 35-46).

Catharine Beecher and Dio Lewis, each of whom had championed the cause of exercise and fitness prior to the war, continued their crusade, calling for an awakening of concern for physical health and vitality. The most important physical educators of late nineteenth-century America, however, were a group of medical doctors associated with colleges and universities. They were the early pioneers in establishing and expanding the principle that health and exercise were important elements of student life and that a responsibility existed toward their promotion and maintenance. Among the most prominent medical physical educators were Edward Hitchcock, Dudley Allen Sargent, William G. Anderson, and Edward M. Hartwell.

Edward Hitchcock in time came to be looked upon as a leader in the field of anthropometry, a basic discipline in the field of scientific foundations for approaches to physical exercise. Hitchcock, associated throughout his long career with Amherst College in Massachusetts, organized a program of physical education for students based on health instruction and practice, calisthenics, apparatus exercise, and bathing (Gerber, 1971, pp. 277–78).

Dudley Allen Sargent's career in physical education was associated chiefly with the Hemenway Gymnasium at Harvard. As Director of the Hemenway Gymnasium he was a responsible guardian of the physical training of Harvard students from the time of his appointment in 1879 until his retirement in 1919, and his work served as a model that became widely copied by other universities in dealing with the subject of physical education. Sargent himself had been a noted gymnast and oarsman at Bowdoin College in Maine (Sargent, 1927 pp. 112–13) and had served a valuable apprenticeship in gymnasium direction while a medical student at Yale University (Sargent, 1927 pp. 136–44). He espoused the use of strength-developing machines in helping individuals who had specific developmental shortcomings. Such an approach, focused as it was on individual needs and differences, represented a sharp departure from the large-group exercise patterns characteristic of German, Swedish, and Dio Lewis gymnastic exercises. Perhaps the crowning achievements of Sargent's influence on American physical education concerned: (1) his practice of insisting on a preliminary medical examination for each student engaging in exercise classes, and (2) preparing qualified teachers of physical education. In 1881 he opened a normal school in Boston which became popularly referred to as the Sargent School of Physical Education; it continues to exist today, in modified fashion, as the Boston University Sargent College of Allied Health Professions (Gerber, 1971, p. 292). No other school for the preparation of physical educators has had such a sustained history.

There is little doubt that one of the most important events in the history of American physical education occurred on November 27, 1885, at Adelphi Academy in Brooklyn, New York, when Dr. William G. Anderson, Director of Physical Training at Adelphi, convened a meeting of 60 Americans interested in the development of physical education in the United States. Among the noted figures present were Dio Lewis, Dudley Sargent, and Edward Hitchcock, along with representatives of sports clubs, private agencies, men's and women's educational institutions, and writers on the subject of exercise. The intent of the conference was twofold: (1) to survey the various methods of physical education in America and explore means leading to a standardized approach, and (2) to develop plans for forming an association of individuals interested in the subject of physical education (Weston, 1962, p. 36). Subsequent meetings, organizational plans, and implemented action produced in embryonic form what is today the largest single organization in the world dealing with health, physical education, recreation, and sport—The American Alliance for Health, Physical Education, Recreation, and Dance. It has been known by several names throughout its history, but its intent has remained consistent over the years: the organization, promotion, and evaluation of America's physical health and vitality. To William G. Anderson—gymnast, physical educator, originator of the Chautauqua Summer School of Physical Education Normal Training, and man with a vision—must go the credit for convincing early American physical educators and leaders of particular gymnastic movements to come together and direct their resources toward a common goal.

Edward M. Hartwell, a former student of Hitchcock's, became American physical education's first historian/analyst. Hartwell, a New Englander by birth who studied at Amherst and Johns Hopkins University (where he became Director of Physical Training), was perhaps the first American physical educator to travel widely in Europe with the express purpose of studying and evaluating European approaches to the subject of physical education. Hartwell's visits to Germany, France, Sweden, Austria, and England provided him with data on which to base many of his messages to his American colleagues (Gerber, 1971, pp. 320-24). A prolific writer from 1885 until well into the twentieth century, Hartwell authored a large number of reports and analyses of the history and role of physical education in America—the first definitive record of America's physical education heritage.

Other individuals joined with Hitchcock. Sargent, Anderson, and Hartwell in playing leading roles in the development of American physical education during this era. Many of their efforts began in the late nineteenth century and continued to have impact until well into the twentieth century. Such an honor role must include Delphine Hanna, "family-tree matriarch" of a group of prominent physical education leaders educated at Oberlin College in Ohio (Gerber, 1971, pp. 325–31); R. Tait McKenzie, transplanted Canadian, supreme sculptor, and rehabilitative exercise specialist, associated for many years with the University of Pennsylvania (Gerber, 1971, pp. 339–47); and Luther Halsey Gulick, espouser of the YMCA movement, conceiver of the YMCA's *red triangle* connoting mind, body, spirit, and founder of the American Academy of Physical Education (Gerber, 1971, pp. 348-56).

Apart from the efforts of American physical educators utilizing what might be called an eclectic approach to exercise—combined elements of various systems of calisthenic and apparatus gymnastics—certain European systems of exercise expression gained wide acceptance in the United States during the latter part of the nineteenth century. German enthusiasm for the *Turnverein* gymnastics of "Father Jahn" led to their implementation wherever German emigrants to America settled in their adopted land. The Mississippi River Valley corridor, from Milwaukee to New Orleans, proved to be the scene of the strongest and most far-reaching German-American influence (Barney, 1978 and 1984). Milwaukee, Chicago, St. Louis, Cincinnati, Indianapolis, Louisville, and New Orleans were but a few midwestern cities which could count large German populations. From such centers sprang the essence of German *Turnverein* exercise, characterized by an addiction to apparatus of all types—vaulting horses, parallel bars, climbing ropes, and horizontal swinging bars. German-American *Turnverein* organizations played key roles in introducing German gymnastics to the midwestern schools as a major form of physical education. In 1880 agitation by German *Turners* led to the introduction of German gymnastics in many American schools (Van Dalen and Bennett, 1971, pp. 401-2). *Turners* also played a key role in the scenario which produced America's first state legislation for mandatory physical education in public schools, that of California in 1866 (Barney, 1973, pp. 352-57). *Turners* undertook a systematic campaign to acquaint American educators and the public in general with the merits of the German system of exercise expression. A normal school dedicated to preparing teachers of this system was established initially in New York City in 1866. Planned as a "traveling entity," the German normal school concept flourished in Chicago, Cincinnati, and Milwaukee. Of those systems of physical education extant in America prior to the twentieth century, the German system was the best organized, maintained the largest following of active participants and, more than any other singular form of physical education, captured the imagination of American public school authorities (Barney, 1974, p. 118).

A prominent gymnastics expression practiced in America proved to be the Swedish approach to exercise. Unlike the German system, the Swedish form of exercise did not achieve its prominent place in nineteenth-century American physical education as a result of a large Swedish population. Rather, the exercise movement, based largely on the developmental work of Sweden's Pehr Henrik Ling and his son Hjalmar, was first introduced to America by Hartwig Nissen (a Norwegian) in 1883. The most important spokesman for the cause of the Lings' gymnastics in America, however, was the Swedish aristocrat Baron Nils Posse. He was joined in his enthusiasm by Mary Hemenway, wealthy Boston philanthropist. The teaching of Swedish gymnastics to prospective physical educators became the mission of the Boston Normal School of Gymnastics, founded by Hemenway and Posse in 1889. The Swedish gymnastics, which featured light exercise in calisthenic form for the development of flexibility and grace of movement, became a popular basis for physical education in New England and other areas of the East. With many of its teachings founded on practical applications of anatomy and physiology, aspects of Swedish gymnastics found a ready reception from American medical figures involved in physical education practice.

The pioneering era of American physical education was climaxed by an effort in 1889 that brought together the leaders of the various forms of physical education present in the United States to debate and discuss the merits of each system in a search for commonality on which to base future development. Promoted and financed by Mary Hemenway and her associate, Amy Morris Homans, the so-called Boston Conference of 1889 was convened on the campus of The Massachusetts Institute of Technology in November. The most important figures of nineteenth-century American physical education were present to represent their particular viewpoints (Weston, 1962, pp. 37–39). The most tangible result of the conference was the development of a more enlightened attitude on the part of the participants toward America's diverse exercise systems. Dudley Allen Sargent, in his conference statement on the subject of exercise, speculated:

> What America needs is the happy combination which the European nations are trying to effect; the strength-giving qualities of the German gymnasium, the active and energetic properties of the English sports, the grace and suppleness acquired from French calisthenics, and the beautiful poise and mechanical precision of the Swedish free movements, all regulated, systematized, and adapted to our peculiar needs and institutions. (1890, pp. 62–76)

Oddly, no representative of the sports and games movement in America played a role at the Conference of 1889. But as the century closed, the concept of sports and games as expressions of formal physical education was being tested in progressive California. At Stanford University the young and enlightened Thomas D. Wood became an early champion of individual involvement in sporting activities as a significant agent of social development (Gerber, 1971, pp. 376–77). Indeed, Wood and physical educator colleagues of the same mind laid the foundations for what would be called in the twentieth century "the New Physical Education."

As the century drew to a close, American sport and physical education had assumed a prominent place in the milieu of national development; indeed, a sport and health mentality had been engendered (Mrozek, pp. 226-225). The practice of health and fitness exercise in educational settings emerged from its pioneer era to stand poised on the brink of shedding a largely European image and moving towards becoming a truly American expression. Because sport received such widespread public attention, its growth was staggering. Publicized by the nation's newspapers, magazines, and other literary works, all of which were most sensitive to the public's interest; aided in no small measure by the nation's swiftly growing transportation and communication systems which provided the means to get to and from recreation and sporting sites, as well as to learn results of events in rapid order; and abetted by the continued efforts of sporting entrepreneurs to galvanize Americans toward embracing sport ardently, sport thus became a social factor fully as important in the lifestyle of Americans as its former antagonist and suppressant— religion.

Twentieth-Century America:
Sport Spectacle and the Professionalization of Physical Education

Perhaps more than in any other period of modern history, the events of the twentieth century have sorely challenged the problem-solving abilities of nations. Two types of general problems have emerged for America, as for all nations: (1) national and international crisis in the form of war, economic dislocation, and international ideological difference; and (2) the advancement of science, specifically as that advancement has been pertinent to technological growth and development.

To date, the most urgent crises have been: (1) two world wars in the first half of the century; (2) the economic depression of the 1930s; (3) the military conflicts carried out in Korea and Vietnam, and postwar deterioration of social values inherent with each; and (4) the capitalism/communism confrontation, and the struggle of each to withstand the encroachment of the other. The institutions of sport and physical education have played important roles in helping to provide solutions to these four crises of America's twentieth century. In times of war and international discord, a nation's concern is aroused naturally toward ensuring that the overall fitness of its citizens is a high priority. During eras of economic dislocation when work habits are altered drastically, a country turns its attention toward those problems associated with the boredom and inactivity of its citizens. The overtones of fitness and leisure occupation for physical education and sport are obvious.

The advancement of science and explosion of technology in the twentieth century have also produced new challenges for sport and physical education. Developments in the fields of transportation and communication—the impact of the automobile, airplane, radio, and television—have led to striking changes in the American lifestyle. Such changes have had a significant relationship to the direction taken by sport and physical education—a direction which has connoted demands for specialization and, at least in the case of sport, attractive entertainment spectacles.

If America's "Gilded Age" marked the rise of college sport and the clash of gymnastic exercise systems, the twentieth century has quite clearly signaled: (1) the accenting of sport in its various forms toward becoming an entertainment extravaganza in the sense of the literal meaning of the word "spectacle"; and (2) the professionalization of physical education along the lines of a typically American sports and games approach.

Prodded by entertainment and entrepreneurial motives and by the rise of a national sporting hero concept, sport, in all its ramifications, became one of the most viewed, most discussed, and most widely read-about dimensions of American life. "King football" dominated the college sporting scene, even though other sports also developed markedly and at least one of them (basketball) realized a measure of success in draining college sporting attention away from football. Interscholastic sport for high school youths evolved early in the century and grew rapidly, even tending sharply toward emulating the model of its college brethren. Amateur sport, spurred by the Olympic movement and by a number of sports-related agencies and organizations, notably the AAU, YMCA, and municipal recreation associations, also contributed to the American sporting scene. And finally, the rise of professional sport in its various parameters completed the nation's sporting mosaic. Professional basketball, ice hockey, football, golf, tennis, and a host of other activities joined nineteenth-century-established baseball and boxing in giving credence to the concept of sport as big business—the business of entertainment and profit—a fitting "motive-theme" for promoter/manager and athlete alike in a society dedicated toward an ever-increasing degree of materialism.

Emerging from the throes of its evolutionary organization in the last quarter of the nineteenth century, American college sport continued to feature football as its most popular activity. Football's exalted position in the spectrum of American sport, however, was tested at the outset of the century due to an increasing amount of concern expressed by educators and other observers over the alarming number of injuries sustained by football players. Rough and brutal in its execution, early twentieth-century football play featured the concept of massed interference for the ball carrier which, when coupled with the fact that protective equipment had hardly begun to be developed, produced an alarming 1905 statistic of 18 players dead from football injuries (Danzig, 1956, p. 29). A public outcry resulted, and President Theodore Roosevelt, a Harvard alumnus and an enthusiastic follower of the Crimson's football fortunes, added his voice to that of the concerned faction. "Brutality and foul play should receive the same summary punishment given to a man who cheats at cards," exclaimed Roosevelt (Danzig, 1956, p. 29). Behind the stimulus of Henry B. McCracken of New York University and Walter Camp of Yale, representatives from a number of the nation's colleges and universities met in New York in December 1905 to seek solutions to the problem (Lewis, Dec. 1969, pp. 720–24). Two critical developments evolved from the 1905 meetings: (1) the blueprint plan for a closer supervision of college athletics through the formation of the Intercollegiate Athletic Association of the United States, later known as the National Collegiate Athletic Association (NCAA); and (2) a revision of the football rules, making the game safer to play and a more exciting spectacle to watch. The most significant change in the rules was the legalization of the forward pass, a maneuver which soon captured the imagination of the American football-viewing public as has no other aspect of the sport.

College teams directed by students, recently graduated players, and "seasonal" coaches soon learned the advantages to be gained by hiring full-time, year-round coaches. To such coaches—Haughton of Harvard, Warner of Carlisle, Rockne of Notre Dame, Zuppke of Illinois, Stagg of Chicago, and others of similar stature—can be extended the major credit for the development of football into a sport which has rivaled baseball and basketball as the chief satisfiers of America's urge for exciting sports entertainment. Except for the years of World Wars I and II, college football's growth traced a quite predictable path. College stadia developed from pasture-like surroundings to huge, magnificently designed and constructed edifices which could, and often did, accommodate crowds in excess of 50,000. Sectional rivalries became time-honored traditions in American college football: Harvard-Yale, Army-Navy, Michigan-Minnesota, California-Stanford, Texas-Oklahoma, Alabama-Tennessee, and many others. The age-old argument as to which team might be the best in any given year was at least partly resolved by the development of the New Year's Day bowl game concept which began in 1916 in Pasadena, California, with the first Rose Bowl game.

As the century progressed, a subtle shift in the seat of football power began to take place. Traditionally powerful schools such as Harvard, Yale, Princeton, and their eastern colleagues found their positions of prominence impinged on by midwestern, southern, and Pacific Coast institutions. Notre Dame, coached by the inimitable Knute Rockne and featuring George Gipp and the celebrated combinations known as the "four horsemen" and the "seven mules," dominated college football in the 1920s. During the Depression-ridden 1930s college football was only slightly less "glorious" than it was during the 1920s, an era which has been referred to as America's "golden age of sport." The 1940s featured service-oriented elevens—Army, Navy, and the Great Lakes Naval Training Center. Midwestern squads, especially Oklahoma and Michigan, were consistently among the nation's best during the 1950s. Since that time Alabama and Southern California have established themselves consistently as among the very best in the nation.

Not only football, but other college sports as well underwent growth in participation and spectatorship during the twentieth century. College swimming, given impetus by aquatics in the Olympic program, developed rapidly and was dominated by those institutions that built the first competitive natatoria—Yale, Ohio State, and Michigan. In contemporary times, Indiana University, and the University of Southern California (whose swimming team trains and competes in outdoor pools), have assumed preeminence in college swimming. As might be expected, those colleges and universities located in states along the "sun belt"—the South, Southwest, and southern Pacific Coast—have in general developed most successfully in those sports which are at least partly dependent on a climate allowing for long outdoor seasons: baseball, tennis, golf, and track and field. Wrestling, a consistently popular sport on the frontier and in the American West, has continued to be dominated by the midwest and southwest; its finest college traditions have been built by Iowa, Iowa State, Oklahoma, and Oklahoma State. College lacrosse developed along the nation's eastern seaboard, as did ice hockey in the northeastern and north central portion of the United States. Gymnastics and cross-country running, each of which became a viable athletic program component, conclude the list of the core activities of twentieth-century college sport, except for basketball, an "equal partner pretender" to football's superiority.

By the opening of this century, basketball had achieved stature as the sport likely to have the most appeal in spanning the gap between outdoor fall and spring sports. Prior to 1914 organized basketball in America was administered largely by three agencies: The Amateur Athletic Union, The Young Men's Christian Association, and The National Collegiate Athletic Association. Subtle differences in interpretation of the rules by the three governing bodies were significant enough to spur a demand for uniformity of playing rules. Consequently, these three factions formed a joint committee in 1914 and brought the rules of the game into a framework of common interpretation (Krout, 1929, p. 268). From a game featuring an element of undesigned roughness and the dribbling and shooting antics of one or two superior players on a team, basketball rapidly developed into an activity emphasizing teamwork. The concepts of short, fast-passing maneuvers and the development of troublesome zone defenses became focal parts of the game. Dr. Walter Meanwell, who coached at the Universities of Missouri and Wisconsin during the pre- and post-World War I period and throughout the 1920s, was perhaps the leading experimenter and innovator of basketball development. Meanwell's syndicated newspaper column "Winning Basketball" helped in the diffusion of basketball knowledge and technique to all parts of the country.

To many students of basketball history, the single most important skill development in the sport has been the one-handed method of shooting, either from a stationary position or from the circumstance of a "jump shot." Perfection of the skill by Stanford University's Angelo "Hank" Luisetti and others in the 1930s demanded that the defensive aspect of the sport be developed strongly. The post-World War II era of basketball history has featured the so-called "big man." Players approaching 7 feet in height, and a few even exceeding that, have come to dominate the game. George Mikan of Depaul and Bob Kurland of Oklahoma A & M were among the very first of the giant pivotmen, and a more contemporary era has witnessed Bill Russell, Wilt Chamberlain, Lew Alcindor (Kareem Abdul-Jabbar), Bill Walton, Moses Malone, and Ralph Sampson.

There have been several dynasties recorded in American college sporting history, but perhaps the most remarkable was that of UCLA in winning ten national collegiate basketball championships during the twelve-year span between 1964 and 1975.

Athletic sport for college women was prompted by the invention of basketball. From the time of the first campus women's athletic associations in the early 1890s, basketball has been the chief preoccupation of college women interested in sport. First at Bryn Mawr in 1891 (Ainsworth, 1930, p. 76) and subsequently at a growing number of eastern institutions, women's athletic associations flourished during the early part of the twentieth century. Track and field, field hockey, and swimming joined with basketball to form the thrust of women's athletics prior to the 1930s. Tightly bound to college departments of physical education and highly critical of the "method and manner" of men's intercollegiate athletics, college sport for women was influenced and regulated by a number of organizations, the most prominent of which was the Athletic Conference of American College Women (ACACW), organized in 1917 under the leadership of Blanche Trilling of the University of Wisconsin (Gerber, et al., 1974, pp. 76–79). Over the years, however, college sport for women has experienced cyclic changes in basic philosophy. In its infancy the sporting experience was directed toward interschool competition, following to some extent the model then quite prevalent in men's athletics. From the post-World War I years until the late 1960s, women's collegiate sport followed a pattern featuring play days, sport days, telegraphic meets, and jamborees under the direct sponsorship of the Division for Girls' and Women's Sports (DGWS) and its antecedents. The desire for competition, however, is not solely the province of men. The urge to test skills in a more superior competitive atmosphere sparked the beginning of a movement toward emulating what was only too apparent in men's intercollegiate athletics: national and regional conference championships, media exposure, athletic scholarships, and gate receipts. The beginnings of such a drift led to the establishment in 1972 of the Association for Intercollegiate Athletics for Women (AIAW), an organization which counted 278 colleges as charter members (Gerber *et al.*, 1974, p. 84).

A significant aspect of college sport in America has been the intramural athletics movement. During the nineteenth century, *intracollegiate* sport existed on college campuses in the form of obscure and generally disorganized informal games and pastime sport. Not until the twentieth century were intramural athletics noticed by university athletics officials. Shortly before World War I the NCAA, America's intercollegiate athletics governing body, gave approval and support for recognition and stimulus of campus intramural sports programs. In 1913 the University of Michigan and Ohio State University achieved special distinction as pioneers in the intramurals movement when each appointed a Director of Intramural Athletics to its staff. A survey taken in 1916 indicated that 140 colleges and universities in the United States had organized at least some form of intramural sports programs for students (Athletic Research Society, 1918, pp. 189–212). In 1919 Elmer D. Mitchell, the most significant figure in the growth of intramurals in the early twentieth century, accepted an appointment as Michigan's Director of Intramural Sports. A decade later Michigan opened the first campus building ever constructed solely for the purpose of intramural athletics. The growth of intramurals in colleges and universities prompted a similar development in junior and senior high schools during the late 1920s.

America's passion, indeed need, for recreational activities during the Depression of the 1930s proved to be a major factor in transforming intramurals from a highly competitive orientation to a concept of recreation and pastime "sport for sports sake," A National Intramural Association was formed in 1950, providing an organizational framework which stimulated wide expansion of intramurals during the 1960s and 1970s. Sports clubs, competitive leagues, instructional classes, and fitness opportunities became commonplace for students, faculty, and staff on American campuses.

Although college athletics gained a major share of attention from the public, the realm of amateur sport was capably reflected in other dimensions. Interscholastic athletics for high school students gained momentum before and after World War I, and by 1925 state high school athletic associations existed in every state (Van Dalen and Bennett, 1971, p. 448). The concept of high school athletics, ushered into perspective by the New York City experiment of 1903—the Public School Athletic League—has progressed to the point where it now receives extended treatment on the sports pages and on radio and television. Amateur athletes under the organizational supervision of the AAU, YMCA, various athletic clubs, and municipal recreation associations have played important roles also in focusing attention on sport in general. The most outstanding of such athletes became national sports heroes. Their exploits endured in the memories of their contemporaries and created a cultural sporting heritage which was transmitted to younger generations who never saw them perform. Among those gaining the most distinction were: (1) Johnny Weissmuller, peerless swimmer of the 1920s who realized Olympic titles as well as Hollywood fame as the cinema's most enduring Tarzan; and (2) Jesse Owens, a black sprinter-jumper whose exploits in track and field at the 1936 Berlin Olympics astounded a sports record-conscious public and presumably embarrassed Adolf Hitler, Germany's exponent of Aryan supremacy. However, Jim Thorpe, an American Indian who became an All-American football player and an exciting track and field performer at Pennsylvania's Carlisle Indian School, will perhaps be the longest remembered—the controversial usually are. Thorpe won the decathlon event in the 1912 Olympic Games at Stockholm, a distinction which was nullified by proven charges of so-called professionalism. Later, Thorpe spent six seasons in major league baseball as a pitcher and became a gridiron performer on whom much of the early success of professional football was dependent (Claassen, 1963, p. 25). Jim Thorpe possessed immense natural athletic talent, but his nature prompted him to rise to the challenge only when the occasion demanded. He was accused of being lazy and temperamental, but few will argue the point that the title bestowed on him by American sportswriters as "America's athlete of the half century" (1900–1950) could not rightfully have gone to any other individual (Kaye, 1973, pp. 64–66).

America's twentieth-century involvement in the Olympic Games has been characterized by a dedicated effort to achieve an optimum number of medal performances, particularly in those sports which have been important in the nation's sporting heritage. In almost a century of Modern Games history, the United States has hosted three editions each of the summer and winter competitions. In 1904 the Games were held in St. Louis in conjunction with that city's hosting of the World's Fair. In 1932 the winter Games were staged at Lake Placid, New York, and the summer spectacle occurred in Los Angeles. The Los Angeles competitions attracted 2,500 athletes from more than 40 nations (Menke, 1969, p. 736). Squaw Valley, California, was the site of the 1960 winter Games, an event which was notable in American sport history as a result of the gold medal won by the United States ice hockey team. In 1980 Lake Placid once again played host to the Winter Olympics. The American ice hockey team again surprised the world by winning the gold medal, prevailing over its chief rivals, Canada and the Soviet Union. Although much of the Western World boycotted the Summer Games of 1980, and most of the Eastern European countries did likewise four years later, the XXIIIrd Olympiad in Los Angeles in 1984 proved to be a glorious economic and visual success. Although its record in swimming, track and field, basketball, and eight-oared shell racing has been consistently exemplary, America's dominance of the Olympics from a team-scoring perspective has been seriously eroded, largely because of the emergence of the Soviet Union and East Germany as world leaders in the early identification of young athletes, and the subsequent systematic exposure of such youngsters to programs based on scientific principles of training and performance.

Clearly the strongest explosion of sport in twentieth-century America has been that organized and conducted by professionally oriented business enterprise. Professional baseball and prizefighting continued to hold the public's attention, as did affairs of the turf. But other sports, some of them emerging from well-developed amateur circumstances, rose in intensity to capture the imagination and pocketbooks of individuals bent on sports entertainment. Football, basketball, golf, "pro" wrestling, auto racing, and ice hockey became well established by mid-century. Since then, tennis, bowling, soccer, skiing, figure skating, and even track and field have become creditable business enterprises. Promoters and participants alike have extracted millions of dollars from them over the past 25 years.

Professional baseball has been faced with numerous dilemmas in the twentieth century, but somehow has managed to find the necessary solutions. The Black Sox Scandal of 1919 placed the game in jeopardy of losing its credibility with the public, but the appointment of Kenesaw Mountain Landis, a testy, resolute Illinois judge, as Commissioner of Baseball led to a full investigation and a restoration of confidence (Wallop, 1969, pp. 177–78). Baseball boomed during the 1920s and the Depression years of the 1930s, providing to millions both radio and live entertainment that lent to a retention of confidence in those American values that the Depression and its unemployment had damaged. World Wars I and II drained baseball's player personnel drastically, but the postwar years of "moral release" from the rigors of wartime social and economic restrictions were more than enough to compensate baseball for its hard times. The effects of television were disastrous for the widespread, carefully constructed minor league baseball system which groomed future major league stars, but the rise of college baseball in the 1950s and 1960s substituted adequately as a reservoir for new talent. Large salaries and huge bonuses for signing contracts were attractive lures in beckoning college players to forsake careers in business and the professions for the instant security and prestige of being in the highest range of American wage earners.

Developments in transportation and communication have made professional sport "global" in its national context. Teams representing cities from coast to coast, and from the Great Lakes to the Gulf of Mexico, have become permanent and semi-permanent fixtures on the American sporting scene. The profile of professional baseball, especially since World War II, has changed rapidly in the form of major league expansion and the shifting of franchises from city to city by owners in an attempt to find the elusive goal of financial stability. Several of baseball's established team names have become dim in memory as a result of the rapid series of events which saw the Boston Braves settle fleetingly in Milwaukee and hence move to Atlanta; the Washington Senators shift to Minneapolis; Brooklyn's Dodgers to Los Angeles; New York's Giants to San Francisco; and Philadelphia's Athletics to Kansas City and later to Oakland, California.

There seems to be little doubt that the American sporting hero concept has been promulgated more by professional baseball players than by any other type of athlete. Twentieth-century baseball heroes have been household words to millions of Americans, young and old, men and women. Who among us will forget the deeds of Ty Cobb, Babe Ruth, Lou Gehrig, Joe DiMaggio, Ted Williams, Sandy Koufax, Hank Aaron, and others equally excellent whom we either have seen perform in person or have heard of?

The affairs of the prize ring were important to twentieth-century Americans. With the controversial Jack Johnson, modern boxing history's first black heavyweight champion of the world, there was generated the idea that pugilism could be a lucrative profession. Accordingly, hundreds of youths pursued the paths which led occasionally to record purses, public attention, and social distinction—and at other times to exploitation, serious injury, and social oblivion. The fight promoter became a one-man molder of boxing's gate attraction scenarios, several of which exceeded millions of dollars. The prototype of such a figure was Tex Rickard, creator of the first million-dollar gates and a man whose genius for fanning the public's passion for bloody combat was unparalleled. Rickard's chief drawing cards were Johnson, Jack Dempsey, and Gene Tunney, each of whom played important roles in the history of boxing from 1910 until well into the Depression years of the 1930s. The 1940s, 1950s, and 1960s featured a succession of renowned heavyweight champions, accented by Joe Lewis, Rocky Marciano, and Muhammed Ali. Although heavyweights gained a major share of media and spectator attention, performers in lighter-weight classifications also achieved a measure of fame. Among the notable ones were Stanley Ketchell, Mickey Walker, Henry Armstrong, Willy Pep, Tony Zale, Rocky Graziano, Roberto Duran, Marvin Hagler, and two Sugar Rays—Robinson and Leonard.

Professional basketball, spawned in 1898 by an organization known as the National Basketball League (Menke, 1969, p. 152), had an abortive history until the 1920s and the record of achievement established by the (Original) Celtics. That organization began in 1915 as a semipro team and ultimately became the dominant group in the American Basketball League, which was formed in 1925. Besides competing in the ABL, the Celtics also traveled throughout the nation, playing in small towns and cities for whatever purses might be collected from the crowds of curious onlookers. In the late 1920s the (Original) Celtics were joined in their quest to diffuse the idea of professional basketball throughout rural and urban America by the (Original) Harlem Globetrotters, a barnstorming group of black basketball players under the promotion of Jewish entrepreneur Abe Saperstein. It was not until the late 1940s and 1950s, however, that the bonafide emergence of basketball into the mainstream of professional sport took place. The National Basketball Association, known by various names in the late 1940s, blossomed during the 1950s and 1960s to develop franchises in every section of the United States and to present one of history's records of sports dynasty—the Boston Celtics, a team which won seventeen NBA titles between 1957 and 1986. This record was due in no small way to the colorful and expert play of such Celtic players as Bob Cousy, Bill Sharman, Bill Russell, Dave Cowens, John Havlicek, and Larry Bird.

Turf events continued to arouse the attention and enthusiasm of an ever increasing number of Americans. Horse racing's triple crown (Kentucky Derby, Preakness, and Belmont Stakes) became the supreme test of competitive excellence for three-year-olds. Only eleven thoroughbreds have achieved that pinnacle of distinction: Sir Barton (1919), Gallant Fox (1930), Omaha (1935), War Admiral (1937), Whirlaway (1941), Count Fleet (1943), Assault (1946), Citation (1948), Secretariat (1973), Seattle Slew (1977), and Affirmed (1978).

Oddly, America's horse of the first half of the century, as selected by the Associated Press (Menke, 1969, pp. 568–69), never won the triple crown and never participated in the Kentucky Derby. Nevertheless, Man O'War, a large, stunning, chestnut-colored colt, left an indelible record for American turf history to ponder. "Big Red," as he was affectionately called, won all but one of his career races, being beaten in 1919 at Saratoga by a horse appropriately named Upset (Robertson, 1964, pp.

238–40). In many of his outings Man O'War set world and American records that endured for decades.

A focus on golf was aroused by Francis Ouimet, a young amateur player whose exploits in winning the 1913 United States Open appealed to the Horatio Alger spirit of Americans. The feats of Bobby Jones and Walter Hagen in the 1920s, and the later accomplishments of Byron Nelson, Gene Sarazen, Babe Zaharias, Ben Hogan, and Sam Snead, during the 1930s and 1940s, kept golf coverage a prominent aspect of sports reporting. By the outbreak of World War II over 5,700 golf courses had been constructed in America, prompting millions of men and women to take up the game in earnest (Menke, 1969, p. 455). After World War II, chiefly because of television and sponsorship revenues, professional golf tour prize monies spiraled to dizzying heights, and tournament winners, more often than not Arnold Palmer and Jack Nicklaus, consistently pocketed checks for thousands of dollars.

Enthusiasm for tennis was prompted by the feats of Bill Tilden in the 1920s, by Ellsworth Vines and Don Budge in the 1930s, and by Jack Kramer and Richard "Pancho" Gonzales in the late 1940s and throughout the 1950s. Tennis in the 1960s and 1970s became a sport in which the differences between amateur and professional players were hardly perceptible. The sport became heavily commercialized and its century-old traditions eroded to the point where the very profile of the game was changed dramatically. Vividly colored costumes, richly dyed tennis balls, and carnival-like playing atmospheres replaced the white sedateness of tennis's past era.

Ice hockey appealed to a more limited segment of America's population, mostly to residents of New England, New York, and other states bordering the southern boundaries of the Great Lakes. The feats of the legendary Hobey Baker, Princeton's exemplary hockey captain of 1913 and a player rivaling Canada's best, aroused some interest in the Canadian-adopted sport prior to 1920. However, pronounced spectator enthusiasm for the game did not begin until 1924, when Boston joined Canadian teams in the National Hockey League (Durant and Bettman, 1973, p. 169). The Bruins' entry was followed in rapid succession by that of New York, Chicago, and Detroit. Succeeding eras have seen professional hockey dominated by American business interests capitalizing on Canadian-spawned playing personnel.

From its irresolute beginning in the late nineteenth century, professional football tried diligently but with little success to capitalize on public enthusiasm for the sport engendered by American college teams. Prior to World War I pro football play was limited to Pennsylvania and Ohio, but the signing of Jim Thorpe in 1915 by the Canton Bulldogs paved the way for the game's expansion to cities in Illinois, Michigan, Wisconsin, Minnesota, and New York. The American Professional Foot-

ball Association, precursor of the National Football League, was organized in 1920, and Thorpe was elected as its first president (Claassen,
1963, p. 32). When the magnitude of Thorpe's influence on the game
began to fade in the 1920s, another idol of the times rose to take his place
as the sport's most prominent attraction—the indomitable Harold "Red"
Grange. Displaying the talents of Grange and such "superhero" succes-
sors to him as Ernie Nevers, Bronko Nagurski, and Sammy Baugh, the
NFL survived the troubled years of the Depression and World War II.
The ramifications of the war had the same deteriorating effects on pro
football as they had on major league baseball. League attendance dwin-
dled to 887,920 in 1942, the lowest annual figure of the decade 1935–
1945 (Classen, 1963, p. 86). By the 1950s, the so-called "golden age of
pro football" (Herskowitz, 1974), the NFL had successfully overcome the
challenges posed by a rival league, the All America Football Conference,
and in the process had built a model of marketplace retaliation that was
dusted off in the 1960s and 1970s and used to fend off the encroachments
of still other would-be competitors—the American and World Football
Leagues, respectively. The issues at stake with the imposition of competing leagues were: (1) the signing of "name" players, the very essence of
spectator attraction; (2) the securing of competition-free franchises in the
key urban centers of America; and (3) the accrual of television revenues.
In general, pro football during the third quarter of the twentieth century featured: (1) authentic American sporting heroes in the form of
Otto Graham, Johnny Unitas, Joe Namath, Jim Brown, O. J. Simpson,
the "doomsday defense," and the "steel curtain"; (2) multimillion-
dollar television bonanzas which filled the NFL's coffers and stimulated
nationwide interest for pro football's product—Sunday afternoons of
unrivaled sport spectacle; (3) expansion to the far corners of the United
States; and (4) the establishment of parity with big league baseball as twentieth-century America's most prominent professional sport
forms.

The fabric of American sport in the twentieth century has been
woven from a variety of threads over the years. Many of those threads
have changed in color and composition. Some, such as football and
basketball, have become garish and frenetic in tone. Others, such as
professional wrestling and roller derby, appear humorous and border on
the ridiculous. Still others, such as baseball and golf, have changed only
slightly and have clung to a semblance of sedateness and conservatism.
And sadly, some, such as ice hockey, mirror American societal trends in
general and reflect violence and pugnaciousness. But each fabric lends
itself to the perspective of sport in American society—providing for
healthful activity during times of increasing automation; creating entertainment in an era when mechanization of lives has produced an unprecedented need for outlet of pent-up emotions; stimulating a profit motive

to those involved in the business of sport whether performing, managing, or in ownership; and accumulating social prestige for those who achieve in sport, which must, out of necessity, include the psychic satisfactions engendered in all who have had an identification with the sporting heroes of the times.

If sport played a major role as a form of entertainment for adults in twentieth-century American society, it served a different purpose for the thousands of American schoolchildren enrolled in public school physical education classes. Indeed, sport formed the core of the physical education expression which developed in ever stronger tones as the century progressed.

During the early part of the century, American education was shaped by the tide of progressivism that brought about distinct changes in several other national institutions—government, labor, the judicial process, etc. The progressive movement in education resulted in reforming the mission of the schools towards better serving the best interests of a free, democratic society (Cremin, 1961). The underpinnings of such a mission focused on individual differences in inherent nature, growth and maturation patterns, and readiness to learn various intellectual and physical skills. The published theories of G. Stanley Hall and Edward L. Thorndike, two behavioral psychologists, became the most important pieces of early twentieth-century literature on the subject of learning. Joining Hall and Thorndike as important catalysts in prompting the direction of education was John Dewey, generally recognized as the single most important educational philosopher of the twentieth century. Among the most crucial educational concepts espoused by Dewey was his viewpoint that the school atmosphere and learning process should be based on the larger society outside it (Dewey, 1963). The school, therefore, became a primary shaper of the values and the social development of youth.

Before World War I the sports and games approach of the "new physical education" was largely in its embryonic state, struggling to emerge against the formidable opposition of various European-accented, formal gymnastics systems, the chief thrusts of which were aimed at postural improvement and corrective exercises. However, with the sharp curbing of immigration after the First World War, European influence on such gymnastics programs declined. Then, succeeding generations of American-born children of immigrants, particularly Germans, melted more rapidly and deeply into the mainstream of American life, thus eroding old country values and customs. The Americanization of young Germans was an important factor in the general decline in the number of German *Turnverein* societies (Leonard and Affleck, 1947, p. 310).

Aided by the spectacular rise of sport in America, physical education found it less and less difficult to develop a typically "American approach," one which was rooted in the values of American society and which would influence children to lead productive lives as members of American democracy.

Thomas D. Wood's colleague in the initiation and subsequent development of the "American way" in physical education (see p. 196) was Clark Hetherington, an introspective perfectionist who has been referred to as the first modern philosopher of physical education (Gerber, 1971, p. 389). Hetherington's objective of physical education through natural play activities was inspired by G. Stanley Hall, with whom he had studied at Clark University in Worcester, Massachusetts. Hetherington's ideal, "play is the child's chief business in life" (Gerber, 1971, p. 389), was first implemented in 1913 at the Child Demonstration Play School on the University of California campus in Berkeley. Throughout most of the first half of the century, until his death in 1942, Hetherington was one of the profession's strongest voices for: (1) fair play and sportsmanship in competitive athletics; (2) women's programs in health, hygiene, and physical activity; (3) sophistication of physical education curricula; (4) development of professional preparation programs for prospective teachers; and (5) advancement for the cause of research in physical education. There is little doubt that Hetherington's career, with teaching and administrative posts in Massachusetts, Missouri, California, Wisconsin, and New York, influenced scores of leaders in twentieth-century physical education. Those inspired by his ideals—among them Jesse Feiring Williams, Jay B. Nash, Charles McCloy, and Harry A. Scott—extended many of his theories and practices on behalf of the field.

Both World Wars and the Depression had severe effects on the maintenance of the sports and games framework of American school physical education. The nation's apprehension over the revealing statistic that one-third of the men examined for World War I military service were physically unfit for duty, and that another third had pathological impairments, proved a strong argument for school health and physical education programs (Van Dalen and Bennett, 1971, p. 439). But not all tax monies appropriated for such programs were directed toward development of a sports and games curriculum. Military drill and calisthenic fitness programs at times dwarfed the growing concept of individual development through an approach characterized largely by vigorous games activity. The experience of military drill in the schools as a replacement for sports participation during World War I was not repeated in the Second World War. Secretary of War Henry Stimson argued for the elimination of such a concept, exclaiming that military drill could be administered better by the armed forces after induction than in the school. Stimson felt the schools should instead emphasize physical fitness, a human condition that is more difficult to develop and takes longer to achieve (Van Dalen and Bennett, 1971, pp. 477–78).

⮕ The nation's "social relaxation" during the 1920s was accompanied by the sharp growth of sport, giving further impetus to the active games approach in physical education. But physical education, along with education in general, experienced a setback during the Depression years. Fiscal budgets were sharply restricted, and many schools closed entirely. Indeed, history has shown that during times of financial limitation those school subjects not considered essentials (physical education, home economics, art) are among the first to face elimination or cutbacks.

Among the most significant factors in the rise in status of twentieth-century physical education were developments in teacher education. The academic prestige of several of those nineteenth-century teacher education schools was now raised appreciably by their affiliation with established American universities. Among the best known were the Boston Normal School of Gymnastics, which linked its curriculum to that of Wellesley College in 1909; the Sargent School, which affiliated with Boston University in 1929; and the Normal School of the North American Gymnastic Union (German-American *Turners*), which joined with Indiana University in 1941. Undergraduate programs of physical education teacher preparation were established at several of the nation's finest universities; Illinois (1905), Oregon (1907), Wisconsin (1911), Iowa (1918), and Michigan (1921). Graduate work in physical education commenced in 1901 at Teachers' College, Columbia University. The first doctoral programs of study in physical education were introduced in 1924 at Teachers' College and at nearby New York University (Weston, 1962, p. 55).

Complementing the development of teacher education programs was the active involvement of thousands of American physical educators in professional organizations. The largest forum for the exchange of ideas and the organization most responsible for molding the character essence of school physical education has been the American Alliance for Health, Physical Education, Recreation and Dance, known popularly as AAHPERD. Regional and state associations of the AAHPERD have been effective voices in bringing about needed changes in curricula, sports participation conditions for young people, benefits for teachers, and dissemination of research information through the publication of journals, pamphlets, and manuals. State physical education legislation has placed on the profession a stricter framework of accountability for teaching standards, certification of teachers and facilities, frequency of classes, and evaluation of programs. The first state legislation for physical education was passed in California in 1866, and other states followed suit, particularly in the early part of the twentieth century. By 1930, for example, 39 states had enacted physical education legislation of some form

(Weston, 1962, p. 74). By the mid-1970s every state in the Union had government-legislated physical education standards.

Fundamental to the strength of all cultural forces, of which education is but one, is the impact and counterimpact of philosophy on the direction that development should take. In the late nineteenth century, for instance, the chief issue in physical education's development focused on which system of gymnastic exercise was best suited for American needs. Several systems were so evenly balanced with each other that a clear-cut resolution never materialized. American twentieth-century physical education history has featured a similar "conscience-issue." As has been noted, physical education in this century has been heavily weighted toward contributing to the child's development as a future citizen of American democracy. Such an approach centers on the social development of the individual. The findings of educational and behavioral psychologists which were put into educational philosophical perspective by Dewey and others led to the germination of "education *through* the physical" as the central theme of physical education. Espoused originally by Wood, Gulick, and Hetherington, the movement reached greater fruition under the stimulation and careful guidance of Jesse F. Williams, Jay B. Nash, and physical education's more contemporary progressivist leaders.

On the other side of the spectrum, however, there were those in the profession who argued that physical education was getting too enmeshed in social development and was neglecting what might be termed "education *of* the physical." In its infancy American physical education was rooted in the teachings of medical men whose concern about physical fitness and efficiency was prompted by scientific rather than social motives. Developing young people for a democratic society received only secondary consideration from people of science. The foremost twentieth-century torchbearer of the science-oriented concept of physical education was Charles H. McCloy, the distinguished scholar-scientist whose work in China and at the University of Iowa, in particular, gained wide respect among academics. The biosciences sector of physical education, often essentialist in its philosophical stance (Zeigler and VanderZwaag, 1968, pp. 72–73), associates closely with physical development underscored by vigorous, large-muscle exercise and the strengthening of organic vigor—approaches validated by scientific inquiry rather than by authoritative pronouncements (Gerber, 1971, p. 409). As might be imagined, the science-oriented scholars have produced the major share of physical education literature. From the laboratories of McCloy at Iowa, Karpovich at Springfield, and Cureton at Illinois, among others, flowed a steady stream of scientific research findings related to exercises of all types. The social science dimension of sport and physical education has been trying vainly to match the research output of the sciences and, it must be said, has been gaining a greater measure of respect with each passing decade. Scholarly studies of the philosophy, history, psychology, and sociology of sport and physical education have added much to our perspective.

Recent times have seen the marriage of the two schools of thought into a theme projecting "education *of* and *through* the physical." Enhanced by an abundance of young, professionally trained teachers utilizing the latest developments in scientific research pertinent to health and exercise, contemporary physical education has striven to meet the challenges imposed on society by increasing automation, the invention of thousands of devices that lighten or eliminate the expenditure of physical energy, and the abundance of leisure time. Of concern is the lesson of history which has demonstrated all too well that no civilization has survived for long when the people had too much free time (Zeigler, 1968, p. 99).

Contemporary America: Arrest of the Puritan Ethic

As America surveys her past and reflects with pride on her history's vast record of accomplishment, she ought to be aware of the cost of such achievement. America's arrival at that point in her history when a distinct surplus economy arose, coupled with the nation's economic overgrowth since that time, have had some startling effects on society. The rugged individualism and work ethic orientation characteristic of Americans living in a deficit economy have given way slowly to the inevitable by-products of an accelerated and sustained economic growth pattern underwritten by the development of science and technology. The physical efforts of man have been replaced by the productivity of machinery. Mandatory employment necessitated by the demands of an exacting social and economic environment have been replaced instead by a decreasing need, indeed often a lack of opportunity, to work. The "subpoenas" for the work ethic's "final indictment and execution" are the social welfare schemes of several dimensions (Medicare, unemployment compensation, food stamps, social security, family welfare payments, and the concept of "negative income tax," to name some of the more prominent examples). A distinct shift has taken place in the foundations of the American way, a drifting away from the necessity to maintain the Protestant ethic, and toward a state in which entertainment and the use of leisure become key cultural factors. Americans once worked with only peripheral regard for play. Today, that ethic has been reversed to a significant degree. Such a reversal presents immense challenges to sport and physical education. Entertainment of the idle, the mental and physical rejuvenation of the machine-replaced, and the installment of values in the young for personal fitness are necessarily major considerations in the difficult times ahead of us.

GENERAL BIBLIOGRAPHY

ADELMAN, MELVIN L., *A Sporting Time: New York City and The Rise of Modern Athletics, 1820-70;* Urbana: University of Illinois Press, 1986.

AINSWORTH, D. S. *The History of Physical Education in Colleges for Women.* New York. A. S. Barnes and Company, 1930.

ATHLETIC RESEARCH SOCIETY. "Report of the Committee on Intramural Sport," *American Physical Education Review,* no. 23, April 1918.

BARNEY, ROBERT KNIGHT. "Adele Parot: Beacon of the Dioclesian Lewis School of Gymnastic Expression in the American West," *Canadian Journal of History of Sport and Physical Education,* vol. V, no. 2, December 1974.

———. "German-American Turnvereins and Socio-Politico-Economic Realities in the Antebellum and Civil War Upper and Lower South," *Stadion: International Journal of the History of Sport and Physical Education,* Vol. X, 1984.

———. "German Turners in America: Their Role in Nineteenth-Century Exercise Expression and Physical Education Legislation," *A History of Physical Education and Sport in The United States and Canada.* Ed. Earle F. Zeigler. Champaign, Ill.: Stipes Publishing Company, 1975.

———. "German Turners in American Domestic Crisis," *Stadion,* Vol. IV, 1978.

———. "A Historical Reinterpretation of the Forces Underlying the First State Legislation for Physical Education in the Public Schools of the U.S.," *The Research Quarterly,* vol. XLIV, no. 3, October 1973.

———. "Of Rails and Red Stockings: Episodes in the Expansion of the National Pastime in the American West," *Journal of the West,* Vol. XVII, No. 3, July 1978.

———. "To Breast a Storm: Nathaniel Topliff Allen and the Demise of Military Drill as the Physical Education Ethic in the Public Schools of Massachusetts, 1860-1890," *Canadian Journal of History of Sport,* Vol. XIX, No. 2, December 1987.

BEATTY, EDWARD C. O. *William Penn as Social Philosopher.* New York: Columbia University Press, 1939.

BENNETT, BRUCE. "The Making of The Round Hill School," *Quest IV,* April 1965.

BETTS, JOHN RICKARDS. *America's Sporting Heritage: 1850–1950.* Reading, Mass.: Addison-Wesley Publishing Company, 1974.

CLAASSEN, HAROLD. *The History of Professional Football.* Englewood Cliffs, N.J.: Prentice-Hall, 1963.

CREMIN, LAWRENCE A. *The Transformation of the School: Progressivism in American Education, 1876–1957.* New York: Alfred A. Knopf, 1961.

DANZIG, ALLISON. *The History of American Football.* Englewood Cliffs, N.J.: Prentice-Hall, 1956.

DAVIS, PARKE H. *Football: The American Intercollegiate Game.* New York: Charles Scribner's Sons, 1911.

DAVIS, THOMAS. "Puritanism and Physical Education: The Shroud of Gloom Lifted," *Canadian Journal of History of Sport and Physical Education,* vol. III, no. 1, May 1972.

DEWEY, JOHN. *Democracy and Education.* New York: Macmillan Paperbacks Edition, 1963 (first published in 1916).

DULLES, FOSTER RHEA. *A History of Recreation: America Learns to Play.* New York: Appleton-Century-Crofts, 1965.

DURANT, JOHN, and OTTO BETTMANN. *Pictorial History of American Sports.* New York: A. S. Barnes and Company, 1973.

FAIRS, JOHN R. "Sociocultural Control of the Body in Western Society: An Ethico-economic Interpretation," *Canadian Journal of History of Sport and Physical Education,* vol. III, no. 2, December 1976.

FRANKLIN, BENJAMIN. *Proposals Relating to the Education of Youth in Pennsylvania.* Philadelphia: University of Pennsylvania Press, 1931 (first published in 1749).

GERBER, ELLEN W. *Innovators and Institutions in Physical Education.* Philadelphia: Lea and Febiger, 1971.

————, JAN FELSHIN, PEARL BERLIN, and WANEEN WYRICK. *The American Woman in Sport.* Reading, Mass.: Addison-Wesley Publishing Company, 1974.

GRISWOLD, A. WHITNEY. "Three Puritans on Prosperity," *The New England Quarterly,* vol. VII (September 1934).

HENDERSON, ROBERT W. *Ball, Bat and Bishop: The Origin of Ball Games.* New York: Rockport Press, 1947.

HERSKOWITZ, MICKEY. *The Golden Age of Pro Football.* New York: The Macmillan Company, 1974.

HOLLIMAN, JENNIE. *American Sports (1785–1835).* Durham, NC.: The Seeman Press, 1931.

HUIZINGA, JOHAN. *Homo Ludens: A Study of the Play Element in Culture.* New York: Roy Publishers, 1948.

JABLE, J. T. "The English Puritans: Suppressors of Sport and Amusement," *Canadian Journal of History of Sport and Physical Education,* vol. VII, no. 1, May 1976.
————. "Pennsylvania's Early Blue Laws: A Quaker Experiment in the Suppression of Sport and Amusements, 1682–1740," *Journal of Sport History,* vol. I, no. 2, November 1974.

KAYE, IVAN N. *Good Clean Violence: A History of College Football.* Philadelphia: J. B. Lippincott Company, 1973.

KROUT, JOHN ALLEN. *Annals of American Sport.* New York: United States Publishers Association, 1929.

LARDNER, REX. *The Legendary Champions.* New York: American Heritage Press, 1972.

LEONARD, FRED EUGENE, and GEORGE B. AFFLECK. *A Guide to the History of Physical Education.* Philadelphia: Lea and Febiger, 1947.

LEWIS, GUY M. "America's First Intercollegiate Sport: The Regattas from 1852 to 1875," *The Research Quarterly,* vol. XXXVIII, no. 4, December 1967.
————. "Canadian Influence on American Collegiate Sports," *Canadian Journal of History of Sport and Physical Education,* vol. I, no. 2, December 1970.

————. "1879: The Beginning of an Era in American Sport," *Proceedings—National College Physical Education Association for Men,* January 1969.

————. "Theodore Roosevelt's Role in the 1905 Football Controversy," *The Research Quarterly,* vol. XL, no. 4, December 1969.

LUCAS, JOHN A. "Pedestrianism and the Struggle for the Sir John Astley Belt, 1878–1879," *The Research Quarterly,* vol. XXXIX, no. 3, October 1968.

MANDELL, RICHARD D. *The First Modern Olympics.* Berkeley: University of California Press, 1976.

MENKE, FRANK G. *The Encyclopedia of Sports.* New York: A. S. Barnes and Company, 1969.

MROZEK, DONALD J., *Sport and American Mentality, 1880-1910,* Knoxville: The University of Tennessee Press, 1983.

PAXSON, FREDERIC L. "The Rise of Sport," *The Mississippi Valley Historical Review,* vol. IV, September 1917.

REID, O. LEON. Ed. *Franklin's Autobiography.* New York: American Book Company, 1896.

RICE, EMMETT A., and JOHN L. HUTCHINSON. *A Brief History of Physical Education.* New York: A. S. Barnes and Company, 1952.

ROBERTSON, WILLIAM H. *The History of Thoroughbred Racing in America.* New York: Crown Publishers, 1964.

ROSTOW, W. W. *Politics and the Stages of Growth.* Cambridge: University of Cambridge, 1971.

————. *The Process of Economic Growth.* Oxford: Clarendon Press, 1960.

SARGENT, DUDLEY ALLEN. *An Autobiography.* Ed. Ledyard W. Sargent. Philadelphia: Lea and Febiger, 1927.

————. "The System of Physical Training at the Hemenway Gymnasium," *Physical Training: A Full Report of the Papers and Discussion of the Conference Held in Boston in November 1889.* Boston: Press of George H. Ellis, 1890.

SHANNON, FRED A. "A Post Mortem on the Labor–Safety Valve Theory," *Agricultural History,* vol. XIX, January 1945.

SHERIDAN, THOMAS. *A Complete Dictionary of the English Language.* London: Printed for Charles Dilly, in The Poultry, 1789.

SMITH, RONALD A. "The Rise of Basketball for Women in Colleges," *Canadian Journal of History of Sport and Physical Education,* vol. I, no. 2, December 1970.

STERN, JOSEPH S. "The Team That Couldn't Be Beat: The Red Stockings of 1869," *Cincinnati Historical Society Bulletin,* vol. XXVII, no. 1, 1969.

VAN DALEN, DEOBOLD, and BRUCE L. BENNETT. *A World History of Physical Education.* Englewood Cliffs, N.J.: Prentice-Hall, 1971.

VOIGT, DAVID QUENTIN. *American Baseball: From Gentleman's Sport to the Commissioner System.* Norman: University of Oklahoma Press, 1966.

WALLOP, DOUGLAS. *Baseball: An Informal History.* New York: W. W. Norton and Company, 1969.

WEBSTER, NOAH. *A Collection of Essays and Fugitive Writings.* Boston: I. Thomas and E. T. Andrews, 1790.

WESTON, ARTHUR. *The Making of American Physical Education.* New York: Appleton-Century-Crofts, 1962.

WHORTON, JAMES C., *Crusaders for Fitness: The History of American Health Reformers.* Princeton, N.J.: Princeton University Press, 1982.

ZEIGLER, EARLE F. *Problems in the History and Philosophy of Physical Education and Sport.* Englewood Cliffs, N.J.: Prentice-Hall, 1968.

——— and HAROLD J. VANDERZWAAG. *Physical Education: Progressivism or Essentialism?* Champaign, Ill.: Stipes Publishing Company, 1968.

Sport and Physical Education in Canada

Garth A. Paton

Robert Knight Barney

Canada is a country of open space in an overcrowded world. It is also a country of unmatched geographical variation with scenery that bids to exceed the best offered by a dozen other countries. Nevertheless, Canada is a land with many cosmopolitan cities.[1]

Canada is the second largest country in the world covering over 3.8 million square miles, virtually one half of the entire North American continent. This vast political entity is bordered by three oceans, the Arctic, the Atlantic, and the Pacific. It also possesses the longest fresh-water navigational system in the world — the St. Lawrence-Great Lake system. Further, Canada is rich in natural resources including water power, oil, and minerals.

Despite all of the above, the population of Canada totals only 25 million people. These relatively few people presently have a diverse multi-ethnic base, one that now enriches the founding races of native peoples as well as French and British settlers. What does the future hold for Canada and Canadians? It seems safe to say that Canada is a country with many achievements to its credit, but that looking to the future it still has a great unfulfilled potential.

It may be held by many social historians that the American (United States!) way of life has been little more than an extension of Old World customs and traditions. If this thesis has any basis in fact, then it may be argued that Canada conversely has emphasized a different interpretation of the Old World than that of the United States. The roots of these two major North American countries have many links and similarities, yet the differences are indeed significant.

[1]Garth A. Paton is currently Professor of Physical Education, The University of New Brunswick, Fredericton, Canada. He has incorporated earlier material about Canada from Barney's chapter in the first edition.

Despite the above, it is very difficult to imagine the people of any two countries in the world as being more alike than are Canadians and Americans. There are differences, of course, but the major social institutions of each country are remarkably similar. For example, Canadians are not mystified by American patterns of speech, religion, education, government, and economics because their own concepts and practices of each are roughly the same. Canada and the United States have had quite similar stages of historical development. For instance: (a) each went through a discordant early history affected by the economic interests of other nations, (b) each experienced a period of fundamental British overseership, (c) each underwent large-scale immigration of European peoples, (d) each witnessed the frontier phenomenon and the expansion of the West, and (e) each graduated toward urbanization and industrialization starting in the second half of the nineteenth century. There is an even stronger reason for similarities between Canadians and Americans, especially in contemporary times. Canada, although, is a country far larger than the United States with a population of roughly one tenth as many people, approximately 85 percent of them live within 100 miles of the Canadian-American border, well within range of American radio and television. There is additional influence from American newspapers, magazines, journals, and textbooks in a Canadian market that seems starved for publications. These facts leave little doubt as to the impact of American social and economic institutions.

The differences, as subtle as they may appear to non-Canadians and in particular to Europeans who tend to perceive North America as unitary, take on significant dimensions when viewed more closely. Some of these differences flow directly from the two Mother Countries — Britain and France. Other differences may be attributable to such factors as geography (considerably larger and more northerly), climate (less temperate), stronger ties to the Mother Countries (the British Loyalists and the French culture), ethnicity (multicultural as opposed to a melting pot), or governmental differences (British parliamentary), or the slightly more socialistic tendencies. Most important, however, may be the Canadian belief that there is a difference — one worth maintaining — when compared to the large neighbour to the south.

Canadians tend to accept the view suggested by Gough (1975), "Among the histories of the nation-states of the modern world, that of Canada is likely to be either not well known or misunderstood" (p. 1). This perception is most certainly true of Canada's sporting heritage and history. Canada's sporting past has been a largely neglected subject, but scholars are presently hard at work investigating that important component of Canadian culture. Early signs from such investigations point to the fact that the nation's sporting heritage has been carefully cultivated and developed, not only in the area of winter sports, as might be imagined, but also in the perspective of summer and autumn activities. Given its population numbers in comparison with those of the United States, Canada's sporting past has been every bit as rich and colorful, and perhaps unique in its contributions to the world's sporting mosaic.

The last two decades have been a remarkable period of growth and development in Canadian sport and physical education, It has been a period which has seen Canadians host a variety of international competitions including the XXI Summer Olympic Games, the Olympiad for the Physically Disabled, the XIth Commonwealth Games, World Cup Track and Field, Canada Cup Ice Hockey, the Pan American Games, as well as the 1982 Pan American Wheelchair Games in Halifax, Nova Scotia; the 1983 World University Games in Edmonton, Alberta; and the 1988 Winter Olympic Games in Calgary, Alberta. The same period has seen an equally dramatic growth of sport within the country including summer and winter national games (Jeux Canada Games), regional and provincial games, as well as a significant change in the activity patterns of the population at large. These achievements within the recent past rest upon a solid and rich sporting base.

The World Fair — Expo '67 — hosted in Montreal in 1967 was one aspect of the celebration of the one hundredth birthday of Canada. Clearly a young country by world standards, Canada as an evolving country with a geography required early settlers to virtually carve a society out of a harsh wilderness. Organized sport has been largely a nineteenth and twentieth century phenomenon. The foundations of many of the most popular Canadian pastimes have roots that trace back to the native peoples of North America, the Indians and the Eskimos. As Lindsay (1969) pointed out, "Canadian sport is indebted to the Indian for the toboggan, the snowshoe, the lacrosse stick, and the canoe" (p. 378).

THE DAWN OF THE NATION

The early settlement of Canada was based on the development of the fishing industry and the fur trade carried out by both French and English explorations. John Cabot discovered the shores of Newfoundland for England in 1497 and reported that the sea was teeming with fish. England was slow in colonizing, however, and in 1534 Jacques Cartier discovered the islands and south shore of the St. Lawrence River erecting a cross on the Gaspe. Thus, the duality of Canada and of the two founding races — the French and the English — was established very early. This duality has been a Canadian fact that has both perplexed and enriched the country to the present (Gough, 1975, pp. 13-17).

EARLY SETTLEMENT

The first permanent settlement to survive in Canada was established by Sieur Pierre du Guast de Monts and Samuel de Champlain in 1604 on St. Croix Island located on what is now the Maine border. The settlement was then relocated to the Annapolis Basin in Nova Scotia in 1605 at Port Royal (Gough, 1975, p. 18). This early settlement has proved to be of interest to sport historians because of the development of what is considered to be the earliest social-recreational club established in the new world — L'Ordre de Bon Temps (The Order of Good Cheer).

L'Ordre de Bon Temps was developed by Champlain as a means of maintaining morale and good spirits among the settlers and fur traders, as well as promoting good relationships with the local natives. The members gathered together on alternative weeks to enjoy an evening of feasting, story-telling, singing, and friendship. The responsibility for providing the meal was passed from one person to the next, and it became a point of honour to assure excellent fare. The benefits that accrued appeared to be higher morale, better diet, stronger relationships with the native people, more physical exercise in pursuit of fishing and hunting, and improved physical health. Overall, considering the benefits and the activities, L'Ordre de Bon Temps might legitimately be considered the first physical education/recreation program in the new colony (Salter, 1976, pp. 111-119).

The native peoples provided the spark that developed many of the early sports and games coupled with the European heritage for both French and English. It was from the Indian that early fur traders learned of the canoe, the snowshoe, the toboggan (Howell and Howell, 1981, p. 4). These became a vital part of the settlers' means of travel, commerce, and culture. Also, the Indian provided the game of lacrosse which was adapted and eventually came to be considered the national sport of Canada during the nineteenth century.

EARLY SPORT

Lacrosse was widely played among the Indians of eastern Canada and the United States (Howell and Howell, 1981, p. 4). The common Indian name for the game was "baggataway," but it was referred to eventually as "lacrosse" because of the shape of the playing stick — a shape similar to that of a bishop's crozier. The game was played in various styles along the geographical perimeters of the Great Lakes and surrounding areas. The Indians used it (a) as a means of *sport* and *recreation* in the true sense of those words, (b) as a means of settling war disputes, (c) as a training program for war, (d) as an agent of gambling activity, and (e) as a function of religion, particularly as related to medicinal agents, a medium of divination, or a means of influencing the elements (Salter, 1972, p. 29). Impromptu lacrosse games between Indians and Britons occurred as early as 1843, leading in time to the game being taken up seriously by the British residents of Montreal (Metcalfe, 1976, p. 3). The Montreal Lacrosse Club was formed in 1856, and during the following three decades organized play expanded coast to coast. In the 1860's George W. Beers, a Montreal dentist and an ardent leader of the movement to have lacrosse officially declared by parliament as Canada's national sport (which it never was), became directly responsible for bringing about a codification of the playing rules. Beers was also instrumental in bringing about the game's exportation to Britain, personally arranging for a team of Britons and Caughnawaga Indians to tour the British Isles in 1876.

The historical conflict between France and England was carried to North America in the seventeenth and eighteenth centuries. The Anglo-French dispute in North America centered on the encroachment of the expanding British-American colonial settlement against the spheres of French trading influence in the northern Great Lakes area and along the length and breadth of the Mississippi River Valley. The key to the reduction of French influence in North America can be traced to the British capture of Quebec City in 1759. From that date until the Confederation of Canadian provinces in 1867, the British ruled Canada. The French-Canadian population remained as the majority in Lower Canada (present-day Quebec) as well as significant sections of the present-day provinces of New Brunswick, Nova Scotia and Prince Edward Island.

EARLY INFLUENCES — GUNS AND FUR

Montreal, initially established in 1642, emerged as the pivotal settlement in early Canada. Geographically, it became the crossroads for both north-south and east-west travel. It was natural that Montreal became the centre of commerce, an important military garrison, and the principal hub for sport in the young country. The confluence of the great rivers, the St. Lawrence and the Ottawa, and the connection south to Lake Champlain and the United States, provided natural transportation routes, thus fixing the importance of Montreal in the New World. The waterways and their vehicles, the canoe and later the ships, became the lifeblood critical to survival.

One of the great gifts of the native people was the canoe. Canada, indeed much of North America, relied upon this remarkably versatile craft for transportation, hence, exploration, travel, and commerce. The development of Canada was inextricably linked with the fur trade, and the fur trade prospered on the canoe and the amazing men who paddled them — the voyageur. As Lappage (1984, p. 34) pointed out, " the value of a man was measured in terms of his physical prowess and his ability to endure hardship". The voyageur epitomized these characteristics.

The voyageurs paddled the large Montreal canoes from Montreal to the head of Lake Superior and then returned all in one season with their canoes loaded with up to six thousand pounds of fur bales. Lappage describes their routine:

> The voyageurs' daily routine was arduous to say the least. For the six-to-eight weeks they were on the trail, they were roused as early as two or three a.m. and, provided that no rapids were ahead, they set off without breakfast, stopped about dawn to eat on the water, and about midday lunch was "served" - though often lunch was no more than an opportunity to hack off a piece of pemmican to chew on the way. Between eight and ten in the evening, depending on the light, camp was made, the canoes were repaired, and supper was devoured. The men then dropped down on the turf, moss, or beach with their heads under an overturned canoe. A tarpaulin was stretched from the canoe to give shelter from rain and dew, however, there was no provision made to give protection from insects, except the voyageurs' own grease and dirt, assisted sometimes by a smudge lit up-wind (Lappage, 1984, p. 31).

These remarkable men became legitimate folk heroes. Their competitive instincts and physical skill quite naturally led to the sporting contests of running rapids, racing, and various maneuvering skills.

MID-NINETEENTH CENTURY — WATER AND ICE

The early history of Canada and North America was characterized by a series of armed conflicts and the accompanying necessity of military garrisons. The Seven Years War (1756-1763) involving Britain and France resulted in the bilingual and bi-cultural nature of the country and occasioned the existence of British garrisons for the next one hundred years. The Revolutionary War involving the Thirteen Colonies and Britain soon followed. The War of 1812-1814 between Canada and the United States reinforced the need for military garrisons, as did the American Civil War (1861-1865). The presence of the British military garrisons had a significant impact upon the Canadian cultural development including a variety of Canadian sporting activities (Lindsay, 1970). The British influence through the military resulted in the popularization of many games including, cricket, curling, rugby, and ultimately the game of ice hockey, as well as horse racing and sleigh riding. Keeping in mind that the military had long periods of relative peace, and therefore ample leisure, the personnel were able to serve as organizational catalysts as well. The British shaped many leisure pastimes as well as sports, games, and physical education in early Canadian schools.

Much of the initial development of sport in Canada centered around Montreal. Redmond (1976) points out:

> Despite such understandable discrepancies amongst scholars, and the deserved significant place of Toronto in the history of Canadian sport, there is a consensus of opinion that most of the first clubs in various sports in Canada were formed during the nineteenth century in Montreal, such as: Snow-shoe Club (1840); Montreal Olympic Club (1842/43); Montreal Lacrosse Club (1856); Montreal Football Club (1868); Montreal Golf Club (1878); Montreal Toboggan Club (ca. 1880); and the Montreal Aquatics Polo Club (1887). (p. 45).

In addition, the first gymnasium, under the auspices of Canada's early physical educator, Frederic K.S. Barnjum, was established in Montreal in 1843 (Wise and Fisher, 1974, p. 13). Gymnasiums began to develop, often with support of athletic clubs, during the 1850's and 1860's. McGill College (now McGill University) constructed a gymnasium in 1862, and in 1864 in Toronto a gymnasium was available on the top floor of the Toronto Baths (Lindsay, 1969, pp. 276-278).

Snowshoeing was a sport rivaling lacrosse in pre- and post-Confederation days, an activity which gathered participants from all three cultural factions. The formation of the Montreal Snowshoe Club in 1840 led to the rise of annual showshoe races of varying forms (relays, hurdles, etc.) and distances (Howell and Howell, 1969, pp. 26-29).

Long distance tramps as well as steeple chase events and races of shorter distances maintained variety in competition. The weekly tramp, in Montreal up and over the top of Mont Royal, served as a conditioner and a social event. The snowshoers would tramp to a local hotel where supper would be served, followed by songs and stories and the return journey to the city (Collard, 1976, pp. 221-226).

The sport of curling, which some Americans refer to as "shuffleboard on ice," was imported to North America early in the nineteenth century and had considerable appeal to Lowland Scots wherever they settled in the New World where the climate was favourable (Redmond, 1975, p. 203). Canada, in effect, became an "Eldorado" for the serious curler (Kerr, 1904). Before 1800, Canadian Scots participated in curling on an informal basis. By the mid-1820s the Scots had founded four clubs whose activities featured organized curling: Montreal (1807), Kingston (1820), Quebec City (1821), and Halifax (1824). The activities of more contemporary Scots-dominated organizations spurred curling's growth over the years to a point where the game rivaled ice hockey for the distinctive title of Canada's National Sport.

There is an element of uncertainty regarding the establishment of curling in the new world (Savage, 1974, p. 4). He points out that most

Scottish regiments were from the Highlands rather than the Lowlands. The game of curling, however, was a Lowland activity. The sport was extremely popular with the British settlers and military. The French Canadians did not develop an enthusiasm for the game until the twentieth century. As the frontier pushed westward, the sport of curling spread as well. The game had become popular in the western provinces of Manitoba, Saskatchewan and Alberta by 1876 (Savage, 1974, p. 6).

Ice hockey has been characterized by some as the national religion of Canada. The foundations of the game were based in the activities of bandy, shinty, hurley, and field hockey; hence, a background shared by the Indians, the English, and the Irish. Early forms of hockey were played around Halifax, Nova Scotia; Saint John, New Brunswick; Kingston, Ontario; and Montreal, Quebec about 1837 (Lindsay, 1969, pp. 40-43). Cox (1969, p. 228) presents evidence however, that suggests that the first game of ice hockey as we know it was played in Montreal in 1875. The game soon spread west to Toronto and Winnipeg by 1890. The Stanley Cup, emblematic of professional ice hockey supremacy in North America was first donated in the 1892-93 season for amateur competition. In 1909 it became associated with the professional game.

Salter (1976) in his discussion of L'Ordre de Bon Temps makes reference to the settlers skating on the frozen ponds during that difficult winter in 1604 on St. Croix Island. Skating remained a complicated task for the populous because of the difficulty of attaching the skate to the boot or shoe. In 1865, John Forbes of Dartmouth, Nova Scotia, perfected a re-designed spring skate which simplified the mechanics and permitted much greater participation. The development of the spring skate occurred at about the same time as the Early Closing Movement. The effect of skate technology and increased leisure time led to greater participation. During this period covered rinks were built to accommodate skaters in Quebec City (1852) and Montreal (1863), as well as in Halifax, Saint John (N.B.), Toronto, and Hamilton (Howell and Howell, 1985, pp. 62-64).

Where ice is plentiful in the winter, water is available in the summer! Rowing began early in the development of the new country. Organized regattas were reported as early as 1816, and the sport developed rapidly over the next few decades (King, 1980, p. 15). Canada quickly gained some international success. One of the sporting highlights occurred almost incidentally with the birth of the nation in 1867. A crew of four rowers from Saint John, New Brunswick gained international recognition, as well as enormous national attention, by winning the World Amateur Rowing Championship in Paris, France, during the summer of 1867. The victorious crew were thereafter referred to as the "Paris Crew." Lindsay (1969) described the importance of this event to the new nation by suggesting, "The unifying force of sport had been clearly shown when all of Canada basked in the glory achieved by the New Brunswick crew in Paris. Sport had given Confederation a deeper significance" (p. 311). Down through the years Canada has produced a number of world and Olympic champion rowers.

The confederation of the new nation in 1867 occurred in the midst of the industrial revolution. Lindsay (1969) pointed out that Canada had developed a significant sporting heritage. "In rowing, curling, billiards, and lacrosse, Canada had produced the best players on the continent, while in rowing and lacrosse, Canadians were champions of the world" (p. 311). Improved transportation by rail, water, and later by road permitted the development of intercity competition as well as more extensive involvement of spectators. During the latter part of the nineteenth century, cricket, baseball, lacrosse and football flourished. Outdoor activities during the short Canadian summers and colorful autumns were hunting, fishing, fox hunting, cricket, sailing, track and field contests (associated with the annual picnics of Caledonian and church groups), cycling, baseball, and rowing regattas.

Horse racing was one of the earliest examples of organized sport in Canada. The first horses arrived in Quebec from France in 1665, and horse racing evolved shortly afterwards. By 1871 the sport was considered such a nuisance in Halifax that it was banned on the grounds that it made citizens "idle, immoral and gamblers" (Roxborough, 1966, p. 20). By the eve of Confederation, racing meetings were being staged regularly in towns and cities of Upper and Lower Canada (Ontario and Quebec) and in Nova Scotia. Both French and British were ardent followers of turf affairs.

Codified baseball found its way into Canada from the United States in the late 1850s. Before that time, variations of the ball, bat and base sport were played wherever United Empire Loyalists and other English immigrants from the United States had settled in Canada (Barney and Bouchier, 1987). By 1859 Torontonians were playing the game, igniting an expansion of play to nearby Hamilton, Brampton, Guelph, Woodstock, and London. In 1885 clubs from Toronto, Hamilton, London, and Guelph organized to form Canada's first professional baseball league. At the close of the nineteenth century baseball play in Canada was firmly embedded in the country's sporting culture.

The roots established in many sports early in the nineteenth century began to nurture the bloom of sporting success as the century moved into the third and fourth quarters. Improved transportation, communication, and industrial development enhanced Canada's growth in sport as well as geographically. The population base expanded up the Pacific coast and inland as well as from east to west across the prairies of Manitoba, Saskatchewan and Alberta. As Wilson (pp. 15-32, 1985) pointed out, sports such as baseball had become of almost fanatical importance in towns such as Medicine Hat by the 1880s. Mott (1984, pp. 62-69) identifies the Manitoba Baseball League of 1886 as the first professional league formed on the prairies in any sport. He comments upon the "mania" existing at that time for the sport in Winnipeg.

The influence of the earlier established clubs in sports such as lacrosse, snowshoeing, and gymnastics began to work to the advantage of sport. The Montreal Amateur Athletic Association (M.A.A.A.) was formed in 1881 and represented the unification of these sports (Morrow, 1981, pp. 20-26). Morrow (p. 35) identifies the power and influence of the M.A.A.A. in the establishment of at least ten early sport governing bodies such as lacrosse, cycling, rugby, hockey, baseball, skating, bowling, and water polo. A number of these associations developed as a result of controversy surrounding amateurism and professionalism.

Whereas yachting was a sporting endeavour of the wealthy, rowing became known as "the people's sport." Rowing had a prominent position in the nineteenth-century Canadian sports, and outstanding in that activity were: (a) the stalwart four of Saint John, New Brunswick (Price, Fulton, Ross, and Hutton), who won a double world championship in rigged boats and outrigger shells during the Paris Exposition of 1867; (b) Edward "Ned" Hanlan, "immortalized in bronze and verse" (Cosentino, 1974, pp. 16-17), who won the world's professional championship in 1879 and "stood the rowing world on its ear" during the early 1880s (Wise and Fisher, 1974, p. 101); and (c) Jacob Gill Gaudaur, who eclipsed the records of Hanlan and established himself as the world's premier oarsman during the 1890s.

Hanlan was a rather remarkable story in himself. World champion sculler from 1880-84, he captured the attention of the Canadian public ripe for a figure to cement a feeling of national unity. Hanlan's contests for the Canadian Championship with such figures as Wallace Ross, Fred Plaisted, and Charles Courtney of the U.S., and Edward Trickett of Australia were national and international sensations. The amount of money wagered, the huge crowds, and the colorfulness of the competitors propelled Hanlan into the international spotlight. The "Boy in Blue," as he was dubbed, became Canada's first true national sporting hero (Cosentino, 1974, pp. 5-17). Hanlan was the most impressive, if not the first, of a number of Canadian rowers of international importance such as Jake Gaudaur, Sr., Jake Gaudaur Jr., Jack Guest, George Brown, John O'Neill, and, somewhat later, Roger Jackson and George Hungerford, Olympic medalists in 1964.

Saint John, New Brunswick, fostered the development of some of the world's best speed skaters in the last two decades of the nineteenth century and the first three decades of the twentieth century. Hugh Mc-

Cormick, world professional champion in 1890, was among the first. He defeated Axel Paulsen of Norway over a ten mile course (Flood, 1985, pp. 68-69). Fred Breen, from just outside Saint John, defeated McCormick a few years later in front of four thousand spectators in the Victoria Rink (built in 1865). Fred Logan brought more speed skating honours to Saint John during the first decade of the new century. Charlie Gorman and Willie Logan continued the tradition. William Whelpley, a skater himself, developed the Whelpley "Long Reachers," one of the most popular skates used in competition (Flood, 1985, p. 65). But of all Canadian skaters, speed and fancy (figure) alike, Louis Rubinstein stood alone at the top of national and international figure skating prowess (Rosenberg, Morrow and Young, 1982). A Jew in a world of increasing prejudice, Rubinstein demonstrated enormous decorum and model sport heroism in a career of competition and active sport leadership stretching to 1931, the year of his death.

THE SCHOOLS — SPORTS AND PHYSICAL EDUCATION

There were a number of social factors influencing the development of education in the nineteenth century; however, two principle elements stand out. The first of these was the sheer size of the country coupled with the sparse population. Canada was a country of small rural settlements with few major pockets of sizable populations (this remains true today relatively speaking). The second influence was the concern for survival — both militarily and economically. The military influence shaped physical education into a mold that emphasized drill and gymnastics to some extent. Economic survival, based extensively upon the need to squeeze a living from the land, resulted in little importance being placed upon formal education, and certainly less on anything more than the basic skills. Metcalfe (1970, pp. 29-33) details the heavy reliance on drill and gymnastics, as well as the austerity of the schools in his article on 19th century physical education in Ontario.

The clearly definable bicultural base of the country emerged during the 1800s. The church in French Canada retained strong control of education and developed a foundation in the schools which underlined classical and traditional training lasting until well into the twentieth century. In English Canada a number of important private schools were established. Some were church related, but all were based on the British Public School model. It was within schools such as Upper Canada College, Ridley College, Lower Canada College and similar institutions, that sport began to first be seen as a favorable component of education. Metcalfe (1970, p. 32) points out that it was well into the 1870s and

1880s before high schools of Ontario showed evidence of interschool competition in rugby football and cricket, and then the stimulus came from the students, not the educators.

As the nineteenth century drew to a close, Canadian sport gave ample promise of accelerated growth and development in the century ahead. The tri-cultural establishment of sport had largely given way to British orientation, augmented by the rising specter of American influence. The American thread in Canada's tapestry of sport would be most recognized in college and professional athletics. The Canadian thread in the tapestry of U.S. sport was woven by two Canadians — Naismith and McKenzie.

THE TWENTIETH CENTURY — 1900-1950

The twentieth century has been marked by a number of events that have moved the Canadian sporting scene, indeed the Canadian nation, much closer to that of the United States. Barney (1975) commented upon this phenomenon:

> Twentieth century Canadian sport history has been filled with the richness of activity characteristic of urbanization and industrialization. Following the trend noted in the United States, college and amateur sport rose to become formidable components in the nation's sport fabric. Professional athletics, the inevitable sporting plateau in societies permeated by cultural materialism and competition emerged towards becoming the identical spectacle in Canada as it had in earlier times in the United States (p. 1).

Barney (1975, p. 2) attributes this similarity to a number of factors, including: similar historical ties to Britain, reflecting similar language and customs; and a Canadian population distribution which places approximately eighty-five percent of its inhabitants within one hundred miles of the United States border making them especially prone to the elephantine persuasion of American communication instruments — radio, television, newspapers, magazines, books, and movies.

The preponderance of these influences have moved from the south to the north or from the U.S.A. to Canada. During the latter part of the nineteenth century and early twentieth century, however, there were some significant exceptions. Lewis (cited in Redmond, 1976, pp. 49-50) wrote extensively of the Canadian influences on sport in the U.S.; hockey and lacrosse were two significant Canadian games exported in the United States. In addition, the game of American football was strongly shaped by Canadian football introduced to American colleges by McGill University.

Two noted physical educators, James Naismith, the inventor of basketball, and R. Tait McKenzie, both Canadians by birth, made their most significant contribution to sport and physical education in the United States. McKenzie was Director of Physical Education for Men at McGill

University until 1903 when he moved to the University of Pennsylvania where he remained until his death in 1938. McKenzie is commemorated annually by both the Canadian and American professional associations (CAHPER and AAHPERD). A national shrine, the Mill of Kintail, stands to McKenzie's memory at his former home and studio in Almonte, Ontario.

Sport in Canada during the first half of the twentieth century changed markedly. Baseball increased in popularity with many Canadian teams able to compete against U.S. teams because of improved transportation. Cricket on the other hand began to decline in popularity. Lacrosse, after achieving great popularity during the early part of the century, began to decline following the war years of 1914-1918. The game that once was considered Canada's national game has diminished to the extent that there are now only a few areas remaining as strong lacrosse centers, notably southern Ontario and sections of British Columbia.

The words, "Hello Canada and hockey fans," a Foster Hewitt radio salutation which was first enunciated in 1927 and which regularly captured a spellbound audience of listeners from St. John's, Newfoundland to Victoria, British Columbia, hinted at a national preoccupation with ice hockey, the sport which the rest of the world properly regarded as the special sporting monopoly of Canada. Although hockey and lacrosse experienced parallel chronological and cultural development in their early stages, hockey, unlike lacrosse, has sustained the interest of Canadians. An annual award for the "best team in the Dominion" was donated by Governor-General Stanley in 1894. The Stanley Cup, won for the first time by the Montreal Amateur Athletic Association, had a history similar to that of football's Grey Cup. Originally intended as a distinction for "the best", Lord Stanley had not envisaged the possibility that one day "the best" might mean a professional team. By 1908, however, Canada's most famous sports trophy lay solidly vested in the heritage of professional hockey. Surprisingly, professional hockey did not originate in Canada, but rather in the United States at Houghton, Michigan, in 1903 (Howell and Howell, 1969, p. 206). Using Canadian "imports" to good advantage, Houghton decimated all opponents, Canadian and American alike. The first professional team in Canada was developed at Sault Ste. Marie, Ontario in 1904 (Howell and Howell, 1969, p. 206). The concept of professional hockey spread rapidly through prairie, mountain, and Pacific Coast provinces and to French Canada and the Maritimes. In 1909 the National Hockey Association was formed, including among its original teams hockey's most enduring and majestic entity — the Montreal Canadiens. By 1917 the NHA had become the National Hockey League, and by 1924 American franchises had been added to the league, starting a precedent which led in more modern times to a distinct, over-expansion imbalance between American-based clubs and Canadian organizations.

Hockey benefitted positively from a variety of technological changes during the twentieth century, particularly the advent of indoor artificial ice surfaces and from improved transportation. The advantages of these developments are obvious, but the result was a plethora of rink and arena facilities in virtually every town of any size across the country. The natural climate greatly encouraged this sport to the point where Canada produced most of the finest hockey players in the world, and Canadian teams or Canadian players dominated world professional and amateur hockey. It wasn't until post-1950 that other countries, Russia, Czechoslovakia, Sweden, and the United States, overcame Canada's advantage in ice hockey. Hockey is still one of the few sports with very strong programs at all levels including minor or youth hockey, amateur hockey, programs in educational institutions — in high schools, colleges and universities, and semi-professional and professional hockey.

A history of Canadian football provides a model for witnessing the development of Canadian college and professional sport. The Rugby Union game which formed the basis for the creation of American football was developed by McGill University in the 1870s. Teams representing sporting clubs from various Ontario and Quebec cities, together with a small number of universities, engaged in rugby-type play throughout the remainder of the nineteenth century. In 1909 the first Grey Cup game took place, matching the Ottawa Football Club with the University of Toronto. The Grey Cup spectacle, symbol of national football prominence and largely amateur in early Canadian football, often featured the championship play of Toronto, McGill, and Queen's Universities before 1925. Keen inter-city and inter-sectional rivalries led gradually to the professionalization of the game, including the dimension of importing skilled American players. "Professional football is going ahead by leaps and bounds in the United States and we intend to have a shot at it," stated Lionel Conacher, the organizer of Toronto's 1932 Cross and Blackwell Chefs, Canada's first all-professional football team (Consentino, 1969, p. 98). By 1939 the Winnipeg Blue Bombers could boast a $40,000 annual team budget (p. 117). As the years passed, the Canadian rugby football game became more and more Americanized, influenced heavily by players and coaches from the United States. In 1958 the Canadian Football League was formed. Today, professional football in Canada is quite the same spectacle to Canadians as it is to Americans. The style of play and rules are roughly similar. Unlike their American cousins who lean toward the animal kingdom in choosing their nicknames, Canadians curiously demonstrate a penchant for selecting the human element — Argonauts, Stampeders, Roughriders, Eskimos, Blue Bombers.

The professionalization of football marked the retreat of universities to the sphere of inter-university competition. For almost three decades, commencing in the late 1920s, Queen's, Toronto, McGill and the University of Western Ontario dominated Canadian college sport, especially football, The "exclusive four" decided national football titles among themselves and shunned all official competition with smaller schools. By 1961 a growing measure of unrest among western universities, together with expressions of concern from Ontario, Quebec, and Maritime institutions, signaled the demise of "the Big Four's spirit of exclusiveness" and led to the development of the Canadian Intercollegiate Athletic Union in true national context.

Basketball, for both men and women, quickly caught on as a major Canadian sport. As the YMCA spread across Canada, so did the game of basketball. It was quickly picked up by the universities as well (Jones, 1981, p. 193). Indeed, one of Canada's most renowned and successful teams, the Edmonton Grads, a women's basketball team, played worldwide competition between 1915 and 1940. Playing in Canada, the United States and Europe, the Edmonton Grads during the years from 1922-1940 compiled a record of 355 wins and 20 losses (McDonald, 1981, p. 60). These victories included an undefeated record in Olympic competition in the years 1928, 1932, and 1936.

The proximity of competition in the United States has reinforced the quality of basketball in Canada. Many Canadian teams, both men's and women's, have had the opportunity of competing, and training, in American situations. This cross-fertilization has been a major impetus to the Canadian basketball scene.

Women's intercollegiate athletics have also flourished in Canada. Stimulated initially by the development of basketball competitions, later by public attention focused on the achievements of the superlative Edmonton Grads and Olympic gold medalists Ethel Catherwood and Fanny Rosenfeld, women's competitive athletics in college settings gained momentum. The Canadian Women's Intercollegiate Athletic Union realized a strong evolution during the 1960s and 1970s, and its mission of organizing high-level competition on a local, regional, and national basis reached fruition well before such an accomplishment in women's athletics in the United States.

It is not surprising that soccer has continued to be a popular sport in Canada given the strong British heritage of the country. Soccer benefitted from the early establishment of a national association and has maintained a consistent level of popularity over the years. The strength and interests of many of Canada's ethnic groups has given soccer a renewed impetus in the country. The relatively low cost of the sport, the skill, and demands of the game have made it popular from coast to coast from the elementary school level, to high school, colleges and universities, and it was further enhanced by several Canadian cities fielding professional teams.

It was mentioned earlier that the first truly Canadian world championship was in the sport of rowing, achieved by the "Paris Crew" of Saint John, New Brunswick, shortly after Confederation in 1867. Rowing continued as a vital part of Canadian life through the 1930s before losing popularity, and now has made a strong comeback within the last decade. Much of the popularity of rowing was attributed to interest maintained by betting on the outcome. In 1880 for example, it was estimated that over $300,000 was bet on a Ned Hanlan race, the Canadian and world champion sculler (King, 1980, p. 27).

Hanlan, the World Champion sculler from 1880-1884, continued actively in rowing for many years afterward. In 1896, Jake Gaudaur, taught by Hanlan, became World Champion as well and held the title until 1901. King (1980, p. 30) reports that he was greeted by 100,000 people upon his triumphant return to Toronto after his victory.

Lou Scholes, an amateur rower from Argonaut Rowing Club of Toronto won the Diamond Sculls trophy at Henley, England, in 1904. He was greeted by a crowd of 70,000 upon his return home (King, 1980, p. 32). Of exceptional merit during the period were Joe Wright, Junior, who won the Diamond Sculls in 1928 and Jack Guest, who repeated that coveted achievement in 1930. Joe Wright, Senior, also a winner at Henley, remained a prominent figure in Canadian rowing for a period of fifty years.

Track and field has been a sport that Canadians have been able to point to with pride, particularly in the earlier decades of the twentieth century. Names such as Bill Shearring, Etienne Desmarteau, Bobby Kerr, Earl Thompson, Percy Williams, Ethel Catherwood, the 1929 Women's 400 meter Olympic relay team, and Duncan McNaughton, to name only the Olympic Gold Medal winners, were outstanding performers. This list could be considerably lengthened if Commonwealth Games', Pan-American Games', and Boston Marathon champions were included. The double victories of Percy Williams in the 100- and 200-meter sprints of the 1928 Games in Amsterdam marked Canada's most notable Olympic triumph (Cosentino and Leyshon, 1975, pp. 74-76). In winter Olympic competition the nation's performance has been far better. Figure skaters, skiers, and hockey players have regularly performed at world class levels. Currently the government is dedicated to improving Canada's international status in a number of athletic sports, particularly those which are highly regarded in North America.

As a country with a northern climate, typically receiving ample snow and an extended winter season, it would seem natural that Canadians would succeed in the sport of skiing. In recent years a number of Canadians have indeed achieved noteworthy success in skiing, particularly Lucille Wheeler, Anne Heggtveit, Nancy Greene, Betsy Clifford, all having won World or Olympic Championships, and more recently the Canadian Men's Downhill Team. These successes have all been since 1956. Skiing started in Canada around the turn of the century in Western Canada. The Montreal Ski Club was formed in 1904 (Jones, 1981, p. 106). International success has been a more recent phenomenon, and skiing has been one of the fastest growing sports in recent years.

Similar to skiing, curling is a sport for which the extreme cold of the Canadian winter was ideally suited. The popularity of the game increased and, by the beginning of the twentieth century, curling clubs had been established from coast to coast. Early in this century artificial ice was first used for curling in Vancouver in 1912. Notwithstanding the fact that curling has tended to be of greatest appeal to the middle and upper class, Jones (1981, p. 199) reported that curling was Canada's most popular winter sport by 1920. It still retains that popularity and the Brier, the Scott Tournament of Hearts, and the Silver Broom, emblematic of the Canadian men's, women's championships, and the men's world championships respectively, attract enormous attention.

The depression period of 1930-1940, followed by the Second World War (1939-1945) was an unsettling time in Canadian sport. The search for employment, followed by concerns of national security, disrupted the sports scene considerably. The period was characterized by the seeds of government intervention in sport with the British Columbia Pro-Rec movement in the 1930s and then Canada's National Physical Fitness Act of 1943. These will be discussed more extensively in the following section.

Following World War II the first sport heroine of the post-war period emerged — Barbara Ann Scott, a remarkable figure skater, and a new role model for Canadian women in sport (McDonald, 1981, pp. 69-73). She was indeed the toast of Canada and the world, winning the European Championships in 1947 and 1948, the World Championships in 1947 and 1948, and the Olympic Championship in 1948.

THE EDUCATIONAL SETTING

Games and sports, the legacy of British settlers in Canada, proved to be a constant adversary of foreign gymnastics systems for the attention of physical education authorities. A strong deterent to the growing games and sports-oriented physical education movement in early twentieth century Canada resulted from that form of school-sponsored physical activity characterized by a military drill and exercise regimen. Known simply as the Strathcona Trust program and first implemented in 1909, the Trust was far-reaching in its impact on school physical education. The Federal Government, with assistance from the Department of Militia, transferred the interest gained from a $500,000 donation by Donald Smith (knighted as Lord Strathcona), wealthy Canadian businessman with interests in the Hudson's Bay Company and the Canadian Pacific Railroad, to the Dominion's provinces to be used for school physical education programs. The terms of the Trust stipulated that monies be employed to help underwrite the costs of establishing Ling's Swedish system of gymnastics augmented by military marching drill and musketry (Cosentino and Howell, 1971, p. 28). Initially, some provinces were reluctant to accept such government help under the imposed circumstances, but eventually all succumbed to the dollar attraction of underwriting a "non-essential" school program. Although Ontario was tardy in entering into the Trust program (1911), that province's experience with the Strathcona experiment was pronounced and enduring — to the eve of World War II, in fact (Morrow, 1977, p. 80). In a system whereby each province qualified for Strathcona Trust grants in proportion to the number of school-age children in residence, populous Ontario gained a major share of the fund's annual grants. For instance, in 1911 Ontario received 38 percent of the total national disbursement (Cosentino and Howell, 1971, p. 29). It was not until World War II and after that the damaging efforts of the trust started to be eroded by a rising interest in a sports and games motif as the chief form of school physical education activity.

GOVERNMENT INVOLVEMENT IN SPORT

The immensity of the country, the regionalization of the country, and the relatively small population which is so unevenly distributed, are factors that have encouraged government involvement in sport and physical education. The decisions by provincial governments and by the federal government to enter the sports field has been one of the most important developments in Canadian sport history. Government involvement in sport was not completely new, but remained largely indirect at both the federal and provincial level until the 1930's. The intrusion of government increased slightly in the latter part of the 1930s, and even further during the 1940s.

Broom and Baka (undated, p. 2) summarized the federal pattern of initiative from 1909 to 1939:

Throughout the first half century federal involvement was extremely low-key and catalytic, and centered on the themes of physical fitness for national security through the Strathcona Trust, 1909, and the National Physical Fitness Act, 1943; rehabilitative training for the unemployed through the Youth Training Act, 1939; and the fostering of national prestige through international sport as reflected by grants to the Canadian Olympic Committee, which were first made in 1930 (p. 2).

The Youth Training Act, though encouraging school physical education, had negligible impact. The National Physical Fitness Act which superseded it, had more. Though terminated, the NFFA laid a strong fundamental platform on which far more vigorous and effective government initiative would be based.

One of the early entrances into the sport field, aside from education, was initiated in the Province of British Columbia with the Pro-Rec program (Provincial Recreation). Initiated during the depression period, the program was intended to stimulate and occupy the thousands of unemployed men and youth of the Province. The program became a model emulated by other governments (Broom and Baka, pp. 6-7). Various provinces developed programs of their own, but needed stimulus from the federal level. In 1961 this stimulus was provided.

AN ACT TO ENCOURAGE FITNESS AND AMATEUR SPORT

The fitness movement, triggered in part by the Kraus-Weber fitness results and the American Association for Health, Physical Education and Recreation Youth Fitness Tests, plus the 'Zeitgeist' of the time, had a definite impact on Canada. Parliament became concerned about the well-being of the youth of the country. Reinforcement for the lack of fitness was provided by a statement made by the Duke of Edinburgh in an address to the Canadian Medical Association in 1959. In brief, he chastised Canadians for their unfitness and encouraged them to do something about it (Westland, 1979, p. 13). Following extended debate in Parliament the Act to Encourage Fitness and Amateur Sport, Bill C131, was passed, September 15, 1961.

The early years of the Fitness and Amateur Sport Directorate, which was created by the Act, were characterized by efforts to promote cooperation between the provinces and the federal government in regard to sport. Achieving this type of cooperation in Canada was very difficult because of the respective responsibilities of the levels of government and competitive party policies. Nevertheless, within two years a Federal-Provincial cost-sharing agreement had been reached, and a National Documentation Centre on Fitness and Amateur Sport had been established (Westland, 1979, p. 21).

Prior to 1970 a number of important steps were achieved by Fitness and Amateur Sport including: the establishment of fitness research centres at the Universities of Alberta, Montreal, and Toronto; the establishment of the first "Jeux Canada Games"; initiation of administrative grants to national sports-governing bodies; the beginnings of National Teams; the completion of a study on amateur hockey; the initiation of an experimental sports program in the far north; and bursaries were provided to further upgrade physical education and coaching personnel (Westland, 1979, pp. 22-24). Within the next decade even more striking progress was made. The Report of the Task Force on Sport for Canadians was tabled in the House of Commons; two conferences on Leisure in Canada were held; further Jeux Canada Games were conducted; Hockey Canada was established; grants-in-aid were provided to so-call "carded athletes"; the first Arctic Winter Games were held; the Canadian Academy of Sports Medicine was established; an Administrative Centre for Sport and Recreation was opened in Ottawa; the National Coaches Association was formed; A Canada Fitness Award program was established; Sport Participation Canada (later Particip*Action*) was created; considerable progress was made in fitness programs; the Northern Games were begun; the Olympics were held in Montreal; and the Commonwealth Games were held in Edmonton (Westland, 1979, pp. 24-27). Clearly, significant progress was made and is continuing. Several of the unique aspects of these accomplishments will be discussed further including, national and international games, the Sports Information and Resources Centre; the Administrative Centre for Sport and Recreation; the National Coaching Program; and the Particip*Action* program.

GAMES, GAMES, GAMES

One of the important outcomes of the involvement of the federal government in sport has been the incentive provided in the development of provincial, regional, national and international games. Many provinces have developed both summer and winter provincial games; there have been Western Provinces regional games; and there have been both Arctic Winter Games and Northern Games. The capstone from the national perspective has been the Jeux Canada Games, initially held as winter games in Quebec City in 1967 and then expanded to include summer games in Halifax-Dartmouth, Nova Scotia during August, 1969.

The Jeux Canada Games have come to be recognized as a "Canadian Olympics." A product of national concern for Canada's poor showing in Olympic competition, the games had been suggested as early as 1924 (McLaughlin and McDonald, undated, p. 2). Since that time the games have been held, alternating winter and summer.

The Jeux Canada Games have served to link the country in a true national sports festival. The games have triggered many provinces into developing provincial teams or provincial competitions to select competitors in individual sports. Even more important and lasting has been the development of sports facilities to host the games. The provinces and cities serving as host have developed elaborate facilities to stage the games, generally with monies from all levels of government. These facilities have remained to be used recreationally and competitively within the respective communities.

The Arctic Winter Games, initially held in 1969, and the Northern Games, held first in 1974, were attempts to provide a regional sport festival appropriate for the northern regions of the country. The Arctic Winter Games were composed of a more typical "Euro-Canadian" sports. The Northern Games, however, were based on the traditional aboriginal activities; hence, they included competition that was quite different than the more common types of sport competition (Paraschuk and Scott, 1980, p. 50). Many activities were incorporated that have been a part of the Eskimo heritage for generations.

The hosting of international sport competitions has become a part of the Canadian sport panorama. In 1967 Canada hosted the Pan American Games in Winnipeg, Manitoba. The hosting of the Olympics in 1976 was clearly a highlight, as were the Commonwealth Games in 1978 in Edmonton. Edmonton again served as the host city for the 1983 F.I.S.U. World University Games, and the 1988 Winter Olympics were held in Calgary.

The frequency of hosting competitions of international importance within one country is without parallel. Sport has remained very much in the public eye. The spin-off benefits to all of sport have been extremely significant. Aside from the impact of sport facilities, sport programs, and sport administrators, a system of finance — lotteries — has developed. Lottery money has served as the primary means of financing sport at the provincial and federal level since the first National Lottery was established to support the Olympics prior to 1976.

SOME SPECIAL PROGRAMS

During the past two decades some special programs have been developed that have been very successful and possess unique characteristics. Four of these programs, Particip*Action*, the Coaching Association of Canada and the National Coaching Certification Program, the National Sport and Recreation Centre and the Sports Information Resource Centre, deserve special comment.

One of the remarkable success stories during the past two decades has been the story of Particip*Action*, the promotion and marketing organization devoted to improving the activity lifestyle of Canadians. Subsidized by the government, the goal was to create a semi-private organization that could sell fitness advertising. In fact, most of the active lifestyle advertising has been presented as public service announcements. Virtually every medium has been used — posters, sign boards, radio, television, magazines, newspapers, etc.

One of the early projects used to demonstrate the effectiveness of the material centered on the city of Saskatoon. This city in Western Canada was used as a test in 1973 with enormously successful results. Activity patterns changed drastically, and the resulting publicity influenced much of the country. A market study conducted in 1978 indicated that 79% of Canadians were aware of the ParticipAction symbol and 72% thought it to be an effective organization (Government of Canada, 1981, p. 7).

Another very successful program, this one under the auspices of the Coaching Association of Canada, has been the National Coaching Certification Program (NCCP). Over fifty sports are included in the national program which is designed to develop coaches in over fifty sports. The program includes a series of levels, eventually Level I through Level V, with Level I for beginning coaches and Level V for national coaches. There are three distinct packages — Theory, Technical, and Practical. The material focuses on areas such as administration, special topics, sport medicine, psychology, physical training and strategy. The program has provided vital training and information to hundreds of coaches across the country.

Closely related to coaching and sport information has been the development of the Sport Information Resource Centre (S.I.R.C.). S.I.R.C. has become one of the most comprehensive sport libraries in the western world. Information is catalogued from books, periodicals, theses, etc., and is available through a computerized sport data base. Reproductions of these materials are available by mail enabling sport scientists to assess this information quickly and conveniently.

In 1969 the *Report of the Task Force on Sport for Canadians* was completed. One of the most important elements contained in this report alluded to the fact that Canadian sport organizations had suffered from "kitchen-table" administration (Rae, Des Ruisseaux, and Green, 1969, p. 58). Major changes in sport administration occurred in the following years because of this report.

The federal sport structure was modified, indeed modified several times over the past decade, but presently consists of two distinct units answering to the Minister responsible for Fitness and Amateur Sport; one unit is Sport Canada and the other is Fitness Canada. As the names suggest, the former deals primarily with elite or high performance sport, whereas the latter, Fitness Canada, is concerned with recreation, mass sport and fitness.

Relating to these two major units, but at arm's length, is the National Sport and Recreation Centre. Funded by the government, this unit houses and provides services for over sixty-five national sport governing bodies and professional associations. Sport bodies availing themselves of this support are able to receive secretarial and reproduction assistance, financial support for an executive director and a technical director, and assistance for travel and the staging of national championships. This type of assistance has permitted dramatic growth and administrative development of sport governing bodies in Canada. The National Sport and Recreation Centre has been a great step forward for sport administration.

EPILOGUE: CANADA AND THE UNITED STATES — SIMILAR BUT DIFFERENT

It is apparent that the underlying Victorian, middle-class Canadian societal values expressed in work, perseverance, and self-help were necessary conditions for an emerging industrial society in nineteenth-century Canada (Metcalfe, 1974, p. 72). The same might be said for late nineteenth-century United States. But modern times have seen the erosion of that common European-inherited Protestant ethic shared by both countries. What, then, is to be the future of each under the imposed conditions of city and industry? Whatever those futures, a safe assumption is that there will be similarities.

A strong argument for such speculation is the fact that both Canada and the United States share common geographical boundries, similar social institutions of critical importance, similar economic frameworks, national security destinies, and, indeed, common professional sport endeavours. Given the foregoing profile of North America's sport and physical education heritage, there is little to suggest dissimilarity. Historical traditions prevail! Canada's triculture development of Native, French and British still exists. Canada, possibly more than in the past, has begun to extend these heritages. The contrasting development of Loyalist emigration to Canada in 1783 as opposed to American Revolution has left a different ethos. The French culture, protected in the British North America Act, closer to being enshrined in the Canadian constitution, reinforces this difference. The slightly greater social welfare orientation in Canada produces different government involvement in sport. There are differences — 'vive la difference'!

The character of the sports, games, and physical education of each country demonstrates a tendency to adapt successfully to social environmental changes, the ultimate mark of intellectual and practical achievement. The challenge of the future for Canada lies in the continued pursuit of such achievement.

REFERENCES

ALLEN, E. JOHN B., "Early Canadian Skis: Notes From Europe", *Canadian Journal of History of Sport,* Vol. XVII, No. 1, May, 1986.

BARNEY, R.K. Reflections on Canadian Sport: Images of yesterday, the forecast for tomorrow. In *Proceedings,* North American Society for Sport History, 1978, 1-2.

BARNEY, R. K., "To Breast a Storm: Nathaniel Topliff Allen and the Demise of Military Drill as the Physical Education Ethic in the Public Schools of Massachusetts, 1860-1890", *Canadian Journal of History of Sport,* Vol. XV, No. 2, December, 1987.

BARNEY, R. K. AND BOUCHIER, N. B., "Before Doubleday and Cartwright: The Reminiscences of Adam E. Ford and a Canadian Claim for the Origin of Baseball," *Proceedings: North American Society for Sport History,* 1987.

BROOM, E.F., AND R.S.P. BAKA. *Canadian Governments and Sport.* Ottawa, Canada: Canadian Association for Health, Physical Education and Recreation, undated.

COLLARD, EDGAR A. *Montreal: The Days That Are No More.* Toronto: Doubleday Canada Ltd., 1976.

COSENTINO, FRANK. *Canadian Football: The Grey Cup Years.* Toronto: Musson Book Company, 1969.

CONSENTINO, FRANK. "Ned Hanlan — Canada's Premier Oarsman, A Case Study in 19th Century Professionalism." *Canadian Journal of History of Sport and Physical Education,* Vol. V, No 2, December 1974.

COSENTINO, FRANK AND MAXWELL L. HOWELL. *A History of Physical Education in Canada.* Toronto: General Publishing Company, 1971.

COSENTINO, FRANK AND GLYNN LEYSHON. *Olympic Gold: Canadian Winners of the Summer Games.* Toronto: Holt, Rinehart and Winston of Canada, 1975.

COX, A.E. A History of Sports in Canada, 1868-1900. Unpublished doctoral dissertation, University of Alberta, 1969.

FLOOD, BRIAN. *Saint John, A Sporting Tradition, 1785-1985.* Saint John, N.B.: Neptune Publishing Company, 1985.

GOUGH, B. *Canada.* Inglewood Cliffs, N.J.: Prentice-Hall, Inc., 1975.

GOVERNMENT OF CANADA, FITNESS AND AMATEUR SPORT. *A Challenge to the Nation — Fitness and Amateur Sport in the 80s.* Ottawa: Ministry of Supply and Services, 1981.

HOWELL, NANCY, AND MAXWELL L. HOWELL. *Sports and Games in Canadian Life.* Toronto: Macmillan Company of Canada, 1969.

HOWELL, M.L., AND R.A. HOWELL. *History of Sport in Canada.* Champaign, Illinois: Stipes Publishing Co., 1981.

HOWELL, M.L., AND R.A. HOWELL. *History of Sport in Canada.* Champaign, Illinois: Stipes Publishing Co., 1985. Revised edition.

JONES, K. "Sport and games from 1900-1920." In M.L. Howell and R.A. Howell (Eds.), *History of Sport in Canada.* Champaign, Illinois: Stipes Publishing Co., 1981.

KERR, J. *Curling in Canada and the United States.* Edinburgh: G.A. Morton Publishers, 1904.

KING, P. *Art and a Century of Canadian rowing.* Toronto: Amberly House Limited, 1980.

LAPPAGE, RONALD S. "The Physical Feats of the Voyageurs." *Canadian Journal of History of Sport,* Vol. XV, No. 1, May, 1984.

LEWIS, GUY M., "Canadian Influence on American Collegiate Sports," *Canadian Journal of History of Sport and Physical Education,* Vol. I, No. 2, December, 1978.

LINDSAY, P. L. A History of Sport in Canada, 1807-1867. Unpublished doctoral dissertation, the University of Alberta, 1969.

LINDSAY, P. L. "The Impact of the Military Garrisons on the Development of Sport in British North America." *Canadian Journal of the History of Sport and Physical Education,* Vol. I, No. 1, May, 1970.

McDONALD, D. *For the record.* Toronto, Ontario: John Wiley, 1981.

McLAUGHLIN, P. AND D. McDONALD. *Jeux Canada Games, the First Decade.* Montreal: Pierre des Marais Inc., undated.

METCALFE, ALAN. "Physical Education in Ontario during the Nineteenth Century." *CAHPER Journal,* Vol. 31, No. 1, Sept.-Oct., 1970.

METCALFE, ALAN. "Some Background Influences on Nineteenth-Century Canadian Sport and Physical Education." *Canadian Journal of History of Sport and Physical Education,* Vol. V, No. 1, May, 1974.

METCALFE, ALAN. "Sports and Athletics: A Case Study of Lacrosse in Canada, 1840-1889." *Journal of Sport History.* Vol. III, No. 1, Spring, 1976.

MORROW, DON. "The Strathcona Trust in Ontario, 1919-1939." *Canadian Journal of History of Sport and Physical Education,* Vol. VIII, No. 1, May, 1977.

MORROW, DON. "The Powerhouse of Canadian Sport: The Montreal Amateur Athletic Association, Inception to 1909." *Journal of Sport History,* Vol. 8, No. 3, Winter, 1981.

MOTT, MORRIS. "The First Pro Sports League on the Prairies: The Manitoba Baseball League of 1886." *Canadian Journal of History of Sport,* Vol. XV, No. 2, December, 1984.

PARASCHUK, V.A. AND H.A. SCOTT. "Games Northerners Play — the Arctic Winter Games and the Northern Games." In *Proceedings,* North American Society for Sport History, 1980.

RAE, W.H., P.W. DES RUSSEAUX AND N. GREEN. *Task Force on Sport for Canadians.* Ottawa: Queen's Printer, 1969.

REDMOND, G. "The Olympic City of 1844 and 1976: Reflections Upon Montreal in the History of Canadian Sport." *Canadian Association for Health, Physical Education and Recreation Journal.* 42, 4, 1976.

REDMOND G. Developments in Sport since 1939. In M.L. Howell and R.A. Howell (Eds.), *History of Sport in Canada.* Champaign, Illinois: Stipes Publishing Co., 1981.

ROXBOROUGH, HENRY. *One Hundred — Not Out: The Story of Nineteenth-Century Canadian Sport.* Toronto: The Ryerson Press, 1966.

SALTER, MICHAEL A. "The Effect of Acculturation on the Game of Lacrosse and on Its Role as an Agent of Indian Survival." *Canadian Journal of History of Sport and Physical Education,* Vol, III, No. 2, May, 1972.

SALTER, MICHAEL A. "L'Ordre de Bon Temps: A Functional Analysis." *Journal of Sport History,* Vol. III, No. 2, Summer, 1976.

SAVAGE, PAUL. *Canadian Curling "Hack to House".* Agincourt, Ontario: Sportbook Ltd., 1974.

WESTLAND, C. *Fitness and Amateur Sport in Canada — An Historical Perspective.* Ottawa, Canada: Canadian Parks/Recreation Association, 1979.

WILSON, L.J. ROY. "Medicine Hat — 'The Sporting Town' 1883-1905." *Canadian Journal of History of Sport,* Vol. XVI, No. 2, December, 1985.

WISE, S.F., AND DOUGLAS FISHER. *Canada's Sporting Heroes.* Don Mills, Ontario: General Publishing Company, 1974.

Section Six

Physical Education and Sport in a Historical Perspective

Earle F. Zeigler

INTRODUCTION

A truly qualified professional in physical education and sport must start from the beginning to comprehend the role of his or her own specialized field in society. For this reason we will take a brief excursion into the area of philosophy of history (see Zeigler, 1964, pp. 3–9; 1968, pp. 3–7; 1973, pp. 341–57; and Zeigler, ed., 1975, pp. 363–78). A philosophy of history could be described as a systematic body of general conceptions about history. Before studying physical education and sport philosophy (Zeigler, 1977), a student would be well advised to have at least a reasonable acquaintance with the field's history, thus placing it in historical perspective.

Living our lives from day to day, we sometimes forget that the planet Earth originated some four billion years ago. Early man, we are told, had his beginnings a million years ago and has used crude tools for something less than half that time. Some 300,000 years have elapsed since the mutation of subhuman into human being. The beginnings of the first civilizations were actually less that 10,000 years ago, which means that there was a gap of 290,000 years more or less. The great religions are the products of the past 2,500 years. Democracy, the youngest of infants, had its origins during past several centuries. Is it any wonder that perfection appears to be a long way off?

TEN PEACEFUL REVOLUTIONS

During the second half of the twentieth century we are told that at least ten *peaceful* revolutions are having a significant effect on our nation and on the world. Political candidates with an eye to the future discuss

Earle F. Zeigler is currently Professor of Physical Education, Faculty of Physical Education, The University of Western Ontario, London, Canada.

such problems and the resultant implications. The so-called peaceful revolutions are as follows: (1) the "exploding" cities, [from the standpoint of population and territorial growth]; (2) the mechanization of the farm; (3) the vastly increasing birth rate [which many governments and agencies have now been able to control]; (4) the extended life expectancy; (5) the technological improvements in production; (6) the use of electrical and atomic energy; (7) the development of a higher standard of living, [which now needs to be limited primarily to those nations where improvement is desperately needed]; (8) the development of weapons, [which is hardly a "peaceful" revolution item]; (9) the rapid [and continued] growth of population in underdeveloped nations least able to support it; and (10) a developing nationalism evident throughout the world.[1]

QUESTIONS AND ANSWERS

As we think about the past and the present, we begin to realize that there are a large number of unanswered questions. We—both individually and collectively—must come up with answers that satisfy us. We might ask the question, "What is history?" Is everything historic? Are we referring to the actual order of events or to the order of events as seen by an interpreter (the historian)? A student of history might well ask whether the philosophy of history challenges the democratic way of life. This would imply that there is just one way of looking at history or that there is simply one philosophy. If there are indeed many philosophies of history, can we say that one is paramount? (The author, for example, subscribes to an interpretation that concedes the unattainability of perfect objectivity, "but yet remains hostile to rigid or dogmatic historical theories. . . . This school is pragmatic and pluralistic, assuming always multiplicity of causation, and prepared to use *ad hoc* whatever general theories may illuminate a particular point" [Zeigler, 1973, p. 349].)

Approaching this issue from another angle, we might question the validity and reliability of historical research. Is it possible to construct a valid philosophy of history that is fact and not fiction? Is it possible, for example, for historians to record facts scientifically? It has been said that good history has depth as well as surface. Historian Theodore Mommsen, however, has asserted that "history is neither made nor written without love or hate."

An example of this is given by Woody when he deprecates the fact that those who have written about education and its history have slighted, perhaps through bias, what he designates as "physical culture":

> Despite the fact that lip-service has been paid increasingly to the dictum "a sound mind in a sound body," ever since western Europe began to revive the educational

[1]From an address by President J. F. Kennedy, Detroit, Michigan, Spring 1958.

concepts of the Graeco-Roman world, there is still a lack of balance between physical and mental culture, both in school programs and those who write of education. This is evident in many quarters, even where a certain universality of outlook ought to reign. Turn where one will, it is impossible to find physical culture adequately presented in books dealing with the general history of education. Written in keeping with a dominant rationalism, these books have been concerned chiefly with intellectual movements and institutions for mental improvement. (1949, p. vii)

History appears to have begun with the ancient Greeks. It was written also, but perhaps not quite so well, by the Romans. We have to decide, of course, whether a disinterested observer can write history as effectively as someone who has lived through the passing events. This introduces a disturbing problem which is difficult to answer. What constitutes acceptable history? Is a simple chronological listing of events satisfactory? Some would argue that history must show the connection between a series of events, and that, furthermore, it should cover a broader field and should extend over a fairly long period of time.

And then we find some histories of the world with religious overtones that would have us believe unequivocally that God's purpose is gradually coming to pass. Indeed we must ask ourselves if there has been moral evolution. Despite the fact that history is destructive as well as cumulative, many do feel that the history of mankind shows strong trends toward emergence. Are we gradually—*very* gradually—evolving a formula that will help all the people of the world live together in relative peace and harmony?

THE POSSIBILITY OF HISTORICAL RESEARCH

There is no argument but that historical writers need to uncover as many primary sources as possible to write the best history. If only one mind passes between the historian and the material about which he is to write, there is a much greater chance of an accurate report. The possibility of a forged document, for example, or of a first-hand observer's inaccurate report only increases the difficulty of writing fine history. Because it may be so difficult also to locate an objective observer, some historians have felt it necessary to retrace the steps of the incidents which the historians themselves hope to describe later. Witness the historian of the twentieth century who felt it advisable to hire an elephant to prove that it had been possible for Hannibal to cross the Alps by this means of transportation. One further step may be required: the historian may find it essential to employ the highest type of reflective thinking before completing the work.

Experimental researchers, and even those who undertake survey research, may repeat and check on their earlier observations. Unfortunately (for the historian at least) history does not repeat—at least never in *exactly* the same way! Because historians cannot themselves "see" what has happened, their attitude will undoubtedly influence their work. They must make some assumptions as to the rationality of the universe, for example. Presumably this assumption of underlying rationality would have to be true if a human being hoped to make sense out of the world in which he or she lives. (And now that this is the so-called "Age of Analysis" in philosophy, I will have to qualify the above statement by stating that implying rationality to the universe may be somewhat different than ascribing rationality to a particular human being!)

Thus we might agree that complete objectivity of history is an impossibility. Perhaps our best hope is that someone with penetrating insight will have flashes of intuitive genius while writing and interpreting the history of mankind. And yet I must confess that such a hope is to me dubious at the very best. If such an occurrence were to take place, however, such a person would undoubtedly be employing a type of speculative philosophy as part of his or her approach to the highly complex problem of historical interpretation. Certainly we do have already a number of unproven philosophies of history, some of which are highly speculative and extremely interesting albeit as yet substantially unproven.

Having employed empirical methods involving experiment and experience, scientists in many of the more exact sciences have been able to predict future developments. In this respect historians are fighting against a severe handicap, but in recent years definite progress has been made toward improving the scientific base of historical investigation. By attempting to meet the exacting requirements of the more empirical sciences, it has been possible to develop a type of philosophy of history. As a result many kinds of history may be examined today using these improved criteria for adequacy and accuracy. History makes a stout effort to define the future. Any such definitions reflect the mood of the times and the predispositions of the historian. People must continue to strive and, although many may not like it just that way, it appears that they must continue to act on at least a certain amount of faith.

ASSISTANCE FROM RELATED DISCIPLINES

Those working in the area of sport and physical education history should be relating both directly and indirectly to the related disciplines of sociology, anthropology, social psychology, and philosophy. We should know what these people are doing and why they are doing it.

Conversely, they should be taking more cognizance of what has been occurring in the subdisciplinary area of sport and physical education history. That body of knowledge, albeit not typically genuinely interpretative, is much larger than that which is available in the other four subdisciplines. They need the background material that we have provided and will continue to provide in substantive quantity. However, we really should begin to employ established methodology and accompanying techniques when and where possible from these subdisciplines to strengthen our investigative base. This will become the best possible way to make a comparative analysis and interpretation of the historical role of sport in society. All of this stands to reason. People have employed a variety of psychological or learning processes to gain knowledge about the present and the past, notably (1) thinking (rationalism), (2) intuiting (intuitionism), (3) sensing (empiricism), and (4) believing (authoritarianism) (Royce, 1964, adapted with slight change). As the discipline has become more scientific, placing increased emphasis on research techniques with a more empirical approach, there has been a marked tendency to turn to a variety of related disciplines for assistance. The late Allan Nevins, writing in 1968, reaffirmed the idea that the discipline of history was employing "Many powerful new forces ... and few men understand half of them" (1968). He was referring to such aspects as new studies from archeology, advancements in epigraphy, development of the carbon-dating process, comparative ancient literature, and so forth.

Sociology

The discipline of sociology can be extremely helpful to the sport and physical education historian, especially in analysis and interpretation of the values and norms of the various social systems and cultures of the past. Parsons' theory of action, a structural-functional theory, has been described by Johnson as "a type of empirical system" (1969). Four levels of social structure are postulated as (1) values, (2) norms, (3) the structure of collectivities, and (4) the structure of roles. These proceed from highest to lowest, with the higher levels being more general than the lower ones. Values, for example, are categorized, and values in sport would of necessity reinforce the important societal values and shared, sanctioned norms of a particular social system.

To arrive at an accurate interpretation of the historical role of sport in a society, there would appear to be a prior need to achieve an acceptable synthesis of the history of the social system being considered. The functional interchanges between and among the subsystems of the social system should be understood (e.g., how its economy serves as an effective adaptive subsystem), as should the means whereby a social system maintains its equilibrium (e.g., how the social processes whereby a society maintains a given structure *or* changes it) (Johnson, 1969, pp. 46–58). If, as is typically postulated by many, sport, games, and physical activity exert significant social force within a society (and vice versa, of course), a knowledge of these factors will offer increased explanatory power to the sport historian. Obviously, those offically engaged with the discipline of sociology are not concerned with an analysis of sport at present, and it also appears that so-called sport sociologists haven't shown much inclination to relate to so-called sport historians. For these reasons it behooves us in this subdisciplinary area to make an effort toward cooperative effort because of what such an inclination could mean to sport and physical education history.

Anthropology

The field of anthropology includes the study of the physical, cultural, and social development (and the behavior) of men and women since they appeared in the evolutionary development of the planet that has been designated as Earth. Since this is obviously an enormous discipline, that subdivision within it which treats the cultural heritage of the human animal has been named social or cultural anthropology. This deals with the interrelationship of cultural values and human behavior within the various social units that have existed on earth, such a relationship being a perennial concern for the members of any particular society.

Cultural anthropology has only recently been recognized as a science by some, and anthropological theories about sports and games as dynamic processes of social life have perhaps not been given suitable attention. Of course, the work of the cultural anthropologist would often not even be sufficiently exact to warrant the employment of complex statistical procedures (and for that matter may never be, in instances when someone is studying the processes that occasion the development or change of cultural patterns). This is not to say, however, that games and sporting patterns of early cultures cannot, or should not, be described with care, or that *ad hoc* theories may not be applied to them wherever possible. It seems reasonable to assume that certain types of games and sports will appear as identifiable elements in the culture complex of a society, e.g., the concepts of "sportsmanship" and "fair play" in the games of a democratic society (Herskovits, 1955, pp. 33–85).

One investigation in which game theory was related to so-called cultural complexes was that in which R. G. Glassford sought to prove an interrelationship between a culture and its game forms. He postulated that the *nature* of sports and games would undergo changes depending upon the possible changes in values and norms of a culture undergoing transition. On the basis of a theory of games and economic behavior outlined by Von Neumann and Morgenstern (1947), Glassford developed a game classification model which he then tested on a culture (Eskimo) which was undergoing a marked transition. Basically he hypothesized that "the orientation of the traditional generation toward the values of reciprocity and sharing would be reflected in their game preferences," and that "the new-era generation would express a stronger preference for competitive games." The findings enabled Glassford to verify his postulations, at least tentatively, and also confirmed the hypotheses that the traditional generation seems to prefer self-testing games more and also preferred a game strategy which afforded "tolerable satisfactions" with minimum risk (Glassford, 1970).

Social Psychology

There is no doubt either but that the historian will need to keep the investigation of social psychologists increasingly in mind in the future as he hypothesizes about the historical role of sports and games in various civilizations. Fundamentally, the present concern in this subdisciplinary area is with "the development of the social phases of personality, attitudes, and values by means of" these activities (Cowell, 1960). The challenge of explaining how personality and/or character is developed and maintained in a culture is such that fully adequate explanations or theories may not be available for some time to come. The many variables involved greatly complicate the possibility of investigation. And yet society seemingly readily accepts the hypothesis that physical activity in competitive sport situations does lead to desirable social development. It seems true further that social behavior and personality growth can be influenced positively or negatively according to a society's values and norms, and that such development may well depend upon the quality of the leadership and the opportunities for participation afforded.

A really good beginning has been made on the development of an inventory of findings about human behavior (Berelson and Steiner, 1964), and there soon will be research efforts in this area that may well serve to assist sport and physical activity historians with their analyses. This highly important aspect of the disciplinary approach to sport deserves continuing support. The classification of games based on socio-psychological phenomena should be developed further (e.g., Roberts and Sutton-Smith, 1962), as should the "people experiments" encouraged by Martens (1971) and broadened in his plea for "a social psychology of physical activity" (1970).

Philosophy

The field of philosophy—especially the *history* of philosophy, but also the *philosophy* of history—offers a storehouse of data to the sport and physical education historian. The difficulty is to determine how and on what basis the historian can or should approach all of this information. Presumably such an approach would depend almost completely on the historian's background and experience within the culture in which he or she is living. Pragmatists would tend to be concerned about learning theory prior to questions about the nature of reality. Another person might wish to study the many histories of philosophy in which theories and so-called schools of philosophical thought would be presented chronologically. (Some of this second group might be in the form of biographies of great philosophers of the past.) A third approach for the historian might be to read progressively from the actual works of the philosophers themselves, an approach usually based on the location of the best translations available. Another highly useful method would be the determination of the major recurring issues or problems with which philosophers have concerned themselves over the centuries. It was this approach that Brubacher used with the departmental philosophy of education (1969). This approach, I feel, is an excellent one to adapt to physical education and sport because of its seemingly effective application (Zeigler, 1964, pp. 247–82; 1968; and 1977) through the employment of a so-called structural analysis research technique (Fraleigh, 1970).

It is possible to conclude with some confidence that philosophers have over the centuries approached their work speculatively (or synthetically), normatively, or analytically—or with some combination of these approaches. The historian is presumably in as good a position as anyone to sense the spirit of the times in which the philosopher was writing (and who can argue that the philosopher was not influenced by the values and norms of his period?). Lauwerys recommends, for example, that an investigator should make an effort to understand at the very least the dominant philosophy *and* philosophy of education in the culture that is being studied. The assumption is that such an assessment will provide a truer insight concerning the reasons why certain sporting patterns or a specific and/or definitive pattern of education were being carried out (1959, pp. 283–90).

THE BASIC NATURE OF MAN

All of this investigation should eventually lead us to a better understanding of the basic nature of man. At least it may help us to "get a fix" on man's basic nature as it was conceived in a particular period of time during man's development within recorded history. There have already been a variety of postulations made along these lines. Writing in 1956, for example, Van Cleve Morris offered a fivefold definition of man on a historical time scale: (1) *a rational animal,* a classical Greek definition in which man was subdivided into body and mind, thus requiring an educational system that provided a curriculum balanced between these two entities; (2) *a spiritual being,* in which St. Thomas Aquinas described man as being made up of three dimensions (mind, body, and soul), and with which appeared a hierarchy of values in which "animal nature" assumed the lowest position; (3) a *"receptacle of knowledge,"* in which man as a sentient creature was obligated to absorb as much knowledge as possible in order to make a better life for himself on earth and, inasmuch as the body developed "naturally," physical education could provide a change of pace for students; (4) *a dualistic body and mind person,* in which a redefinition of Platonic-Aristotelean man was postulated, and in which both aspects of the seemingly organic unity were to be exercised (with the result that often only "lip service" was given to bodily exercise in a weak effort to preserve some balance in the curriculum); and (5) a *problem-solving organism,* in which man is regarded as an animal or creature in the process of evolution whose capabilities have come from a developing capacity to solve problems, and in which mind and body are simply considered "instrumental extensions" of one another. Within such a pattern physical education's task could be to teach a person to move efficiently and purposely (with *meaning*) within the context of his or her socialization in an evolving world (Zeigler, 1975, p. 405).

Then in the 1960s Berelson and Steiner carried out a significant inventory of Human Behavior (1964) in which they presented ordered generalizations based on the findings of 1,056 selected studies. They finally traced six images of man throughout recorded history, but more from the standpoint of the behavioral sciences than Morris's philosophically oriented definitions. The first of these was the so-called *philosophical image* (1964, pp. 662–67), in which people of the ancient world distinguished virtues through the employment of their reason. This was followed by what they called the *Christian image,* where there was added the concept of original sin and salvation became possible through the transfiguring love of God for those who controlled their sinful impulses. The third delineation was the *political image* during the Renaissance in which man, through the introduction of power and will, managed to take greater control of the social environment. In the process sufficient energy was liberated to bring about numerous political changes, the end result being the creation of national ideals which coexisted with somewhat earlier religious ideals. During the eighteenth and nineteenth centuries a fourth image emerged. This *economic image* provided an underlying rationale for economic development in relation to people's possession of property and things along with improved monetary standards. Efforts were being made to equate the concept of "individual good" with that of the "common good," while at the same time the third basic political division, class, was more sharply delineated.

The early twentieth century saw the development of a fifth, *psychoanalytic image,* which introduced another form of love—with ego and self, as the instinctual impulses were delineated more carefully than ever before. An effort was made to understand the role of childhood experiences in man's life, and to comprehend how nonconscious controls often ruled man's actions because of the often incomplete gratification of certain human drives related to libido and sex. Finally, because of the belated (but now rapid) development of the behavioral sciences, Berelson and Steiner postulated the *behavioral science image.* This view characterized man as a creature who is continually and continuously adapting reality to his own ends. In this way he seeks to make it more pleasant and congenial —to the greatest possible extent *his own* reality.

THE PERSISTENT HISTORICAL PROBLEMS

The earlier chapters of this book presented a brief overview of the history of physical education and sport on earth. It is now appropriate to place the subject in slightly different historical perspective, by recasting unilateral historical narrative into an approach to the teaching of physical education and sport history that delineates the persistent, recurring problems that have emerged throughout recorded history in sufficient quantity for reasonably intelligible qualitative analysis. Within this pragmatic approach, an inquiry is conducted to ascertain, for example, what influence a type of political system in a culture had on the structure and function of the culture's educational system—and perhaps concurrently on the program of physical education and sport offered. All history can, therefore, be viewed with an eye to the persistent problems (social forces or professional concerns) that seem to reveal themselves as a result of a searching, in-depth analysis. Thus, no matter which of a number of historical theories or approaches is employed, such a "persistent problems" approach guides one to search for the interpretive criterion, to seek out underlying hypotheses, to ask how a particular historical treatment aids in the analysis of past problems, and to inquire whether new insight has been afforded in the search for solutions to problems that people will perhaps always face.

Delineation and description of these problems as they might relate to this field has been one of this author's more important investigative goals. How this idea came to him may be traced to a period of study at Yale University. The credit for this unique approach in educational history and philosophy must therefore go to John S. Brubacher, long-time professor of the history and philosophy of education at Yale and Michigan. Many of the ideas for the specific problems listed in Figure 5–1 originated with him (and with some of his colleagues and graduate students), although some adaptations and a few additions have been made. Thus, the approach has been adapted to the specialized field and this *adaptation* is this author's own contribution to a very large extent (Brubacher, 1966; Zeigler, 1977).

Such an approach as this does not really represent a radically different approach to history. The typical major processes are involved in applying historical method to investigation relating to physical education and sport as follows: (1) the data are collected from primary and secondary sources; (2) the collected data are criticized and analyzed; and (3) an integrated narrative is presented, with every effort made to present the material interestingly and solidly based upon tentative hypotheses established at the outset. This approach does differ markedly, however, in the organization of the collected data: it is based completely on a presentation of individual problem areas—persistent or perennial problems of the present day that have been of concern to people over the centuries. The idea is to illuminate them for the student of physical education and sport. A conscious effort is made to keep the reader from thinking that history is of antiquarian interest only. The student is in a fine position to move back and forth from early times to the present as different aspects of a particular subject (persistent problem) are treated. This technique of "doing" history may be called a "vertical" as opposed to a "horizontal" traditional approach—a "longitudinal" treatment of history in contradistinction to a strictly chronological one. These persistent problems will in all probability continue to occur in the future along with others that may appear from time to time. A problem used in this sense (based on its early Greek derivation) would be "something thrown forward" for man to understand or resolve.

Values and Norms

The persistent problem of values and norms seems to possess a "watershed quality" in that an understanding of those objects and/or qualities desired by people through the ages can evidently provide signifi-

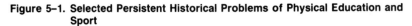

Figure 5–1. Selected Persistent Historical Problems of Physical Education and Sport

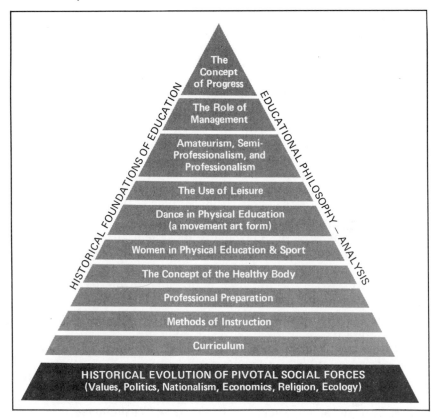

cant insight into this particular problem—and also into most if not all of the other recurring problems that will be discussed. From a sociological standpoint, *values* are typically conceived as the institutions, customs, or ideals of a society or culture, and they exert a great influence on the direction in which a particular society is moving. Of course, I am referring here to the positive values, but it must be kept in mind that people generally have an "affective disdain" for a society's negative values as well as an affective regard for the positive ones. In philosophy, in the subdivision of ethics, the ultimate meaning of the term "value" has a direct relationship to the above description. People typically ascribe value to those objects and/or qualities which they find desirable in life either as means or as ends in themselves.

So-called *norms* have an interesting relationship to a society's values, but they are not identical in certain regards. A norm has several meanings based on the specific context in which it is being employed. Typically we

257

think of it as a general level or average, but it is used also to describe a model, pattern, or standard that prevails in a social system or culture.

It seems wise to review the roles of values and norms both individually and comparatively at the outset, and here we can look to the analysis of their relationship by the sociologist Johnson in his review of Parsons' general action system on these points. This may be regarded as a type of empirical system that is composed of four subsystems (culture, the social system, the personality, and the behavioral organism). The theory is that these subsystems compose a hierarchy of societal control and conditioning (Johnson, 1969, pp. 46–58).

Culture as the first subsystem of the action theory provides the basic structure and its components "and, in a sense, the 'programming' for the action system as a whole." (These quotations, and others in this section are from Professor Johnson's paper.) The structure for the "social system," of course, "has to be more or less attuned to the functional problems" of social systems, and the same holds for the structure and functional problems of the personality subsystem and the behavioral organism subsystem, respectively. Further, you should keep in mind that the subsystem of culture exercises "control" over the social system, and so on down the scale. Legitimation is provided to the level below or "pressure to conform" if there is inconsistency. Thus, there is a " 'strain toward consistency' among the system levels, led and controlled from above downward."

The terms "conditioning" and "strain" are used by Parsons to explain the hierarchy of conditioning that is theorized. The higher systems depend on the lower ones, and the "strain" that may occur at the lower level "works" to change the very structure of the system above. Of course, as might be expected, "incipient strain" at the lower level may well be resolved prior to the creation of such an effect that change takes place above. Generally speaking, a change in culture is apt to take place when important scientific or religious beliefs are challenged or negated. This can in fact bring about structural change in larger social systems, while change in personality could well bring about change in somewhat smaller social systems.

To return to direct consideration of values and norms in relation to the social systems of the United States (or perhaps Canada), proceeding from the highest to the lowest level (or from the general to the more specific), the social system itself has four levels of structure within it: (1) *values*, (2) *norms*, (3) *the structure of collectivities*, and (4) *the structure of roles*. Keep in mind that all of these levels are normative in that the social structure is composed of sanctioned cultural limits within which certain types of behavior are mandatory or acceptable.

Note that values are the highest level, and that there are many categories of values according to this theory (scientific, artistic, and values for personalities, etc.). "*Social* values are conceptions of the ideal general character of the type of social system in question." As Johnson explains, "For the United States as a society, important societal values are the rule of law, the social-structural facilitation of individual achievement, and the equality of opportunity" (1969, p. 48).

Further, it is most important to keep in mind the difference between the values and the shared sanctioned norms that are the second level of the social structure. In the U.S. social system, for example, the basic *norms* are the institutions of private property, private enterprise, the monogamous conjugal family, and the separation of church and state. These are different in type from the *values* explained by Johnson above. (It would not serve our purpose at this point to discuss either the structure of collectivities or that of roles, other than to state that the Democratic Party, or the Liberal Party in Canada, would be examples of *collectivities*, and the fourth-level *roles* would similarly be the possible unique influence of a John F. Kennedy or a Pierre Trudeau.

Without going into detail about Parsons' so-called interchange processes and the various subsystems of the larger social system, it can be stated that Parsons' action theory suggests that the most important cultural aspect of any society is its value system. In the United States, for example, there has been, according to Parsons, a remarkably stable value system with gradual value generalization such as that which accompanies structural differentiation. Progress toward these values has obviously not been a straight-line movement, mainly because of various types of resistance that have arisen over the decades. Johnson outlines four of these obstacles (1969, p. 55) as follows:

1. Many mistakenly identify norms with values and react indignantly to reform because to them this represents a subversion of values. Parsons calls this "fundamentalism."
2. Reform is most difficult because it comes into conflict with vested interests bent on preventing a redistribution of the benefits and burdens of the system.
3. So-called ideological distortion often develops, a situation in which many citizens hold a distorted view of the state of the system and of the probable effect of the proposed changes.
4. Because of the rapid change in the culture and the social systems of the United States, there exist a great many needs for change. Some of these needs are not being met, or are being met insufficiently at best. This is producing strain with a resultant "need" to restore solidarity (an integrative problem).

It is interesting to note that truly significant change can take place at the three lower levels without actually "doing violence" to the value level itself. The reason for this is the hierarchy of control and conditioning that prevails. It takes a thoroughgoing social revolution—one in which a new value system becomes the source of legitimation, guidance, and control—to bring about a sufficient amount of disequilibrium to force the social system to adopt new or basically altered values.

Parsons' action system does not state that history is the unfolding of a predetermined cultural value system—the possible error of those who hold teleological beliefs, and who may even believe fully in the implementation of an idealistic philosophy of education. It does provide historians with a framework or model with which to view any or all of the civilizations since recorded history. The interesting point, still further, is that there is an opportunity to relate and identify the scientific methodology underlying Parsonian theory with that of scientific pragmatism. Both Parsons and Dewey (when he was alive) envision an actor-situation frame of reference in a world characterized by ever-present change and novelty. And in this dynamic relationship the crucial position and importance of values, and especially the approach to the determination of *specific* values, is paramount.

Values from a Philosophical Perspective. The study of values *(axiology)* may be regarded historically at least as the fourth and most important subdivision of philosophy. Many would assert even today that it is the end result of philosophizing. Presumably the effort to become knowledgeable on the subject of values involves the development of a system of values that is consistent with one's beliefs in the other three major subdivisions of philosophy: (1) metaphysics, questions about reality; (2) epistemology, acquisition of knowledge; and (3) logic, exact relating of ideas. There have been various theories throughout history about the subject of values. Some believed that values exist only because of the interest of the valuer (the *interest theory*). The *existence theory,* conversely, is one in which values are assumed to exist independently of man: that is, they are essence added to existence. The *experimentalist theory* explains the concept of value somewhat differently: values which yield practical results that have "cash value" bring about the possibility of greater happiness through more effective values in the future. One further theory, the *part-whole theory,* is explained by the idea that effective relating of parts to the whole brings about the highest values.

Axiology itself has various domains. First and foremost, we must consider ethics, which includes morality, conduct, good and evil, and the ultimate objectives of life. There are several approaches to the problem of whether life as we know it is worthwhile. A person who goes around all the time with a smile on his or her face looking hopefully toward the future is, of course, imbued with optimism. Those who get discouraged easily and who wonder if life is worth the struggle are victims of pessimism. In between these two extremes we find the golden mean of meliorism, which implies that one faces life striving constantly to improve one's situation. This position assumes that a person is not capable of the wisdom or foresight needed to make any final decisions about whether good or evil will prevail ultimately on earth.

A second most important problem that has been considered historically under ethics is what has been regarded as most important in life for the individual. This might be described as the ultimate end or highest values of our existence. Here there has been the belief that pleasure is the highest good *(hedonism)*. One approach related to hedonism that has developed in the modern period of history is known as *utilitarianism.* In this theory society becomes the focus: the basic idea is to promote the greatest happiness for the greatest number of people in the community. Thus, although there are types of pleasure which range from intense, momentary, emotional pleasure to a pleasure that is reflected in a placid life of contentment, a hedonist believes that the seeking of this type of pleasure will eventually result in the fulfillment of his or her required moral duty.

Another important way that men have viewed the highest good *(summum bonum)* in life was called *perfectionism.* This person aims at complete self-realization, while at the same time envisioning a society characterized by the highest achievement as well.

A logical progression that followed from a person's decision about the greatest or highest good in life was the standard of conduct that he or she subsequently set for life fulfillment. It was typically presumed that the philosophical position or stance that one held gave direction and purpose in this regard. Certain interests did guide people's conduct in life. Thus, if we are too self-centered today, people will say that we are egotistical *(egoism).* Some that we know go to the other extreme; they feel that a person is best fulfilled when playing down the realization of personal interests to serve society at large—or some social group or collectivity therein *(altruism).* Aristotle's difficult concept of the "golden mean" enters at this point for possible guidance.

Throughout the course of history there developed other aspects of value over and above ethical considerations that treated moral conduct. One of these areas under axiology had to do with the "feeling" aspects of one's conscious life *(aesthetics).* Aesthetics may be defined as the theory or philosophy of taste, and people have inquired over the centuries whether there are indeed principles which govern the search for the beautiful in life. Because there was a need to define still other values in the life of people, we now have specialized philosophies of education and religion—and even a philosophy of physical education and sport. When we refer to a person's social philosophy, we are referring to the decisions that have been made about the kind, nature, and worth of values which are intrinsic to, say, some aspect of one's life as a social creature in a social environment (e.g., the best educational process).

Physical Education and Sport. In *primitive* society there was probably very little organized, purposive instruction in physical education and games; any incidental education was usually a by-product of daily experience. The usual activities of labor, searching for food, dancing, and the games were essential to the development of superior bodies. Physical education activities, in addition to promoting physical efficiency, helped to strengthen membership in the society and served as a means of recreation.

In the ancient *Chinese* civilization, physical education and sport presumably had little if any place in a culture whose major aim was to preserve and perpetuate a traditional social order. At that time no strong military motive existed, although physical training was used sporadically when it did become necessary to increase military efficiency. As a type of classical education grew and various religious influences were felt, even less emphasis was placed on physical development, and health standards were poor indeed. In later Chinese history the value of training to bear arms was appreciated much more because of the changing nature of the type of combat in which the men engaged. In ancient *India,* the climate and religious philosophy forced a relative rejection of physical activity for all save the ever-present dancing girls of the ancient world. Further, those men in the military caste were trained physically to bear arms in defense of their society. Certain hygienic rules and ritualistic dances were common to the Hindus, but typically they were connected with religious ceremonies.

In early *Egypt,* physical education was not part of the typical educational system, although the average person did receive a greater or lesser amount of exercise depending upon his or her daily work activities. As the social life grew in complexity and a class structure developed, the upper class received a level of education that was not available to the great majority of people. Sports and dancing were popular with the nobility, the latter activity being included in religious life for common people as well. The Tigris-Euphrates civilization (*Babylon* and *Assyria*) did not seem to give physical education much status except for the perennial warrior class and for those other occupations that demanded varying levels of physical fitness for their adequate execution. The *Hebrews* promoted certain physical education activities and hygienic practices mainly because of the influence of their religious heritage and their desire to preserve their national unity, but it may not be assumed that they valued physical education highly for all. Later, under the influence of the Greeks and then the Romans, this attitude changed in some sections. However, sports were never popular among *all* Hebrews of the ancient world. In contrast, the *Persians* rivaled Greece in many of its methods of physical education. Physical fitness was very valuable to them because it helped to produce the stamina needed for great armies. They went to extremes in developing excellent hunters, horsemen, and warriors. Thus, it is obvious that their concept of physical education was very narrow because of this desire for military supremacy.

Physical education and athletic games were valued very highly in ancient *Greek* society. From 1100 to 700 B.C., the Homeric Age, athletic games held a prominent place. The aim of physical education was to produce a man of action, and great concern was shown for individual excellence. The well-rounded man–citizen–soldier was the ideal, a person who steadily increased in wisdom as well. The *Spartan* Greeks were almost completely concerned with the development of devoted citizens and outstanding soldiers or warriors. They placed great stress upon almost unbelievably difficult physical training and hardship as part of the training at arms; the end product was an almost invincible soldier in single combat. Athletics were not considered important unless they contributed directly to soldierly prowess. In *Athens,* however, where harmonious development of body and mind was of paramount concern, physical education was valued most highly in the development of the ideal individual. Although such overall development was available only to free men in a society where slaves were ordinarily kept because of military victories, there has probably never been another culture—if this city-state may be so designated—in which the development of the all-round citizen was more cherished. In later Athenian Greece gradually increasing emphasis was placed on intellectual excellence; the majority of youth lost interest in excellent physical development, and eventually extreme professionalism in athletics grew to such an extent that the former ideal was lost forever.

The *Romans* were much more utilitarian in their attitude toward physical training; they simply did not grasp the concept of the Greek ideal. They valued physical training for very basic reasons: it developed a man's knowledge in the skills of war, and it kept him healthy because of the strict regimen required. It helped to give a man strength and endurance and made him courageous in the process. Later in Roman history as their army became more specialized, the value of physical training for all became less apparent, although it was still practiced by most citizens to a degree for the maintenance of health and for recreational pursuits. Athletic festivals and games, often of a highly barbaric nature, were held for the entertainment of the masses and to gain political support for the various political office holders.

The *Visigoths* began their successful invasions to the south in 376 A.D., and the end of the Roman Empire has usually been designated as 476 A.D. The period following has been commonly, but now seemingly incorrectly thought of as the "Dark Ages," a time when most literature and learning came to a standstill and might have been completely lost save for the newly organized monasteries. "Ill blows the wind that profits nobody" is a proverb that applies to this era. The Visigoths did possess abundant energy and splendid bodies and are presumed to have helped the virility of the civilized world of the West at that time. The Moslem leader Tarik ended the Visigothic kingdom in 711 in the battle at Guadalete.

As the immoral society of the declining Romans became a mere memory, Christianity continued to spread because of the energy, enthusiasm, and high moral standards of its followers. The Church managed to survive the invasion of the barbarians and gradually became an important influence in the culture, and its continued growth seemed a certainty. Although the historic Jesus Christ in many ways was said to be anything but an ascetic, the early Christians envisioned the individual's moral regeneration as the highest goal. They became most concerned about their souls and the question of eternal happiness. Matters of the body were of this world, and consequently of Satan; affairs of the soul were of God. This way of life was given the name of asceticism, the main idea being to subdue the desires of the flesh, even by means of torture if necessary. The belief has prevailed that most churchmen were opposed to the idea of physical education or training, but recently this has been called "The Great Protestant Legend." On balance it seems more logical that these Christians would not be opposed to the idea of hard work and strenuous physical activity, but that they would indeed be violently opposed to all types of sports, games, and athletic festivals associated with earlier pagan religion that had led to so many harsh evils. And so for hundreds of years during this period known as the Early Middle Ages, physical education, as it is typically known today, found almost no place within the meager educational pattern that prevailed, a very sterile period indeed for those interested in the promulgation of physical education and sport of the finest type. Eventually even much of the physical labor in the fields and around the grounds of monasteries was transferred to nonclerics. Thus, even this basic physical fitness was lost to this group as more intellectual pursuits became the rule. As is so often the case, the pendulum had swung too far in the other direction.

Physical training was revived to a degree in the period known as the

Age of Chivalry. Feudal society was divided into three classes: (1) the masses, who had to work to support the other classes and to eke out a bare subsistence for themselves; (2) the clergy, who carried on the affairs of the Church; and (3) the nobles, who were responsible for the government of certain lands or territories under a king, and who performed military duties. During this time a physical and military education of the most strenuous type was necessary along with a required training in social conduct for the knight who was pledged to serve his feudal lord, the Church, and, presumably, all women as well as his own lady in particular. Such an ideal was undoubtedly better in theory than in practice, but it did serve to set standards higher than those which existed previously. The aim of physical education was certainly narrow according to today's ideal, and understandably health standards were usually very poor. The Greek ideal had been forgotten, and physical education once again served a most practical objective: to produce a well-trained individual in the art of hand-to-hand combat with all of the necessary physical attributes such as strength, endurance, agility, and coordination. With the subsequent invention of machinery of war, the enemy was not always met at close range. As a result, death in battle became to a larger extent accidental and was not necessarily the result of physical weakness and ineptitude in warfare techniques. Naturally, some divergence took place in the aims and methods of military training and allied physical training.

Just prior to the Renaissance a transitional period occurred accompanied by a decline of feudalism and a rise in nationalism. With more vigorous trade and community growth, a stronger middle class gradually arose, with a resultant demand for an improved educational system designed to prepare the young male for his lifetime occupation. Some informal physical exercise contributed to the social and recreational goals of the young townspeople. Such physical activity also enhanced military training, and it is interesting to note that games and informal sports were accompanying features of the frequent religious holidays.

The period that followed feudalism was known as the *Renaissance.* At this time it was natural that learned people should begin to look back to the periods in history that were characterized by even roughly similar societies. The Church was solidly entrenched, and there was much enthusiasm for scholarship in the fields of law, theology, and medicine. Understandably this scholasticism and emphasis on intellectual discipline found little if any room for physical education. Unorganized sports and games were the only activities of this nature in the cathedral schools and in the universities. In the late fourteenth and in the fifteenth century, however, a type of humanism developed which stressed the worth of the individual—and once again the physical side of man was considered. Most of the humanistic educators appreciated the earlier Greek ideal and emphasized the care and proper development of the body. Vittorino da Feltre set an example for others in his school at the court of the Prince of Mantua in northern Italy. One of his aims was to discipline the body so that hardship might be endured with the least possible hazard. His pupils were some day to bear arms and had to know the art of warfare. Individual and group sports and games were included because of the recreative nature of such activity. Vittorino believed that the ability of youth to learn in the classroom depended to a considerable extent upon the physical condition of the individual.

In what has been called the *Early Modern Period*, there followed a decline in liberal education as the schools lost their original aim and began the exclusive study of the languages of Greece and Rome while unfortunately neglecting the other aspects of these civilizations. The importance of physical training for youth again declined, as preparation for life work was crowded out by preparation for university education. Thus, when the spirit of Italian humanistic education reached into Europe, the Greek ideal of physical education was realized by only a relatively few individuals. Those involved with the Protestant Reformation did nothing to encourage physical education activities with the possible exception of Martin Luther himself, who evidently realized a need for the physical training of youth. Some educators rebelled against the narrow type of education which came into vogue, but they were the exception rather than the rule.

Rabelais satirized the education of the time in his depiction of the poor results of the typical Latin grammar school graduate. His Gargantua was a "dolt and blockhead," but subsequently became a worthwhile person when his education became more well rounded. Michel de Montaigne, the great French essayist of the sixteenth century, believed that the education of man should not be dichotomized into the typical mind-body approach. Other educators such as Locke, Mulcaster, and Comenius recognized the value of physical exercise and attainments. Some educational leaders in the seventeenth century stressed character development as the primary aim, but a number of them believed in the underlying need of health and physical fitness. John Locke, for example, even stressed the importance of recreation for youth. However, his ideas were far from being accepted as the ideal for all in a society characterized by a variety of social classes.

The *eighteenth century* in *Europe* was a period of change to what might be called more modern political, social, and educational ideals. In France Voltaire denounced both the Church and the State. Rousseau decried the state of society also, as well as the condition of education in this period. He appeared to desire equality for all (except his wife) and blamed the civilization of the time for the unhappiness in the world. He urged the adoption of a "back to nature" movement, because it seemed to him that everything had degenerated under the influence of man in so-called organized society. In his heralded educational treatise *Emile*, he described what he considered to be the ideal education for a boy. From the age of one to five, he stressed, the only concern should be for the growth and physical welfare of the young person. From five to twelve years of age, the idea of *natural* growth was to be continued as the sturdy, healthy youngster learned about the different aspects of his environment. Rousseau did consider the person to be an indivisible entity and was firmly convinced of the developmental growth of the entire organism. For him it was difficult to determine when an activity lost its physical value and began to possess so-called intellectual worth.

The opinions of both Rousseau and Voltaire, combined obviously with many other strong social forces, led to the ruination of the political and social structure of Europe, the reconstruction of which did not take place until the following century. For example, Johann Basedow started a naturalistic school in Dessau based on the fundamental ideas of Rousseau. This school, called the Philanthropinum, was the first in modern Europe to admit children from all social classes and to give physical education a place in the daily curriculum. A number of other prominent educators in the late eighteenth and early nineteenth century expressed what they felt to be the proper place of physical education in the curriculum, thereby helping to influence public opinion. Outstanding among these men were Guts Muths, Pestalozzi, and philosopher Immanuel Kant. Friedrich Froebel, who ranks along with Pestalozzi as a founder of modern pedagogy, offered the first planned program of education through play.

Emerging nationalism had a direct relationship to the development of physical education in modern Europe. Both the French and American revolutions sparked these feelings of strong loyalty to country in many parts of the world. Gradually education was recognized as a vital means of promoting the progress of developing nations. Education for citizenship stressed the obligation of youth to develop itself fully for the glory of the nation. Historians have pointed out that nationalistic education is probably a necessary step toward subsequent internationalism.

In *Germany* the *Turnvereine* (gymnastic societies) originated during the first decade of the nineteenth century. Friedrich L. Jahn, a staunch patriot of the time, is considered the father of this movement. He wished fervently that his people would become strong enough to throw off the yoke of the French conquerors. Jahn believed that exercise was a vital means to employ in the ideal plan of growth and development for the individual. He held also that there was a certain mental and moral training to be derived from experience at the *Turnplatz*. The War of Liberation for Prussia was waged successfully in 1813, and his work undoubtedly helped the cause. *Turnen* underwent periods of popularity and disfavor during the next forty years. Later the *Turnen* societies accepted the games and sports of the newer period cautiously.

Adolph Spiess did a great amount of work in planning and developing school gymnastics as he strove to have physical training included as an important part of the child's education. In 1849 he established normal classes in this type of gymnastics at Darmstadt. Since 1860 Germany has fully recognized the importance of school gymnastics, and this subject has continually grown in prominence for the pre-university years. The military motive was very influential in shaping the development of physical training in a number of other European countries, with certain individual variations. Scientific advances have gradually brought about the inauguration of new theories in keeping with the advancing times.

The isolated position of *Great Britain* in relation to the European continent made rigorous training for warfare and national defense somewhat less necessary and tended to foster the continuance of interest in outdoor sports. In feudal England archery was the most popular sport, and in the fifteenth century golf rivaled it until the king banned it by proclamation because of the disturbance it was creating. A bit later, however, it was accepted by nobles as well, and the ban was lifted. Field hockey, cricket, bowling, quoits, tennis, rugby, hammer throwing, and pole vaulting all had their origins in the British Isles. Many of the other traditional sports originated elsewhere but soon were adopted by the English people. In the early nineteenth century an urgent need was felt for some type of systematized physical training. Clias, Ehrenhoff, Georgii, and Maclaren were some of the men who introduced varied methods of physical training and culture to the British people. Any stress on systematized school gymnastics and the movement for improved health did not, however, seem to have discouraged sport participation in any way. Down through the years England has encouraged active participation by all schoolchildren and avoided the overtraining of the few.

The revival of the *Olympic Games* in 1896 was brought about largely through the efforts of Baron Pierre de Coubertin of France. Certainly much interest has been created with the successive holding of these Games every four years in countries all over the world. Although some are concerned about the media's preoccupation with team scores, it probably can be argued successfully that international goodwill has been fostered in this way. The cynic would counter by declaring that all of this "goodwill" resulted in two worldwide wars being fought since the advent of the modern Games, but assuredly it is worthwhile to promote athletic competition in the hope that such "friendly strife" might foster the development of peace and international goodwill. Throughout the twentieth century, therefore, sports and games for men, and then for women too, have become increasingly popular initially throughout Europe and then in many other parts of the world as well. At the same time European interest in varying types of gymnastics has not declined.

Finally in this substantive review of the values for which people strove in sport and physical activity, we will take a look at the role that they played in the educational pattern of the *United States*. We shall see how these activities have been incorporated into our system of education as certain individuals and groups felt that they had something valuable to offer.

Because the population of colonial United States was mostly rural, one could not expect organized gymnastics and sport to find a place in the daily lives of the settlers. Most of the colonies, with the possible exception of the Puritans, engaged in the games and contests of their mother lands to the extent that they had free time. Even as today, the significance of play and its possibilities in the educative process were not really comprehended; in fact, the entire educational system was opposed to the idea of what would be included in a fine program of physical education and sport today.

The national history of the United States ran quite parallel to the history of the academies. The aim of these schools was to prepare youth to meet life and its many problems. With such an emphasis, it is natural that the physical welfare of youth gradually was considered to be more important than it had been previously. Some of the early academies, such as Dummer, Andover, Exeter, and Leicester, were founded and incorporated before 1790. This movement reached its height around 1830, when there were said to be approximately 800 such schools throughout the country.

Many of the early American educators and statesmen supported the idea that both the body and the mind needed attention in our educational system. Included among this number were Benjamin Franklin, Noah Webster, Thomas Jefferson, Horace Mann, and Henry Barnard. Further support came from Captain Alden Partridge, one of the early superintendents of the United States Military Academy at West Point, who crusaded for the reform of institutions of higher education. He deplored the entire neglect of physical education.

In the early nineteenth century German gymnastics came to America through the influx of such men as Charles Beck, Charles Follen, and Francis Lieber. However, the majority of the people were not ready to recognize the values of these activities imported from foreign lands. The *Turnverein* movement before the Civil War was very important for the advancement of physical training. The Turners advocated that mental and physical education should proceed hand in hand in the public schools. As it developed, they were leaders in the physical education movement around 1850 in such cities as Boston, St. Louis, and Cincinnati.

Other leaders in this period were George Barker Winship and Dioclesian Lewis. Winship was an advocate of heavy gymnastics and did much to convey the mistaken idea that great strength should be the goal of all gymnastics, as well as the notion that strength and health were completely synonomous. Lewis, who began the first teacher training program in physical education in the country in 1861, was a crusader in every sense of the word; he had ambitions to improve the health of all Americans through his system of light calisthenics—an approach which he felt would develop and maintain flexibility, grace, and agility as well. His stirring addresses to many professional and lay groups did much to popularize this type of gymnastics, and to convey the idea that such exercise could serve a desirable role in the lives of those who were weaker and perhaps even sickly (as well as those who were naturally stronger).

After the Civil War the Turnvereins continued to stress the benefits of physical education within public education. Through their efforts it was possible to reach literally hundreds of thousands of people either directly or indirectly. The Turners have always opposed military training as a substitute for physical education. Further, the modern playground movement found the Turners among its strongest supporters. The Civil War had demonstrated clearly the need for a concerted effort in the areas of health, physical education, and physical recreation (not to mention competitive sports and games). The Morrill Act passed by Congress in 1862 helped create the land-grant colleges. At first the field of physical education was not aided significantly by this development because of the stress on military drill in these institutions. All in all, the best that can be said is that an extremely differentiated pattern of physical education was present in the post-Civil War era of the country.

The beginning of American sport as we now know it dates back to the days of this unfortunate but necessary internal conflict. Baseball and tennis were introduced in that order during this period and soon became very popular. Golf, bowling, swimming, basketball, and a multitude of other so-called minor sports made their appearance in the latter half of the nineteenth century. American football also started its rise to popularity at this time. The Amateur Athletic Union was organized in 1888 and, despite the controversy which has surrounded this organization almost constantly ever since, it has given invaluable service to the promotion of that changing and often evanescent phenomenon that this group has designated as "legitimate amateur sport."

The Young Men's Christian Association traces its origins back to 1844 in London, England, when George Williams organized the first religious group; this organization has always stressed as one of its basic principles that physical welfare and recreation were helpful to the moral well-being of the individual. Some of the early outstanding physical education leaders in the YMCA in the United States were Robert J. Roberts, Luther Halsey Gulick, and James Huff McCurdy.

It was toward the middle of the nineteenth century that the colleges and universities began to think seriously about the health of their students. The University of Virginia had the first real gymnasium, and Amherst College followed in 1860 with a two-story structure devoted to physical education. President Stearns urged the governing body to begin a department of physical culture in which the primary aim was to keep the student in good physical condition. Dr. Edward Hitchcock headed this department for an unprecedented period of fifty years until his death in 1911. Yale and Harvard erected gymnasiums for similar purposes, but their programs were not supported adequately until somewhat later. These early facilities were soon followed elsewhere by the development of a variety of "exercise buildings" built along similar lines.

Harvard was fortunate in the appointment of Dr. Dudley Allen Sargent to head its famous Hemenway Gymnasium. This dedicated physical educator and physician led the university to a preeminent position in the field, and his program became a model for many other colleges and universities. He stressed physical education for the individual, and his goal was the attainment of a perfect structure—harmony in a well-balanced development of mind and body. From the outset, college faculties had taken the position that games and sports were not necessarily a part of the basic educational program. Interest in them was so intense, however, that the wishes of the students, while being denied, could not be thwarted. Young college men evidently strongly desired to demonstrate their abilities in the various sports against presumed rivals from other institutions. Thus, from 1850 to 1880 the rise of interest in intercollegiate sports was phenomenal. Rowing, baseball, track and field, football, and later basketball were the major sports. Unfortunately, college representatives soon found that these athletic sports needed control as evils began to creep in and partially destroy the values originally intended as goals.

The years from 1880 to 1890 undoubtedly form one of the most important decades in the history of physical education in the United States. The colleges and universities, the YMCA's, the Turners, and the proponents of the various foreign systems of gymnastics all made contributions during this brief period. The Association for the Advancement of Physical Education was founded in 1885, with the word "American" being added the next year. This professional organization was the first of its kind in the field and undoubtedly stimulated teacher education markedly. An important early project was the plan for developing a series of experiences in physical activity—physical *education*—the objectives of which would be in accord with the existing pattern of general education. The struggle to bring about widespread adoption of such a program followed. Early legislation implementing physical education was enacted in five states before the turn of the twentieth century.

The late nineteenth century saw the development also of the first efforts in organized recreation and camping for children living in underdeveloped areas in large cites. The first playground was begun in Boston in 1885. New York and Chicago followed suit shortly thereafter, no doubt to a certain degree as a result of the ill effects of the Industrial Revolution. This was actually the meager beginning of the present tremendous recreation movement in our country. Private and organization camping started before the turn of the century as well; it has flourished similarly since that time and has been an important supplement to the entire movement.

In the early twentieth century Americans began to do some earnest thinking about their educational aims or values. The earliest aim in United States educational history had been religious in nature, an approach which was eventually supplanted by a political aim consistent with emerging nationalism. But then an overwhelming utilitarian, economic aim seemed to overshadow the political aim. The tremendous increase in high school enrollment forced a reconsideration of the aims of education at *all* levels of the system. It was at this time also that the beginnings of a scientific approach to educational problems forced educators to take stock of the development based on a rationale other than the sheer increase in numbers of students.

There then followed an effort on the part of many people to consider our aims and objectives from a sociological orientation. For the first time, education was conceived in terms of *complete* living as a citizen of an evolving democracy. The influence of John Dewey and others encouraged the viewing of the curriculum as child-centered rather than subject-centered—a rather startling attempt to alter the long-standing basic orientation. The Progressive Education movement placed great emphasis on individualistic aims. This was subsequently countered by a demand for a theory stressing a social welfare orientation rather than one so heavily pointed to individual development.

The relationship between health and physical education and the entire system of education strengthened remarkably during the first quarter of the twentieth century. Health education in all its aspects was viewed seriously, especially after the evidence of the draft statistics of World War I. Many states passed legislation requiring varying amount of time in the curriculum devoted to the teaching of physical education. National interest in sports and games grew at a phenomenal rate in an era when economic prosperity prevailed. The basis for school and community recreation was laid well.

Simultaneously with physical education's achievement of a type of maturity through such legislation, the struggle between the inflexibility of the various foreign systems of gymnastics and the individualistic freedom of the so-called "natural movement" was being waged with increasing vigor. Actually the rising interest in sports and games soon made the conflict unequal, especially when the concept of "athletics for all" really began to take hold in the second and third decades of the century. The natural movement was undoubtedly strengthened further by much of the evidence gathered by many natural and social scientists. A certain amount of the spirit of Dewey's philosophy took hold within the educational environment, and this new philosophy and accompanying method and techniques did appear to be more effective in the light of the changing ideals of an evolving democracy. However, the influence of idealism certainly remained strong also, with its emphasis on the development of individual personality and the possible inculcation of moral and spiritual values through the transfer of training theory applied to sports and games.

School health education was developed greatly during the period also. The scope of school hygiene increased, and a required annual medical examination for all became more important. Leaders were urged to conceive of school health education as including three major divisions: health services, health instruction, and healthful school living. The value of expansion in this area was gradually accepted by educator and citizen alike. During this period there became apparent a tendency to separate health education from physical education. For example, many physical educators began to show concern for a broadening of the field's aims and objectives, the evidence of which could be seen by the increasing amount of time spent by many on coaching duties. Conversely, the expansion of health instruction through the medium of many private and public agencies tended to draw those more directly interested in the goals of health and safety education away from physical education and athletics.

Progress in the recreation field was significant as well. The values inherent in well-conducted playground activities for children and youth were increasingly recognized; the Playground Association of America was organized in 1906. At this time there was still an extremely close relationship between physical education and recreation, a link that remained strong because of the keen interest in the aims of recreation by a number of outstanding physical educators. Many municipal recreation centers were constructed, and it was at this time that the use of some—relatively few, actually—of the schools for "after-hour" recreation began. People began to recognize that recreational activities served an important purpose in a society undergoing basic changes. Some recreation programs developed under local boards of education; others were formed by the joint sponsorship of school boards and municipal governments; and a large number of communities placed recreation under the direct control of the municipal government and either rented school facilities when possible, or gradually developed recreational facilities of their own.

It is extremely difficult, if not impossible to assess properly the historical period from 1930 to the present day. The fact that it is so close to us makes the achievement of historical perspective a dubious possibility. The Depression of the 1930s, World War II and its aftermath, the Korean and Vietnam conflicts, and the continuing Cold War with the many frictions among countries have been very strong social forces directly influencing physical education, sport, health education, and recreation in any form and in any country. To what extent these various fields and their professional concerns have in turn influenced the many cultures, societies, and social systems remains yet to be determined.

It would be simplistic to say that physical educators want more and better physical education and intramural athletic programs, that athletics-oriented coaches and administrators want more and better athletic competition, that health and safety educators want more and better health and safety education, and that recreation personnel want more and better recreation—and yet, this is probably what has occurred to a large degree. The American Association (now the American *Alliance*) for Health, Physical Education, and Recreation has accomplished a great deal in a strong, united effort to coordinate the various allied movements largely within the framework of public and private education. It seems destined to succeed with those functions which properly belong within the educational sphere. Of course, there are many other health agencies and groups, recreation associations and enterprises, physical education associations and "splinter" disciplinary groups, and athletics association and organizations moving in a variety of directions. Each of these is presumably functioning with the system of values and norms prevailing in the country (or culture, etc.) and the resultant pluralistic educational philosophies extant within such a milieu.

We have seen teacher education and professional preparation for recreational leadership strengthened through accreditation and self-evaluation. The dance movement has been a significant development within the educational field, and those concerned are still determining the place for this movement within the educational structure. A great deal of progress has been made in physical education and sport research since 1960. Certainly very few people still regard physical education and military training as being synonymous. The national interest in all kinds of sport has continued to grow unabated. In a world with an uncertain future, there has been an ever-present demand for an improved level of physical fitness for citizens of all ages. Despite financial stringencies and overemphases in certain areas, there is evidence for reasonable optimism. There is obviously a value struggle going on that may well increase unless a continuing search for a consensus is carried out. Such understanding will come only through greater understanding and wisdom, and it is in this regard that science and philosophy can make their contributions. The members of the allied professions need to be fully informed as they strive for a voice in shaping the future development. It is essential that there be careful study and analysis of the questions of values as they relate to sport, dance, play, and exercise—and, of course, the allied fields of health and safety education *and* recreation.

The Influence of Politics

The second social force or influence to be considered is that of politics. The word "politics" is used here in its best sense—as the theory and practice of managing public affairs. When we speak of a politician, therefore, the intent is to describe a person interested in politics as a most important profession, and not one who through maneuverings might attempt to amass personal power.

From the standpoint of sociology, government might be defined as a form of social organization. This organization becomes necessary as a means of social control to regulate the actions of persons and groups. Throughout history every known society seems to have developed some measure of formal control. The group as a whole has been termed the state, and the members are known as citizens. Thus, the state is made up of territory, people, and government. If the people eventually unify through common cultural tradition, they are classified as a nation. They develop a pattern of living called social structure. Political organization is but one phase of this structure, but it exercises a powerful influence upon the other phases. A governmental form is usually a conservative force that is slow to change; inextricably related to the rest of the social structure, the political regime must adapt to changing social organization or anarchy results. The three major types of political state in the history of the various world civilizations have been (1) the monarchy, (2) the aristocratic oligarchy, and (3) the democracy or republic.

Patterns of Education. Aristotle's classification of the three types of political states, mentioned above, holds today largely as it did then. The kind and amount of education offered to young people has indeed varied in these societies depending upon the type of political state extant. In a society where one person rules, for example, it would seem logical to assume that he or she should have the best education so as to rule wisely. The difficulty with this situation is that there is no guarantee that a hereditary ruler is the best-equipped person in the entire society to fulfill this purpose.

If the few rule, then *they* usually receive the best education. These people normally rise to power by demonstrating various types of ability. That they are clever cannot be doubted; it is doubtful, however, that the wisest and most ethical people become rulers in an oligarchy.

If the many rule through the power of their votes in democratic elections, it is imperative that the general level of education be raised to the highest degree possible. It becomes part of the ethic of the society to consider the worth of human personality and to give each individual the opportunity to develop his or her potential to the fullest. In return, in order to ensure smooth functioning of the democracy, the individual is asked to subjugate extraordinary personal interests to the common good. Harmony between these two antithetical ideals would seem to require a very delicate balance in the years ahead.

All of this raises a very interesting question: Which agency—the school, the family, or the church—should have control? In a totalitarian state there is but one philosophy of education permitted, whereas other types of government allow pluralistic philosophies of education to flourish. Under the latter arrangement the state could conceivably exercise no control of education whatsoever, or it could take a greater or lesser interest in the education of its citizens. When the state does take an interest, the question arises as to whether the state (through its agency the school), or the family, or the church shall exert the greatest amount of influence on the child. When the leaders of the church feel very strongly that the central purpose of education is religious, they may decide to take over the education of the child themselves. In a society where there are many different religious affiliations, it is quite possible that the best arrangement is for the church and the state to remain separate.

Physical Education and Sport. There appear to be a number of different inferences here that should be considered in regard to the field of physical education and sport. A progressivistic approach to education, and to physical education and sport in particular, would not be permitted in a totalitarian or fascist state. A progressivistic position, one that envisions physical education and sport as an integral experience in the curriculum, would be realizable only in an evolving democracy. The many objectives for physical education emphasizing the concept of "total fitness" can be projected only where students' progress is evaluated in terms of the starting point of the individual.

Where physical education is regarded as education "of the physical" —a matter merely of muscle strengthening and development of cardiovascular efficiency—it seems possible for such attitudes to prevail no matter which kind of political regime is involved. With this approach to education, physical education yields to intellectual education, and sports —although regarded as extracurricular—can be a school for the development of loyalty and courage. Such a philosophic stance may be designated as essentialistic.

Another typically essentialistic position is not as straightforward. Physical development can take place in any kind of state, although it must be admitted that physical fitness appears to suffer in a *laissez-faire* democracy except when war becomes imminent. The development of all other aspects of human nature presupposes a society in which individuals and their needs and desires rank high. The idealistic concept of the whole personality is negated by the totalitarian state's emphasis on intensive participation in sport competition or the focus of physical education on the development of strength, endurance, and other physical attributes for purely militaristic purposes.

A fourth position encountered quite often today is existentialistic in nature and would typically show little relationship to the question of an ideal political state. Individuals espousing such a stance would presumably revolt against any totalitarian state, and yet such a person might feel like a "homeless creature" in the era of "organization man" living in a democratic, capitalistic society. People imbued with such an orientation would undoubtedly decry the failure of physical education programs to help a child feel at home within the school physical education curriculum. Most certainly the exploitation of athletes in most interschool programs negates an educational ideal that stresses self-motivation and a "self-determining posture."

To summarize, the basic question remains: Which agency—the school, the family, or the church—should exert the greatest amount of influence on the child's education? As explained above, a somewhat different pattern of physical education and sport is possible and probable under each type of political state.

The Influence of Nationalism

The third social force or influence to be discussed is that of nationalism. The word "nation" is usually used synonymously with country or state—a type of governmental rule under which a population of human beings is more or less united. We tend to say that such-and-such a group of people have a certain "nationality." The word "people" often has a broader connotation (and often somewhat ambiguous too), since it may be used to refer to an ethnological unit within several nations. The term "nationalism" is employed often to describe an attitude or feeling that someone might have as a citizen of a nation. The person might hold a strong or weak feeling of nationalism, or varying degrees along a scale. It may be defined as patriotism or love of country, or even as a political philosophy in which the nation's good is paramount. The reader should keep in mind that the word "chauvinism" implies blind or overzealous nationalism, and the two terms should therefore not be used synonymously.

Some type of nationalism has been present throughout the recorded history of man, from the simplest organization of the early tribe to the highly complex nation-states of the modern world. Some scholars believe that nationalism, as they define it, began relatively recently, because until the so-called modern period nations were not unified enough for such a feeling to be engendered. However, if the term is defined somewhat more loosely, the desire of the ancient Greeks and Romans to perpetuate their culture by the promotion of citizenship ideals can be identified as being nationalistic. And presumably the same statement could be made about the ancient Hebrews and a number of other cultures down through the ages.

An examination of history reveals that the Roman Catholic Church developed many far-reaching loyalties over a period of many centuries. During the period of medieval history, and then on into the Renaissance, a number of rulers and their related nobles struggled with the established Church for control. It was at this time that people began to think of themselves as French, or German, or English. Eventually it became possible for representatives of the developing middle class to serve on the many parliamentary bodies as their structures changed. And so it is quite understandable that in time a new and different type of patriotism would be engendered, and that such attitudes might develop into what is now called nationalism.

Nationalism evidently got quite an early start in England, and subsequently such feelings about one's country were transferred to the new land of America by the early settlers. In France, feelings of nationalism were evident even before the Revolution. After Napoleon crushed the Germans at the Battle of Jena, many Germans naturally regretted the plight of their homeland and attempted various means of reestablishing a large degree of self-determination for their country. Linking nationalism with a concept of power has typically fostered chauvinism characterized by hatred of other nations, and this has been most unfortunate. Some have intimated that nationalism is a necessary step en route to enlightened internationalism, but too often the passage through these presumed stages of development has occasioned untold hardship and disaster to evolving civilization.

Even the Industrial Revolution through its accompanying doctrine of mercantilism encouraged the idea of nationalism. With the subsequent rejection of free trade among countries, a force was unleashed that actually retarded progress of all peoples everywhere. Then and even today people are exhorted to follow a pattern of blind allegiance to their country, whose leaders in most cases equate greatness with military might. As a result the whole idea of individual freedom in a democratic social environment is typically a dream for the future, one that may actually be utopian in the sense that we are unaware of the next step to take along the way to such a halcyon state of affairs. We are finding instead patterns of ruthless nationalism often raised to the status of a religion, and these are presently more than counterbalancing the hopes of many in the world for a broader concept of internationalism that could conceivably save us from the devastation of nuclear war between the so-called superpowers. This is not to say that nationalism, and nationalistic education, has no place in the political spectrum, but rather, that it should be a "healthy nationalism" in which every effort is made to preserve a possibly higher goal of individual freedom within an evolving democratic social environment.

Patterns of Education. Reasoned and controlled nationalism has allowed the educational aims of the Church to coexist with its own, probably because these goals were seemingly taking place in somewhat different spheres. But when nationalism grows disproportionately, it sweeps aside everything in its path. During wartime in the United States, for example, we find a great many incidents of unreasoning nationalism that rock the very foundation of our democratic republic. Nationalism flourishes in the totalitarian state, but a strong nationalism is a very difficult state for strong-minded leaders to bring about in a pluralistic society. Citizens living in a democratic society would seek in a variety of ways to reject a nationalistic education that had been dictated by a minority. Conversely, if it were possible for the "right kind" of nationalism in education to emanate from the goals of a truly free people, then the common good of all mankind in a democratic republic would be best served. The ideal at present would seem to be a democracy that is far enough advanced to have the necessary stability to consider sharing its culture fully and freely with other interested countries. Such an enlightened society—one that is well on its way toward a mature concept of internationalism—could well point the way to the idea of "one world," which is perhaps the only method of ensuring permanent peace and possible subsequent prosperity.

Physical Education and Sport. What are the implications of nationalism for the field of physical education and sport? There are a number of inferences that can be considered. If a strong state is desired, for example, the need for a strong, healthy people is paramount. This has been evident throughout history. The United States went through various stages of nationalism in the early nineteenth century and then developed a firmer nationalism after the Civil War with some indication that internationalism was a possibility as more stability was achieved. As the ties with other cultures began to lessen, people began to inquire about the development of an *American* system of physical education. However, it cannot be said that physical education had been cultivated for purely nationalistic purposes at that time. As a matter of fact, except during war periods when all-out mobilization of manpower was necessary, the United States has witnessed the development of a physical education program based largely upon sport skills as well as an informal program characterized by elective and voluntary physical recreational activities.

A progressivistic program of physical education and sport can flourish only in a democratic society, and it is almost impossible to promote nationalism in health and physical education when it must emanate from the goals of a free people. With fifty different autonomous state programs of physical education, it is not possible to require a certain standard of physical fitness. To enforce such a dictum during peacetime would threaten the very foundations of the republic.

Conversely, it is quite possible for an essentialistic type of physical education and sport to function under various philosophies of state with differing gradations of nationalism. If the people were to decide that young people must be physically fit, such a change could be effected. Similarly, if a nationalistic leader or oligarchy decided to improve physical fitness in youth of either or both sexes, it would be relatively simple to effect such an improvement.

Keeping in mind that even the most advanced states possessing a high degree of "enlightened internationalism" still demonstrate elements of nationalistic behavior, it is evident that professional physical educators will find a continuing demand for a reasonable level of physical fitness for youth within the school system. We can only hope, however, that our profession will never be warped beyond recognition by overly aggressive nationalists removing the play and recreative elements from a well-rounded program of physical education and sport.

The Influence of Economics

The fourth social force to be treated in this chapter is economics. Broadly interpreted, economics is a field concerned with what we produce and what formal and informal arrangements are made concerning the usage of the products. Economists inquire about the consumption of goods that are produced, and they want to know who takes part in the actual process of production. They ask where the power lies, whether the goods are used fully, and to what ends a society's resources are brought to bear.

For thousands of years people lived in small, relatively isolated groups, and their survival depended on their own subsistence economies. Early civilizations had to learn how to create a surplus before any class within a given society could have leisure for formal education or anything else that might be related to the "good life." Athens, for example, did not have a golden age until it became a relatively large commercial and cosmopolitan center. During the Early Middle Ages the economy again became agrarian in nature. Later, with the surge in trade and industry, a group of middle-class merchants developed.

The long-established social order was greatly disturbed later by the advent of the machine age and the factory. Men left their homes and their private enterprises, and then in the course of the twentieth century women followed them. Even the farmer became an entrepreneur and, from simple bargaining at the outset, the complex structure known as the "market" developed. With the progress of the machine age, the division of labor was tremendous, and families were often no longer self-sufficient. Industrial organizations mushroomed, and the articulations among these various groups were often disorganized. New inventions and products became part of the evolving culture and in turn created new demands. As a result of all this, people seem now to be seeking stability, or at least a reasonable semblance of order. Such stability is not yet in sight.

Paradoxically, change has become the only relatively certain factor in life. Such greater or lesser social forces as automation, small wars and possible large wars, space travel, the energy crisis, the ecological crisis, the exploding body of knowledge in all subjects, to name only a few, are continually disturbing the economic organization within, between, and among societies. Other influencing factors within the field of economics itself have been organization in the production of goods, mass production, organized research, and the general organization of business, labor, and consumers.

Patterns of Education. The history of education can be directly related to a society's economic status. Although the Romans amassed great wealth and developed an extensive educational system, their education remained basically of instrumental, rather than intrinsic, value to that culture. When the empire declined politically and economically, educational decay set in as well. Then it became necessary for the Roman emperors to subsidize education from the central treasury.

During the Early Middle Ages, education suffered with the return of an agrarian economy. Later, with the surge in trade and industry, vocational education was provided for the sons of middle-class merchants. The gradual intellectual awakening and then the rise of a spirit of scientific inquiry during the Renaissance, coupled with more profitable commerce and industry, revived education still further for at least a small portion of the population.

The marked social and economic changes of the Industrial Revolution were very great indeed. Gradually the masses, whose level of income had risen considerably, clamored for more educational opportunities for their children. Their efforts were supported by educational theorists, although class-structured education remained a problem and is still evident in many quarters even today. A boy or girl can rise above the economic and social level of his or her family, but it is still quite difficult, especially for most minority groups. The United States has now reached a stage where approximately 60 percent of its young people go on to some form of higher education, but there are still many obstacles to be overcome. For the many to receive educational opportunities a country must have a surplus economy. Also, people tend to lose faith in education when the economy turns downward and good jobs are not readily available for graduates of the various programs. They seem to forget or be unconcerned about the value of a broad general education and its relationship to quality of life generally. In summary, the evidence indicates that educational aims will tend to vary depending upon how people make their money and create surplus or shortage economies.

Advancing civilization has brought many advantages, but accompanying industrialization and technology have created many problems as well. One of these has to do with specialization in function: some people manage and others labor, and typically this has resulted in an uneven distribution of wealth in capitalistic societies. Of course, there has always been some specialization of function in various cultures, and the leaders have invariably seemed to end up with the lion's share of the good things of life. The labor movement (and increasing socialistic tendencies within the several types of political states) is striving mightily to reverse this result to what is considered a reasonable degree. It is not difficult to understand why the social welfare state concept has been popular with the middle and lower classes. Although this is a great oversimplification of what is taking place, the trend is definitely there. However, the seemingly inevitable existence of classes has had a definite effect on the educational structure. People with more money have been able to afford longer periods and different types of education for their children.

Essentialistic education has tended to preserve the culture of the past—the cultural heritage—and its advocates would not be striving for the same sort of change, and certainly not at the same rate as the progressivists. If it is inevitable that there will always be sharply divided classes of society, and that those who work with their hands will be considered inferior (really a most unfortunate connotation), the only hope for the masses is probably in increased educational advantages made possible through continued technological advancement and automation. However, we must somehow help *all* people to understand fully the advantages that can accrue to them and their children if they obtain a sound general education prior to subsequent professional or technical specialization—no mean task to accomplish.

Physical Education and Sport. What are the implications of this fourth social force of economics for physical education and sport? Unfortunately, professionals in our field rarely give much consideration to the influence of economics until they begin to feel the pinch of economy moves. Then they find that some segments of the society consider their subject matter area to be less important than others and that these groups decide that physical education, if not varsity athletics, for example, should be eliminated or at least sharply curtailed. Such a move often comes as a distinct shock; it is frequently rationalized by our claim that some of these people are simply using athletics as a lever to pry more money from a pleasure-seeking public who would not wish to see the various entertainment spectacles discontinued.

Physical education, especially as it connotes education of the physical, has a good chance for recognition and improvement under either an agrarian or an industrial economic system. In largely agrarian societies physical fitness normally results automatically through hard work. An industrial society, on the other hand, must prescribe some programs to ensure a minimum level of physical fitness for all, either through manual labor or some other type of recommended physical activity. However, the more democratic types of political states find it difficult to actually *require* such a vigorous program. If so-called post-industrial society has indeed arrived—one in which a percentage of the population is paid not to work or is guaranteed a minimum wage if no work is available—it may be even more difficult to demand that people of all ages maintain a level of physical fitness.

If a sufficiently high level of capitalistic democracy is retained, and the distribution of wealth continues on a markedly uneven basis, the more prosperous groups may be motivated to achieve their physical fitness through a variety of sometimes costly means. In the welfare state, where a person would enjoy a relatively longer period of educational opportunity and improved health benefits that could well result in improved longevity, society will simply have to decide to what extent it must legislate a minimum level of physical fitness for all. The place of physical education and sport will depend upon the values and norms held by the particular society in question.

The Influence of Religion

The fifth social force to be presented is that of religion. Religion may be defined broadly as "the pursuit of whatever a man considers to be most worthy or demanding of his devotion" (Williams, 1952, p. 350). However, the more usual definition of religion explains it as a belief in a Supreme Creator who has imparted a spiritual nature and a soul to us, and who may possibly guard or guide our destiny. Because there are so many types of religion in the world, and these are in various stages of development, it is almost impossible to present a definition that would be meaningful and acceptable to all.

This century has seen the advent of one devastating war after another, as people's ability to destroy each other increases. Our world leaders are on opposite sides of a fence making threatening gestures, often while pointing ominously to their enormous stockpiles of armaments. It is obvious that our ability to live together in harmony must be fostered at every opportunity through increased educational opportunities and research designed to help us learn more about ways of improving human relations at all levels. Actually the very foundation of a world order is predicated by people's beliefs and understandings about the universe which they inhabit. Even though many may not know it, they may all have a theology which they have difficulty in explaining. This important attribute, however, is an important influence in the determination of the type of social order that each attempts to create.

In all probability the nature of the universe has not changed at any time in the conceivable past and will not change in the predictable future. But people's attitude toward the world in which they live has changed, albeit gradually, a number of times. Theology usually forges somewhat ahead of the political institutions, however, and we may theorize that there is a definite relationship between these two sets of phenomena. Originally, the primitives were filled with fear and apprehension about the world. They could not understand adverse natural phenomena and attributed their misfortunes to devils and evil spirits. Somewhat later, people looked upon God as a type of all-powerful king, potentially benevolent, but certainly a power to be feared. Approximately 3,000 years ago the concept of "God, The Heavenly Father looking after his children" began to develop. We were to obey his laws, or else we would be punished. Certain orthodox religions today hold this position to some extent.

Now we find a fourth position emerging clearly (Zeigler, 1965, p. 24, based on Champion and Short, 1951). People look at reality (which they may call God) and conceive that some sort of partnership is in process. Some consider God to be a friendly partner, if we proceed according to His physical laws. As a result of this belief, many churchmen, and scientists too, are expressing a relatively new theological approach, offering us the concept of a "democratic, cooperative God" as a foundation for a new and improved world order. Religious liberals are finding considerable difficulty reaching common agreement on this fourth position. While recognizing—in the Western world—their debt to Christianity and Judaism, they appear to be uniting on a "free-mind principle" instead of any common creed. The ideal of the liberal is therefore a free spirit who gives allegiance to the truth as he or she sees it. The individual is anxious further to join with all liberals in a very loosely knit consortium, no matter to which of the world's dozen or so great religions they nominally belong.

Certain others have taken a possible fifth position, an existential approach, which has emerged as a significant force during the past hundred years. Kierkegaard, prior to 1850, had become concerned about the number of influences within society that were taking away one's individuality. Since that time many others have felt a similar concern. Originally, existentialism started as a revolt against Hegel's idealism, which was a philosophy affirming that ethical and spiritual realities were accessible to one through reason. Kierkegaard decided that religion would be next to useless if one could simply reason one's way back to God. Then along came Nietzsche who wished to discard Christianity since science had presumably shown that the transcendent ideals of the Church were nonsense. A person's task was, therefore, to create his or her own ideals and values. After all, one was only responsible to oneself. Twentieth-century existentialists, such as Sartre, are furthering such individuality, and their efforts are meeting with considerable acceptance both abroad and in North America.

Patterns of Education. In this discussion about religion, there has been no conscious effort to indoctrinate in any way. The premise is that each and every educator should work this religious problem out for himself or herself, and that the solution must of necessity have an influence on the person's development as an individual and as an educator.

The Christian contribution to the history of the world, and especially to education, has been enormous. For the first time, at least in the Western world, the idea of a universal God and of brotherhood took hold. In addition, the Christian emphasis on the afterlife entailed a strict moral preparation. Actually, the basis for universal education was laid with the promulgation of Christian principles emphasizing the worth of the individual.

The early Church was concerned with moral reformation. The previous, strongly pagan centuries of the Roman Empire had introduced vices that were difficult to obliterate. The Christians set up many types of schools to accomplish this purpose, and for a long period the main concerns of monastic life and education were asceticism, chastity, poverty, and obedience. It wasn't until later that the monastic school became interested in the expansion of knowledge and became more tolerant of inquiry. The theological philosophy known as Scholasticism aimed (1) to develop faith and (2) to discover truth through the method of logical analysis. Thomas Aquinas (1225?–1274), like Aristotle, shared the spirit of the realist. After serious consideration, he stated his belief in the reality of matter as the creation of God. He saw God as the first cause—an Absolute with eternal and infinite qualities.

The Protestant Reformation influenced education greatly, while lessening to a considerable degree the all-powerful position of the Catholic Church. The authority of the Bible was substituted for that of the Church, and individual judgment was to be used in the interpretation of the Scriptures and Christian duty. This outlook required the education of the many for the purposes of reading and interpreting God's word. Thus the groundwork was laid for democratic universal education in place of the education of the few for leadership.

In the mid-nineteenth century in the United States, as the educational ladder extended upward, religious education was removed from school curriculums because of many conflicts. Catholics felt so strongly about the need for religious instruction for their children that they began their own system of education. Protestants went along with the secularization of the schools, however, a great boon for the developing country but perhaps not for Protestantism in the long run. The home has done reasonably well in the inculcation of morals, but with rising materialism and the seeming recent decline of the family as an institution, certain problems have arisen. Discussion often arises concerning (1) which agency shall educate the individual—the home, the church, the state, or some private agency; and (2) whether or not any agency is capable of performing the task alone. In a democracy each agency would appear to have a specific function to perform in completing the entire task.

Physical Education and Sport. Relatively few significant studies have been conducted within our field relative to the historical influence of religion on physical education and sport, although there is some evidence of this situation changing recently. Historians themselves have occasionally provided insight into this question, and with this help we can turn to a number of fine sources still available. It is true that in the early cultures the so-called physical and mental education of the people could not be viewed separately. Many ancient rituals and ceremonies included various types of dance and physical exercise that may well have contributed to physical endurance and skill. The development of these attributes may have been incidental, or it may have been by actual design on the part of the priests and elders.

Many early religions placed great stress on a life of quiet contemplation, and this philosophy may well have contributed to the disesteem of certain bodily activities. Continuing emphasis on intellectual attainment for certain classes in various societies must have strengthened this attitude. Yet the harmonious ideal of the Athenians had esthetic and religious connotations that cannot be denied, and physical education and athletics ranked high in this scheme. The same cannot be said for the practical-minded Romans, however, where the "sound mind in a sound body" concept meant that the body was well trained for warlike pursuits and similar activities.

Many have argued that the Christian Church was responsible historically for the low status of physical education and athletics in the Western world, but lately some evidence has been accumulating to the contrary. It is seemingly true that Christian idealism furthered the dualism of mind and body and introduced the concept of "spirit" as well, and the effects of both concepts have been detrimental to physical activity ever since. Furthermore, the doctrine of original sin, with the possibility of ultimate salvation if asceticism were practiced, tended to negate the fostering of the Greek ideal for well over a thousand years. However, it now seems probable that the Church was truly harsh only against professional sport and the barbarity of the arena, and not to amateur sport and physical training per se. Thus it seems that the earlier blame placed upon the Church should be tempered, and that later on in the Middle Ages the problem was more a lack of leadership in this regard.

The fact still remains, however, that physical education and "the physical" did fall into disrepute until certain humanistic educators revived the Greek ideal during the Renaissance. Once again, though, this improvement was not general and in most cases was short-lived. Insofar as the churches are concerned, however, the situation has been gradually improving in the past hundred years. It could be argued that spreading materialism has brought about a secularization of life and has weakened the influence of the earlier sterner approaches to living, and that church leaders are acceding to the popularity of physical recreation in order to maintain a reasonable level of congregational attendance with accompanying contributions. However, it seems reasonable to hypothesize further that Protestants and Catholics are becoming increasingly aware of the role that physical recreation can play in the promulgation of the Christian idealistic way of life. An example of this belief that organized Christianity has taken the role of sport much more seriously in recent years has been the establishment and rapid development of the Fellowship of Christian Athletes, a quite fundamentalist organization whose purpose is to relate athletes directly to the help that can be obtained from a strong and vital Christian commitment.

Everything considered, it seems reasonable to say that Christianity had undoubtedly hampered the fullest development of sport, physical education, and physical recreation in the past, but it now appears that the situation is changing generally, and that many religious leaders (in Judaism as well) are revamping their earlier positions as they belatedly realize the potential of these activities as spiritual forces in our lives.

The Influence of Ecology

The sixth and last of what are claimed to be the major or pivotal social forces is ecology. Ecology is usually defined as the field of study that treats the relationships and interactions of human beings and other living organisms with each other and with their natural environment. As a matter of fact, the influence of ecology has been felt significantly only for the past five or ten years in North America.

There are now approximately 4 billion people on earth. At the beginning of the Christian era that figure was only 250 million. By the time America was settled by Europeans, the figure had been doubled to about 500 million. And now, in just the past fifty years, the total number has jumped from 2 to 4 billion! What makes this sharp increase so potentially dangerous is that it is in the underdeveloped countries that the rate of increase is so much higher than the average. It will presumably not be possible for such nations to move ahead to full industrialization because of the inevitable drain on their resources caused by such rapid growth.

In another realm, that of poor land and animal husbandry, our careless and ignorant abuse of the planet probably goes as far back as 8,000 years ago when we first began to farm the land. There are today innumerable archeological sites that were once thriving civilizations. For a variety of reasons, including poor use of land, most of these locations are now dusty, desolate ruins. An example of such an area is North Africa, which was once exploited extensively by the Romans. Here, valuable topsoil was eroded by poor farming techniques, incorrect grazing of livestock, and flagrant abuse of timberland. One can go back to ancient Greece to find another example of once fertile land with an abundant supply of water and forested hills; now much of the area seems blighted, with rocky hills and barren lowlands denuded of topsoil, and wildlife is almost extinct as well.

Much the same story can be related about Turkey. Early port cities, such as Ephesus and Tarsus, offer no evidence today of their history as trading ports. The Fertile Crescent of biblical times has long since gone, and the "land between the rivers" (the Tigris and the Euphrates) shows almost no evidence of its former luxuriant vegetation. Thus, turn where one will—to areas desolated by fifteenth-century sheep raisers in Spain, to the pre-Columbian American civilization on Monte Alban in Mexico —one is apt to find examples of poor management and land and forest degradation. Obviously, some peoples have managed their resources wisely—The Netherlands (Holland) and Japan, for example, and lately the Israelis, who have reclaimed a desert area through great diligence and husbandry—but they are rare exceptions in an otherwise bleak picture.

What then is the extent of the environmental crisis in modern society? Very simply, we have achieved a certain mastery over the world because of our scientific and technological achievement. We are at the top of the food chain because of our mastery of much of the earth's flora and fauna. However, because of the explosion of the human population, increasingly greater pressures "will be placed on our lands to provide shelter, food, recreation, and waste disposal areas. This will cause a greater pollution of the atmosphere, the rivers, the lakes, the land, and the oceans" (Mergen, 1970, p. 36). This bleak picture could be expanded, yet perhaps the tide will soon turn. Certainly the gravity of prevailing patterns of human conduct is recognized by many, but a great many more people must develop attitudes that will lead them to take positive action in the immediate future. It is time for concerted global action, and we can only hope that it is not too late to reverse the effects of a most grave situation.

Patterns of Education. We can all appreciate the difficulty of moving from a scientific "is" to an ethical "ought" in the realm of human affairs. There are obviously many scientific findings within the environmental science that should be made available to people of all ages whether or not they are enrolled in an educational institution. Simply making the facts available, of course, will not be any guarantee that strong and positive attitudes will develop on the subject. It is a well-established fact, however, that the passing of legislation in difficult and sensitive areas must take place through responsible political leadership, and that attitude changes often follow behind, albeit at what may seem to be a snail's pace. The field of education must play a vital role now, *as it has never done before,* in the development of what might be called an "ecological awareness." (It can be seen why it is impossible to state that this problem has been a *historical* persistent problem. Never before has the eventual magnitude of poor ecological practices been even partially understood, much less fully comprehended. Now some realize the urgency of the matter, but others are telling them that they are exaggerating and simply pessimistic by nature.) This is obviously much broader than what was called the conservation movement within forestry and closely related fields that was bent on the preservation of this or that feature of nature. Now ecology, or environmental science, places all these individual entities in a total context in which the interrelationship of all parts must be thoroughly understood.

Sound educational planning should take place at all levels, from early childhood education through the university courses now being offered to many older citizens. As Mergen states, "The knowledge that has been accumulated is vast, and ecological principles should be made part of the educational menu for economics, city planners, architects, engineers, the medical profession, the legal profession, religious groups, and all people concerned with the public and private management of natural resources, as well as politicians and governmental employees" (1970, p. 37). Obviously, those concerned with the professional preparation of practitioners in physical education and sport, health and safety education, and recreation and park administration have at least an equally important stake in the total educational process in this regard.

Presumably the usual struggle will take place among those who will want to introduce a new subject into the curriculum, those who will demand that environmental science be taught incidentally as part of existing subjects, and those who will see no need at all for the study of environmental interrelationships. Further, some will want the subject matter taught as facts and knowledge in a subject-centered curriculum based on a logical progression from the simple to the complex, whereas others will stress that interest on the part of the learner should dictate if and how the subject should be introduced, because this is the way that people learn best. The urgency of the ecological crisis would seem to warrant an approach that does not veer too far in any direction. The point would seem to be that a literally devastating problem is upon us, and that we should move ahead rapidly to see that some of the basics of environmental science are made available to all. These issues have been with us for so many centuries that they undoubtedly will not be solved tomorrow, no matter what approach is taken.

In a pluralistic society it is difficult to state that certain information and attitudes should be taught, with any confidence that such a directive will be followed throughout the land. This is simply not the way things happen in countries like the United States and Canada, for example, where educational autonomy prevails in the individual states and provinces. All that can be hoped is that they will be exposed to the conflicting positions on economic growth—on the one hand the calling optimistically for a continuous growth economic system, as opposed to what some regard as a pessimistic argument for a no-growth system. They should understand that certain ecological and economic theories and recommendations are diametrically opposed, and those that should be followed and how far is something the people must very soon decide.

Physical Education and Sport. If the field of education has a strong obligation to present the various issues revolving about what has rapidly become a persistent problem or social force in North America, this duty obviously includes teaching professionals at all educational levels and in all subject matter areas. Physical educators and sport coaches have a certain general education responsibility to all participants in their classes or sport programs. Thus, they are directly concerned with our relationship with ourselves, our fellow human beings, other living organisms, and the physical environment. Since all responsible citizens and educators should have an understanding of worldwide population growth and its resultant problems, students should be able to expect that instructors will have a reasoned position about this controversial issue.

As matters stand now, physical educators are confronted daily with the fact that for a variety of reasons modern, urbanized, technologically advanced life in North America has created a population with a very low level of *physical* fitness, with a resultant decrease in overall *total* fitness. We have somehow created a ridiculous situation in which people on this continent are to a large extent overfed and poorly exercised. It is the profession of physical education and sport that is *uniquely* responsible for the exercise programs that will enable men and women to withstand the excessive wear and tear that life's informal and formal activities may demand (Zeigler, 1964, p. 55).

In addition, people at all stages of life show evidence of a variety of remediable physical defects, but there is an unwillingness on the part of the public to make exercise therapy programs readily available through both public and private agencies. Many temporary physiotherapy programs are available after operations or accidents, but out concern here is with the unavailability of exercise therapy programs in the schools and certain private agencies under the supervision of qualified physical educators after the physiotherapist has served his function and the physician prescribes further maintenance exercise. This should include a program in which the circulo-respiratory condition is raised to a desirable level, along with stretching, strengthening, and poising exercises. Further, it is highly desirable for the person to become involved in an adapted physical activity and sport program, because such involvement can play an important role in the social and psychological development of the individual throughout life.

Space does not permit more than a brief mention of each of the remaining ten persistent historical problems, although the final problem —the idea of progress—will be discussed in somewhat greater detail than the others because it has some earmarks of being both a social force *and* a professional concern.

The Curriculum

The seventh persistent historical problem, and the first problem designated as a "professional concern," is the curriculum in physical education and sport. In primitive and preliterate society, physical education, like all education was typically incidental, a by-product of daily experience. Nor was physical education in early Egypt part of a formal educational system. Sports and dancing were popular with the nobility, but the masses simply had to master the many physical skills necessary to earn their living. As was often the case throughout history, fishing, hunting, and fowling were engaged in for pleasure by some and as business by many. Much the same can be said about the other early civilizations. Soldiers were training to fight in a variety of ways, and the masses had occasional opportunities for dancing, music, informal games, and rudimentary hunting and fishing activities. Thus, any informal or formal educational curriculum, or physical education activity, has been and still is influenced by a variety of political, economic, philosophical, religious, scientific, and technological factors. Those subjects included for the education of youth are selected because of their recurring interest and use among educators and the public. The persistent problem, therefore, is: On what basis is the formal or informal curriculum to be selected? The Cretans were surrounded by water, so they learned to swim; the Spartan Greeks emphasized severe physical training, but they did not stress noncombative sport; the Athenians, on the other hand, believed that harmonious development of body, mind, and spirit was most important; the Roman ideal was based on the preparation of a citizen to bear arms for his nation; and so on up through the various ages. Basically, the values that are held in a society will be reflected directly and indirectly in the curriculum. Thus, the task of the physical educator and coach today is to ascertain the values which are uppermost in the society and to attempt to implement them to the greatest possible extent through the medium of sport and related physical activities. To accomplish this task efficiently and according to best educational goals is obviously a most important professional concern (and also a persistent problem as identified in this volume).

Methods of Instruction

The second so-called professional concern, and the eighth persistent historical problem, is that of methods of instruction in physical education and sport. Keeping in mind that curriculum and method should go hand in hand as they usually have in the past, if effective education is a desired end product, it is quite logical to consider methods at this point.

Primitive and preliterate people undoubtedly learned through imitation and through trial and error. When writing was invented in the early civilizations, memorization played a large part in the educational process. Tradition and custom were highly regarded, and precept and proper example were significant aspects of both physical and mental culture. In the Near East we are told that Jesus was a very fine teacher, and undoubtedly the same might be said about other great religious leaders. The religious leaders who followed Jesus presumably employed less exciting teaching methods with an emphasis on formality and dogmatism. Toward the end of the Middle Ages, educational methodology is said to have improved considerably. With the onset of the Renaissance, there was greater recognition of individual differences, and the whole spirit of the period is said to have been more humanistic. Physical educators need to understand that the concept of a "mind-body dualism" has prevailed in many quarters down to the present day. A physical educator/coach should determine what influence that content has on method, and whether they go hand in hand on all occasions. Shall physical education and sport be taught formally, semiformally, or informally? The persistent problem remains: How can the student be motivated so that learning will occur most easily, so that it will be remembered, and so that it will change attitudes and produce beneficial change in all who become involved?

Professional Preparation

Preparation for professional service is the third professional concern to be considered. Although professional preparation had its origins in antiquity, professional preparation of teachers is a fairly recent innovation. In early times the most important qualification for the teacher was a sound knowledge of the subject. In the Middle Ages there was no such thing as professional education to be a teacher, at least in the sense that certification is needed today to teach in most public institutions. In Prussia, much headway was made in improving teacher education in the late eighteenth and early nineteenth centuries, and this system was copied extensively elsewhere. Significant advances in the theory of pedagogy occurred through the influence of Pestalozzi. In America, for example, the "normal school" became a well-established part of the educational system. In the twentieth century this type of school progressed to college or university status. Professional education eventually achieved status at the university level as a subject to be taught, but university-level teachers are not required to take a certain number of courses in it as are those who wish to teach at the lower educational levels.

Generally speaking throughout the world, professional preparation for physical education has been offered at the normal and/or technical school level. University recognition has been achieved at many institutions in the United States with the first doctoral degrees being awarded in 1924. The first two doctoral degrees were awarded in Canada in 1969, and developments at this highest level began in both the Federal Republic of Germany and Great Britain in the 1970s. Japan has made significant progress in the field of physical education and now does award the doctoral degree in physical education at one university.

The Healthy Body

The concept of "the healthy body" is the fourth professional concern (and the tenth persistent historical problem). The condition of our bodies has undoubtedly always been of concern. Early peoples found that a certain type of fitness was necessary for life. Physical efficiency was necessary for survival. A study of past civilizations indicates that the states of war or peace have had a direct bearing on the emphases placed on personal and/or community health. Strength, endurance, and freedom from disqualifying defects are important to men who want to win wars. When a war has ended, a society may then be able again to focus greater attention toward a healthful environment at home.

Modern people in the developed countries have been more successful than their forebears in making an adjustment to their environment, and consequently they live longer on the average. Their success, however, is dependent on complicated procedures, and it is profoundly disturbing that so many people in the world are not able to profit from the outstanding progress that has been made in public health science. Much of the disagreement over the role of school health education today stems from differing educational philosophies and the various resultant concepts of health. There is the ever-present question as to which agency—the home, the school, or the community agency—should play the greatest role in the area. In the twentieth century Jesse Feiring Williams offered a broadened concept of health in which he defined it as "that quality of life which enables the individual to live most and serve best." According to this definition, the ultimate test of health is the use to which it is put for individual and social service.

Women in Physical Education and Sport

The place of sport and physical activity in the lives of women is the fifth so-called professional concern and the eleventh persistent historical problem. Throughout history women's sport and physical activity has been hampered not only by people's ideas of the place of physical education in a particular society, but also by the place that women themselves have held in most societies. It has been believed, by both sexes, that a woman had severe limitations because of her anatomical structure and because of her role in the reproductive process. Aristotle, for example, felt that women were generally weaker, less courageous, and less complete than men, and they therefore had been fitted by nature for subjection to the male. Conversely, Plato believed that women should have all types of education similar to the pattern he prescribed for men (including the highest type of liberal education, and even preparation for warfare). Throughout history, with notable exceptions in the cases of Crete, Sparta, later ancient Rome, and certain other individual instances, practically all women were considered inferior.

Certainly one of the significant social trends of the twentieth century has been women's "emancipation." Women are now more likely to be evaluated in terms of intellectual function and individual qualification. The democratic and socialistic theories of state have fostered equalitarianism. Many people feel that men's and women's physical education and sport programs should more nearly approximate each other. The norm projected by society for women tends to be retrogressive, and it has often been modified by what many consider to be unfortunate societal influences, for example, excessive concern about external appearance. If the field of physical education and sport has advantages to offer to women, society and its educators should see to it that women receive these opportunities to the greatest extent possible.

Dance in Physical Education

The sixth professional concern, and the twelfth persistent historical problem, is the role of dance in physical education. In all ages people have danced for personal pleasure, for religious purposes, for expression of the gamut of emotions, and for the pleasure of others. An analysis of the dance forms of a civilization can frequently tell a qualified observer much about the total life pattern therein. In primitive societies various types of rhythmic expression were "instinctive satisfiers" of people. Dance was most often serious in nature and only incidentally served physical fitness, health, and recreation. It served a purpose in Roman civilization, but its status was below that accorded to it by the Greeks. During the Middle Ages dance had very low status, probably because of its corruption in the later Roman era. The place of dance began to rise again during the Renaissance.

Different types and forms of dance have waxed and waned over the centuries. The twentieth century has witnessed a truly remarkable development in the dance, the body gradually being rediscovered as a means of communication through the dance medium. Yet there is still much room for progress. For example, a significant body of scholarly research is not yet available, although there has been some progress along these lines. Furthermore, better interaction between the dance teacher (professor) and the professional performer would add further strength to the overall development of the field. Articulation within the dance curriculum among the various educational levels is certainly needed. On the North American continent so-called modern dance especially still seems unacceptable to the majority of male physical education teachers and coaches, and their attitude is conveyed to the boys and young men in their classes as well. However, such opinions and attitudes can change, and a vigorous effort should be made along these lines. Recently there has been somewhat of a trend toward dance being shifted from the physical education unit to a relationship with the fine arts. There is some justification for such a move, but it does seem that interrelationships should be maintained so that dance can function most effectively within, say, a university's units for physical education, education, and fine arts. As both an art and a social function, dance will probably always be with us, and it will undoubtedly reflect the dominant influences of the age in which it is taking place.

The Use of Leisure

The use of leisure has been designated as the seventh professional concern (and the thirteenth persistent historical problem). Citizens in the industrialized world now are said to have more leisure than ever before in history, but the promotion of the concept of education for leisure depends a great deal on whether the prevailing educational philosophy will support such programs. An unfortunate development also is that economic inflation has forced many men to take second or part-time jobs, and has forced women out of the home to seek employment. Such pressures have affected leisure patterns significantly.

Thus, just as throughout history, the use of leisure has been strongly influenced by the economic status of society. Both education and recreation have prospered in times when there was a surplus economy. However, in most past and present civilizations the average man has had to work very hard to earn a meager living. Certain classes—rulers, priests, and nobles—were the first to enjoy anything like extended leisure. Even in the Middle Ages life still held many inequalities for the masses, although recreation did begin to take on a broader significance. Persistent war-making, the fact that times change slowly, and the power of the Church prevented the concepts of political democracy and socialism from taking hold. Then, too, the natural sciences had to be advanced sufficiently so that developing technology could direct people to what was called the Industrial Revolution, a development which has lowered people's working hours markedly. Now we hear about cybernation and automation, and most certainly the concept of "education for leisure" warrants serious consideration. The term "recreation" seems now to have a broader meaning than "play," although they are commonly used interchangeably. We need to articulate within our concept of "leisure" a definition of recreation which embodies all those experiences that people engage in during their leisure for purposes of pleasure, satisfaction, or education.

Amateur, Semiprofessional, and Professional Athletics

The eighth professional concern, and the fourteenth persistent historical problem, is the matter of amateur, semiprofessional, and professional athletics. The relationship of these three areas to one another, to the educational system, and to the entire culture must be more fully understood before improvements can be made in the light of changing circumstances. The motivation for people to participate in games and sports through the ages has been so complex that there is really no general agreement on the matter. People have taken part for fun, for re-creation, for self-expression, for self-arousal and adventure, for health, for exercise, for competition, for money, and probably for still other reasons not readily discernible. There was an important early relationship of sporting competition to religious observances. Even in the earlier days the aspect of overspecialization because of the desire to win, and presumably the desire for material reward, has tended to "tarnish the luster" of what has become known as "the amateur ideal." There are so many different definitions of an amateur that it is next to impossible for one person to comprehend them fully. We are steadily but surely reevaluating some of our treasured, basic assumptions about the amateur code in sport, a position which categorizes the matter on the basis of polarities (i.e., if you "take a nickel," you're a "dirty pro"). There is an urgent need for the recognition of a semiprofessional category in which the athlete will not be viewed as a "dirty and degraded" person by the amateur sport authorities. There is a need further for professional athletes (called "sportsmen") who will be taught to devote their lives to a social ideal— to serve their fellow human beings through their contributions to the many phases of sports' development. The assumption is that all types of sport can hold value for people under the finest auspices with the best professional leadership (i.e., that which develops a fine set of professional ethics not dominated primarily by the thought of financial gain). The theory is that sport can be employed as a "socially useful servant."

The Role of Management

The role of management or administration is the ninth professional concern and the fifteenth persistent historical problem. As our society continues to grow in complexity, amazing social changes are taking place. The continuing Industrial Revolution, and now the imminence of a so-called post-industrial society, has placed our most modern societies in a highly difficult situation. Because of these factors, along with the exploding population and the resultant development of immense urban and suburban areas, coupled with fantastic advances in science and technology, a steadily growing percentage of available human resources has been necessary to manage the efforts of a large majority of the people. Such a development has been called the "Administrative Revolution."

Social organizations of one type or another are inextricably related to people's history as human and social animals. Superior-subordinate relationships evolved according to the very nature of things as people produced goods, fought wars, organized society politically, formed churches, and developed a great variety of formal and informal associations. As societies became more complex, role differentiation increased greatly. A central theme seems to have been that of *change,* such change being made presumably to strengthen the organization administratively. It was only recently, however, that "administrative thought emerged as a differentiated field of sustained writing, conscious observation, abstract theory, and specialized terminology" (Gross, 1964, p. 91).

Education has become a vast public and private enterprise demanding wise management based upon sound administrative theory. The "organizational revolution" has meant that educational administrators have been forced to create a greater amount of bureaucracy. Educational traditionalists have tended to believe that there are valid theoretical principles of administration that should not be violated. Many with a more progressive orientation view administration as a developing social science. If and when a truly definitive inventory of administrative theory and research becomes available, such knowledge can then be of use to all administrators and managers.

In many educational institutions the administration of physical education and athletics is now big business within big education, and the same can be said for the management of professional athletics and private exercise establishments. Unfortunately, there is practically no tenable theory or ongoing research about the administrative task taking place. For example, the professional preparation of physical education and athletics administrators is being carried out by physical educators almost universally in a haphazard and poorly articulated fashion. Where possible, administrators of athletics are receiving assistance from seminars in which knowledgeable people from other disciplines are brought in as leaders. Changes in professional preparation for adminstrative leadership are coming about very slowly, and we can only hope that increasingly the administrator's practice will be based on the knowledge available to us through the behavioral sciences specifically.

The Idea of Progress

The idea of progress is offered as both the tenth professional concern and the sixteenth persistent historical problem. As a matter of fact, this topic can indeed be viewed from two standpoints: first, it does seem to be a persistent problem that relates closely to the values that a society holds for itself; second, it can also be introduced as a professional concern for every physical educator and coach.

Any study of history inevitably forces a person to conjecture about human progress. Certainly there has been progression, but can this be called "progress"? To ascertain if change may be called progress, it is necessary to measure, for example, whether advancement has been made from worse to better. Then a criterion must be recommended by which progress may be judged. It is true that humans have made progress in adaptability and can cope with a variety of environments. It is probably safe to assume that the human being on the whole is the pinnacle of evolutionary progress *on this earth.*

Throughout the course of history until the Golden Age of Greece, a good education had been based on the transmission of the cultural heritage. During the Roman Empire and the Middle Ages such an educational pattern continued, despite the fact that from time to time certain educational theorists offered proposals, both radical and reactionary. Thus, when a society declined, those involved in the educational system had relatively few useful ideas about social rejuvenation. Despite the forces of the Renaissance and accompanying humanism, followed by the gradual introduction of science into the curriculum, the same traditional educational pattern kept the school from becoming an agent of social reconstructionism.

In the field of physical education and sport, it is vitally important for us to search most diligently for some consensus along the conflicting positions or philosophical stances extant today. The field has been proceeding "amoeba-like" for far too long considering the body of knowledge that is amassing. There are some common denominators that may be suggested at this time within the specialized fields of physical education and sport, health and safety education, and recreation education (the general education of citizens for creative recreational participation) as follows:

1. The large majority of physical educators believe that regular physical education periods should be required for all schoolchildren through grades ten or eleven.
2. It is important that a child develop certain positive attitudes toward his/her own health in particular and toward community health in general.
3. Leisure should be put to worthy use. It is understood that in North America many people are presumably enjoying a greater amount of leisure than has ever been available before.
4. Physical vigor is extremely important, but there is no general agreement among the men, or between men and women in the profession, about what really constitutes physical fitness. There are national norms in both the United States and Canada, but no national standards (or agreement on whether there should be standards).
5. There should be an experience in competitive athletics. This applies both to boys and girls, but the amount of time and emphasis that should be devoted to it are points of contention.
6. Boys and girls who need therapeutic exercise for remediable physical defects should be helped.
7. Character and personality development is important. We believe generally that our specialized fields can make a definite contribution toward the achievement of this objective, but we have very little scientific evidence to support this claim. (Zeigler, 1977, p. 235)

The time for agreement on what it is that we do is long overdue!

CONCLUSION

In concluding this volume it seems best to be melioristic (that is, to hold a belief that it is still possible for humans to work for the betterment of man and woman's position in the world) rather than to be either solely optimistic or pessimistic. In 1960 Heilbroner stated a concept of "the future as history" (1960, pp. 176 ff.) which can be paraphrased as: America—the United States—acquired the belief that it had a personal "deity of history"; this led a great many people to hold a blind philosophy of optimism about history's malleability and compatibility in keeping with American ideals; this optimistic position has turned out to be very shortsighted, and truly significant changes loom ahead in the immediate future.

Keeping in mind the concept Heilbroner has postulated, whether you believe it or not, it seems to me that it is absolutely imperative that each of us at least seek to comprehend better the great movement of history including the various forces which are shaping and directing it; that we understand further the manner in which Americans have tended to develop a philosophy of history based upon a successful blending of scientific, technological, geographical, political, and economic forces; that we consider the argument that the resultant optimism was very unrealistic and shortsighted because the historic model being created could not be transposed into a theory of historic development that had general applicability; and that we now should make every effort to promote among our citizens the concepts of "malleability" and "flexibility" so that we will be ready to share with our fellow humans everywhere according to urgency of need as we work together for long-range goals still thousands of years away.

What implications do all of these factors have for sport and physical education? I believe that it is most realistic to argue that the pivotal social forces mentioned above (e.g., the influence of economics, etc.) definitely influence sport and games within our culture. But what about reverse influence? It is my belief that sport and games have reached such a level of acceptance in our society that they themselves have now become social forces to be reckoned with because of their many influences on attitudes and conduct. Further, sport has been operating within our schools and colleges as part of a social system known typically as physical education. More recently, however, physical education has declined as a social system, in the United States especially, while at the same time intercollegiate and interscholastic athletics, disguised as sport and games, have made steadily increasing inroads on the shaky physical education structure. The pivotal social forces at work in our culture today and their interrelationship with the sixteen persistent historical problems enumerated, including the ten professional concerns, individually and collectively "confront" the field of physical education and sport. How we and society cope with these problems, forces, or concerns will determine whether sport and physical activity are social forces for good or evil, whether they will serve this culture as socially useful servants, or whether they will simply develop into symptoms and causes of the society's eventual disintegration.

302 PHYSICAL EDUCATION AND SPORT IN A HISTORICAL PERSPECTIVE

Somehow we must bring ourselves to an assessment that may rock our very social foundations while causing us to reaffirm what is sound in the traits that make up our national character. Progress is probably no longer in the direction which we have been following somewhat blindly. Now what do we do? Have we the energy, the intellect, the foresight, the attitudes, the concern for each other at home and abroad, and the will to change our course the required number of degrees so that the ship of state will follow the correct course at a crucial juncture in the world's history?

We can only hope that such will be the case, while we as individuals and as collectivities within society work to realize a "North American dream" in a world setting. Sport and physical activity under highly professional leadership can be a powerful social force. The future of sport and physical education can, in the Heilbronerian sense, be shaped by its history. Let's give it a chance.

GENERAL BIBLIOGRAPHY

BERELSON, BERNARD, and GARY A. STEINER. *Human Behavior.* New York: Harcourt Brace Jovanovich, 1964.

BRUBACHER, JOHN S. *A History of the Problems of Education* (2nd ed.). New York: McGraw-Hill, 1966.

———. *Modern Philosophies of Education* (4th ed.). New York: McGraw-Hill, 1969.

CHAMPION. S. G., and D. SHORT. *Readings from World Religions.* Boston: Beacon Press, 1951.

COWELL, CHARLES C. "The Contributions of Physical Activity to Social Development, *Research Quarterly,* 31, no. 2 (May 1960, Part II), 286–306.

FRALEIGH, WARREN P. "Theory and Design of Philosophic Research in Physical Education," *Proceedings of the National College Physical Education Association for Men,* Portland, Oregon, December 28, 1970.

GLASSFORD. R. G. "Application of a Theory of Games to the Transitional Eskimo Culture." Ph.D. Thesis, University of Illinois, 1970.

GROSS, BERTRAM M. *The Managing of Organizations,* 2 vols. New York: Crowell-Collier, 1964.

HEILBRONER, ROBERT L. *The Future as History.* New York: Harper & Row, 1960.

HERSKOVITS. M. J. *Cultural Anthropology,* pp. 33–85. New York: Alfred Knopf, 1955.

JOHNSON, HARRY M. "The Relevance of the Theory of Action to Historians," *Social Science Quarterly,* June 1969, pp. 46–58.

KENNEDY, JOHN F. Address by the President in Detroit in the spring of 1958. (At that time he was a U.S. Senator.)

LAUWERYS, JOSEPH A. "The Philosophical Approach to Comparative Education," *International Review of Education*, V (1959), 283–90.

MARTENS, RAINER. "Demand Characteristics and Experimenter Bias." Paper presented at the AAHPER Convention, Detroit, April 5, 1971.

———. "A Social Psychology of Physical Activity," *Quest*, 14 (June 1970), 8–17.

MERGEN, FRANÇOIS. "Man and His Environment," *Yale Alumni Magazine*, XXXIII, no. 8 (May 1970), 36–37.

MORRIS, VAN CLEVE. "Physical Education and the Philosophy of Education," *Journal of Health, Physical Education and Recreation*, 27 (March 1956), 21–22, 30–31.

NEVINS, ALLAN. "The Explosive Excitement of History," *Saturday Review*, April 6, 1968.

ROBERTS, J. M., and B. SUTTON-SMITH. "Child Training and Game Involvement," *Ethnology*, vol. 1, 1962.

ROYCE, J. R. "Paths to Knowledge," *The Encapsulated Man*. Princeton, N.J.: Van Nostrand, 1964.

VON NEUMANN, J., and O. MORGENSTERN. *The Theory of Games and Economic Behavior* (2nd ed.). Princeton: Princeton Univ. Press, 1947.

WILLIAMS, J. PAUL. *What Americans Believe and How They Worship*. New York: Harper & Row, 1952.

WOODY, THOMAS. *Life and Education in Early Societies*. New York: The Macmillan Company, 1949.

ZEIGLER, EARLE F. *A Brief Introduction to the Philosophy of Religion*. Champaign, Ill.: Stipes Publishing Company, 1965.

———. Ed. *A History of Physical Education and Sport in the United States and Canada*. Champaign, Ill.: Stipes Publishing Company, 1975.

———, Ed. *A History of Sport and Physical Education to 1900*. Champaign, Ill.: Stipes Publishing Company, 1973.

———. *Personalizing Physical Education and Sport Philosophy*. Champaign, Ill.: Stipes Publishing Company, 1975.

———. *Philosophical Foundations for Physical, Health, and Recreation Education*. Englewood Cliffs, N.J.: Prentice-Hall, 1964.

———. *Physical Education and Sport Philosophy*. Englewood Cliffs, N.J.: Prentice-Hall, 1977.

———. *Problems in the History and Philosophy of Physical Education and Sport*. Englewood Cliffs, N.J.: Prentice-Hall, 1968.

SELECTED REFERENCES FOR HISTORICAL BACKGROUND

BALLOU, RALPH B. "An Analysis of the Writings of Selected Church Fathers to A.D. 394 to Reveal Attitudes Regarding Physical Activity." Ph.D. Dissertation, University of Oregon, 1965.

BENNETT, BRUCE L. "Religion and Physical Education." Paper presented at the Cincinnati Convention of the AAHPER, April 10, 1962.

BURY, J. B. *The Idea of Progress.* New York: Dover, 1955.

BUTTS, R. F. *A Cultural History of Education.* New York: McGraw-Hill, 1947.

COMMAGER, HENRY STEELE. "A Quarter Century—Its Advances," *Look,* 25, no. 10 (June 6, 1961), 80–91.

DURANT, WILL, and ARIEL DURANT. *The Lessons of History.* New York: Dover, 1968.

ELLIOTT, RUTH. *The Organization of Professional Training in Physical Education in State Universities.* New York: Teachers College, Columbia University, 1927.

FLATH, A. W. *A History of Relations Between the National Collegiate Athletic Association and the Amateur Athletic Union of the United States (1905–1963).* Champaign, Ill.: Stipes Publishing Company, 1964. (Includes a Foreword by E. F. Zeigler entitled, "Amateurism, Semi-Professionalism, and Professionalism in Sport: A Persistent Educational Problem.")

HAYES, C. J. *Nationalism: A Religion.* New York: The Macmillan Company, 1961.

LEONARD, F. E., and G. B. AFFLECK. *The History of Physical Education* (3rd ed.). Philadelphia: Lea & Febiger, 1947.

MARROU, H. I. *A History of Education in Antiquity.* Trans. George Lamb. New York: New American Library, 1964.

MCINTOSH, P. C., *et al. History of Physical Education.* London: Routledge & Kegan Paul, 1957.

MULLER, HERBERT J. *The Uses of the Past.* New York: New American Library, 1954.

MURRAY, BERTRAM G., JR. "What the Ecologists Can Teach the Economists," *The New York Times Magazine,* December 10, 1972, pp. 38–39, 64–65, 70, 72.

NEVINS, ALLAN. *The Gateway to History.* Garden City, N.Y.: Doubleday, 1962.

REISNER, E. H. *Nationalism and Education since 1789.* New York: The Macmillan Company, 1925.

SIGERIST, HENRY E. *Landmarks in the History of Hygiene.* London: Oxford University Press, 1956.

SIMPSON, GEORGE G. *The Meaning of Evolution.* New Haven and London: Yale University Press, 1949.

WILLIAMS, J. PAUL. *What Americans Believe and How They Worship.* New York: Harper & Row, 1952.

ZEIGLER, EARLE F. "A History of Professional Preparation for Physical Education in the United States (1861–1961)," *Professional Preparation in Health Education, Physical Education, and Recreation Education,* pp. 116–33. Washington, D.C.: The American Association for Health, Physical Education, and Recreation, 1962.

Index

Academics, 251
Acrobatics, 8, 11, 14, 20, 21-22, 30
    36-37, 38, 39, 42, 48
Action Games, 41, 48
Act to Encourage Fitness and Amateur
    Sport, Canada, 237
Administration, 297-298
Aesthetics, 260
Age of Enlightenment, 107, 119
Agricola, Rudolph, 86
Alberti, Leone Battista, 81, 84
Altruism, 260
Amateur athletics, 199, 201, 204, 269
    296-98
American Alliance for Health, Physical
    Education, Recreation, and Dance
    195, 213, 274
American Association for the
    Advancement of Physical Education,
    270-71
Amoros, F. 117, 120
Ancien Regime, 105, 107, 119
Anderson, William G., 194, 195
Animal sports, 142
Anthropocentrism, 109
Anthropology, 248, 250-51
Antoniano, Silvio, 91
Aquinas, St. Thomas, 60, 253, 285
Archery, 5, 7, 8, 9, 10, 26, 41, 45, 67-68,
    69, 90, 94, 267
Aristotle, 60, 71, 260, 274
Armour, 30, 33, 39, 48
Asceticism, 63, 71, 173-74, 180, 264, 276
Ascham, Roger, 90
Ascolia, 38, 39
Assyrian civilization, 4-5, 9-10, 45-46,
    261
Athenians, 36, 245, 294 (see also Greece,

    ancient
Athleticism, 104, 109, 144
"Athletics for all," 272
Atomic energy, 246
"Audience habit," 181
Augastolia, 48
Australia, 126
"Austrian School," 123
Authoritarianism, 249
Auto racing, 205
Axiology, 259-60

Babylon, 261
Bacon, Francis, 92-93
Badge systems, 116-17, 118, 119
Badminton, 136
Ball games, 9, 14, 15-16, 20, 27, 30, 37,
    39, 41, 48, 49, 51, 65, 69, 83
Balneae, 41
Bardenflith, 127
Baseball, 51, 127, 139, 153-54, 161,
    182-83, 190, 191-92, 201, 205-206,
    209, 269, 270
Basedow, Johann, 108, 120, 126
"Basic Teaching Plan," 124
Basketball, 129, 139, 147, 188, 189, 190,
    199, 201-202, 205, 207, 209,
    270
Beck, Karl (Charles), 113, 186, 268
Beecher, Catharine, 187, 193
Beers, George W., 223
Behavioral science, 254
Berelson, Bernard, 253-54
Bergman-Oesterberg, M. 122
Bicycling, 51
Billiards, 136
Biocentrism, 108-09, 119-26

Birth rate, 246
Blood sports, 40, 176, 178
Blue Laws, 178
Board games, 3, 7, 11, 14, 19-20, 27, 28
    30, 33, 38, 42, 46, 47, 49, 51,
Boating, 191
Bobsledding, 147
Bode, Rudolf, 123, 124
Borsa, 38, 39
Boston University, Sargent College of
    Allied Health Professions, 194, 212
Bowling, 39, 136, 177, 205, 267, 269
Boxing, 5, 8, 25-26, 29, 30, 33, 34, 35,
    38, 39, 41. 42, 44, 45, 48, 49, 67
    136, 141, 176, 179, 182-83, 191, 192,
    206
Bull games, 22-23, 42, 44, 45, 48, 51,
    142

Caber tossing, 69
Calvin, John, 88-89
Calvinism, 76-77, 79, 175
Calisthenics, 194, 196, 197, 211, 269
Canada, 50, 51, 137, 148-149, 151, 159,
    219-21, 222, 222-23, 223-24, 224-229,
    229-230, 230-235, 235-236, 236-237,
    237-238, 238-239, 239-241
Canoe, 223-24
Capitoline Games, 41
Cardano, Girolamo, 81
Castiglione, Baldassare, 84, 90
Cathedral schools, 61, 62, 68, 88
Catholic Reformation, 90, 91, 95
Championships, 152-55, 156-58
Chantry schools, 62
Character and personality development, 299
Chariotry, 5, 6, 7, 8, 9, 10,33, 35, 38, 40
    45, 48, 51
Children's games, 37, 42
China, 42-43, 116, 261
Chivalry, 62-63, 66, 70, 264
Christian, image, 253
Christianity, 61, 62,
    63-64, 65-66, 68, 69
    70, 263, 264
Circus, 40, 185
City-states, 72-73
Civilization, historical perspective, 245
Class structure, 75-76, 95, 141-42, 175
    177, 296
Clias, Phokion, 117, 120, 267
Climbing, 113, 119
Club of Rome, 109
Club throwing, 14
Cockfighting, 45, 142, 176, 177, 178

Collectivities, 249, 257, 258
College sport, 188-90, 200, 201, 203,
Comenius, 92, 265
Communications, 187, 198, 199, 206
Community-school concept, 130
Comparative sport and physical educa-
    tion, U.S. and Canada, 258
Competitive sport, 68, 147, 151-52, 153,
    154-58, 282
Cottabus, 36-37, 42
Coubertin, Pierre de, 128, 130, 144, 145,
    147, 148, 156, 191, 267
Cricket, 51, 127, 136, 137, 142, 161,
    224, 267
Croquet, 136
Culture, 257
Cup games, 28-29
Curling, 135, 136, 148, 224-26, 252
Curriculum, 66, 67, 74, 80, 95, 186, 271,
    289, 291-92, 298-99
Cycling, 191

da Feltre, Vittorino, 74, 81, 82, 83-84,
    89, 96, 265
Dalcroze, Émile, 108, 122
Dancing, 3, 7, 8, 9, 11, 16, 20, 24-25, 30,
    33, 38, 39, 46, 49, 51, 65, 69, 83, 84,
    90, 94, 96, 122, 125, 142, 178, 179,
    185, 261, 273, 286, 294-95
da Verone, Guarino Guarini, 81, 84
Deaths, sport, 162
Delsarte, François, 122, 123
Democracy, 245, 250
Denmark, 104, 106, 109-10, 127
Descartes, René, 78
Dewey, John, 94, 210, 213, 259, 271, 272
Diaulos, 34, 35, 48
Dice, 8, 10, 11, 30, 39, 83, 178
"Discovery" concept, 124, 125
Discus, 30, 33, 35, 38, 41, 47
Diving, 39
Dog races, 42
Dolichos, 34, 35
Draughts, 19, 20, 37
Dualism, 76, 253, 292

Ecology, 287-91
Economics, 96, 174, 188, 193, 219, 254
    279-83
Education, 61-63, 68, 70, 78-80, 81-91,
    95, 106, 107, 113, 124-26, 144, 210,
    252, 255, 264-66, 269, 271, 274-75,
    278, 280-81, 284-85, 288, 297-99
Educational values, 151-157

Egocentrism, 126-28, 129
Egoism, 260
Egypt, ancient, 11-20, 46, 47, 48, 261
Elyot, Thomas, 90
Empirical methods, 248, 249
Encyclopedia, sport, 142-43
England, 124, 126-28, 134-39, 144, 267, 277, 293
Ephidrismos, 30
Episkyros, 37
Epistemology, 259
Equestrianism, 6, 7-8, 10, 35, 45, 48, 67, 83, 90, 94
Erasmus, Desiderius, 74, 87, 89
Ethics, types of, 108-28, 259-60
Ethnocentrism, 109-19
Etruscan civilization, 37-39, 46, 47, 48, 50, 51
Eurhythmics, 122, 123
Exercise, 14, 16, 20, 38, 41, 44, 45, 46, 47, 83-85, 90, 92, 110, 120, 123, 186-187, 188, 193, 194, 196-97, 237-38, 266, 285, 290-91, 299 (see also Calisthenics, Gymnastics, Turnen)
Existence theory, 259
Experimentalist theory, 259

Fair play, 250
Falcon movement, 114-16
Falconry, 8, 67
Fellenberg, Phillip Emmanuel von, 108
Fencing, 88, 90
Fénelon, François, 91
Festivals, athletic, 8, 20, 34, 148-52, 176, 179, 263
Field Hockey, 136, 137, 147, 202, 267
Field sports, 177
Finger games, 16-17, 20
Finland, 123
Fishing, 3, 7, 9, 12, 26, 30, 33, 38, 41, 44, 49, 83, 176, 177, 191, 291
Follen, Karl (Charles), 113, 186-87, 268
Football, 42, 51, 129, 136, 139, 142, 147, 148, 153, 188, 189, 199-201, 208-209, 269, 270
Fowling, 176, 177
France, 104, 131, 266, 277
Franklin, Benjamin, 175, 186, 268
Frisbee, 46
Froebel, Friedrich, 119, 122, 126, 266
Funeral games, 33, 38, 151
"Future as history," 299-300

Gambling, 176, 178, 179, 181, 184, 185
Games, 3, 8, 14, 15, 16-17, 20, 28-29, 30, 33, 34, 37, 38, 41, 42, 44, 45-48, 49, 51, 109, 113, 119, 125, 126-28, 135, 138, 148-52, 191, 235-36, 238-239, (see also Board games; Olympic Games)
Gaulhofer, Karl, 108, 119, 123, 124
Germanic tribes, 58-59, 65
Germany, 112-13, 116, 266-67, 258-59, 277
Gilgamesh Epic, 5, 6
Gladiatorial combat, 8, 38, 40, 44, 45, 50, 51
"Golden mean" concept, 243
Golf, 135, 137, 191, 201, 205, 208-09, 267, 269
Gorlitz Plan, 127
Governmental influence in fitness and sport, Canadian, 236-38, 238-39, 240
Grey Cup, Canada, 231
Great Britain (see England)
"Great Protestant Legend," 63, 263
Greece, ancient, 29-37, 38, 44, 47-48, 51, 109, 160, 247, 253, 262, 277, 291, 295, 298
Greek ideal, 68, 87, 262, 264-65, 286
Gulick, Luther Halsey, 196, 270
Guts Muths, Johann, 108, 113, 119, 120-22, 126, 221, 267
Gymnasia, 9, 30, 36, 41, 47, 48, 110, 113, 187, 194, 270
Gymnastics, 14, 16-17, 20, 39, 41, 106, 108-09, 110-16, 11, 120, 122, 123, 124, 186-87, 196-97, 201, 210, 212, 266-67, 268-69, 272

Hall, G. Stanley, 210, 211
Hammer throwing, 267
Handball, team, 164
Hanna, Delphine, 195
Hartwell Edward M., 194, 195
Health education, 96, 271, 272, 274, 293, 299
Health standards, 68, 70, 261
"Healthy body" concept, 177-78
Hebrews, ancient, 8-9, 261-62, 277
Hedonism, 260
Hegel, Georg Wilhelm, 284
Hemenway, Mary, 197
Hetherington, Clark, 210
Hieronymians, 86-87
Highland Games, 135, 148, 149
High school athletics, 199, 204
Hiking, 191

Hippodromes, 9
Historical objectivity, 246, 248
Historical problems, 254-99
History, philosophy of, 245, 246-48, 252, 300
Hitchcock, Edward, 194, 195
Hitler, Adolf, 117
Hittite civilization, 5, 7-8, 45-46, 47, 48, 65, 69, 94, 113, 119 (see also Track and Field)
Hockey, 44, 51
Holm, Hanya, 122
Hoop games, 14, 15, 30, 33, 37, 42, 46
Hoplite race, 34, 35
Horse racing, 35, 38, 40, 177, 178, 179, 181-82, 191, 207, 227
Humanism, 60, 71, 81-91, 95, 264-65, 286, 292, 298
Hungary, 116
Hunting, 3, 6, 7, 8, 9, 10, 12, 26, 30, 33, 38, 41, 44, 46, 49, 65, 83, 84, 94, 137, 142, 176, 177, 191, 291

Ice hockey, 139, 147, 148, 177, 190, 201, 205, 208, 209, 226
Ice skating, 226
Idealism, 272
Iliad, 33
India, ancient, 271
Industrialization
Industrial Revolution, 105, 106, 134, 136, 141, 158, 271, 278, 281, 296, 297
Injuries, sport, 162
Instruction, methods of, 292
Intercollegiate athletics, 183, 188-90, 199-203, 270, 300
Intercollegiate athletics, Canadian women, 233
Interest theory, 259
International Council on Health, Physical Education, and Recreation, 129, 130
Interscholastic athletics, 283
Intramural athletics, 203
Intuitionism, 249
Isthmian Games, 30, 34

Jahn, Friedrich, 104, 107, 108, 112-13, 114, 118, 120, 123, 129, 196, 266
Japan, 5, 17, 18, 42, 43, 293
Javelin, 30, 31, 35, 38, 41
Jefferson, Thomas, 268
Johnson, Harry M., 249, 257, 258
Joos, Kurt, 122
Jousting, 11, 16, 20, 27, 42, 67
Jumping, 20, 30, 31, 35, 38, 39, 41, 47,

65, 69, 94, 113, 119 (see also Track and Field)

Kant, Immanuel, 266
Kennedy, J.F., 246-47
Kierkegaard, Soren, 283
Kinanthropology, 131
Kinesiology, 131
Kingsley, Charles, 109, 127
Knife throwing 14, 17
Korea, 42-43
Knucklebones, 3, 8, 28, 37, 42, 49, 51

Laban, Rudolf, 108-109, 119, 122, 123, 124, 125
Lacrosse, 49-50, 139, 148, 201, 222
Legislation, physical education, 196, 212, 271-72
Leisure, 3-4, 74, 106, 131, 143, 214, 279-80, 295-96
Lesgaft, P.F., 117
Lewis, Dioclesian, 186, 193, 195, 269
Life expectancy, extended, 246
Ling, Per Henrik, 104, 107, 108, 110, 112, 113, 118, 119, 120, 129, 196, 197
Literature, sport, 142-43
Living, standard of, 246
Locke, John, 107, 108, 248
Logic, 259
Luther, Martin, 76, 87-88, 265

Maclaren, Archibald, 117, 267
Man, basic nature of, 253-54
Management, 297-98
Mann, Horace, 268
Mao Tse-tung, 117
Martial arts, 118, 130, 139
Mass entertainment, 40, 50-51
Materialism, 286
McKenzie, R. Tait, 195, 230, 231
Meanwell, Walter, 202
Mechanization, 246 (see also Technology)
Meliorism, 260, 299
Mercurialis, Hieronymous, 81
Metaphysics, 259
Middle Ages, 44, 57, 58-97, 280-81, 292, 295, 296, 298
Military, 5-6, 8, 62-63, 94, 117, 118, 193, 211, 229, 261, 262, 264, 266, 267, 269, 273
Milton, John, 84, 93
Mind-body dualism, 253, 292

Minoan civilization, 44, 45, 46, 48, 51
Minoan-Mycenaean civilization, 20-29
Mitchell, Elmer D., 203
Monastic schools, 61, 62, 68
Monasticism, 70
Montaigne, Michel de, 93, 94, 148
Montessori, Maria, 108
Mora, 30, 37
Morrill Act, 193, 269
Morris, Van Cleve, 253
Moto-cross, 140
Movement, 110, 119-126, 272
Mulcaster, Richard, 92, 265
Muscular Christianity, 88, 109, 117, 127,
    144, 160
Music, 3, 7, 8, 9, 11, 38, 39, 42, 83, 88,
    94, 178, 187

Nachtegall, Franz, 107, 108, 110, 111, 113,
    118, 120, 129
Naismith, James, 230
National Physical Fitness Act, Canada, 237
Nationalism, 107, 108, 109-19, 120, 129,
    254, 264, 266-67,
    271, 276-79
Natural growth, 266
Nietzsche, Friedrich Wilhelm, 274
Normal schools, 212, 293
Norms, 249, 251, 255-274
Nude competition, 48

Obstacle races, 15
Odyssey, 33
Olympic Games, 30, 33, 34, 35-36, 51,
    109, 128, 144-47, 151, 155-56, 163,
    190-91, 204-205, 267-68
"Organizational revolution," 297
Organizational, international, 151
Ostrakinda, 30
Outdoor education, 109, 125-26
Overspecialization, 296
Owens, Jesse, 204

Palaestra, 47
Palmieri, Matteo, 81
Pankration, 30, 32, 34, 35, 41, 48
Parachuting, 140
Paralympics, 151
Parson's general action theory, 249, 257,
    258, 259
Partridge, Alden, 186, 268
Part-whole theory, 259
Pavement games, 28-29
Pedagogy, 293

Pedestrianism, 181, 191, 192-93
Penn, William, 178
Pentathlon, 30, 34-35
Perfectionism, 260
Persian civilization, 10-11, 262
Personality development, 297
Pestalozzi, Johann, 108, 119-20, 122,
    126, 266, 293
Phersu, 40, 48, 50
Philanthropinum, 120, 266
Philosophy, 248, 252, 253, 259, 260, 274
Physical education, 1-2, 63-71, 80-94, 95,
    108-33, 186, 187, 193-98, 210-14,
    220-22, 249, 254-55, 256, 260,
    261-63, 264-67, 268-74, 275-76
    278-79, 281-82, 285-87, 290, 291,
    294-95, 298, 299, 300, 301
Physical fitness, 66, 69, 70, 84-85, 87, 91,
    96, 107, 109, 110, 116, 118, 119,
    131, 193, 211, 222, 270, 274, 275,
    276, 279, 282, 286-87, 290-91, 293,
    299
Physically disabled, 151
Piccolomini, Aenaes Sylvius, 81
Plato, 71, 294
Play, 2-3, 5-6
Playground movement, 127, 271, 272
Poland, 116
Pole vaulting, 267
Politics, 50-51, 96, 161, 162-63, 253,
    263, 271, 274-76
Polo, 10, 42
Population growth, 246, 287, 288, 297
Posse, Nils, 197
Post-industrial society, 280
Pragmatism, 252
Primitive society, 126, 261, 291, 292, 295,
Private schools, Canadian, 229-30
Problem-solving organism, man as, 253
Professional athletics, 199, 205, 296-97
Professional performers, 36-37, 262
Professional preparation, 79, 132-33, 194,
    196, 289-90, 292-93, 298 (see also
    Teacher education
Professionalism, 41-51, 130-33, 199, 291-99
Progress, 298-99
Progressive education movement, 271, 272
Progressivism, 210
Protestant Reformation, 73, 75-80, 87-89,
    95, 265, 285
Protestant work ethic, 173-74, 175, 176
Prussia, 107, 266-67, 292-93
Psychoanalytic image of man, 254
Public health science, 293
Puritanism, 175, 176, 177, 179, 188, 214
Pythian Games, 30, 34

Quakers, 178-79
Quarter staff, 69
Quoits, 267

Rabelais, François, 93-94, 265
Rationalism, 249, 253
Realism, 91-94, 95
"Receptacle of knowledge," man as, 253
Recreation, 69, 70, 83-85, 90, 94,
    141-42, 143, 143, 174, 256-57, 274, 276,
    299
Regattas, 183
Religion, 49-50, 158-59, 160-61, 264,
    285-87, 296
Renaissance, 71-74, 91-94, 253-54,
    264-65, 281, 276, 292, 298
Research, 43-52, 131, 247-52
Revolutions, peaceful, 245-46
Riding (see Equestrianism)
Rites de passage, 126
Roles, 249, 257, 258
Roller derby, 209
Roman Catholic Church, 61, 62, 68, 75,
    201, 284-85
Roman civilization, 39-43, 44, 47, 48,
    50-51, 247, 262-63, 277, 280, 285,
    291, 295, 298
Rousseau, Jean Jacques, 107-108, 119,
    120, 122, 126, 265-66
Rowing, 127, 182, 189-90, 205, 226-27,
    228, 234, 270
Rugby, 44, 127, 136, 189, 267
Running, 11, 14-15, 26-27 29, 30, 33,
    34, 35, 41, 47, 48, 65, 69, 90, 94,
    113, 119, 182, 201 (see also
    Track and field)

Sack races, 69
Sadoleto, Jacopo, 91
Safety education, 299
Sailing, 183
Salzmann, C.G., 108, 120, 121
Sargent, Dudley Allen, 194, 195, 197,
    270
Sartre, Jean-Paul, 284
Scholasticism, 68, 70, 93, 285
School camps, 109, 126
Scotland, 135, 148, 149
Scott, Barbara Ann, 235
Scuba diving, 140
Sebistia, 48
Secularization, 286
Seesaw, 30, 37
Semiprofessional athletics, 296-97

Seven Free Arts, 67
Seven Liberal Arts, 66, 70, 94
Shinny, 177
Shooting contests, 176, 178, 179
Skating, 147, 177, 205, 228-29
    235 (see also Ice hockey)
Skiing, 139, 147, 234-35
Skittles, 177
Skydiving, 140
Slave athletes, 38
Sleigh riding, 177
Snowmobiling, 140
Snow schools, 109
Snowshoeing, 65
Soccer, 127, 129, 136, 147, 154, 189,
    205, 233-34
Social classes, 68, 69-70, 73, 75-76, 181,
    191, 193, 262, 264, 280, 281
Social philosophy, 261
Social psychology, 248, 251-52
Sociology, 248, 249-50, 256, 257
Sokol, 114-16
Soviet Union (see U.S.S.R.)
Spartans, 36, 262, 291
Specialization, 36, 85, 131
Spectators, 25, 26, 29, 36, 38
Spielfeste, 127
Spiess, Adolf, 120, 267
Spinning disc, 30, 37
Sport history, 249, 254-55
Sport industry, 141-42, 143
Sport literature, 142-43
Sports, 48, 49-51, 133-64, 199, 249-50,
    256, 261, 262, 300, 301 (see also
    Games; Physical education)
Sports and games, triumph in Canada, 220-
    222
Sports festivals, 129
Sportsmanship, 126-28, 250
Sports promotion, 176, 178-79, 181, 185,
    191, 199, 205, 206
Sports schools, 117-18, 119
Sprinting, 27, 30
Squash, 136, 137
Stade, 34, 35, 48
Stadia, 9, 36, 141, 154, 200
Stanley Cup, Canada, 231
Steiner, Gary A., 253-54
Stick fighting, 14, 17, 20, 48
Stone casting, 65, 69
Strathcona Trust program, 252-53
Streicher, Margarete, 108, 119, 123
Sumerian civilization, 4, 5-7, 44, 45, 46,
    47, 48, 51
Summum bonum, 260
Sweden, 103, 110, 112, 116

Swimming, 8, 9, 10, 14, 18, 20, 27, 30, 37, 41-42, 44, 45, 48, 67, 129, 201, 202, 205, 269, 291

Table tennis, 136
Tavern-sponsored sport, 176, 178-79
Teacher education, 68, 130, 134, 269, 270-71, 273 (see also Professional preparation)
Teaching methodology, 68
Teaching profession, 62, 74, 79
Team sports, 129, 147
Technology, 140-41, 143-44, 246
Television, 141
Tennis, 90, 136, 137, 161, 190, 191, 201, 205, 208, 267, 269
Theatre, 178
Thermae, 41, 44
Thorndike, Edward L., 210
Thorpe, Jim, 204, 208
Tightrope walking, 42
Toboganning, 147, 147
Tom Brown's Schooldays, 109, 127, 144
Tournaments, 142
Track and field, 129, 190, 191, 201, 202, 205, 251, 270
Trade, 60, 63, 75-76
Transportation, 106, 140-41, 143, 188 198, 199, 206
"Trespass sport," 176
Troy, game of, 39
Tug-of-war, 69
Tumbling, 20, 21, 22, 51
Turnen, 104, 113, 123, 212, 266, 267, 268-69, 270
Turners (see Turnen)
Turnverein, 187, 196, 210, 268-69
Tyrs, Miroslav, 114

Underdeveloped nations, 246
United States, 173-87, 188-214, 215-16, 258, 268-74, 277, 285, 293
Universities, 62, 68, 74, 80, 96

Urbanization, 141-42, 180-81, 193, 219 297
U.S.S.R., 116-17, 205
Utilitarianism, 260, 271

Values, 249, 251, 255-74
Vanves study, France, 131
Vegius, Mapheus, 81
Vergerius, Petrus Paulus, 81, 83
Vikings, 65
Visigoths, 263
Vocational education, 68, 70, 80
Volleyball, 129, 139, 147
Voltaire, 265, 266

Walking (see Pedestrianism)
War, 45, 143-44, 158, 205, 211, 271
Water polo, 136, 147
Water skiing, 140
Weapons, 6, 7, 8, 10, 26, 246
Webster, Noah, 268
Weights, 20-34, 41, 90
Weissmuller, Johnny, 204
Wigman, Mary, 122
Wild beast fighting, 40
Williams, Jesse Feiring, 3, 211, 283, 292-94
Win(d)ship, George Barker, 269
Winter carnivals, 177
Women, 23, 38, 65, 79, 91, 123, 138, 145-47, 149, 187, 202-203, 294
Wood, Thomas D., 197, 211
Wrestling, 5, 8, 11, 14, 17-18, 20, 26, 29, 30, 32, 33, 34, 35, 38, 41, 42, 44, 45, 47, 48, 49, 67, 69, 88, 90, 94, 113, 176, 179, 205, 209

Yachting, 153, 183-84, 191, 228
YMCA, 160, 190, 196, 199, 201, 204, 269-70

Zwingli, Ulrich, 88-89